GREGORY BATESON
The Legacy of a Scientist

GREGORY BATESON
The Legacy of a Scientist

by David Lipset

Beacon Press   Boston

Grateful acknowledgment is made for
permission to reprint the plates from *Balinese Character*
by Gregory Bateson and Margaret Mead,
photographs by Gregory Bateson, published by
the New York Academy of Science.

Gregory Bateson: The Legacy of a Scientist, by David Lipset
Copyright © 1980, 1982 by David Lipset
First published as a Beacon paperback in 1982 by
arrangement with Prentice-Hall, Inc.
Beacon Press books are published under the auspices
of the Unitarian Universalist Association,
25 Beacon Street, Boston, Massachusetts 02108
Published simultaneously in Canada by
Fitzhenry & Whiteside Limited, Toronto

Printed in the United States of America

(paperback) 9 8 7 6 5 4 3 2 1

Library of Congress Cataloging in Publication Data
Lipset, David, 1951–
Gregory Bateson : the legacy of a scientist.
Bibliography: p.
Includes index.
1. Bateson, Gregory. 2. Bates family.
3. Anthropologists—Biography. 4. Psychologists
—Biography. I. Title.
GN21.B383L56 1982 309'.092'4 [B] 81-70493
ISBN 0-8070-4663-9 (pbk.)   AACR2

Contents

To My Parents, EBL and SML

Preface

This book began unexpectedly. I had known vaguely of Gregory Bateson when the opportunity came to spend the academic year of 1971–72 studying in Asia with him. I knew that he had created the double bind theory of schizophrenia and that he had been the former husband of Margaret Mead, the anthropologist. But I knew nothing about *Naven,* Bateson's classic 1936 theoretical ethnography. I had no idea that Claude Lévi-Strauss lauded his culture theory, or that Ray Birdwhistell and Erving Goffman felt that his powers of observation were exceptional, or that family therapists considered him one of the theoretical founders of their profession, or that the antipsychiatry of R. D. Laing was quietly foreshadowed in his thinking, or that Konrad Lorenz admired the brilliance of his theoretical ethology. I did not even know Bateson was English.

When I met him (I was twenty, and he was sixty-seven), the authorless rhetoric of public discourse in academic life was disturbing me. Particularly often in the social sciences, it seemed that disciplinary or political ideologies were implicitly advocated or that features of individual character were covertly dramatized—all in the passive voice of objectivity. Having grown up among American university intellectuals, I thought I had seen much of this dramatization firsthand. When I met Gregory Bateson, I was also bothered by my sense that the subjects I had tried to study all seemed concluded, and I felt angry and inadequate.

Listening to Bateson discuss his life and science, the compassion, confidence, and dauntless candor of the man impressed me deeply. I was drawn to him initially because aspects of his adolescence sounded familiar to me. Moreover, his antireductionism contrasted enigmatically with the conventional predictive aims of social science, and contrasted starkly with my sense of being at a dead end. To Bateson, science was not nature, abstraction was not phenomenon, and questions were meant only to pose other questions.

The following year, 1972–73, I wrote an undergraduate thesis, "A Tear Is an Intellectual Thing," in which I tried to relate the shape of Bateson's thinking to his family background. He cooperated with my interests. This sort of issue had concerned him as an anthropologist, although the detail of historical narrative did not absorb him. On the other hand, he enjoyed my questions. Perhaps he also noticed that then my understanding of him exemplified his belief that an observer who identifies with his subject to some extent, can draw upon his identification as one source, among many, of insight. At Harvard College, where I was affiliated with the Committee on Social Studies, my project received crucial encouragement from Judith Bierman, David Riesman, and Jay Wylie, as well as from George Marcus, Richard Suzman, Sherry Turkle, and Nur Yalman. But after graduation, I did not work on it for two years.

In the autumn of 1975, having obtained a measure of financial support from the Youthgrants program of the National Endowment for the Humanities, I picked up the project again. In the meantime, Bateson had given me access to a large amount of private material: trunks full of family letters and musty field notes, and his professional correspondence. While sorting through these documents, I interviewed Gregory—which is what he is called—extensively. I used the most significant letters to stimulate his detailed memories about the events and ideas which they concerned. His recollections enriched the letters, and the letters provided me with a check on his recollections.

Besides this, while studying the Victorian and Edwardian history of science and society, I arranged to visit England in order to conduct interviews with some of the people Bateson was telling me about. Then, I perceived my project as a biography, and I assumed that contemporary attempts at this genre were influenced by the great modern explanations of human action. My purposes were not theoretical, however. I was looking at historical and personal processes which were involved in what I considered to be the outstanding feature of Bateson's life—conceptual discovery.

On the whole, probing Bateson's English relatives, close friends, former neighbors, and colleagues proved to be the most provocative stage of my research. During these conversations, I explained my project and tried to elicit an oral history of each person's contact with Bateson. Happily, the majority responded enthusiastically to my interests. Although suspicion is a common contemporary attitude toward tape recorders, I tried to use one whenever possible. In England, I interviewed Mary Adams, Nöel Annan, Horace and Lady Nora Barlow, F. W. Bateson, P. P. G. Bateson, Mrs. Miles Burkitt, Mr.

and Mrs. C. F. Cornford, C. D. Darlington, Sir Raymond Firth, Meyer Fortes, Reo F. Fortune, Sir Geoffrey Gorer, Francis Huxley, Sir Geoffrey Keynes, R. D. Laing, Sir Edmund R. Leach, E. J. Lindgren-Utsi, Mrs. Helena Wayne-Malinowska, and Oliver Zangwill.

Between January 1976 and January 1979, while the tasks of transcribing my tapes and composing this biography occupied me, I conducted further interviews with a part of Bateson's familial and professional network in the United States. This group included: Elizabeth Sumner-Bateson, Eric Vatikiotis-Bateson, Lois Bateson, Mary Catherine Bateson, Stewart Brand, Cora Dubois, Erik H. Erikson, William F. Fry, Philomena Guillebaud, Jay Haley, Mr. and Mrs. Joseph Henderson, Anatol W. Holt, G. E. Hutchinson, John C. Lilly, Margaret Mead, Rhoda Metraux, Steven M. Nachmanovitch, William Newman, Lita Osmundsen, Roy A. Rappaport, Jurgen Ruesch, S. P. Heims, Judith Van Slooten, Paul Watzlawick, John H. Weakland, and Mr. and Mrs. Joseph B. Wheelright.

During this three-year period, I also had the good fortune to have helpful correspondence with a number of generous people: W. S. Bristowe, Robert Edgar, Robin Hill, J. W. Lesley, the Hon. Ivor G. S. Montagu, Mrs. Margaret Penrose Newman, Mrs. Joseph Omer-Cooper, E. E. V. de Peyer, Grace E. Pickford, David Saxon, Mrs. C. H. Waddington, Carter Wilson, Marjorie Woolman, and E. B. Worthington. A handful of institutions made pertinent letters available to me: the libraries of St. John's College; Cambridge University; the London School of Economics and Political Science; the University of London; Yale University; and the American Museum of Natural History. My special appreciation goes out to the librarians of these institutions.

With limited means at my disposal, I did not have the opportunity to inspect the scientific letters of Gregory's father, William Bateson, which are on deposit at the American Philosophical Society in Philadelphia. However, William Coleman, a historian of science, allowed me to see the annotated index he prepared of them. Judging from this, and from my correspondence with A. G. Cock, who is writing a biography of the elder Bateson—essentially the founder of the discipline of genetics in England—I think my presentation suffers only in that the themes I stress are less well documented than they might have been had I seen the Philadelphia APS letters.

Despite this gap in my research, by summer 1976 I had collected a great deal of material. As Bateson called me a "data mongerer," my attention was turning to his relations with the many disciplines to which he has contributed innovative concepts. At this time, I met George W. Stocking, the leading

American historian of anthropology, whose generous suggestions entailed more than I could accomplish. I also met Robert K. Merton, the father of sociology of science in the United States. Discussing ideas with these men— about scientific careers in terms of the interplay among history, family, and discipline—broadened my original interests considerably. Thinking especially about the views of derivative and rival sociologists, I found that one component of the Mertonian view—a sense of the competitiveness of scientific life—sharpened much of the most crucial material in the lives I was trying to re-create. I then thought that tensions of late Victorian science and culture combined with the tragedy of his Edwardian family to direct Bateson toward the science of man. I also thought that this background continued to form his imagination during the unique course of his ensuing career. Moreover, I felt I had come across a striking incident—among Bateson, Margaret Mead, and Reo Fortune—in which Mertonian competition appeared only too intimately.

In the autumn of 1976, I became a graduate student in the Department of Anthropology at the University of California in San Diego. Under its influence, I started calling the people I had interviewed, "informants," and gladly began to compare the sort of biography I was doing with ethnography. Was research upon the life of a living subject akin to fieldwork in a native culture? Might such work benefit from anthropological thinking about biography or about the general relationship between the individual and society? And, reciprocally, did my project have relevance to the discipline I was learning? Bateson, of course, was an admired, if not major, figure, but did he merit such prolonged attention? Amid the droning of modern theories of culture, I began to wonder, again, about the culture of science. My work, branching out from Bateson's life, suggested that at least in the social sciences, theoretical change was shaped by threads of history, personal relationships, choice, and accident. My interests were not so much in anthropological biography at this point, as in the possibility and value of investigating cultural patterning in scientific life and thought.[1]

This is not the sort of concern which yields immediate results. But for allowing me to pose it, I am indebted to three years of critical and financial support provided by this department and university. I must specifically mention the interest of Kevin A. Avruch, F. G. Bailey, Kathleen Barlow, Roy G. D'Andrade, Robert I. Levy, Michael E. Meeker, Manuel Rotenberg, George Saunders, Theodore Schwartz, Melford E. Spiro, Julie M. Taylor, and the tireless eyes of Donald F. Tuzin.

Clearly, then, this book is the product of a complex of institutions and people. However, since it fell to me to mediate between panegyric and exposé, to distinguish between cause and creativity, and, most concretely, to cull the material, I alone am responsible for it.

Another of my initial reasons for writing this book was antiromantic. Bateson had impressed me as an immensely gifted intellectual. He combined realms of thought—e.g., biology with aesthetics, or ethology with philosophy—in ways that I had not anticipated. I felt challenged to find a view which showed the man, not as some sort of phoenix conceived out of its own ashes, but in the more human light of his own individual and cultural history. Accordingly, this biography portrays the central roles of Bateson's life drawn from observations, interviews, and letters: from brother-naturalist, ethnographer, husband, father, theoretical convert, teacher, psychotherapist, dolphin ethologist, disciplinary utopian, finally to public man. I also suggest the effects other people, institutions, and ideas had upon him as well as the sense Bateson himself made of the world. Drawing upon his publications and a literature too plentiful for simple characterization, I fit Bateson's intellectual development into the trends of his life, and fit it into some of the broader scientific and cultural trends of his times.

Although I maintain that this is a comprehensive view of Bateson's life, I do not claim it to be a complete one—he died after publication of the hardcover edition. I have dwelled insufficiently upon certain personal and scientific dimensions of his life. This is conspicuously true of my accounts of Bateson's married lives and of the critical status of double bind theory. To evaluate the latter, I am not qualified. To describe the former more fully would have required a degree of social skills with some of my informants which I was perhaps hesitant about testing. Thanks must go to my editor, Robert Sussman Stewart, in this connection. Acutely conscious of these deficiencies, I took a certain solace from the truism that, whether he or she is living or dead, a biography can only approximate its subject. The reassurances of friends—who know who they are—also restrained me from doubt.

Piecing together Bateson's life brought me into contact with an intimidating bibliography drawn from literature about the great Victorian antagonism between science and religion, the early history of modern genetics, the history of modern social and psychoanalytic anthropology, learning theory, the cybernetic modeling of social and biological phenomena, schizophrenic communication, ethology, and ecological theory. But if living informants can restrict one somewhat, they can also lend their expertise to the work in progress. Bateson typified the attitude that these people adopted when reading what I had written about them: he attended to inaccuracies of fact but respected the interpretations. (Actually, it would be naive to suggest that for

Gregory reading my biography was merely a matter of correcting factual errors. After he had procrastinated with a part of the manuscript, I asked him what the problem was. "Oh," he said, "that's a difficult question. Stage fright, I suppose—but that's a very poor answer." For once, his response did not surprise me.) It is a pleasure to acknowledge the contributions of those who were both informants and critics: Lois Bateson, C. D. Darlington, Robert Edgar, Ray Fogelson, William F. Fry, Jay Haley, G. E. Hutchinson, E. J. Lindgren-Utsi, Margaret Mead, Rhoda Metraux, Lita Osmundsen, David Riesman, Jurgen Ruesch, Theodore Schwartz, Carter Wilson, John H. Weakland, and Joseph B. Wheelwright.

Recently, Bateson has been celebrated by Americans who share his moral and ecological concerns. Yet this is not the biography of a man who found his niche, nor of one who fit neatly within social and professional life. Rather, this is the biography of a doubly anachronistic man, who was both ahead of and behind his times. To begin to understand him, we must recall England between the years 1860 and 1900 when ecclesiastical society was strained by the emergence of modern knowledge, statuses, sex roles, family, and education. An abundance of highly charged polarities marked thinking then: spiritualism–evolutionism, idealism–materialism, and classicism–modernism. On both sides, many of those involved were uncompromising. This kind of rigid opposition is well known to have occurred between priests and scientists, and in painful tension between fathers and sons. However, a few rebels existed who were obliged to reconcile the dualisms—as a result of which they too became doubly out of step with their times.

This book will begin by glancing at the struggles of Samuel Butler, the quintessence of these matters in later nineteenth-century England, and an important metaphor of and in the life of Gregory Bateson.

The hardcover edition of this biography was published before Gregory Bateson died. Therefore, in this paperback edition, I have corrected errata and made a few minor changes to account for Bateson's death. A brief discussion of the final eight months of his life has also been added to the last chapter.

David Lipset
February 1982
Murik Lakes
Papua New Guinea

The Batesons of
St. John's College

1859-1922

1. Between Determinisms: Samuel Butler

During the middle of the nineteenth century, when Samuel Butler was an undergraduate at St. John's College, Cambridge, the scope and purpose of education was set by the Church of England. In particular, it seemed to Butler, this consecrated domination subjugated and demeaned the fledgling science of biology.[1] "All our masters in school, all our tutors in College confirmed us in our belief—not one of them ever gave us a word of warning that there was another side to the question of Christian evidences; all books in which any attempt was made to state the other side were [so] excluded from our... training that we did not even know their names."[2]

Then in 1859, not only education but all English life began to come under prismatic and sneering scrutiny, from men under the influence of *The Origin of Species*. In the years following the appearance of that book, both within and without the emerging profession, the prestige of biology rose appreciably. "Who will deny," Beatrice Potter Webb recalled of her youth during the 1870s and 1880s, "that the men of science were the leading British intellectuals?" Their theories demanded the attention of the philosophers. Their inventions captivated the capitalists. Their certainty stood out against the theologians and mystics. At the same time, they were "snubbing the artists, ignoring the poets and even casting doubts on the capacity of the politicians."[3] By 1880, totally secular life seemed possible. T. H. Huxley, the biologist, could boast of "a new culture created by science," and widely benefiting from its innovations.[4] And Francis Galton, the eugenicist and statistician, hoped that a "scientific priesthood"[5] would assume leadership of society. Choosing between right and wrong, choosing between courses of action, and choosing objectives were all said to be part of a rational process, perhaps eventually a scientific one. The spirit of materialism invaded even the Church itself. Bishop Colenso's attack on the arithmetic of the Pentateuch, which so enraged his fellow bishops, was no anomaly.* The tomb of Newton still stands in Westminster Abbey, surrounded by the graves of Victorian scientists, attesting to their accomplishment but also to the secular sacredness their profession sought and, for a moment, came to achieve.

Nevertheless, enmity fragmented relations between religion and science during this period, and it concerned just the matters about which Charles Darwin was unversed. He himself had little to say about heresy or orthodoxy. "I do not attack Moses," Darwin once remarked to his friend, the vicar of Down. "I think Moses can take care of himself. . . . I endeavor to discover the facts without considering what is said in the Book of Genesis."[6] If at all agonistic, *The Origin* was meant to expose the errors of dead naturalists: Lamarck, Linnaeus, Cuvier, or his grandfather, Erasmus Darwin. "I have never systematically thought much on religion in relation to science," he answered an inquisitor in 1891, "and without keeping my mind on such subjects for a long period, I am really incapable of writing anything."[7] The origin of species lay unexplained in Darwin's thinking. Variations were selected when they happened to arise, and they did so by *chance,* a term he used explicitly to "acknowledge ignorance of the cause of each particular variation."[8] Still, contemporary theologians took even this confession as catastrophic to their creed. Bishop Wilberforce, in his review of *The Origin,* accused Darwin of offering a "degrading notion of the brute origin of him who was created in the image of God."[9]

The spirituality of the universe was not reconcilable, especially when the opposition denied the very reality of any experience incompatible with their assumptions and methods. Materialist scientists held that phenomena were either available to the senses objectively or nonexistent, and they were susceptible of and reducible to immutable laws or mechanical form.[10] R. G. Collingwood, the philosopher, has observed that this perspective, "though it actually was a philosophical system, refused to claim that title. It claimed only

---

*In 1853, John Colenso was elected bishop of Natal, having done missionary work there among the Zulus. He composed a grammar, a dictionary, and a translation of the New Testament into Zulu. He had a reformist approach to doctrine. Indeed, disturbed by questions posed by converts, Colenso was led to abandon certain aspects of the faith. He doubted the historical accuracy of the Pentateuch, arguing that it was a postexilic forgery and not a contemporary account of Jewish life. He also maintained that numerical discrepancies throughout Genesis warranted dismissal of the entire Bible. For this position, for his opposition to the doctrine of eternal punishment, and for his tolerance of polygamy among Zulus, Colenso was summoned in 1863, and convicted of charges of heresy. The charge was later dropped, but then revived. Colenso stayed at his post in Natal, supported by a dwindling band of followers. (P. B. Hinchcliff, *John William Colenso.*)

to be scientific. It was in fact nothing but the methodology of natural science identifying itself with knowledge."[11] The "natural" determination of a mindless and godless universe progressing according to chance and natural selection—which most understood to mean without purpose at all—encouraged reductionist perspectives in diverse fields of inquiry. And the ideas which took shape then appear in retrospect like tactics directed toward an ambitious strategy. In Biblical studies, a search for the historical Jesus seemed to sustain the antimiraculous impulse which Tylor's anthropology of animistic beliefs no less supported.[12] Perhaps the most striking example of these attitudes of the time appeared in 1872. Examining the longevity of persons whose health was widely prayed for, Francis Galton found it no greater than that of common people. And missionary ships, similarly the object of many prayers, did not receive favorable insurance rates, even from Quaker companies.[13]

To many then, the choice seemed to be either biology or theology. Yet there were a few in England who strained to fit into the cramped space between the two. Viewing a universe conceived without purpose and mind as dismal, they found themselves unable to return to one conceived in terms of external and transcendent Design. In their lifetimes, such men were isolated intellectuals. They were ignored because their project—to integrate the opposing conceptions—was offensive to the adherents of both. Their voices were only heard after they and the initial dogmatism had died. To begin a biography of Gregory Bateson, we must turn to one of these voices, Samuel Butler (1835–1902), author of *Erewhon*. Butler's ghost will haunt this book— not only in Bateson's thought but in the family culture from which it grew.

Butler was of yeoman stock, the child of a provincial rectory. From an early age, his father bullied him with lessons, sin, and beatings. His mother was obsequious and confidence-betraying. They conspired to make Butler's childhood "one long process of dissimulation."[14] He had two sisters and a younger brother. Evidently, the girls formed a little group with their mother. The second boy, though, came to hate his father so thoroughly as to make Sam's feeling's seem reasonable by comparison. In later years, Canon Butler answered his younger son's repulsion in kind. "I don't care about knowing where he is, so long as we hear of his death."[15] After completing undergraduate education at St. John's College, Cambridge, Sam Butler went to do parish work in London, assuming he was to enter the ministry.

One of the pupils in a Sunday school class he taught had not been baptized. When Butler discovered that this was widespread among his students, his faith in infant baptism collapsed, as did career plans. The idiom of intellectual and political leadership was shifting in England, and as it did family life became one of the stages upon which the enmity between religi and science appeared. In the spring of 1859—again the crucial year—father and son began their notorious negotiation. Sam wanted to take up painting—an occupation of the unconsecrated spirit—which Canon Butler refused to support financially. If this meant he was being disowned, Sam was ready to accept. On 12 May, his father wrote:

> Most fathers would I believe on the receipt of this morning's letter have been intensely angry.... I am much distressed—distressed at your obliquity of vision, distressed at your opinion of myself, distressed at your seeming callousness of heart.... I judged that it was wisest for your good that I should not encourage you in your artist's career. This is my sole motive for refusing to assist you in it. You have shown no decided genius for drawing.... The notion that I should disinherit you is yours not mine. I said only that I would not contribute to this career of folly. P.S....I do not want to make your life miserable. Why should I? I don't think my conduct is like that. Nor probably will you think it if this correspondence comes into your hands after my death. I will try however once more. Will you go as soon as term is over and learn farming with someone who will take you as a pupil. I will consent to find funds for your doing so.... [They had discussed the possibility that Sam go to New Zealand to farm.]

On 17 May, Butler answered: "Your letter misunderstood me tremendously on many points but it is no use entering into them."

On 3 August, after a number of intervening letters, Canon Butler wrote:

> I have every wish to meet your desires as far as they seem not likely to be injurious to your self. I will therefore so far consent to emigration that I will continue your allowance while you are away for 12 months and then advance capital needful.... The artist scheme I utterly disapprove. It will throw you into very dangerous society. I have no doubt at the end of a year's trial you will draw well enough to be encouraged to go on but this is not becoming a painter, and you may very likely learn to draw very nicely and yet come short of the excellence which alone would give station and respectability to your career. Neither will it be clear whether you will or won't attain this for some considerable time. Meanwhile your society is cast in with a set of men who as a class do not bear the highest character for morality, are thrown into the midst of the most serious temptations and if it is possible that you may stand, it is possible you may fall. I can't consent to it.... I don't want to press the bar, though I should have liked.... I have one last proposition to make. Could you feel inclined to take up with diplomacy?[16]

Behind his attack on mindless science and dictatorial religion was a longing to penetrate the unseen kingdom, to behold the core of existence. Having lost faith in the major currents of his epoch, or as he put it "in the general right mindedness of one's age,"[36] Butler had not lost faith itself. The conventions of professional intellectuals might be delusory, but this was no reason to give way to some sort of pre-modern nausea. It was instead justification of humor and of an end to dogmatism. Butler thought that his ideas about psychical heredity were "as nearly important as any theories can be which do not directly involve money or bodily convenience."[37] His ideal man was no nihilist. He was fraught with contradiction: certain despite uncertainty, uncertain despite certainty; reasonable despite faith, and full of faith despite relying upon reason. Butler's god was similarly construed. "What can approach more nearly to a rendering of that which cannot be rendered—the idea of an essence omnipresent in all things at all times everywhere in sky and earth; everchanging yet the same yesterday, today and forever; the ineffable contradiction in terms whose presence none can either ever enter or ever escape?"[38] There was no retreating to the Creator of *Genesis*. Butler strode between biological and religious determinisms. The designer was the design itself. He spoke of his religion as a "modest pantheism," according to his biographer Henry Festing Jones, in which god was immanent in all things. "Although we cannot see the bowl and the water as part of the goldfish, yet . . . their material is not without intelligence, and . . . God, who is life, is in everything."[39] Enjoying oneself was thus a manner of prayer. "To love God is to have good health, good looks, good sense, experience, a kindly nature and a fair balance of cash in hand."[40]

Throughout the latter part of his life, Butler was composing an autobiographical novel, *The Way of All Flesh*. In the book, Butler personified many of his ideas, and caricatured many of his adversaries. The novel was an account, in brief, of the spiritual and financial career of Ernest Pontifex, as he prevails painfully over parental despotism by following his unconscious. "You are surrounded on every side by lies," an inner voice warns Ernest at a young age, "the self of which you are conscious, your reasoning and reflecting self, will believe these lies and bid you act in accordance with them."[41] Central to the novel was Butler's aching assault upon the oppressiveness of Victorian

---

within much that I have said, but the texture of the world is a warp and woof of contradiction in terms. . . . As in the development of a fugue, where when the subject and countersubject have been introduced, there must henceforth be nothing new and yet all must be new, so throughout organic life—which is as a fugue developed to a great length from a very simple subject." (S. Butler, *Life and Habit*, p. 234.)

family life—an assault foretelling a pattern of interaction about which we shall have more to say in succeeding chapters.

In one instance, Overton, the narrator, watches the Pontifex family on a Sunday evening. The children were not to play during the Sabbath; however, they were allowed one treat—to choose their own hymns. Ernest chooses one beginning with the words, "Come, come, come; come to the sunset tree for the day is past and gone." But he is not yet able to sound a hard *c,* and instead of "come," he sings "Tum, tum, tum." The Reverend Theobald Pontifex, his father, asks Ernest if he does not think it proper to say "come" like other children. (Overton thinks that clergymen, being as bored with the Sabbath as their parishioners, are always in bad temper on Sunday evenings.) Ernest answers his father that he had said "come," although he continues to mispronounce the word. Contradicted, Theobald stands up. Ernest must apply himself, he says, to this simple task.

> The boy remained silent a few seconds and then said "tum" again.... I laughed, but Theobald turned to me impatiently and said, "Please do not laugh, Overton; it will make the boy think it does not matter, and it matters a great deal"; then turning to Ernest he said, "Now, Ernest, I will give you one more chance, and if you don't say 'come,' I shall know that you are self-willed and naughty."... He looked very angry, and a shade came over Ernest's face, like that which comes upon the face of a puppy when it is being scolded without understanding why. The child saw well what was coming now, was frightened, and, of course, said "tum" once more. "Very well, Ernest," said his father, catching him angrily by the shoulder.... "I have done my best to save you, but if you will have it so, you will," and he lugged the little wretch crying by anticipation, out of the room. A few minutes more and we could hear screams coming from the dining room, and knew that poor Ernest was being beaten.... "I have sent him up to bed," said Theobald, as he returned to the drawing room, "and now, Christina, I think we will have the servants in to prayers," and he rang the bell for them, red-handed as he was.[42]

Butler finished *The Way of All Flesh* by 1885. Two years before, a friend said of the book that it had spread man's tenderest family feelings out on the floor, and had stamped upon them until they were reduced "to an indistinguishable mass of filth."[43] Fearful of the personal consequences, Butler did not permit publication while he lived. Only afterward, at the beginning of the twentieth century, did his self-centered, paradox-oriented, tragic sense of satire become acceptable—among the offspring of those he mocked.

II. A Geneticist's Ancestry

In 1909, William Bateson became absorbed in his family's genealogy. Some years before, his scientific interests had veered, with his introduction of Mendel's principles to England, into the study of heredity and variation. Since this was not yet an organized subject, W. B., as students and colleagues called him, proposed in 1905, to name it Genetics. Being that lineage and descent were the subjects of the emergent science, Bateson was led to his own pedigree by more than a meandering curiosity. During this research, he identified forebears back to the beginning of the eighteenth century, obtained a copy of the coat of arms which had been granted to his father's father 100 years earlier, and briefly characterized his aunts and uncles. Despite the efforts of W. B., early Bateson lineage is just barely visible. We know little more than names. The record begins with the 1719 marriage of David Bateson, and indicates that his third child, James, married Margaret Bracken in 1754. They had six boys, of whom three died young. Their last, Richard, born in 1770, became a well-to-do cotton merchant in Liverpool. He married Lucy Wheler in 1806, the daughter of a professional soldier. She gave birth to a family of twelve children, many of whom did poorly in the world. Indeed, three died in childhood. W. B. described two others as "criminal" and "occasionally insane." One died at the age of twenty-four, and another, said to be a "melancholic," died in an asylum. The youngest child, Honora Glynne, had an infertile marriage, "lost her memory in old age and was insane for some years before death."[1]

However, the fifth son, William Henry (1812–1882), became master of St. John's College, Cambridge, and fathered England's first geneticist. He was educated at the Shrewsbury Grammar School, an obscure public school which had been transformed by the strict discipline of Samuel Butler's grandfather into one of the most successful institutions of its kind. In 1829, Bateson went up to St. John's College and found his place, spending most of the rest of his life there. As an undergraduate, he read classics and mathematics and was a sound scholar. But Bateson was to become known chiefly for his work as a libertarian and university politician whose main aim it would be to instigate and to force reform onto one of the most conservative of Cambridge colleges. Even as a student he fought against rules which excluded impoverished undergraduates called sizars from the college cricket and boat clubs.[2] Bateson began administering college life in 1837 when, as senior bursar, he astutely reorganized financial policy. This was a prelude to the reputation he made a few years later in his role as secretary to the royal commission of 1850—a critical and crucial reexamination of British education. A long series of liberalizations occurred in its wake, which transformed the traditional college—independent, celibate, and quasi-monastic—into the modern university in which secular, competitive scholarship took place. The royal commissioners passed statutes calling for the integration of college assets, the establishment of new curricula, the improvement of teaching and, in certain subjects, the abolition of required religious oaths. John Roach, a historian of British higher education, has written that their report "permitted the election of professors and University lecturers into fellowships without the obligation of taking orders, an obligation which had forced J. C. Adams, the discoverer of the planet Neptune, to abandon his fellowship."[3] Sons of nonlanded professionals soon came to outnumber those of clergymen in the colleges, and graduates took a wider range of jobs outside the church.

Until William Henry Bateson became master in 1857, "St. John's was more likely to be found in the rearguard than in the van of reform." Indeed, the curriculum which Samuel Butler condemned might well have been specifically that at St. John's, where he was an undergraduate when W. H. Bateson began his reformist mastership. Edward Miller, a historian of the college, has called the third quarter of the nineteenth century "the age of Bateson,"[4] for the sweeping change over which he presided as master, and as one of a handful of activist liberals in the university as a whole. In 1860, Bateson altered the social position of his college within Cambridge when he invited Bishop Colenso—well known as the leading church modernist of the day—to dedicate the new chapel which had been constructed under Bateson's auspices. Official action had yet to be initiated against Colenso. Nonetheless, his presence, which indicated that he had the support of the master, created such a storm that a number of titled fathers removed their sons from the college.[5]

A man of intense enthusiasms, Bateson was said to have been an excellent chairman, keenly able to sense a committee's feelings. To a large extent then, by his own managerial skill, William Henry Bateson was the last master of St. John's College who was required to be in holy orders. After his death, William

Bateson would describe his father as contentious and political, but also as a gentle, unworldly man.

> I know now that his ways must have been of the old régime, courtly and delicate—and yet he was essentially a man of action. Most of the changes in Cambridge bringing in the things of the new knowledge, have been more or less helped on by him. A very few weeks before he died he sat day after day at the Arts School where the changes of the last Commission were being debated, and stood up and tackled the enemy on point after point, till at last no one could be got up against him. I have heard many men say that it was a regular rout; of course, I knew nothing about these things then.[6]

The year after he was elected to the mastership, Bateson, released from the celibacy imposed by his fellowship, married Anna Aiken (1829–1918). Her grandson remembered her as "a tiny, little woman ... [who] was one of the first suffragettes. She supported not only votes for women, but women's membership in the university. ... She was a beauty."[7] A woman of pioneering vision and widely expressed vitality, Anna wrote poetry and patronized music. For women's enfranchisement, she was militant, and for the poor and infirm, she was caring.

> The contrast she presented to the generality of Cambridge women, especially the wives of Heads of Colleges can hardly be measured by the present generation [it was written of her in 1918]. The Heads of Colleges in those days lived in a sort of Olympian grandeur, apart from the rest of the University: their wives ... emulated their husbands' aristocratic seclusion. But St. John's Lodge knew nothing of this and all the most forward movements for women had an ardent missionary in Mrs. Bateson, aided by the trained political sagacity of her husband, the Master.[8]

Anna Aiken's background was similar to her husband's. She too was of actively liberal, professional stock which, in addition, contained notable diversity. Anna's father, James Aiken, was a prosperous and prominent Liverpool shipping merchant of Scottish descent. A political man and staunchly liberal, he was also something of a municipal leader. It was said of him that "there was not a man who could so effectively silence an opposition by the vigour and readiness of his repartee."[9] Strong, formidable, and energetic, he died at the age of eighty-six, after his usual prebreakfast swim in the ocean. Aiken was self-made. He had built up a successful shipping business, for which he made numerous voyages to the United States. During one of them he married an American, Anne Harrison of Charleston, South Carolina, whose father and brother had fought on opposite sides of the American Revolution, and who was distantly related to the ninth American president, William Henry Harrison. The Aikens produced twelve children, some of whom grew up to be alcoholics. Another committed suicide and another died young in India. However, one of the brothers did become a fellow of Jesus College, Cambridge. In his notes, W. B. wrote that he was "respectable and gifted, but did little."[10] It was Aiken's seventh daughter, Anna, who became William Henry Bateson's wife.

During the first ten years of marriage, four girls and two boys came into the world. Margaret, the first child, was born in 1860. She was followed a year later by W. B., and then by three daughters, Anna, Mary, and Edith. Edward, the youngest, was born in 1868. They grew up strong willed, disputative, and intellectual. The girls all became pioneering feminists. Anna and Mary did not marry and were among the first of their sex fully enrolled in Newnham, the women's college in Cambridge. Anna studied botany. Mary, who read history, became an eminent scholar. Edward was a colonial judge in Cairo and later in Mauritius.

Given the domineering, prescient, and individualistic character of both parents, it is little wonder that they reared their children to be unorthodox and atheist. These were the years, after all, during which there were bitter battles between Darwinian evolutionists and orthodox Anglicans. William Henry Bateson, despite his own ordination as a clergyman in the Church of England, knew enough of the new biology to realize that the religious position had been made untenable. Similarly, his wife Anna continued to attend services, although she did not believe. A story revolved for years in the family that one Sunday after the regular morning rites, there was to be a communion service. Someone whispered to Anna, "You will not be remaining?" and she is said to have replied, "I shall not partake but I will obsairve [sic]."[11]

The Bateson children doted on Willie, who spent his youth surrounded by admiring sisters. He grew up tall and large, with intense—according to the photographs—somewhat dazed eyes. Even when young he was supposed to have had curiosity for the natural world. As a little boy of seven, it was said of him that he once parried an unfavorable comment about a disreputable looking figure who haunted Cambridge ditches, exlaiming reverently, "That man is a naturalist!" He was also an avid collector and would fondly recall an illustration of his childhood ways when "he made prolonged inspection of the humbler contents of a Cambridge curiosity dealer's shop and finally decided to purchase a Roman coin for two pence, and how this conclusion of the matter drew from the proprietor the crushing utterance: "Sir, I do not thank you for your custom!"[12] However, when Willie went to Rugby school, his interests found no expression. He was distinguished there for his misery, for his lack of purpose, for the mediocrity of his work, and for generally being disliked. At one point, the headmaster was given cause to write his father that the boy's schoolwork was "scandalous," and that he thought it doubtful whether "so vague and aimless a boy will profit by University life."[13] Willie's fascination for nature sustained him through what he later called "a time of scarcely unrelieved weariness, mental starvation, and despair."[14]

At least part of his problem then involved a disjunction of interests. Until approximately the end of the nineteenth century, British middle-class public schools stressed the Greek and Latin classics and mathematics to the exclusion of all else. Young Willie Bateson, the budding naturalist, had little curricular outlet for his concerns. At school, daydreams occupied him more than schoolwork. What might he do during chapel services if some rare hawk moth flew through the open window? Catch it or not? And if he tried, would he be allowed, and what would be thought of him? From boyhood onward, his wife would recall, the problems related to the general theory of evolution held him in thrall.[15] His father saw only that his boy struggled with mathematics and had little taste for classics. The master remarked to a friend when Willie was sixteen, "I regard you as fortunate in one respect with regard to your son; that he has a distinct and decided inclination in life. . . . We have been wishing that our eldest boy could manifest some special propension but as yet there are no signs of any."[16]

In 1879, Will Bateson enrolled in his father's college, St. John's, and read zoology, then a recently established curriculum. His career began under the influence of the morphologists Alfred Newton, F. M. Balfour, and Adam Sedgwick. "At Cambridge in the eighties, morphology held us like a spell," Bateson wrote in retrospect. "That part of biology was concrete. The discovery of definite, incontrovertible fact is the best kind of work, and morphological research was still bringing up new facts in quantity."[17] Principally, young naturalists were taught to seek evidence of ancestral histories, using comparative embryology as their paradigm or guiding analogy. The recapitulation theory underlay this approach, justifying close observation of the transformations which an embryo underwent. It was held that those which were experienced by the individual organism were reproduced in its evolutionary development. Phylogeny could be reconstructed from ontogeny. Bateson was introduced to these methods and assumptions, recalling that "morphology was studied because it was the material believed to be most favourable for the elucidation of the problems of evolution, and we all thought in embryology the quintessence of morphological truth was most palpably presented. Therefore every . . . aspiring zoologist was an embryologist, and the one topic of professional conversation was evolution."[18]

At St. John's, the young Bateson prospered—allowed, for the first time in his life, to study subjects for which he had a sincere interest. From his undergraduate days onward, he was known for his effulgent personality and striking figure. "It must have been in 1879, when I first became conscious of the presence in College of a large and rather untidy undergraduate," said one contemporary.

> [He] was pointed out to me as the son of our honored Master, Dr. Bateson. I did not at once get to know this youth, but I was from the first attracted by his appearance, even in his bodily movements unconventional. He seemed a sort of living protest against the "average" quality of his contemporaries. Acquaintance soon affirmed the suggestions of his outer bearing, and I found myself in touch with a man of frank independence in thought, word, and deed.[19]

Not an indecisive young man, Will was boisterous and he had, except for mathematics, a notable catholicity of interest. He threw himself into a parliamentary election during these years, canvassing for a Liberal candidate so enthusiastically that forty-five years later, his political reputation still preceded him. This was his only political foray however. He would later conclude that politics were simply without foundation in reality. Similarly, he considered the fields of law, political history, and economy too trifling to be worth his time. Will applauded his sister Anna when she began to study botany, supposing that she would have "despised ... success" in Mary's subject, history. The study of natural science, being closest to "the origin of things," was a "purer" endeavor. It had transformed Bateson's life and had enabled him to take control of his personality. In homage, he would say:

> We are all men born into a splendid and terrible world in which our lot is to enjoy and to suffer. . . . The one reasonable aim of man is that life shall be as happy as it can be made, with as much possible of joy and as little possible of pain. There is only one way of attaining that aim: the pursuit of natural knowledge.[20]

But though the young man's scientific fascinations were closely related to the materialism of the day, like Samuel Butler (then laboring anonymously in the Reading Room of the British Museum), Bateson had little affection for the utilitarian values of his contemporaries. At the age of twenty-one, a sense of aesthetics began to form Bateson's intellectual life. He read French literature ardently and dedicated himself to Balzac and Voltaire. It was his rule never to travel without a copy of *Candide*. The pleasures of the eye came to underlie seemingly divergent aspects of his life. On vacation in 1882, Bateson visited Dresden, where he first expressed devotion for paintings and especially for Old Master drawings. He was overwhelmed by what he saw there. "To see anything in perfection," he wrote Anna, "is a treat, even if it is only skill. Just try to think what it means, to be able to paint a heap of clothes absolutely perfectly!"[21] He preferred the artist's sketch to the final painting, because he felt that the former was done for love while the latter was meant for public consumption and for reward.

> When you see [the drawings] you see well enough why lots of things in pictures don't come up to scratch, simply because they were done for the world, while the man did the drawings for himself. All the drivel and half-heartedness of the pictures is away from the drawings. The fellows that did them, did them for outright love of them, and because they couldn't help it, and not for money and fame, as they did their pictures.[22]

Will Bateson valued the transcendent in human creativity. His critical catchword was "ephemeral," which he continually used to condemn the products and issues of English intellectual life. Although as a child he had suffered because of compulsory Greek and though the theory of evolution had fortified those who now challenged traditional education, at thirty Bateson came to respect classical learning. On a number of occasions he took up somewhat conservative, antiutilitarian positions when that curriculum came under attack by modernists holding that it was irrelevant and useless. Bateson would argue that Greek enriched the otherwise dull lives of the common man, "who by instinct and training is savage and would fain destroy what it cannot understand."[23] The classics benefited the man of science as well, "if only that he may know the greatness of his own calling." Thinking, perhaps, of Lucretius' prophetic poem *The Nature of Things*, Bateson expressed remarkable doubts about the professional scientist of 1891.

> He, forsooth, will read the riddle of nature. In the fullness of time he has set himself up to solve old problems. . . . It is right then, that he should know that his are those which the poets have put. *If there had been no poets there would have been no problems, for surely the unlettered scientist of today would never have found them.* [italics added]. To him it is easier to solve a difficulty than to feel it. It is good, besides, that the Science man should be made to know that there was a people as sharp as he is, who saw the same Nature as he sees, who read it otherwise with no less confidence than he.[24]

His first scientific venture involved "a lowly worm of dubious nature called *Balanoglossus*,"[25] which had previously eluded classification. Was it the last of the invertebrates or the first of the vertebrates? Bateson's close friend, W. F. R. Weldon, and one of his teachers, F. M. Balfour, thought that the answer to this question might shed light on the origin of the class of vertebrates. In 1883, William Bateson, then twenty-two, proceeded to America to spend the summer collecting worms in Chesapeake Bay, where they were plentiful. Besides getting formerly unrecorded morphological information, Bateson came under the influence of a philosophical naturalist and morphologist, W. K. Brooks. The young man was much taken with this pipe-smoking American scientist and fondly recalled his ability to spit from a distance into a spittoon. "I wonder," he later wrote of Brooks, "if any university professor ruminates spacious ideas as Brooks used to do daily through long vacant hours of leisure, to the delight and elevation of a youthful listener. Those are the times of true education."[26] Brooks discussed heredity as if it were a problem demanding solution. To Bateson, whose undergraduate days had come within the harmony of early Darwinism, the notion that one might pursue a set of questions concerning the actual physiology of the hereditary process was entirely new. "As [Brooks] talked of them," Bateson recalled, "the insistence of those problems became imminent and oppressive. . . . I know it was through Brooks that I first came to realize the problem which [became] my chief interest and concern."[27]

Bateson's scientific heterodoxy was encouraged if not engendered in the United States, and the result of his research there was his classic paper, "The Ancestry of Chordata."[28] In it, Bateson argued that *Balanoglossus* was the first of the vertebrates in the evolutionary scheme, demanding a new subdivision of the entire class. At the age of twenty-five, he had reordered the canons of evolutionary classification. His college rewarded him by electing him to a fellowship. But Bateson was not content to pursue comparative embryology. Critical of the suppositions upon which that subject rested, he maintained a skeptical attitude. Using "modern" morphological interpretation did "not in any way prejudge the question as to the possible or even probable error in these methods."[29] And with that flourish, Bateson set aside all further phylogenizing, to seek a new field for inquiry. Having learned from Brooks that Darwin's account of the evolutionary process was incomplete, Bateson became concerned with the effects of environmental change on heredity and variation in species. In the 1880s this pursuit was an isolating one, so sedentary was scientific opinion in Cambridge about the Darwinian corpus. William Bateson's youth and skill, though, seem to have been best suited to standing against the tide. A colleague later wrote of this stage of his career that "the desertion of orthodox morphological methods of enquiry by the most brilliant of its younger exponents caused [him] to be regarded by many as little better than a renegade. But Bateson was never deterred by other men's opinions."[30]

In 1886, he set out to explore the effects of environmental change in marine organisms residing in the lakes of central Russia. On the basis of his *Balanoglossus* work, he had won financing for this entirely different field. It was known that some lakes were drying up, while others were getting saltier. By comparing mollusks, Bateson hoped to witness the effect of these shifting environments upon the organisms. He wandered about the Russian steppe for two years, collecting specimens of three genera of living and fossil mollusks. He returned to Cambridge in the autumn of 1887, only to depart again on a short expedition to the brackish waters of northern Egypt. The scientific results of all this travel were insignificant. By his own admission, Bateson had followed a false lead and had entertained overly narrow expectations. Although plentiful, the evidence collected was inconclusive. He concluded that the diversities of environment, for the most part, had not produced variations in his Russian and Egyptian mollusks. He became distrustful of environmental explanation and again sought to reformulate his methods and to focus his attention elsewhere.

Bateson's expedition had also offered the rich opportunity of living with and observing natives (who called him William Williamitch). Learning Russian enabled him to gain entry throughout the culture. He sent home amusing ethnographic letters, which showed in him candid descriptive ability but little or no social insight.[31] While in Turkestan, for example, he concluded that "anything like chivalry or personal honesty is unknown and not ever appreciated. In short, it is like living among the criminal classes."[32] Will Bateson was outspoken and good humored. In Pavlodar, he observed the afternoon bath which the population normally took

> entirely unclad—promiscuously and without distinction of sex or age, without even the costume which French indecency demands. I have seen many things among foreigners but never anything to touch this. I would respectfully ask whether, on encountering young ladies who take a high place in local society (and whom one has escorted on a boating expedition), should one take off one's hat or not? I had not considered the problem, and did so, as I saw others also did, but I think it was perhaps a mistake.[33]

Disappointed by the outcome of his travels, Bateson remained absorbed by the problem that had motivated it—variation in species. "All naturalists are agreed that the process by which the result has been achieved is one of Evolution," but he upheld that many questions still remained unanswered.

Whether we believe with Lamarck that adaptations are the direct result of environmental action, or with Darwin that they have been brought about by natural selection, it is admitted by all that the progression has come to pass through the occurrence of variations. This is common ground. Hence, if we seek the steps in the sequence of animal form, we must seek by studying the variations which are now occurring in them, and by getting a knowledge of the modes of occurrence of those variations and, if possible, of the laws which limit them.[34]

In 1890, Bateson phrased his purposes morphologically, in terms of the recurrence of organic pattern: what were the laws of symmetry and segmentation by which, for example, repetition of parts in an organism was made possible? The production of regular repetitions stood in his mind, in fair comparison to hereditary phenomena, and per contra, when they were disrupted, anomalies or variations appeared. Bateson was looking for laws which governed organic form. In doing so, he disclosed that theoretical materialism was no less repellent to him than utilitarianism, its lay counterpart. Heredity and variation were not to be based in "form'd Matter in solid, massy, hard, impenetrable moveable Particles" spoken of by Newton. In nature, Bateson maintained, "the body of one individual has never *been* the body of its parent."[35] Instead, "the new body is made again new from the beginning just as if the wax model had gone back to the melting pot before the new model began."[36]

He viewed the organism as an integral, coordinated whole and not as an atomic assemblage of "characters." Variation, therefore, when it occurred, would have effects on other parts of the organism. He tried to express this in terms of visual and formal analogies to phenomena which possessed rhythmic order and contained undulatory motion, or what he came to call vibrations.* Sand ripples on the beach, the zebra's stripes, waves, and organic segmentation all offered themselves as instances of both form and periodic oscillation which Bateson suggested, were "comparable" to the series of segments formed by

---

*William Coleman, a historian of science, has argued that Bateson's emphasis on rhythmic order was a part of his "long and intimate friendship with ... Alfred North Whitehead. They shared not only interest and understanding of art and the classics but concern for a pressing problem, how to reconcile pattern or form, the product or companion of changeless geometry, with the inescapable dynamism of nature. From the rhythmic model Bateson aspired to derive biological form from physical process; Whitehead's interest in the matter implicates his entire metaphysics." (W. Coleman, "Bateson and chromosomes: conservative thought in science," *Centaurus* 15 (1971): 268.)

"the communication of vibrations in an Elastic body."[37] By 1891 he was heatedly describing a new "VIBRATORY THEORY OF REPETITION OF PARTS" in a letter to his sister Anna.

> It is the best idea I ever had or am likely to have.... Divisions between segments, petals, etc., are *internodal* lines like those in sand figures made by sound, i.e., lines of maximum vibratory strain, while the midsegmental lines and the petals, etc., are the *nodal* lines, or places of minimum movement. Hence all the *patterns* and *recurrence of patterns* in animals and plants—hence the perfection of symmetry—hence bilaterally symmetrical variation, and the *completeness* of repetition whether of a part repeated in a radial or linear series, etc., etc.... Of course Heredity becomes quite a simple phenomenon in light of this.[38]

At the core of Bateson's analogies was the idea that the mechanics of heredity and variation was fundamentally one of division—that is, of dynamism within form. "The geometrical symmetry of living things is the key to a knowledge of their regularity, and the forces which cause it," Bateson wrote in 1909.

> In the symmetry of the dividing cell the basis of that resemblance we call Heredity is contained. To imitate that morphological phenomena of life we have to devise a system which can divide. It must be able to divide, and to segment as—grossly—a vibrating plate or rod does, or as an icicle can do as it becomes ribbed in a continuous stream of water; but with this distinction, that the distribution of chemical differences and properties must simultaneously be decided and disposed in orderly relation to the pattern of the segmentation.[39]

He attributed the source of the "rhythms of division" to the concept of "polarity," which was generally understood to be an ideal force existing between binary, opposing poles in a sort of dynamic relation. Disruptions of balance gave rise to corrective tendencies, although new modes of equilibrium could be established. Stability in such a polarized system was marked by constant oscillations. Bateson therefore had the notion that "the rhythms of segmentation may be the consequence of a single force definite in direction and continuously acting during the time of growth ... *This polarity cannot be a property of ... material, as such, but is determined by a force acting on that material, just as the polarity of the magnet is not determined by the arrangement of its particles, but by the direction in which the current flows*" [italics added].[40]

There were not a few vibratory models of inheritance abroad in the 1890s. Bateson's provided him with a means of sidestepping matter, but it also brought him into the company of men like Samuel Butler and James Ward, who openly asserted the alluring analogy between heredity and memory. Confessing his attraction, Bateson refused to accept any species of psychophysical postulate. "It is tempting," he wrote in 1915, "to suppose that the apparatus, the readiness to make the right response to various stimuli, is a manifestation of unconscious memory, but since . . . there is no good reason to suppose that even the simplest experiences of the parent are . . . transmitted to a succeeding generation, the suggestion of continuous memory . . . can only be defended on grounds which to the biologist are mystical and unconvincing."[41] Publicly at least, William Bateson was a master at leaving the greatest things unsaid; his youngest son would later say of his father. "If you want to put salt on a bird's tail, you will be advised not to look at the bird while you approach it. He was always trying to put salt on the tail of nature and particularly to catch that component of nature which we might as well call Mind."[42]

But however diffident or simply unaware he was about what perhaps was the heart of his science, nonetheless he was completely immersed in it. At times his "brain boil[ed]" with evolution, so completely did the work take hold of him. "It is becoming a perfect nightmare to me," he wrote his sister, in "a great fluster" and "giddy" from thinking about his vibratory theory of heredity.[43] For the most part, W. B. reserved his emotions for his science. Having broken through some vexing problem, for example, he informed his future wife, "I feel rather like I did on the morning of [our engagement], very pleased with myself—only perhaps a little more certain I am on the right track. Also the risks are not so great, because hypothesis can be amended— wives less easily."[44] Some years later, she recalled the great affect that her husband brought to his science.

> Research was one long delicious adventure to him. He was patient, painstaking and ingenious—the drudgery was nought compared to the exhilirating thrill of treasure-trove, which sure enough awaited him. And yet as he worked, in the white heat of excitement, judgment sat within him cool and critical. Emotion could not compel him to unwary haste. [45]

Reacting against the hard-and-fast conception of species as unchanged since Creation, Darwin had stressed continuity and subtle mutability within and between species. Variation in evolution occurred by means of a smooth series of intermediate forms. Large mutations, called sports, were discounted because they could only confound adaptation rather than contribute to it. In any case, sports were likely to be "swamped," as it was said, by the numerous normal forms among which they existed. Bateson opposed this position. "In all the older work on evolution," he countered, "it is assumed, if the assumption is not always expressly stated, that the variations by which species are built are small. But if they are small, how can they be sufficiently useful to their possessors to give those individuals an advantage over their fellows?"[46] In a manner that was characteristic of him, Bateson took up a scientific cause by inverting theoretical consensus. For seven years he collected biological monstrosities—cases of extra limbs and fingers, inverse symmetries, and dwarfs—as illustrations of large, sudden discontinuous variations in species. His methods brought him into contact with "all sorts and conditions of men."[47] He sought out anyone who had intimate dealings with multiple generations of life—stock breeders, horticulturalists, amateur gardeners, shepherds. Taking Darwin's lead, he looked especially to those whose interest in heredity was practical and whose knowledge of it was theoretically untainted. Bateson attended flower shows and animal exhibitions. He scoured museums and libraries, amassing an unrivaled knowledge of zoological facts.

In 1894, Bateson published the fruits of his massive labors—*Materials for the Study of Variation, Treated with Special Regard to DISCONTINUITY in the Origin of Species*.[48] Over six hundred pages long, it was a catalogue of more than eight hundred illustrations of variations in animal form. It included examples of excessive number (supernumerary digits, anthropoid segmentation) and oddities of symmetry (such as radial and bilateral monstrosities). Bateson had spent these last years convincing himself of the frequency and significance of specific diversity. He stated flatly that there were no transitional forms between most species, and presented his *Materials* as a teratological handbook to represent the relentless occurrence of sharp distinction between parent and offspring. He meant it to be a fresh start, nothing more than a compilation of new facts presented entirely free of theoretical discussion. Although the preface and introduction to *Materials for the Study of Variation* were sprinkled with filial disclaimers in homage to Darwin, Bateson's book was undeniably a bold and original attack on a crucial part of the theory of natural selection. Though more than thirty years had passed since *The Origin of Species* was published, the hereditary process was still a mystery.

> In owning that it is so, we shall not honour Darwin's memory the less; for whatever may be the part which shall be finally assigned to Natural Selection it will always be remembered that it was through Darwin's work that men saw for the first time that the problem is one which man may reasonably hope to solve. If Darwin did not solve the problem himself, he first gave us the hope of a solution, perhaps a greater thing. How great a feat that was, we who have heard it all from childhood can scarcely know.[49]

The book was little read and even more rarely purchased. Indeed it attracted more critics than converts. Its early failure, in part, can be laid to lack of theoretical formulation. Bateson had presented no basis from which to view his ample demonstration of discontinuity. None yet existed. His famous conclusion was terse: "Inquiry into the causes of variation is as yet in my judgment premature."[50] But, further, the book's poor reception was related to its ill-timing. The piety of the tones in which Bateson called on his fellow naturalists to reexamine problems most believed Darwin had solved reflected both the rigidity of the orthodoxy against which he stood, and his own quasi-religious zeal.

> The priest and the poet tried to solve [the problem of variation] each in his turn, and have failed. If the naturalist is to succeed he must go very slowly, making good each step. He must be content to work with the simplest cases, getting from them such truths as he can, learning to value partial truth though he cheat no one into mistaking it for absolute or universal truth; remembering the greatness of his calling, and taking heed that after him will come Time, that "author of authors," whose inseparable property it is ever more and more to discover the truth, who will not be deprived of his due.[51]

Materials established William Bateson as the leading anti-Darwinian, enfant terrible of British biology. "His conclusions were unwelcome, and his outspoken manner, conveying harsh and ironic assaults upon Britain's pride, Darwinism as it triumphed in the second generation, further reduced the young man's appeal."[52]* At thirty, struggling with problems and methods which isolated him both from orthodox biologists of the day and from their sources of support, Bateson relied on his college, St. John's, for financial backing. Fortunately, the college was loyal to a former master's son. In addition to a meager fellowship, he was offered the job of college steward. The combination of these two provided him with adequate income. His responsibilities included charge of the college kitchen, whose chaotic state he promptly reorganized. "Always keeping the end in view, [Bateson] made as a rule, short work of obstacles.... Truth is," it was later written, "he had

---

*The Marxist journalist, J. G. Crowther, has proposed a third element: "Bateson's contest was not purely scientific. He belonged to the Liberal rentiers, descended from the trading and commercial classes, whereas his opponents . . . belonged to the Conservative landed aristocracy. The spirit of the Liberal rentiers was centered in St. John's whereas that of the Conservatives . . . was centered in Trinity. The rivalry between these two colleges reflected the struggle between these two social classes. Bateson's ideas and work were influenced by and were in some degree a part of this struggle." (J. G. Crowther, *British Scientists of the Twentieth Century,* p. 256.)

grasped with unacademic firmness the fact that situations occur in which *the prompt exercise of crude authority* offers the only real solution of a difficulty."[53] Bateson also supervised St. John's farm and gardens, which allowed him to conduct some small-scale experiments in plant hybridization. His forceful reputation in the college grew.

> Our undergraduate life was stirred, one day, by a portent. We passed through the front gate of the college on our way to laboratories and all was as usual. But on our return, to our dismay and confusion, there stood before us firmly rooted in the pavement, close to the gateway and affronting its mellow time-stained purple brickwork, a flaunting vermillion pillarbox of the royal mail. Its insolent stance was, however, fated to be of short duration. Before our emotions had taken form, it was removed as suddenly as it had come, and the brickwork glowed softly as of old. Eagerly, we asked to whom did we owe this deliverance: soon there percolated down to us from higher strata of College life the name of Bateson. Clearly a man of action as well as of taste! Round the name thus impressed upon us, legends soon accumulated; that his views on evolution were heterodox; that he disapproved of attempts to reconcile science with religion; that he had shot a man on his Eastern scientific travels; that he had been the proud owner of a bulldog and then given him away to a porter at Waterloo Station. Clearly a man of more heroic mold than we expected to find among the dons of our college! A few years later I came to know the actual William Bateson and was nowise disappointed.[54]

III. Early Genetics

In January 1889, soon after returning from Russia and Egypt, Will Bateson met his future wife, Caroline Beatrice Durham. She was a tall, socially awkward, shy girl who was "one of the Durham sisterhood," of which there were six members. Their father, Arthur Edward Durham (1834-95), was senior surgeon at Guy's Hospital in London, where it was said that his fingertips had eyes.[1] In later years, however, Durham was evidently seen as a bit slothful and procrastinating. A reticent man and exceedingly deaf, he never confessed to daily attacks of nausea, or to his continual drinking.* Years later, Bateson boys would hear of the understanding within the Durham family that, in fact, the "coachman was an alcoholic. The coachman and [her father] the surgeon would come in arm in arm in the middle of the night. But in fact it was the coachman supporting the surgeon and not vice versa."[2]

Securing parental approvals, Bateson and Miss Durham were engaged. To celebrate, the twenty-eight-year-old biologist decided to give a dinner party with college wine, over which he had charge as steward of the St. John's cellar. Like his fiancée, Bateson was quite uninformed about her father's problems—and the times discouraged that sort of inquisitiveness. During the course of the evening, Miss Durham's somewhat puritanical mother, Mary

---

*Curiously, Florence Durham, one of his daughters, later became involved in research concerning the interplay between alcohol and heredity in cats. Miss Durham concluded that "the litters of young obtained from alcoholic parents, or from their descendants, have been as numerous and as heavy as those from the control matings, and have shown no excess of still-births or of deformities. Their offspring for several generations have exhibited no transmitted defects. ... It is hardly necessary to point out that these negative findings have no relation whatever to the effects of alcoholic parentage on the upbringing, as distinct from the inherited qualities, of children in an organized human society." (F. M. Durham and N. M. Woods, "Alcohol and inheritance," Privy Council, Medical Research Council, Special Report Series 168 [1932]: 3–4.)

Ellis, observed that Will himself was drinking a glass or two more than was acceptable. He later denied it, but to a household already camouflaging one alcoholic, the distinction between giddiness and inebriation was minimal. Will received word that his engagement was terminated. Letters were intercepted, and almost seven years passed before Bateson heard from Caroline Durham again. In the interim, her mother and father died. In September 1895, three months after the surgeon's death, she published a short story in the popular monthly *The English Illustrated Magazine,* using "Beatrice Durham" as a pseudonym.

The piece was in the form of a late-night conversation between two sisters. One is just returning from a party chaperoned by Sophie, their retiring, spinster aunt. She had expected to suffer through another dull affair, when suddenly the old aunt steps foward across the room and introduces herself to "Sir William Collins . . . [the man] who went on that expedition." Overcome, Collins interrupts his conversation to kiss her hand. They assure each other that neither is married, and straightaway Collins proposes. Sophie blanches at the thought, as the gloom of lost years appears on Sir William's face. It is too late, she laments, and we are too set in our ways. Instead, she gives him permission to visit her. So promised, Sir William leaves the party and Sophie explains the situation to the narrator:

> "When I was your age and wanted to—he was plain William, then, my dear, and had not won a title—poor Will, poor Will! . . . Mother—your grandmother, I mean . . . had other views for me. She said he was not eligible, and she was a hard woman in her way. . . . [She] disliked him too, and I—well—we never met again—never until tonight; but I might have been Lady Collins. I was right all the time, only I gave way, and now it is too late."[3]

The story of the party concluded, the one sister asks the other if she thought Collins would call again. " 'I'm sure of it,' was all the answer."[4]

Prose with a purpose this was, and if so judged, successfully composed. Miss Durham's message was hardly hidden in the story but rather in the publication. As Will Bateson was not in the habit of reading popular magazines, he did not come across the piece. Half a year after it appeared, Mrs. Whitehead, the philosopher's wife, passed a copy of the magazine on to him. The urgency of the note he then wrote betrayed its reserve.

> From things that have lately reached me I have been led to think it possible that you may be willing to see me again.
>
> If it is not so, you tell me and that will be all; but if it is so, will you some day meet me?

If we meet, it must, I think, be as friends simply, that we may see each other after the changes seven years have worked, freely and without committal of any kind on either side. I think that would be the right way.

Unless you choose otherwise I would suggest we should meet in some open place and that we should have a walk together. It would be less trying so. I will not say any more now, save that it has been for a long time my earnest desire to meet you again, if only as one who was once my dear friend, without regard to the future at all. . . . P.S. I shall be out of town most of tomorrow returning to this lodging in the evening. W. B.[5]

The engagement was renewed. At thirty-five, Bateson again delighted in the prospect of marriage and introduced his fiancée in Cambridge circles, with high excitement. As their wedding day approached, Will wondered where their presents were.

I can't think what's got the givers. I know several will *have* to give, who are hanging back. You wait and see . . . But no sensible person buys in Cambridge, and we must wait till term ends. There ought to be a general holiday to enable people to discharge their duties towards us. Margaret [his sister] says I must not give you a pipe, that it will lead to great trouble . . . that servants won't stop in a house where there are such goings on.[6]

In June 1896, they were finally married. Caroline Beatrice Durham decided for the occasion to simplify her name to Beatrice Bateson. Tall and formidable looking, the two made a handsome couple. If W. B. was aggressive and extroverted, Beatrice was rather reserved and self-deprecating. She adored him. "I began to learn what life may be," she wrote of the day of their marriage.[7] Her character was quite unlike the other Durham sisters in this regard. Florence, Hermia, and Edith were all fierce, intellectual ladies. They were "advanced" women, as it was said. Florence became a considerable geneticist. Hermia did historical work. Edith, called Dick, wrote ethnological accounts of the Balkans, throughout which she traveled extensively. Like generations of Cambridge dons, none of them married. In comparison to her sisters Beatrice was shy. She also thoroughly enjoyed her husband's company and quickly fell in not only with his ambition but with his prejudices as well. Will thought lactation "obscene." Utilitarian values had begun to threaten classical education, now the body was being made useful. Their children were wet-nursed.

Beatrice was an earnest woman and more so in contrast to the playfulness of her husband. "Under a . . . dignified manner," she would say of him, "lurked mirth and jollity. His intense and learned interest in life creamed over in gaiety."[8] By nature histrionic, Bateson excelled, for example, at charades. He was also a skillful opponent at croquet, which he never played without a fez perched on his head. Unendingly energetic, "he played as he worked, with a kind of special concentration of attention."[9] His quickness made him impatient. He attributed incapacity to simple lack of volition. Geoffrey Keynes, then a medical student and sometime visitor to the Bateson home, recalled the two of them. "I was very fond of her," he said. "She was . . . an extremely intelligent person, whom W. B. used to treat rather roughly." Keynes laughed at the memory.

> I remember once . . . she was offered a cigar, and she'd taken one (hesitantly), and William said, "Don't be so sheepish, Beatrice!" He was always apt to say what he thought. . . . A very straightforward person . . . Gwen Raverat [née Darwin] was very fond of Beatrice. William wasn't a person you were fond of, you admired him. . . . He was a rough character. I once said something rather "ticky" to him and he strapped me on the back, and it hurt. . . . I can't remember what it was now. I made some jokes against him. . . . He was a big man.[10]

Family repeatedly deferred to science. When the Batesons moved to a small house at the corner of Norwich and Panton Streets, they chose the new location for its proximity to the University Botanical Gardens, where W. B. had undertaken some experiments in the hybridization of plants and poultry. There they started a small family. In the last years of the nineteenth century, Beatrice gave birth to two boys. John was born first, on 22 April 1898, and sixteen months later on 1 September 1899, Martin arrived. To commemorate the birth of his first son, W. B. bought an original copy of William Blake's *Book of Job*. Beatrice soon enough hired Delphie Ann Taylor to tend the boys. Her husband had meager financing from the Evolution Committee of the Royal Society and needed her help with the peas and chickens. They settled on a family of four, but seeking larger quarters after Martin's birth, they moved to Grantchester, a small village on the periphery of Cambridge.

The new home, called Merton House, was surrounded by five acres of land, which in turn was enclosed by a high brick wall. With more space, they spent the first years of the new century, Beatrice recalled, in "hard manual labor from the merest menial drudgery to high flights of scientific speculation, hand and brain were hard at work."[11] Following publication of his *Materials for the Study of Variation,* Bateson turned his interest upon the appearance of anomalous form in experimental conditions. "The breeding pen is to us what the test-tube is to the chemist—an instrument whereby we examine the nature of our organisms and determine empirically what . . . I may call their genetic properties," he would later explain.[12] W. B. bought oil-burning incubators, capable of holding one hundred eggs, and stocked poultry pens. The baby chicks he kept in an upstairs bedroom until Beatrice pointed out that the boys' nanny might object to sharing the room. Will moved them into a large outhouse. When her husband was out of town, Beatrice took charge of the fowl, detailing the goings-on for him in correspondence. In the spring of 1902 for example, she wrote:

> Old J. B. 59 has done your poor wife grievous injury. Whilst occupied with the dead hen in his pen he attacked me with fury and caught me a good one on the foot. I felt bruised but took no serious notice. However as the day wore on, my foot felt so stiff and painful and hot that I retired to inspect its state. To my surprise the stocking stuck to my skin and removing it with a pang I found a small but bloody wound. I then examined my boot and beheld it was pierced— presumably with a spur. By bedtime my foot was so hot and painful that I could not be bothered to flash the eggs. I wrapped the wound in cold wet handkerchiefs and pitied myself for a long time. The inflammation is better this morning but the hurt is still prominent in my mind. The little boys are very happy. . . . It has aged John a good deal having an [older friend] visiting. The weather is horrible—bitterly cold and everlastingly windy. . . . Yrs. ever and ever.[13]

In 1903, W. B. lost Beatrice's assistance. She was pregnant and without her, research would be severely curtailed. Bateson invited a young biologist, R. C. Punnett, to join the work. "The matter has become urgent," he wrote Punnett. "My wife has hitherto done a large part both of the recording and of the many menial operations that such work involves, but I am sorry to say she will be more or less incapacitated this next season, so that help in some form or other I must get."[14] Punnett became confidant and lieutenant, arriving early every morning with a copy of the *Morning Post,* "a paper of which Bateson approved since it contained the best account of art sales."[15] The two men would talk and collect the day's eggs. Many were not allowed to hatch because the characters which they were observing were sufficiently developed for prenatal inspection. Before opening the shell, they often bet each other on the sex of the embryo. W. B. generally gave his assistant two to one odds and, more often than not, lost the bet. Except when pregnant, Beatrice kept very efficient notes of their findings. Punnett recalled the scene.

Having settled her in a chair at the trestle table with the "dead" book and a large bowl, Bateson ... took off his coat and produced his knife with the big, blunt blade, while I stood by with a pair of scissors. He then took up an egg, read off the numbers of the pen, then hen and the date of laying, and after, "Have you got that Beatrice?" proceeded to stab and peel off the shell into the aforesaid bowl, and to call out the peculiarities of that particular embryo.... After which the chick was handed to me, who slit it so as to expose the sex glands and give Mrs. Bateson the sex to complete the entry.[16]

Hardly the cloistered don, William Bateson pressed himself through each day. There was a ruggedness about the man, a physicalness. "His attention," Beatrice later said, "was strained and alert asking at every instant how the new knowledge c[ould] be used in a further advance, watching continually for fresh footholds by which to climb higher still."[17] Punnett called him "an intensely virile personality."[18] Attracted by his passion and by his endless curiosity, a small group of students began to surround him, in awe certainly but also a little in fear, for his scientific standards were high and rigid. Each involved himself in breeding experiments. Mice, pigeons, guinea pigs, goats, rabbits, oxalis, and snapdragons were bred under Bateson's scrutinizing eye. One of them later wrote, "I never had an argument with him—and I had many—without the absolute conviction that he would no more hesitate to admit himself in the wrong if I could convince him, than to tell me that I was talking nonsense if, as was more usual, I failed to do so."[19]* Beatrice added wistfully after her husband's death, "With his fine sensitive hands ... he was a beautiful manipulator. To watch him work, delicately dissecting some fragile blossom, was a splendid lesson. He seldom bungled."[20] Bateson had the high Victorian gift of concentration. In either work or play he could immerse himself totally. "One could not imagine, whilst working with him," his wife said, "that he had any trouble or anxiety greater than the sterility of a pea or the death of a valued chick.... In the same way he could completely absorb his attention in a game of chess or bridge."[21]

The central problem during the first decade of the twentieth century was financial. Students and colleagues all worked out of their own incomes, and

---

*However, J. G. Crowther has disagreed. Bateson's "qualities appeared to some as a model of absolute honesty and fearlessness inspired by a burning passion for truth. To others, these same qualities seemed to show a lack of self-control and an inability to enter into other people's points of view, and cooperate with them." (J. G. Crowther, *British Scientists of the Twentieth Century*, p. 306.)

Bateson himself struggled without firm basis of support. He continued to depend on money he received for looking after the kitchen at St. John's, and on the pittance sent by the Evolutionary Committee. Enthusiasms constrained by insufficient funding, W. B. despaired often. He kept a file of "begging letters" —of correspondence which had not produced support—and even pondered leaving biology. He weighed becoming head of the London Zoo, but then declined, concluding, "my proper place is on the land."[22] Twice, he seriously considered emigrating to the United States, where he had been well received. "I think I am cosmopolitan enough not to decline a handsome offer from the mere inertia that most people call love of their country," he wrote his American patrons, having decided to stay in England. "But being here, in the midst of a going concern—if slowly going—I see all sorts of risks that would follow a great break of continuity at my time of life, and before incurring those risks I am going to make a serious attempt to get, over here, the kind of opportunities I want."[23]

W. B. towed Beatrice. "In earlier days," she recalled, "he walked with a long rapid stride, with which I could never keep pace; he once turned to me in the Strand exclaiming: 'Really, Beatrice, you are the only man's wife I know who always walks two yards behind her husband,' to which I made the obvious retort, and we both laughed and walked together for some way until he gradually slid ahead again."[24] They attended flower shows together. The two of them, rising before dawn, would tend to the incubators, catch the eight o'clock train to London, and visit an art gallery or two before the show opened. After taking in the flowers, they rushed to the library to check some references, and then moved on to a number of art sales. They might visit the National Gallery. By late afternoon, back among the flowers, the show now less crowded, Bateson would confer with the exhibitors. "We tried once or twice," Beatrice remembered, "to finish with a theatre, but the midnight ride back to Grantchester from Cambridge station—the eggs still to be turned, the lamps adjusted—taught us to be content without this extra pleasure."[25]

Their second experimental preoccupation was with sweet peas. In search of the regularities of heredity and the exceptions of variation, each year W. B. and Beatrice bred and harvested thousands, until again lack of space intervened. Beatrice required some land to grow vegetables for their own consumption. Neighbors offered access to sections of their private gardens, and W. B. acquired use of the university farm, four miles away. Bateson's interest in plant hybridization led him to the affairs of the Royal Horticultural Society. In the summer of 1899, he addressed that organization, calling upon members to do breeding experiments and to compile statistical records of generational differences and similarities. Moreover, he made the provocative suggestion that the results of heredity might not be a blend of parental components, as was conventionally accepted. "The recognition of the existence of discontinuity in variation," W. B. said, "and the possibility of *complete integral inheritance* [italics added] where the variety is crossed with the type is . . . destined to simplify to us the phenomenon of evolution, perhaps beyond anything that we can yet foresee."[26] At this moment in the history of biology, before the rediscovery of the Mendelian laws, being so disposed put Bateson in a strange position. He was both behind and ahead of his time. He had hit on a conception of heredity which had already been verified, but no one knew it yet. Bateson candidly exposed his own ignorance: "We have no glimmering of an idea as to what constitutes the essential process by which the likeness of the parent is transmitted to the offspring."[27]

On 8 April 1900, Bateson was to address the Royal Horticultural Society again on the general subject of heredity and agriculture. Typically a cautious lecturer, he prepared some notes. He also brought along a paper which had just arrived from a Dutch colleague, the botanist Hugo de Vries. It was a recently uncovered article from *The Proceedings of the Natural History Society* of Brünn, then in Austria, on the experimental hybridization of peas by an unknown Augustinian monk, Gregor Mendel.[28] Originally published in 1865, it had been ignored after that time. On the train down to London, Bateson read the paper through. Immediately, he appreciated the consequence of Mendel's conclusions, and rewrote his entire lecture.

In eight years of experimentation, Mendel had crossed thousands of peas *(Pisum sativum)* of "differential characters,"—e.g., talls with shorts, or ones with differing pod shapes, or rough-skinned seeds with smooth skins. Mendel explained the results of his assiduous hybridization. Departing from the notion that hereditary process blended traits, so that the offspring presented a form intermediate between both parents, Mendel argued that the outcome of a cross between "antagonistic" characters was *either* the unaltered appearance of one trait in the hybrid *or* the entire disappearance of the trait from somatic expression. The underlying units of heredity were seen as unmalleable but capable of repeated combinations and separations. If the hybrid generation was bred with itself, the secondary character which had been absent could reappear unchanged. This was Mendel's crucial point. Though singular in outward, somatic appearance, the hereditary units, when crossed, were joined into a duality. Bateson outlined this view, a few years later:

> The fact that two cells are concerned in the production of all the ordinary forms of life was discovered a long while ago, and has been part of the common stock of elementary knowledge of all educated persons for about half a century. The full consequences of this double nature seem nevertheless to have struck nobody

before Mendel. Simple though the fact is, I have noticed that to many it is difficult to assimilate as a working idea. We are accustomed to think of a man, a butterfly, or an apple tree as each *one* thing. In order to understand the significance of Mendelism we must get thoroughly familiar with the fact that they are each *two* things, double throughout every part of their composition. There is perhaps no better exercise as a preparation for genetic research than to examine the people one meets in daily life and to try in a rough way to analyze them into the two assemblages of characters which are united in them.[29]

The hereditary elements, according to Mendel, were particulate. They maintained their identity unaffected through generations of breeding, in changing relations of precedence. The character which occurred in the first generation Mendel termed "dominant," and the latent character became "recessive." For example, when pure tall and pure dwarf varieties of the common edible pea were crossed, all the hybrids were tall, and "tallness" was said to be "dominant" over the "recessive" character "dwarfness." But when the tall hybrids were allowed to self-breed, the resulting generation was mixed. Dominant to recessive progeny appeared in a ratio of three to one—three-quarters were tall while one-quarter was dwarf. The dwarfs in turn, upon self-fertilizing, produced a generation of dwarf-size plants, whereas the talls continued to beget mixed offspring, about which Mendel provided further ratios.

Having argued so long in defense of the importance of discontinuous variation, and having already begun to do his own experiments in hybridization, William Bateson was uniquely prepared to assess the value of these new-old ideas. Indeed, he had himself come so close to discovering the Mendelian principles independently that one of his later disciples, J. B. S. Haldane, supposed that "if the Proceedings of the Brünn Natural History Society had been a little rarer ... Bateson would now be lying in Westminster Abbey."[30] Fundamentally, what struck W. B. was the utter significance of Mendel's contribution: "These experiments will certainly play a conspicuous role in all future discussions of evolutionary problems."[31] His rewritten paper to the Horticultural Society began with the proclamation that an "exact determination of the laws of heredity will probably work much more change in man's outlook on the world, and in his power over nature, than any other advance in natural knowledge that can be foreseen."[32] And before anyone else in England, Bateson knew that Mendel had pointed the way. Dazzled by the rediscovery, he hailed it, his wife said, "with a kind of triumphant gladness."[33] Bateson would later include the moment on the train to London, during which he read through Mendel's paper, as one of the half-dozen most intensively emotional experiences in his life. Immediately, he set himself the task of translating the paper into English.

Mendel also appealed to W. B. for reasons which were not strictly scientific. Aspects of the monk's life made personal sense to him, expressing many qualities which he himself possessed and which he most admired. Bateson did biographical research into Mendel's scientific development and found that he too had been isolated from and ignored by his contemporaries. "Two years ago," Bateson announced in 1902, "it was suddenly discovered that an unknown man, Johan Gregor Mendel, had, alone and unheeded, broken off from the rest. This is no metaphor, it is simple fact."[34] W. B. became devoted to chess, understanding that the monk had played the game ardently and took up cigars in his honor. But more seriously, Mendel was illustration of Bateson's belief that intellectual progress rested primarily on the contributions of highly gifted individuals. "The great advances of science," he wrote, "are made like those of evolution, not by imperceptible mass-improvement, but by the sporadic birth of penetrative genius. The journeymen follow after him, widening and cleaning up, as we are doing along the track that Mendel found."[35] Further, Mendel's work was a marvelous example of the importance of pure research. Bateson despised knowledge in the service of utilitarian ideals, and here was a case in point—a man who had sought only to gratify his curiosity. "Untroubled by an itch to make potatoes larger or bread cheaper, he set himself in the quiet of a cloister garden to find out the laws of hybridity, and so struck a mine of truth, inexhaustible in brilliance and profit."[36] The most startling instance of the depth of coincidence between the personal and scientific for which Mendel then stood in W. B.'s life can be seen in the birth of his third son on 9 May 1904, whom he named Gregory after the monk.

Bateson became Mendel's apostle in the English-speaking world, assuming a position similar to that T. H. Huxley had taken in defense of Darwinism. "It is to [his] missionary voice... that we look for the interpretation of Mendelism to the rising generation of the new century," the geneticist C. D. Darlington wrote, overviewing the history of the subject.[37] Moreover, as the genetist A. H. Sturtevant has pointed out, it was W. B. who coined the new English terminology.

> Many of the now familiar terms were introduced by Bateson—such as genetics, for the subject itself, and zygote, for the individual that develops from the fertilized egg, as well as for the fertilized egg itself (which was the older usage). Homozygote, heterozygote, and the adjectives derived from them followed. Mendel had spoken of the hybrid and the first generation from them; Bateson

suggested that these be designated "F1" and "F2" respectively—to stand for first and second filial generations. The term allelomorph (later and especially in the U. S. shortened to allele) also dates from Bateson's early work. Mendel usually used the word Merkmal for what we now term gene, and this was translated as character, often appearing as unit character; Bateson usually used the word factor. It was somewhat later (1909) that Johannsen introduced the word gene.[38]

In 1936, R. A. Fisher, one of his contemporaries, described Bateson's interest in the rediscovery as that of a "zealous partisan."[39] Beatrice, on the other hand, attributed her husband's behavior to a selfless "passion for truth."[40] Like the knights errant of old, she wrote, "he took to the field, full of chivalrous and honorable ardor to defend the truth as he knew her: possibly a disappointed expectation of the same ideal of conduct in others added some sting of contempt to the battery of knowledge which he brought to bear on his opponent.[41] Darlington, perhaps, was more even-handed when he recalled that Bateson "was pugnacious. He had opinions. He disagreed with certain of the prevalent, established views, and being pugnacious he asserted his opinions, and he found that he could assert them eloquently, and convincingly, and of course when he had Mendel behind him, overwhelmingly. This swept him forward and gave him the drive of his life."[42] W. B. realized that in defending Mendel he had gained an agonistic reputation, but was hardly bothered. "The term controversial," he said in 1907, "is conveniently used by those who are wrong to apply to the persons who correct them."[43]

Correcting those who refused to accept the new paradigm embroiled Bateson, during the first six years of the new century, in venomous and at times violent controversy. On one side were W. F. R. Weldon and his mentor, Karl Pearson, who were both statistical and positivist in orientation. They accepted the Darwinian conception of inheritance based on the accumulation of small continuous variations and were attempting to vitiate or minimize the significance of Mendelian laws. On the other side stood W. B., whose thinking so closely paralleled Mendel's own, alone and uncompromising. The intensity of the dispute was heightened because, as undergraduates, Weldon and Bateson had been closest friends, splitting in the early 1890s when the rebellious Bateson began to belittle the importance of continuous variation. In 1902, Weldon published an article attacking Mendel's principles in *Biometrika*,[44] a journal which he and Pearson had established to foster the expression of statistical investigation of Darwinian phenomena. Furious, Bateson responded with a book, *Mendel's Principles of Heredity: A Defense*,[45] about which one reviewer said, "One cannot help feeling that his speculations would have had more value had he kept his emotions under better control; the style and method of the religious revivalist are ill-suited to scientific controversy. ... The strength of Mr. Bateson's reasoning is hardly equal to that of his language."[46] They traded articles across the pages of *Nature* and *Biometrika* until the editors of the former refused to publish any more from either of them. Not surprisingly, Bateson was soon denied access to Weldon's journal. Relentless, he took up the strategy of the Trojan horse. Within an exact replica of *Biometrika's* cover he had a rejoinder privately printed. "To Bateson," it has seemed to the historians of science, P. Frogatt and N. C. Nevin, "preaching Mendelism was a mission—in the event a sacrificial one— but perhaps it was the only cause for which he would have sacrificed so deeply."[47]

The dispute between Mendelians and those who had come to be known as Biometricians, came to a head at the 1904 meeting of the zoology section of the British Association, of which Bateson was then president. Weldon "with voluminous and impassioned eloquence, beads of sweat dripping from his face"[48] attacked the Mendelian corpus. And Bateson, with a volume of *Biometrika* held aloft above his head as "patent evidence of the folly of the biometric school,"[49] asserted that the "gross" statistical method was a misleading instrument when applied to complex phenomena.[50] Through students and co-workers, he presented evidence in support of the Mendelian conception of heredity. Punnett's sense was that the Batesonians won the day. If all this rings too loudly of melodrama, it is by virtue of the presence of a theatrical bent in the antagonists. The hall was packed, both Bateson and Weldon knew it, and their argumentative natures were stimulated.*

The controversy finally subsided in 1906 when Weldon, as if exhausted, died of pneumonia at the age of forty-five. Despite this shock, the resentment which Bateson harbored for Mendel's detractors was felt so deeply that even two years later, he would not acknowledge Pearson as the two sat next to each other at an awards dinner of the Linnaean Society. "Bateson refused my

---

*The magnitude of the conflict brought its personalities and issues onto center stage of the larger English scientific community and even into its families. J. B. S. Haldane's sister Naomi Mitchison, for example, named her pet guinea pigs after Bateson and Punnett, and remembered learning the following limerick:

> Karl Pearson is a biometrician
> And this, I think, is his position:
> Bateson and co.,
> Hope they may go
> To monosyllabic perdition.

(N. Mitchison quoted in *Haldane and Modern Biology*, ed. K. R. Dronamraju, p. 302.)

greeting," Pearson recalled, "and sat sideways on the chair, with his back to me, the whole of the medal distribution"[51] When Pearson was asked to contribute to the Darwin centenary festschrift, Bateson threatened to resign from the organizing committee if Pearson participated. The invitation was withdrawn.

If the discord of these years did much to impel the new science of heredity and variation into both the academic and the public mind, it did little to improve William Bateson's position in Cambridge. His vitriolic defense of largely unaccepted and misunderstood ideas had not ingratiated him in the hearts of senior people in biology. At the age of forty-five, he had gathered around him a group of students but still had not been offered a proper professorship. It was also true, however, that insofar as Bateson was creating his own field, there was no post to be bestowed, for in 1907 no chair dedicated to his subject yet existed. He applied for three positions and was refused for each. In 1905, during one of his attempts, Bateson suggested a new word to stand for the study of heredity and variation. "No single word in common use quite gives this meaning," he wrote in application. "Such a word is badly wanted and if it were desirable to coin one, 'GENETICS' might do."[52] The professorship went to someone else in another subject, and Bateson was bitterly disappointed. Forced to teach informally, he ran a small extracurricular course on Mendel after hours. Nora Barlow (née Darwin), one of the students in attendance, recalled those days:

> My first introduction to the whole subject . . . was when William Bateson was giving what we called his Bible Class, in a remote lecture room, in the back of one of the colleges. It was outside the ordinary curriculum. It was a five or six o'clock lecture. And there he introduced a small set of people into the elements of the new Genetics. Mendelism was just coming in. . . . He was a brilliant lecturer and, of course, he had an entirely new view of ordinary heredity. . . . It was very inspiring indeed.[53]

Geoffrey Keynes, who also admired his pedagogy in those classes, called Bateson "the great teacher of my youth." Curiously, the geneticist's most abiding influence on the young Keynes was not to introduce him to the new science. It was rather to introduce him to the art of William Blake.[54]

W. B. visited America in 1907 to lecture at Yale and to attend the International Zoological Congress of that year. For the second time, he was met with adulation and curiosity. After so many years of ostracism, he wrote Beatrice that it was "an exhiliarating thing to speak to a really large and enthusiastic audience. It [wa]s dreadfully intoxicating! . . . I go about like a queen bee on a comb."[55] But beer was scarce, and the difficulty of finding servants to shine his shoes annoyed him. Returning to Cambridge, Bateson received an offer of a meager readership in zoology. Though humiliated, he consented to the position, resigned that the university could put forth nothing better. In doing so, he vowed to leave Cambridge as soon as possible. Early in 1908, however, in honor of Darwin's one hundredth birthday, money was received from an anonymous donor to endow a five-year chair in biology. The stipulation of the bequest required that its occupant do research in the new genetics—slightly veiled testimony that the post was created with Bateson specifically in mind. He accepted, not knowing that the finances for the chair had come from his friend, the former Prime Minister, A. J. Balfour. It carried a salary of five hundred pounds per year, but W. B., having resigned his stewardship at St. John's, was little better off.

At forty-seven, he had won a measure of recognition and was pleased. Yet the chair "had more of dignity than security," as Beatrice later supposed.[56] It was not permanently endowed and did not provide money for research. When, therefore, the directorship of the John Innes Horticultural Institution, newly founded at Merton Park, outside of London, became available, Bateson could not refuse. The income was five thousand pounds per year. There were to be funds for staff, and research facilities seemed limitless. "A new start in the middle of life is good for a man," he wrote a colleague.[57] The university had honored him, but the John Innes Council presented him with opportunity. Aspiration, not recognition, compelled W. B. at this point in his career. Even two years later, when the title of the chair of biology was changed to genetics,* and he was asked to return to Cambridge, according to Beatrice, "he unhesitatingly declined this tempting invitation."[58]

During the autumn of 1910, Bateson moved affairs and family to Merton. "Whilst these changes were pending," his wife recalled, they went to Happisburgh, for a seaside holiday.

> The attraction of that coast was, he said, its absolute nullity, and without lectures to prepare or even proofs to correct, we did not rightly know how we should bear this absoluteness.... En route came the inspiration—we would paint. We found an artist's colour man and fitted outselves out with paint, boards and brushes.[59]

Then and thereafter, Beatrice and W. B. spent many leisure hours painting.

---

*The change to secular belief partly involved the substitution of an evolutionary explanation of the development of life for that in *Genesis*. Perhaps in the wake of this shift, or perhaps in concert with it, Cambridge University, which, hitherto, had trained those who espoused the sacred version in the world, was transformed. The creation of the new chair of *genetics* for William Bateson thus signaled somewhat more than that a specialized subdiscipline had been carved out and authorized by the university. Surely Butler would have recognized it, had he lived, as the end of one ideological monopoly and the formal sanction of a new one.

IV. A Didactic Family

Favored by material comforts, and attended by inexpensive labor, upper middle-class English academics lived in an unhurried world that was flexible enough to permit idiosyncrasy, yet integrated enough to sustain intense inquiry and generational continuity. According to Nöel Annan, a historian of this intellectual aristocracy, the collective certainty about their place in society was founded in religion.

> Evangelicalism, indeed, was the strongest ingredient in the spirit of the class and though the faith in its purest form might fade, the intellectual aristocracy were imbued with the principles which flowed from the faith. There was the sense of dedication, of living with purpose, of working under the eye, if not of the great Taskmaster, of their own conscience—that organ which evangelicalism magnified so greatly. There was the sense of mission to improve the shining hour and the profession to which they had been called. There was the sense of accounting for the talents with which Providence had endowed them. There was also the duty to hold themselves apart from a world given over to vanities which men of integrity rejected because they were content to labour in the vineyard where things of eternal significance grew—in the field of scholarship where results were solid not transient.[1]

Many, however, did not restrict their consciences to within the academy. A "splendid eccentricity" flourished among them, whose purpose was to expose sham in Victorian conduct.[2]

Family in Cambridge was a relatively recent development. Fellows had only been allowed to marry in 1882. Although the sacred underpinnings of the clerical college had been eliminated, vestiges were yet visible at the beginning of the twentieth century. Between 1905 and 1907, notably, one quarter of all those who matriculated still eventually entered the church. Before World War I, the university community remained small and intertwined. Families differed in intellectual emphasis one to the next, according to the interests of the head of the household, but tended to rather uniform organization. They were inclined to be patriarchal. Severe allowances might be made on a father's behalf, which were yielded less readily to a mother, who was, in any case, accustomed to self-sacrifice. Households relied upon nannies and servants, whose control over domestic affairs was as complete as their ability to preserve the illusion that their employers were in charge. Children were often more intimate with their nannies than with their parents, because proper respect still required them to be mute bystanders of adult activity. Gwen Raverat, who grew up in Cambridge at the turn of the century, complained that parents noticed little of children's lives. "It was perfectly easy to hide anything from them," she remembered, "from love to a bad cold and cough. In fact, if you wanted them to know anything, you absolutely had to shout it at them, and even then they probably would not grasp it."[3]

Perhaps these families offered a somewhat stiff, overly defined, overly protected childhood; nonetheless they were relentless in their eagerness for knowledge. Children of the academic upper middle class grew up soaked in conversation. As infants, Annan has suggested that they extended their vocabulary and learned to talk in grammatical sentences, almost osmotically. From hearing discussions between their elders, they learned how to reason logically. Of course, many of these children did not inherit their parents' intellectual talents and suffered unjustly by feeling inadequate. The ones who did were enriched by acquiring the habit of thinking in concepts at an early age. They were surrounded by ideas and by those who professed them. At the dinner table, when parents sought to consult reference books, children were sent as bearers. And if treated more as students than as children, they were raised with access to magnificent libraries and within houses adorned with objets d'art. Leslie Stephen, Virginia Woolf's father, though he did not allow his daughters to smoke cigarettes, permitted them free reign throughout his unexpurgated books and expected them never to accept the judgment of good form.

By now in their second generation in Cambridge, the Batesons were a well-known, even conspicuous family, with manners and values adhering to the norms of their moment, place, and class. Beatrice kept a diary during the boys' infancy, revealing the interests of both parents and children. John "recognizes drawings of objects known to him. His father yesterday drew him a cat which John instantly greeted with the shrill delight which he reserves especially for the cat. . . . He pets Martin like a pet animal."[4] Something of the day-to-day tenor of the household is also evident in a letter W. B. wrote his wife while she was away on holiday during the summer of 1901.

John has had a stomach-ache all day and consequently been moping. We think the cause is probably no further than the mulberry-bush. I don't suppose much there is much wrong. He is now asleep and seems comfortable.

I have had a thorough clean of all flues, incubators and rearer. The latter had a leaky and empty boiler, now I trust repaired, as the night is cold. My hands reached a level of uniform blackness never, I believe, before endured. They were clear negro tint, smoothly spread and for days they will be imperfectly clear. Martin [then about two and one-half years old] was afraid to pass in the passage and shrank in physical fear. He felt as the children of Israel did when they found that Moses had married "a woman of the Ethiopians." I have been thinking it was small wonder they "murmured" against him. Think how we should feel if the Archbishop of Canterbury did the same. There is a slackening of the household tension which shows me that it is you who are supposed to be the critic of the kitchen. Yesterday I dined off faded hashed mutton and Sunday's pudding, but was borne up by thoughts of tonight's curry. This would have been admirable had the rice been cooked. Soup and potatoes were stopped. Salad is stopped. Veg. marrow has succeeded it, for good and all. *But* this morning I had the prethought to order turnips, which were yellow and excellent. Also we had the long hoped for raisin dumpling, but to one gorged with curry this was only occasion of regret for wasted opportunity.

I gathered the plums, three baskets full and they have been some jammed and some bottled. I have bought nothing but a paper all day.

Seeing that Moses had very little influence with the people at the best of times he ought to have thought twice before marrying a negress. And if any one else had done it, he would have been the first to call out. . . . Yours just came. John much better, though the cause is not yet removed. Wilkes writes asking whether I will go to the Hybridization Conference in New York, September 1902, as one representative of the Horticultural Society. They offer 75 pounds towards expenses. I am rather tempted but shall not write for a few days.[5]

The content of Bateson's unique spirit of inquiry infused family life. Indoors, his children lived in what amounted to a museum, and outdoors, they played among rows of peas, greenhouses, and poultry pens. "I grew up in the middle of natural history and beetle collecting," Gregory would later say.[6] This was a didactic childhood, walks were field trips and conversations were explanatory. The boys were entertained by W. B.'s students. "Please tell Mother I enjoyed being at the Darwin's very much. We had a splendid bonfire; and we baked potatoes in it," Martin wrote his brother John in the fall of 1907.[7] Bateson expressed fatherhood through science and taught his children as he did his students. There was no distinction drawn between science and family. Beatrice maintained that "working as he did almost entirely at home, the children saw much of their father, and he soon established a delightful camaraderie with them. He was keenly interested in their development, and enjoyed helping them."[8] One day, for example, he found his four-year-old son playing in a forbidden flower bed, rubbing some petals together. "Hullo! John! What are you doing there?" he called out. "I'm only vaccinaten' of them [sic]," John answered back happily. The trespass at once forgiven, W. B. put aside the business of the moment to give John his first simple lesson in the structure of a flower. According to their mother—who did also—the children took after their father, full of "curiosity and admiration."[9] The days of the little boys came to be cramped with natural history and natural scientists. His gardens in Grantchester had become a beacon for research in the new genetics. Visitors came from all over the world, and W. B.'s students and colleagues were constantly present at Merton House. Gregory recalled that Punnett worked as his father's "sort of research assistant, coming out all the time, but very much second fiddle. One day two men came visiting, neither of them Punnett, and I am said to have pointed at one of them, and said, 'Is that, that man's Punnett?' as if a Punnett was a sort of a rank and not a high one."[10]

The house swarmed with cats. "W. B. couldn't abide dogs," Gregory recalled, "and he always used to say that they knew he saw through them."[11] Bateson had a sense of fun but many people did not notice it. He was a large man, and perhaps his imposing size may have obscured his intent. Once, he playfully scolded his eight-month-old son Martin "calling him naughty, and the baby puckered up his face to cry." Beatrice wrote in her diary that "this was not intended or expected."[12] Nora Barlow, one of his students in those days, had the impression that "probably W. B. may have been rather an alarming father.... I don't know, I may be quite wrong about this, but the man may have been a dictator, not in the ordinary way, rather in the anti-orthodox way. He had very definite views."[13] In all things—from the inane, it seemed, to the transcendental—the tenor of the family was of Bateson's making, reflecting his beliefs and interests, and evolving out of his commanding and varied personality. Indeed, Edward, his younger brother, was of the opinion that Bateson was a tyrant and "one of the real Victorian autocrats."[14] W. B., for his part, rarely missed an opportunity to transmit his self-assurance to his offspring. We find him gently exhorting John, when the boy began primary school.

> I have just got letters from your mother, which I hear that by now you must be a real schoolboy! That is a great state in life and I hope you have made a good beginning and are working hard. *The great thing is to go your own way and not to bother what other people think or say about you. If you are satisfied that what you do is right, you can't go very far wrong* [italics added]. I am afraid butterflies are quite

over at least for the present. I saw "tufted grouse" in the woods. It was close to me, such a fine big bird. I have seen three kinds of squirrels in the U. S. A.[15]

Except, perhaps, for a devotion to the intellect, there was no religion in the Bateson house. The father was a confirmed atheist and the mother descended from many generations of nonbelievers. "W. B. knew something about the sort of structure of the Anglican creed," Gregory supposed, "about the nature of heresy and things of this kind."[16] Bateson was determined that his children not grow up to be what he called "empty headed atheists," and took care that they received a literary education as well as a scientific one. For many years, every morning after breakfast, he read to his boys—generally from the Old Testament, but occasionally from Bunyan or Shakespeare. Beatrice remembered the scene: "If sometimes, he rose from the table, absent-minded, one of the [children] would say: 'We haven't had our chapter, father,' and back he came."[17]

John and Martin grew up intimately, being close in age and interest. Together, they collected nature. Pursuing beetles, butterflies, fossils, they became field naturalists simply by living out their childhood. The scientific culture of their upbringing was thick. In the spring of 1909, John had been sent to stay with his paternal grandmother, Anna, at the Yorkshire coastal town of Robin Hood's Bay, to recuperate from nagging chest congestion. W. B. wrote him of goings-on at home.

> Martin and I went to the Geological Museum the other day and tried to get the names of our fossils.
>
> The very big Ammonite seems probably to be *A. obtusus*, not *Bucklandi*. The flat, Nautilus-like one from Runswick seems to be *Harpoceras exaratum* and the round ribbed one from Runswick is *Dactylioceras annucatum*. (The "ceras" in these words is of course κέρας a horn.) Your bit of nautilus I take to be *N. intermedius*. The Equisetum is *Equisetites columnaris*. We had not got the shiny Ammonite with us, and there were a good many so nearly like it that we did not get a satisfactory name.
>
> Martin began school again yesterday, and we hope to see you home and well again before long.
>
> I haven't yet taken the bits of the big fossil plant in, we saw nothing like it in the show cases. I find the Plesiosaurus paddles are altogether different from Ichthyosaurus. They have long regularly formed finger-bones like those of a mammal. . . . Ichth. has the round, scale-like bones you saw in our piece and they have generally *six* fingers, not five, as I thought.[18]

Will and Beatrice occupied their days with chickens and peas and little boys—sometimes, it seemed, in that order of priority. Gregory occupied a position even further down in the family's concerns. Indeed, he may have been the result of an unwanted pregnancy, which Beatrice had then tried half-heartedly to miscarry. Tenacious, the child was born on 9 May 1904. W. B. was in the fields, shelling peas, when the news came to him that Beatrice had given birth to another boy. Slightly disappointed that his progeny were all male, he is said to have looked up and remarked, "Too bad, I like 'em mixed like the chickens."[19] Unlike his brothers', Gregory's birth was marked neither by the purchase of a new Blake nor a new house. Beatrice merely made terse entry in her diary, "Son born. Gregory, after Gregor Mendel. Fair. Blue eyes. Very healthy."[20]

Despite being the baby of the family, Gregory was not the subject of adoration. On the contrary, he was "like a third to twins" to his brothers, who were five and six years older. "It was they who received all the attention, and it was they who were considered to be the clever ones."[21] Gregory was a human footnote to his father's appreciation of the Augustinian monk, and a distant other to his brothers intimacy. "We were out for a walk yesterday," Martin wrote home during a vacation when the boys were eight and seven, "as we were coming home we met Gregory and he shouted out: 'John and Martin!'"[22] When he was old enough, the elder brothers took him under their joint wing and, to a certain extent, served in loco parentis. They led him around Cambridge, "beetling," and taught him what they knew about the natural sciences. "I had this funny thing about goats and ghosts that was never quite clear," Gregory remembered of his childhood. "I think they were ghosts. I called them goats. And this led to a whole theory that Gregory was interested in goats. I don't think I ever was. [I recall] Martin taking me all through the wood behind the house in Grantchester to show me there were no goats there.... [I had] a photograph of goats over my bed, for years."[23]

They were often sent to stay with maiden aunts on both sides of the family or to their father's widowed mother. Single women all, and of marked assertiveness, they had a large presence in the boys' childhoods. In retrospect, Gregory would attribute an independence of character to them which he had not noticed as a child. "They filled space. ... I can't tell you how much they didn't belong. They contrived to not belong by combining elitism and a contempt for the efforts of the rest of the world with extreme idiosyncrasy like smoking pipes."[24] As boys, however, John, Martin, and Gregory only received their fondness. Just as Beatrice doted on Will, so the children basked in these ladies' sympathetic attention. One of W. B.'s sisters, Edith, did busts of all three of them during these years. "I have received a letter from Granny," Martin wrote his father from school; "she has written an invitation . . . in poetry . . . about why don't you stir to send us to her, and that the toys are very lonely without us."[25] Gregory recalled visiting W. B.'s sister Anna, once a summer for a number of years: "We collected beetles in the pond. First all of us, then Martin and me, then me alone. . . . She ran a sort of nursery garden for her flowers. Ran it very successfully, was sort of a Grande Dame of the neighborhood, down in Hampshire inside the New Forest. . . . Very sturdy, red-faced, very plain, very worthy sort of face."[26]

In July 1910, so that their parents could prepare to leave Cambridge, the boys were packed off with their nanny to Robin Hood's Bay, to stay with Aunt Edith Bateson. "How is the moving getting on? How are the cats and kittens?" Martin repeatedly asked his mother throughout the summer.[27] The boys fished and played croquet. Gregory was six and with his nanny's help learned to swim. "You would have laughed to see Gregory in the water this morning," she wrote Beatrice. "He said he would bathe, so I found him a nice sandy place and tucked my skirt up and went in with him. He did enjoy it, till the boys saw us, then they came for a little game. They did have great fun, and are really good. They get occasionally high spirits, but soon calm down."[28]

When the move to Merton occurred, John and Martin stayed in town as boarders at a small preparatory school, Saint Faith's. Losing their younger brother, they took charge of a young boy named Evelyn Hutchinson,* who remembered that though he was born and brought up in Cambridge, his initial contact with the Bateson boys came immediately after their parents left town. "I went to school when I was nine, I suppose, where both John and Martin were slightly senior to me," he said. "I got to know them, and they were, at that time, very interested in beetle collecting. They showed me how to collect beetles."[29]

Being in boarding school, correspondence between John and Martin and their mother began in earnest. Letters were sent on a weekly basis, about the cricket they played or about fads for marbles and model airplanes. Sometimes, they told of their visits to their grandmother or to their aunt, Florence Durham, who had stayed on at Newnham. Politics took hold of their dormitory in the fall of 1910, and Martin wanted to know if his new town, Merton, was Liberal or Conservative. "All the boarders but one, besides us, are Conservatives," he noted to his mother. "They all try to convert us here. But

---

*Later Sterling Professor of Zoology at Yale University. (G. E. Hutchinson, *The Kindly Fruits of the Earth*.)

not very successfully."[30] Their letters were strikingly similar. Often written on the same day, their news had the tendency to be word for word. Of course, Saint Faith's was not large, and they were nearly the same age, so one might not suppose there could be great differences between their letters. Still, their voices are difficult to distinguish. Martin, for instance, wrote, "A boy was swished on Tuesday evening for wanton assault on an inkpot! He had four cuts."[31] Just as John's letter of the same date had it that "Lower . . . performed manouvers [sic] with a walking stick this week, it was four cuts, but I did not get it, nor did Martin. It was for upsetting a rather full inkpot on purpose."[32] When, in 1912, John was to go to public school, W. B. and Beatrice chose to send him to Charterhouse. Gregory recalled, "There was some muttering that I took note of. It was felt that they were too close and . . . they were deliberately separated."[33] The following year, Martin, whom his parents considered brighter, was sent to Rugby, his father's old school. The brothers' companionship, so central in their zoological childhood, was thus split up.

V. Before the War

Although moving to Merton represented a radical split from the Cambridge University community, it also served to mark in William Bateson's life a settling of attitudes. From about 1910, there was increasing participation in the mainstream of British professional and intellectual life. He began to accumulate emblems of scientific notoriety. In 1911, he chaired the agricultural section of the British Association for the Advancement of Science, and in 1914 was president of that organization. Further, W. B. became involved in the social trappings of distinction. He was elected to the Athenaeum, the London club whose members shared eminence gained rather than inherited. It is inaccurate, however, to suppose that Bateson was now conforming, whereas before he had eschewed the norms of his social and theoretical moment. More exactly, its shape was shifting to him. In biology, the case for Mendelism had been won, the new language accepted, and the significance of discontinuous variation understood. In society, the Victorian mind was turning in directions of which W. B. had formerly approved.

By the end of the first decade of the new century, the writings of the indomitable Lamarckian vitalist, Samuel Butler, had been uncovered for British intellectuals by his disciple, George Bernard Shaw. In the preface of his new play, *Major Barbara,* Shaw had called Butler "the greatest English writer of the latter half of the XIX century. . . . It drives one almost to despair of English literature when one sees so extraordinary a study of English life as Butler's posthumous *The Way of All Flesh* making so little impression."[1] An enthusiastic vogue for the book followed, so that by 1920 it had been reprinted eleven times. In 1908, to commemorate Butler's struggles, Festing Jones instituted the Erewhon Dinners which were widely and notably attended. W. B., although suspicious of popular attention to most things, had been a longtime admirer of Butler's work and a close friend of Jones. Perhaps Bateson envied his courage and ability as a controversialist. Indeed, the year after

Shaw's play appeared, W. B. was designating Butler the "most brilliant, and by far the most interesting of Darwin's opponents."[2] In the summer of 1911, Bateson gladly agreed when Jones asked him to address the fourth Erewhon Dinner. Of all places it was to be held in the dining hall of St. John's College, and W. B. could not neglect the irony of the location. It pleased him, he said, "to think that Butler's portrait was now hanging in the hall of St. John's College on equal terms with ecclesiastics in wigs and lawn sleeves."[3] Bateson found himself in strange times. Hitherto, his life had been spent as a contentious isolate, in this regard not dissimilar to Mendel, Butler, and Blake, with all of whom he felt affinity. Now, the orthodoxies against which he had stood were re-forming in his own image—a change which reacted on the vigilant and individualist aspect of Bateson's personality and made him distinctly uncomfortable.

His political and sociological views admitted of a similar convolution. Society, which resisted yet relied on change, did not quite allow for free will. "Conditions," he asserted, "give opportunities but cause no variations."[4] At birth, man possessed a range of potentialities, or "appetancies" as he called them, the realization of which was dependent on interaction with the environment. From his early travels though, through the Russian steppe to his death in 1926, Bateson consistently stressed nature over nurture. Progress in civilization, as he believed it did in evolution, depended "upon mutational novelties." Major advances were essentially the work of the exceptional individual alone. Bateson lauded the intellectual elite in 1914, when he gave the presidential address to the British Association, then meeting in Sydney.

> The members of civilized communities when they think about such things at all, imagine the process [of change to be] a gradual one, and that they themselves are agents in it. Few, however, contribute anything but their labour; and except insofar as they have freedom to adopt and imitate, their physiological composition is that of an earlier order of beings. Annul the work of a few hundreds—I might almost say scores—of men, and on what plane of civilization should we be? We should not have advanced beyond the mediaeval stage without printing, chemistry, steam, electricity, or surgery worthy of the name. These things are the contributions of excessively rare minds.[5]

Bateson had no use for egalitarian and democratic trends. His ideal state was almost feudal. Society must maintain hierarchical differentiation, and as far as possible coordinate "the constituent parts of the social organism."[6] The goal was "to set in appropriate social context the qualities, potential, and authority of the uncommon individual, the man of genius."[7] However, W. B.'s conception of political action was limited. "The aim of social reform," he wrote, "must be not to abolish class, but to provide that each individual shall so far as possible get into the right class and stay there, *and usually his children after him* [italics added]."[8]

Yet these were not the views of a shallow apologist for an established order. Bateson would neither simplify nor reduce. In 1912, it was obvious to him that the world was on the brink. "Whatever is doubtful," he said, "this much I think is certain, that we are fast nearing one of those great secular changes through which history occasionally passes. The present order is too unstable to last much longer and he must be callous who greatly desires that it should."[9] Basically, his interest in political matters was minimal. He opposed deliberate human intervention in complex matters best left to natural history, and was horrified by applied science. "It is not the Eugenicists who will give us what Plato called the divine releases from the common ways. If some fancier with the catholicity of Shakespeare would take us in hand, well and good; but I would not trust even Shakespeares, meeting as a committee. Let us remember that Beethoven's father was a habitual drunkard and that his mother died of consumption."[10]

If individual genius was central to Bateson's sociology, its highest expression was found in great art. He was fond of Blake's prayer, "May God us keep from simple vision and Newton's sleep."[11] Science and art were the two great realities of W. B.'s life, but it is a measure of his profound intellectual humility—and peculiar estrangement—that he valued the products of his own profession well below those of the artist. As Coleman has written, Bateson's "unflinching" convictions were focused upon "the realm of commonly unattainable vision [which] the genius might alone approach." Aspiring to them became an isolating endeavor, at times desperate. But "he never assumed for himself either directly or by implication the role of genius,"[12] however nearly he possessed its qualities.

Science was relatively accessible to the ordinary diligent and intelligent man, and Bateson considered it "the one source of rational conduct ... the light which shows man in his natural perspective."[13] Artistic creation, however, partook of the sacred and commanded W. B.'s devotion. He "worshipped art, and regarded it as inaccessible to all but geniuses."[14] He assembled a distinguished personal collection. "As an appreciator of art," his son supposed, "he went for the formal and the representational. For Mozart and against Beethoven. I think 'classical' is the word.... Yet he was romantic about many classical productions, and less romantic about romantic productions.... He did have a weakness for Rembrandt—because Rembrandt was

what W. B. called a 'swell.' W. B. could never resist high grade exuberance."[15]
He sought art just as he practiced science—always assured that he was about to
locate some ignored masterpiece. Auctions, art sales, and isolated galleries
aroused him. "Of all pastimes," Beatrice wrote, "except that of painting, the
hunting and acquisition of Old Master drawings was his favorite. He had an
extraordinarily sure 'flair' for a good thing, and once started, his collection
grew and paid its own way."[16] There were Old Master drawings, Japanese color
prints, Greek island embroideries, lesser collections of Chinese porcelains and
bronzes, and not least, works by William Blake.

> When John Bateson was born, W. B. and Beatrice celebrated by buying a copy
> of Blake's *Job* engravings.... He favored both the pictures and much of the
> poems. The prophetic books were, I think, too turgid and complex for his taste
> and he knew little of the tangled network of Blakian "symbolism." ... I ... do
> not know when he acquired the big painting "Satan Exulting Over Eve." It was
> installed at Merton when I was six, but I cannot remember it at Grantchester.
> My impression, however, is that while he was always fascinated by Blake ...
> with the depression of his later years, Blake became less magical. I do not think
> he acquired any more Blake books or paintings after we moved to Merton. I may
> be wrong about this. I am sure ... W. B.'s protest against contemporary values
> is closely related to that of Blake. We may say in both cases the contemporary
> values won against the protest but this bred despair in W. B. which it never did
> in Blake.[17]

Since Bateson knew the major European museums by heart, members of the
staff of the British Museum consulted him often, and in 1922 appointed him
to a trusteeship of their institution. Thus it was in 1924, when he took his
family with him to attend a horticultural conference in Holland.

> We had absolutely to see these Poussins at the gallery at The Hague, whatever it
> was called, at the far end of the main street there. A blazing August afternoon,
> and he had his walking stick. He had a game knee ... and he liked to rest....
> It was always bothering him in his last years.... We sweat down the whole
> length of the street, walking on the pavement ... and he knew exactly where
> the pictures were.... He led us to the room and it had been entirely rehung
> with the works of Vincent Van Gogh. It must have contained fifty such things. I
> can see him look around, like a rat that somebody's just triggered the trap on.
> ... Then he picks up and walks out into the middle of the room, and with the
> metal-covered stick, beats on the ground, screaming at the top of his voice,
> which was considerable, "I will not admire the works of *Spirochaeta pallida*
> [syphilitic spirochete]!"[18]

Bateson made extensive use of the facilities and funds presented him as director of the John Innes Institution. He subjected the bare fields of the new horticultural station to his acute organizational abilities. Retaining his old Grantchester gardener to supervise planting and discipline staff, "Will's edict that every plant should be well grown was attended to with exactness."[19] To students, however, Bateson applied his distaste for institutional fetters, assuming that individual interest would make restrictions unnecessary. He placed all facilities at their disposal and set them the highest standards of scientific accuracy. Among biologists, the John Innes developed a reputation for concern with problems of an "impossibly difficult" nature.[20] At the time it was the richest private research station in England, but the vast opportunity was not boundless. Trustees criticized Bateson for misusing Innes' bequest. Horticulture was said to be a practical, applicable subject, but under Bateson, the new institute was dedicated only to pure science. When the Innes' trustees sent a group of breeders to tour the fields and greenhouses, Bateson's old reputation among them stood him in good stead. He was a well-known and much-liked figure, having frequented their exhibitions for years. Beatrice recalled that a "party of gardeners had been shown around and told something of the aims of and the work of the Institute by Will, their spokesman made a little speech of thanks, 'They do say, sir, that you are too scientific, but now we have seen around the place we know that is not the case!'"[21]

Bateson's ruthless skepticism, which had spawned his criticism of Darwinian evolutionary theory, now began to turn against his own work. "He had many disciples," said one of his disciples, "but was never himself of their number."[22] From about 1912, Bateson withdrew from the careful enumeration of characters inherited according to Mendelian principles, to the investigation of anomalous cases. "Treasure your exceptions!" he repeatedly advised students. "When there are none, the work gets so dull that no one cares to carry it further. Keep them always uncovered and in sights. Exceptions are like the rough brickwork of a growing building which tells that there is more to come and shows where the next construction is to be."[23] And Bateson, always the preeminent illustration of his own thought, now proceeded by concentrating experiments on non-Mendelian phenomena, such as plant chimeras and color variegation. The first to accept Mendelism in England, he was now among the first to assume it and proceed.

> He ... probably prevented Mendelism from becoming a dogma [according to J. B. S. Haldane]. For example he held that it would not, as some at least of his disciples believed, explain evolution. It is normal for a discoverer to be unduly impressed by the importance of his own discoveries, and it is a thoroughly excusable weakness. There are times in the history of thought, when an idea

must be born, and if it is a great idea it may be expected to overwhelm and obsess the man who gave it birth. He either becomes its slave, or preserves a certain independence only continuing to hold views incompatible with it at the expense of dividing his mind into watertight compartments. William Bateson escaped these fates because he was greater than any of his ideas.[24]

Initially, W. B. was dissatisfied with the location of the John Innes, lest he become professionally isolated. His misgivings filtered down into the culture of his family. Gregory recalled that "living at Merton Park, we had a sort of family myth which lent a crystal halo to Cambridge and especially Grantchester. I grew up feeling in a gentle way that we had been turned out of, or perhaps had deserted, the Garden of Eden. . . . The break with Cambridge was very very serious, much more serious than it rationally should have been. . . . [We had] a nostalgia for Cambridge, that this was really home."[25] Despite W. B.'s fears, the Manor House was frequently crowded with colleagues and students from the world over. At once, Mendelism had involved Bateson with the three co-discoverers of the monk's work—the Dutch de Vries, the German Correns, the Austrian Tschermak, and there was also the Dane Johannsen, who coined the term "gene." In addition, the enterprise to widen the general validity of Mendelian laws went on in France under Cuènot, in America under Castle, and in Russia under Vavilov. The contact with this work gave Bateson's shop a thoroughly international flavor—that all the early geneticists depended upon the mails and upon open borders became painfully evident in 1914.

The Batesons were socially active before the war and entertained often. On weekends, people typically arrived on Saturday and stayed the night. Gregory remembered a normal evening in which there might be nine to twelve people at the dinner table. Co-workers came, such as R. C. Punnett, Edith R. Saunders, Nora Barlow, R. P. Gregory, and C. C. Hurst, and there were the young scientists Julian Huxley, J. B. S. Haldane, and C. D. Darlington. For the most part, though, W. B.'s weekend guests were not scientists. The various Durham and Bateson aunts visited, as did his friends: Lawrence Binyon, the poet; Festing Jones, Butler's biographer; Claude Guillebaud, the economist; Henry Head, the surgeon; Geoffrey Keynes, the physician and Blake scholar; E. V. Lucas, the editor of *Punch;* and Arthur Waley of the British Museum.

Sundays at the Manor House had something of ceremony to them, which Gregory recalled fondly. W. B. usually spent the morning writing, alone in his study, "a great big converted barn, with an enormous table . . . [that] was sort of sacred ground."[26] Beatrice meanwhile was attending to roses in her garden. Those guests who came the night before or early in that morning were left to bide their own time. "For example, Binyon has come for supper Saturday evening ... goes out to the lawn, spends Sunday morning sitting on the lawn, vaguely composing one of [his] patriotic poems."[27] Until midmorning, everyone was "quiet and scattered," then more people would arrive, assembling in the drawing room. "Sherry was not served before dinner. They waited around with nothing to do 'til lunch, talking."[28] Except for the occasional foreign geneticist, guests mostly knew each other. "Noisy," Gregory remembered. "This is pre-World War I—me, ten or less. ... [P]eople used to laugh in those days, roaring with laughter, deep belly laughs from Batesons, Durhams, [and] all sorts of people. ... World War I stopped the belly laugh."[29]

Beatrice and W. B. did not receive their guests, but would arrive in their midst separately. "They would drop in under their own timing, which would be different for the two of them."[30] Gregory was left to his own devices during the moments after the guests', but before his parents', arrivals. In the presence of the latter he behaved himself—quietly out of the way. When the family moved to Merton, he was not permitted to join in meals. "Initially," he said, "I ate in what was called the nursery. I would say all three of us at the beginning of that time [did so]. ... But then the boys went off to boarding school, and I'd be alone up in the nursery ... and ... that became a nuisance, and I would say I joined into the main meals about the same time they did."[31] During Sundays then, Gregory would mingle with the guests, some of whom might amuse themselves with him until either W. B. or Beatrice entered. However brief, this little attention was special to a boy growing up on the periphery of this centripetal family. "I formed funny little quick, sort of ten-minute friendships, with some of these people, with Binyon at one stage ... with Nora [Barlow]."[32]

Guests were directed to their seats, which Beatrice planned so that the sexes alternated. "Somehow we would manage to get to the dining room, more or less in pairs."[33] W. B. presided and Beatrice sat opposite him at the front of the table, which was large enough to accommodate both their conversations. "[My mother] would have [one] at her end," Gregory noticed, "giving way, now and then, to the other conversation, in effect being mopped up by it."[34] Beatrice tended to belittle herself and was, in her son's memory, "sort of rueful," doubting the quality of whatever her activity, in part to protect herself from Will's pressuring eye. So that in all, the conversation "would be about three-quarters W. B. He talked. He talked extraordinarily well. He came out of a tradition of table-talk. ... It was an art form."[35] The overtones at the dinner table were lusty, and the metaphors somatic. Since Bateson had not been among the guests before the meal, the subject would typically not carry over, once everyone was seated. Gregory, in both awe and fear of his father, would watch carefully. "He would tune up and get going on whatever it was," he remembered. "Now, he might defer to experts.... I mean, there's no kidding about, you know an alpha animal when you meet it. It takes over and he took over."[36] Certain of his favorite topics would then recur: the wickedness of the government, the deplorable nature of democracy, his travels in Russia, the arts, and the contribution of individual genius to the progress of civilization. There was also a great deal said about previous meals. "He was a considerable gourmet and somewhat gourmand and talk about food was one of the things he enjoyed. 'You remember, Beatrice, that restaurant—' and this would be ten years back—'that crepes suzette. Superb! Now, in English restaurants, you never see anything like that.' "[37]

The meal itself, Gregory recalled, might be a big rib of beef, "which would have shavings of horseradish on the top. It would ... in American terms, be rather well done. He might fuss about that. Potatoes were roasted with the beef, and he would carve it transversely.... He was very conscious of things manual, like carvings—and very skillful.... Plates were usually passed. Vegetables were carried by the cook, Jessie, an old-old lady.... The wine would be good."[38]

Throughout Will teased Beatrice and their cook. "He criticized the food in front of fourteen people sitting around the table. 'It's overdone today, the beef.... Can't we ever! Now really Beatrice ... ,' he might say."[39] And very rarely, she might return the jibe, squeaking back with a tinge of facetiousness, "You *really* think so, Will?" Conventionally, the Sunday meal concluded with suet pudding—another of W. B.'s affections—coffee, and "a great deal of smoke."[40]

The tempo momentarily subsiding, Bateson would grab his fez and lead guests to the lawn for croquet, a game which he generally won because, unlike them, he played often. Dramatizing his ability but mocking himself, W. B. would decree whether he was "on or off his stroke," that day. "One of the things that used to be characteristic," Gregory recalled, "was that somewhere around three o'clock, the chickens had to be fed, and W. B. would personally conduct [a tour], showing the peas, etc., with considerable pride.... He was a performing, very histrionic character,"[41] and could arouse the interest of the many guests who were not geneticists. By the end of the feeding, dusk would be settling. It was an hour's train ride back into London, and people began to drift home, exhausted by the pace, but amused by this eclectic, somewhat dogmatic, yet very playful scientist.

The guests gone, W. B. would turn to his painting. Beatrice meanwhile played the piano. Although accomplished as a musician, like the rest of her family, she had no gift. Will was completely unmusical, according to Gregory, but would "play at singing," to his wife's accompaniment. John and Martin "sang on one note," and did not learn any instrument. Gregory too had difficulty distinguishing tones, but Beatrice pushed him to the violin. Typically, they practiced together. "Towards the end of the afternoon, Will might wander over to the house [from his study], and I and my mother would be making dreadful noises. He would come quietly into the drawing room, and either go out again—he couldn't bear it—or he would say, 'It seems to be a little more in tune today.'"[42]

Beatrice also had charge of answering the boys' letters, acting as her husband's tacit deputy. Their interests were increasingly abstruse to her, so she was hardly a confidant. W. B. read their correspondence, though, and in the rare circumstance, in crisis or sometimes during vacation, wrote them himself. But their mother had a less demanding ear, the boys felt. "When he went to America at one stage, John and Martin were saying what a relief it was to have him out of the house. He was rather critical."[43]

In 1913, W. B. suffered a minor heart attack or, as Beatrice saw it, "he overstrained his magnificent physique."[44] As if foreshadowing the catastrophe that soon followed, their lives began to change. "We were never quite free from anxiety; he felt pain, lurking round the corner waiting to pounce upon him. The gay sense of physical well-being was lost."[45] Where once Beatrice strode to keep up with her husband, now she slowed herself, "and it was grievous to wait whilst he fussed with his pipe knowing it was not the pipe that was giving trouble."[46] World War I, needless to say, compounded his difficulties. W. B. tried to ignore the situation and continue his work, assuming that science would transcend the collapse of international relations. The departure of students and staff indisposed him, and he brooded over the daily slaughter of the rising generation. "The pitiful thing is the destruction of young men coming on," he lamented in the summer of 1915, "all the best are in it—the pick of the best breeds in the country. Inevitably the succession—in learning, I mean—must be broken throughout Europe."[47] When English libraries deliberately stopped receiving German scientific periodicals, Bateson became irate. "He was genuinely amazed and shocked," his wife recalled, "to find the world of learning and the professional classes shaken by national prejudices. . . . Amidst much else the masking of truth in public announcements of 'news' especially angered him. He thought this unworthy of any governing class and degrading."[48]

Bateson was convinced that the war was almost entirely a matter of commercial and political cabal. National passions, he declared in 1915, were a sickness, the cure for which was a universalistic outlook.

> We are all citizens of one little planet. We are as it were a ship's company on an unknown and mysterious island. There is not time to quarrel about origins. We have food to find and shelter to prepare. Of what that island can provide for our comfort we know still very little. Let us in peace explore the place. It is as full of wonderful things and for aught we know we may yet find the elixir of life.[49]

In 1918, the Ministry of Information asked him to write an article on the advance of English genetics during the war years, which they would translate and distribute among noncombatant countries, to counteract the impression that scientific progress had ceased there. Declining, Bateson denounced propaganda of this kind as incompatible with the spirit of science. "If I found some country, say the United States or Germany, holding forth in various languages on what they had been doing in genetics, I should, without being unduly fastidious, think it not good scientific manners, to say the least."[50] The preceding year, however, he had volunteered to go to France to lecture troops on elementary genetics. After one address, a soldier commented to him that it seemed to be a sort of scientific Calvinism. This remark so startled W. B. that he wrote Beatrice calling it a flash of illiterate inspiration.[51]

VI. Boarding School

As we have said, no conventional faith existed in the Bateson household. Instead, the family revolved around W. B., and developed an idiom derived from his aesthetics as well as from his science. From his model, John and Martin learned a posture of individuated dissent which was tempered by an outward adherence to social forms. For them, Bateson family life provided both a camaraderie and fascination. On the other hand, for Gregory, the little brother, it provided something less fulfilling.

> How did I grow up in that world really not knowing its rules at all? Was I very stupid? Was I insensitive? . . . I was very unhappy. . . . [When?] Oh, I suppose from the beginning of going to school onwards. I never had any idea where I belonged in any of the stuff. I mean, I had been warned and advised and whatnot, to not accept, to distrust and to despise the entire value structure of the school, the athletics, and all that, and the army, and the war, and the middle classes, and the lower classes. . . . But not really, or not seemingly, getting any real idea of how the group to which I supposedly belonged—but who were they?—were supposed to function? But who were they?[1]

The John Innes Institution was located in a working-class town on the edge of London. After a few years there, W. B. became concerned about the friendships his youngest boy was forming. In Cambridge, academic children naturally spent time together, doing no harm to the integration of the larger community. But in Merton, Bateson somehow felt vulnerable, surrounded by people whose values and standards differed from his own. John and Martin were old enough to board when the family left Grantchester, so the move had less effect on them than it did on Gregory, who was six and impressionable. After three years of day school, he began to pick up the local accent which his father, though by birth a solid member of the upper middle classes, found disturbing. It was decided, in the summer of 1913, that Gregory should begin his studies. He had been a sickly child, and the suspicion was that his lungs were weak. With this in mind, his parents sent him to Wardenhouse, a preparatory school situated salubriously in the town of Deal, on the Kentish coast. In other ways, however, the school was not well suited to a Bateson boy, who was accustomed to a rather permissive childhood without God or cane. "My parents were liberal, good people," Gregory recalled, "and not only was there some sort of agreement that the school would accept this little atheist, there was also an agreement not to beat him."[2] Beatrice had promised Mullins, the headmaster, that her son would conform during daily prayers.

> My mother saw that there was a crisis ahead. There was very little use to ask my father about it. So she handed me over to my brothers for religious education. They took me for a walk, and told me that at school I would probably sleep in a dormitory, and that I'd better watch what the other boys did, that when they knelt down to pray, that I should do the same. And that if I said the alphabet over eight times, that that would be long enough and then I could get up. So I went to school with complete authoritarian approval for conforming to that which I did not believe in.[3]*

Middle-class education in England before World War I has been pilloried by many. The schools maintained extensive programs in athletics—held up by Victorian educators as a subliminal source of right character—and taught little

---

*When Gwen Raverat went to boarding school during this period, she also came from a family of atheist biologists—named Darwin—but her resolution of the matter of religious observance contrasted the Batesons'. "So I grew to be sixteen, and went away to boarding school; and on the first Sunday there all the big girls, very old and powerful, got around me in a ring and began asking me questions. 'Don't you really believe in Adam and Eve, Gwen?' 'How do you think you were made then?' 'Do you think we are all kind of monkeys?' 'Don't you believe in the flood?' And so on and so forth. It was quite frightful; it was like being in the midst of a herd of bullocks, all staring at you, and coming closer with their shining horns. . . . Still one can die but once; and I wasn't going to let them see how frightened I was. So I dug my heels and scrunched my hands together, and answered: 'No, I don't,' stoutly, to all their questions; and they were most delightfully horrified and shocked. . . . Therefore, when we went off in a crocodile to church next Sunday, I determined to testify to my faith. And when they all knelt down to pray on first going in, I sat up straight and didn't kneel; and when they all turned to the east for the Creed, I didn't turn; and when they bowed, I didn't bow; and when they mumbled the Lord's prayer, I didn't mumble; and I felt like a real martyr. To my surprise no one said anything to me about this; I imagine that the mistresses must have given the girls a hint to hold their tongues, which was clever of them. This somewhat deflated me; but I could not retreat from the position I had taken up, and all the time I was at school I kept up my silent protest; though, after a time, being a non-conformist became rather a bore. When they asked me to be confirmed, I just said politely but firmly: 'No, thank you'" (G. Raverat, *Period Piece*, pp. 226-27.)

other than mathematics and the classics of Greek and Latin. "No wonder masters had no trouble in channeling boys' energies into sports," Edward Mack, a historian of the subject, has noted. "The extravagant interest they took in school games was largely a dire consequence of their intense boredom in school hours."[4] The rigid social hierarchy, the tyrannical opinion of peers, the cultivation of school spirit, and conservative curriculum all have been condemned for resulting in boys who were incurious and unintellectual, conformist, and deferent.* "It is a question," William Bateson asked in 1915, "whether that almost hypochondriacal interest in the stupid school games which now wastes the intelligence of our young people may not be due to the fact that we give them so little else they care to think about."[5]

His children were well prepared to find adversity in school, coming as they did from a family culture in which radical individualism lionized arts *and* sciences. This seems to have been the case for Gregory at Wardenhouse.

> There was a paper chase. Two of the better runners were sent ahead with bags of paper. It was scattered on the countryside, as they ran, and the school ran behind them, chasing them . . . in the course of which I . . . found a hedgehog. I rolled it up in my handkerchief. A hedgehog is a remarkably difficult thing to carry on a paper chase [laughs]. I brought it home and kept it in my locker. Whether it lived there is unclear. I used to put food in my locker. At any rate, at a certain point, it was evidently dead. I buried it, what did we do with it? There was something terrible about that. I can't remember. I can't reconstruct it now properly. There was an awful sequence of constipation and finally explosive shitting in the middle of the night. . . . Anyway I got my beetle bottle out, and put the cianide in my mouth in the john one day. And I suppose it was fairly well covered with carbonate. Actually, [cianide] deteriorates from the outside inwards. I spat it out again, but it was sort of near [laughs]. I don't think little boys of nine ought to have cianide in school. But I don't see why not, I mean here I am. . . . I can't tell you what sort of tangled horror the whole of the rot Wardenhouse was.[6]

Science, among his peers, was known as "stinks," so there was little else for him to do other than collect beetles. All the boys went to watch King George V review the troops in the spring of 1916. "Whilst we were waiting for the King

---

* "Those who have been taught from an early age," Bertrand Russell in 1932 wrote, "to fear the displeasure of the group as the worst of misfortunes will die on the battlefield, in a war of which they understand nothing, rather than suffer the contempt of fools. The English public schools have carried this system to perfection and largely sterilized intelligence by making it cringe before the herd. This is what is called making the man manly." (B. Russell, *Education and Social Order,* p. 7.)

to come," Gregory reported to Beatrice, "I found a rather nice *Silpha* with a white stripe on each of its wingcases."[7]

Though John's curiosities were no different from those of his younger brother—he too, spent much time "bugging" throughout the countryside around Charterhouse—his experience there by contrast seems to have been bearable. "I have collected hundreds of beetles but have hardly got any set," he wrote in 1912, his first year at Charterhouse. "Also, which is rather a nuisance, monitors have put up a notice forbidding any natural history student to open his killing bottles or otherwise prosecute his hobby within range of Long Room. Long Room is the common-room where one has his meals and generally does things. This notice, you see, practically prevents one setting anything, as it is seldom calm enough out of doors to enable one to do anything."[8] To protect him from the antiscientific trends of public schools, W. B. and Beatrice had John housed in Robbinites, a dormitory whose housemaster, O. H. Latter, was himself something of a biologist. He nurtured the youth's interests. "Mr. Latter has given me a Poplar Hawk," John notified his mother, "and the other fellows, or some of them at least, bring me beetles almost every day."[9]

The two brothers, formerly inseparable, now wrote each other tirelessly. From John's side, perhaps, the letters he sent his mother resembled the ones he sent Martin, save that the latter were denser in botanical and entomological reference. "I went over to the Alice Holt Woods again last Tuesday, I did not strike a good place," he wrote Martin. "I got several *Strangabia armata, Agabus* or *Olybius, Hydroporus* and several *Copelatus agilis* out of a small puddle left in a dried up ditch."[10] John was dedicated. Though he lacked his father's flair for the arts, he had his keen eye and memory. At fifteen, he announced the finding of an extremely rare beetle in the *Entomologist's Record*.[11] "In April 1913, my brother [Gregory] caught a specimen of *Ischnodes sanguinicollis,* and a few days later I caught another in the same situation, namely a hollow in an old elm in our garden [at Merton]. We also found remains of a third and some *Elaterid* larvae, but these may have been of some other species, since there were many elytera of other species found in the hold, together with owl's pellets."[12]

Apart from his passion for natural history, John seems to have been a conventional schoolboy—fagging for older monitors, playing cricket, participating in debates and, despite his parents' objections, marching in the rifle corps. To his teachers, he was intelligent and possessed competent academic talents. Gregory's memory of John had him tempered and gentle. Unlike Martin, he was "not in the least in any sort of battle, and not any sort of show-off. . . . What he was doing in [W. B.'s] house, I don't know."[13] Like his mother in many respects, John was polite and sincere—and good humored. "By the way," he concluded one letter to Beatrice, "if you send clothes and food at the same time again, please pack them apart as the last lot of apples tasted like socks."[14] He left the promising impression at Charterhouse of becoming a great biologist and took the school's prize in that subject in 1916, the year of his graduation and of his entry into war.

At first, Martin's career paralleled his brother's. He entered Rugby in the fall of 1913, similarly absorbed in biology and natural history. A successful student, he became secretary to both the entomological and geological sections of the Rugby Natural History Society. He participated actively in the botanical section, and an essay "Surface Tension" was awarded the chemistry prize in 1916.

Evidently, there was more to him than Lepidoptera. As an adolescent, he was developing into an erratic young man, sarcastic and critical. Martin wrote poetry and adored literature. He assumed a leading role in school politics. While editing Rugby's newspaper, *The Meteor*, he frequently took issue with school policy. Vacuous religiosity, for example, repelled him. Martin accused school authorities of prejudice against clothes when wartime austerities required they suspend the acquisition of new athletic uniforms and evening attire. Why this, he asked, and not the headmaster's weekly sermons which continued to be printed for intraschool circulation? One of these, in which the headmaster affirmed his belief in a literal afterlife was particularly infuriating. Martin disliked any species of theism, other than that of Samuel Butler whom he considered England's greatest thinker. To answer the sermon, he had three of Butler's sonnets published in *The Meteor,* drawing special attention to "The Life After Death," in which men and their earthly struggles are simply held to die.[15]*

---

*   Not on sad Stygian shore, nor in clear sheen
      Of far Elysian plane, shall we meet those
      Among the dead whose pupils we have been,
      Nor those great shades whom we had held as foes.
      No meadow of asphodel our feet shall tread,
      Nor shall we look each other in the face
      To love or hate each other being dead,
      Hoping some praise, or fearing some disgrace.
      We shall not argue saying "Twas this or Thus,"
      Our argument's whole drift we shall forget;
      Who's right, who's wrong, 'twill be all one to us!
      We shall not even know that we have met.
          Yet meet we shall, and part, and meet again
          Where dead men meet, on lips of living men.

According to his biographer, Festing Jones, Butler may have been thinking of his feud with Charles Darwin when he composed the above. (H. F. Jones, "Charles Darwin and Samuel Butler: a step towards reconciliation," in *The Autobiography of Charles Darwin,* ed. N. Barlow, p. 197.)

About the time John was shipped to the trenches in France, Martin, who had very few friends, began to keep a journal. He was then swaying between doubts and egotism. "Whether I am an awful prig or no, I do not know, though I fear the worst," he wrote on one occasion. On another, however, he confessed to "not feeling my companions nearly so oppressively inferior as I have often felt them."[16] To his surprise, Martin also began to write angry poetry at this time. He admitted of two inspirations, Samuel Butler and his father, worrying that he was plagiarizing ideas from W. B. "I sometimes work myself into quite a fervour of wanting to write poems of revolt," he noted privately. "I am filled with fury at the ideas I see put forward as ideals by my own contemporaries."[17] He wrote a number of religious sonnets regretting man's neglect of his intellect, antimaterialist poems, and brooding poems on death and war. "I feel myself continually hampered by the solidity of the world. 'The world is too much with us,' I consider one of Wordsworth's greatest sayings. That art should depend on technique is a forgivable blunder of the Creator. Still worse that it should depend on food."[18]

However critical he tried to be, Martin still became apprehensive in the summer of 1917, when he sent some of his poetry to his parents (see Appendix). Although he claimed they were made of "Blasphemy, Anarchy, Conventionality, Insincerity, Gross sincerity, Infantility," he wanted their reactions.[19] Even before their verdicts though, his uncertainty had diminished, "I would rather make my name as a writer of the poetry in my mind than as a scientist," was his secret resolution. Beatrice replied at first. Liking his verse, she judged it promising, but at his age, schoolwork was the first responsibility: "Keep the poetry for, if I may say, the sacred hours of pleasure. I think you know the divine obsession which at the moment makes you feel it must be one or the other and I feel myself throbbing in sympathy."[20] She urged him to avoid sham in his writing, to aspire to a high ideal, while clinging to direct simplicity, "like an accurate delicate touch to a fiddle string, [which] gives off its harmonics so purely that every sense thrills with delight."[21] In order to achieve this, he must subject his work to stern scrutiny and study the works of the great masters intimately. Contemporaries, on the other hand, could be damaging. "You must not let others jog your arm. It's avoiding these mishaps that distinguish individualities."[22] Not wanting to discourage him, still Beatrice warned her seventeen-year-old that a poetic career might not succeed financially.

> Unless you sell yourself to the ephemeral side of letters, there is not much livelihood, I take it, to be got out of them. The highest flights are their own reward—but they'll hardly keep you in tobacco, let alone a possible wife and family. You must have a bread winning occupation to keep Pegasus fresh and fiery. He's a poor doer between the shafts.[23]

W. B. was similarly reassuring, after Beatrice showed him the poems.

> They seem to me very right and proper—certainly nothing to regret. Butler says that it is best to do nothing unless the thing "hits you in the eye." There is no better rule. So if it hits you in the eye that you *must* turn to verse, turn to verse, but in most of us the "Zwang" wears out in a little while as others take its place. I envy those who keep it and continue to have such feelings in later life.[24]*

Martin turned back to his studies, and to newly acquired duties as dormitory proctor. "My position as Head of the House is now beginning to be a nuisance. I have to watch the whole of every House [cricket] Match. They have a beastly knack of choosing all the best afternoons for this."[25] By the early fall, however, the "Zwang" had reappeared. He sent more of his poetry home. Anxious about his ability, he stopped preparing for his natural science scholarship examination.

> Much of what I send this time is even rougher than before.... Just out of the quarry. But is it ore? Does it contain Poetry? [I] must face the fact ... at this point.... [M]y highest ambition is to write poetry. But I know I cannot unless some of what I have already written is. I could be a humble follower of science; but if I write poetry, I must be a leader.... The point is can I fairly tell myself it is poetry? I can still stop.... Me thinks ... a word from you would be sufficient I think to make me throw it all up and work wholly at science.[26]

Seeing that the poetry was interfering with Martin's studies, W. B. wondered if his boy might be ill. He offered to come to Rugby to discuss the situation. "Many fathers think themselves sufficiently tried when their sons ask to follow pure science. In suggesting literature as the serious occupation of your youth, you go a good way beyond that! Of one thing I am perfectly clear: however good promise your composition may show, the wisest course for you at present is to stick to your work. I don't say shut your mind to verse altogether, though till after your exams I think you should."[27] Learning and experience were the dual priorities of youth, whatever one's ultimate occupation. Writing, after all, could only benefit from a more mature mind. At base, Martin most required

---

*W. B. suggested that Martin read Browning's "Bishop Blougram," as it related to Martin's own "Theist and Atheist," and he enclosed Sassoon's bitter anti-war poem "To Any Dead Officer," which had just appeared in *The Cambridge Magazine,* because he judged it "rather strong." (William Bateson to Martin Bateson, 9 July 1917.)

intellectual companionship, "just as I did at your age."[28] The long term would be served best by friendships in which scientific interests were shared. "If all had gone well [i.e., if there was peace] you would have found [friends] in Cambridge. As things are likely to be, I fear you may not for some time. But don't despair. There are always prophets who have not bowed the knee to Baal and sooner or later, they come to you."[29] The war had completely changed the British economy, W. B. pointed out, and had halved the family's financial worth. "Scarcely anyone lives on letters, least of all poetry, or practical writing in the broad sense. Few make more than a pittance out of pure science."[30] W. B. thought of himself as "extraordinarily lucky," to have prospered through biology. Nevertheless, in science one could expect more openings than in anything else of an intellectual kind. "If you follow it, you will find out that it is just as exciting as poetry! . . . I see no reason why you should not be a leader in science or anything else."[31] Of the poems themselves, he wrote his son:

> You should not ask *"are* they poetry?" There have been many young men who have turned out verse early in life, but I don't remember one who at your age wrote anything that could be so called in the full sense of . . . that mighty word. Certainly the greater poets did not. If you ask have they any poetry in them, I should say yes . . . I can see that they have sincerity and express genuine emotion.[32]

A few of them seemed to flirt with conscientious objection. Responding to these themes, W. B. reminded Martin that, dissent aside, one ought to take part in the war, "at least in outward seeming. Your 'soul' remains your own. I know that is what John feels and rightly so, as I think." But essentially W. B. sympathized with his son's opposition. "If all this had come in my time, I believe I should have struck, but I don't think in later life, I should have been proud of that, or satisfied."[33]

Apologizing, Martin thanked his father for his interest. "I was badly overexcited when I sent mine off, as I fear I not infrequently am. I hope I did not ask if my efforts were *poetry,* I didn't mean to. What I wanted to know . . . [was] whether they have *any* germ of Poetry in them."[34] Above all, Martin offered assurances that his studies were in control. "[I am] resisting the temptation . . . to put into verse my present feelings . . . [and] to destroy all that I have already done. . . . I see no necessity for Father to come down. I think the matter can be laid aside for the present. After this slight wriggle I return to normal quiet pupality."[35]

He passed his exams at the top of his class, despite disdaining them, and won a senior scholarship to St. John's College. Martin was honored as the first science man at Rugby to become student head of the entire school.* "I'm quite popular and am as cynical as ever," he wrote of himself.[36] He was known as something of an enfant terrible, bullying sanctimonious regimentation. Martin's posture now resembled his culture hero Samuel Butler—save that his defiance was directed outward, against circumstances, rather than intimates. The tenor of this rebellion is evident in the pleasure a conversation between the headmaster of the school and his son gave him. He described it to Beatrice.

> In the course of half an hour he [the son] managed to place some very relevant questions. One of them, which he repeated with great determination was "Why do you go to Church on Sunday?" In spite of the repetition of the question, it did not receive an answer from his parents. He also offered the information that his teeth needed cleaning.[37]

For a time, Martin opposed the war, which he thought was the "indiscriminate slaughter of good and bad for the sake of the commercial classes," and raised to himself the possibility of conscientious objection. "Of course, Father and Mother are both conscientious objectors in the spirit, as all decent people must be."[38] Killing itself was not the issue. Martin was willing to dispose of both Germans and Englishmen, priests and military officers, even many labor leaders. "But I would not kill the intellectuals; scientists, artists, musicians, etc. . . . I am for one nation of intellectuals—as man is superior to animals in mental forms only, so man is superior to man in mental powers only. The Devil take the rest of all nations."[39]

Rather, Martin's grudge was against killing for the financial benefit of others. He would tell peers that the White Star Lines (the shipping company which owned the *Titanic*) had more than doubled its annual profits by 1916. "And I am to go and die for them!"[40]

The year before he graduated from Rugby, however, Martin decided not to object. That his brother was already in the army compelled him. "Knowing myself . . . to be physically more cowardly than John," he confessed, "I think that my position at home would become increasingly odious if I refused to take a commission. It would be quite another matter if I was the eldest son and had the first choice, but I have not got it."[41] He left Rugby in the winter of 1918, entering the Royal Air Force in the early spring. Despite being quite nearsighted, he was trained in photographic reconnaissance. Beatrice sent him numbers of the *Times Literary Supplement* and *Nature*. When he asked her for the

---

*Consistent with the traditional antiscientific biases of these schools, this position had been reserved until that time for classics students.

university publication, *The Cambridge Magazine*, she suggested that he only read it in private so as not to create resentment. W. B. agreed, "I expect your mother was right in suggesting that you forgo *The Cambridge Magazine* in your present circle. It might lead to misunderstanding."[42] Lacking biology, Martin's letters to his parents now bore little resemblance to those of his childhood. Transferred from his base at Grantham, to a navy installation at Yarmouth, he disdained military life. "I used to think at Grantham that there was about as little room for me as a photographic officer as could reasonably be expected. I was not quite right, however, because here there is very much less. No aerial photography is being done or very little. The chief work of the section, which consists of one corporal ... [who is] on leave and two men, is photographing knick knacks."[43] The war was in its last year when Martin joined the fight. He never saw action, or went overseas. "Nobody can now say that I have not won a medal in the Great War, because she arrived today," he wrote Beatrice at one point, "I have examined her with a lens and found a somewhat doubtful Lion on her. The grateful donor is the British Chess Federation. I do not know what my title to the medal is, but I believe it rests on the fact that I was Head of Chess at Rugby before I left."[44]

If Martin's military experience just fueled a sardonic nature, John's had the characteristics of an extended, if hazardous, botanical field trip. The politics of the war did not concern him. John did not suppose one side to be more or less justified than the other. Visiting some friends of his parents, he thought them "very jingoistic, and very full of nonsense about spies, hidden hands, etc.... They were convinced that everyone they don't like is a German and (presumably) any Germans that they like are not Germans."[45] John was accepted as second lieutenant in the winter of 1916, "I am alright for a commission of some sort ... and shall probably get a proper one, i.e., not 'on home garrison clerical duty.'"[46] He trained for the artillery and was dispatched to France the following spring. "I am living in a fine deep German dug-out," John wrote home. "It is really a model dug-out in its way, for though deep enough to keep out anything, it is dry and not too stuffy. A *Sirex gigas* came out of one of the planks with which it is lined this afternoon."[47] Beatrice also sent him issues of *Nature,* while John took to mailing her elaborate descriptions and drawings of insects and plants he had failed to identify. A year of war had done little to his character. He had neither closed his naturalist's eye nor lost his humor.

> I found a solitary but unmistakable mole hill the other day in a bit of ground that has been straffed as much as any I have seen. The mole must be an optimist sort at least, I should think. ... About half an hour ago, I saw a hawk hovering about close here, and wondered what on earth he could find hereabouts to

interest him. However, a little field mouse has just made its appearance about ten feet away, so the riddle is solved.[48]

Although John portrayed his first experience of trench warfare almost blandly, he was clearly in some danger.

> I got properly scared my first day up here, before I could judge where shells were going by their sound. I heard one coming, but as they had been shelling a good distance off, I took no notice, didn't even duck. The damned thing, a pipsqueak (77 mm field-gun shell) dropped about five yards away, just in front of me. I got a couple of grazes as big as a finger nail on my thigh, but was otherwise absolutely untouched.... I suppose the thing blew over my head. (You needn't tell mother about the incident, as she is rather liable to get "windy" about such things, as we say.)[49]

Slightly injured in November 1917—shot in the left arm—he was awarded the Military Cross for heroism in battle. His commanding officer, G. E. Tatham, called him "gallant" and "absurdly modest." *The Times* correspondent wrote that when "his battery was being heavily shelled, he twice went through an intense barrage to find a medical officer and assist a wounded man to the dressing station. On the same night, his party was caught in a heavy barrage and all of them were wounded. Though wounded himself, he went forward to the dressing station and brought help back. He showed splendid courage and self sacrifice."[50] He was sent home for six weeks, but by January 1918, was back with his brigade, stationed for the moment, at Ipswich. "Fossil-hunting has been my chief occupation," John alerted his father. "I have got quite a lot of red crag things." He spent the rest of the winter and spring there, recuperating. In June, applying for overseas service, he told Beatrice, "I have been marking time long enough. Moreover, I don't like either the major or the colonel."[51] Reaching Le Havre in July, he got himself transferred back to Tatham's brigade. August was peaceful, but an offensive began in September. "Dear Mother, we are having a rather good time just now pursuing the Boche. Constantly moving the battery position is of course rather a nuisance in some ways, and makes for plenty of work, but one sees a lot of fresh country and clean, unshelled country at that, which is interesting."[52] On 10 October, John was apologizing to Martin for not writing. "This is due to wars and rumours of rain, not to any inherent repugnance to epistolization on my part."[53]

Four days later, he was dead. Amid heavy German shelling of his unit, a bomb exploded at his feet, killing him instantly. Tatham, the commanding officer, wrote Beatrice and W. B. that few soldiers were as painfully thorough, uncomplaining, and cheerful as their son. And one month later, after the Armistice was signed, he added, "When I saw him after his death he had a smile on his face and I like to feel, and I'm nearly sure I'm right, that he enjoyed that morning and was happy at knowing he was a man."[54]

As the poetry expressed (see Appendix), Martin feared the possibility of his brother's death. Now, he was made completely disconsolate by the fact of it. "I know what you must be feeling," his father comforted. "John was a splendid creature.... He would have been a comrade for life for you and his mother. Like all of us, I think he had no illusions [about the war]. I never heard him say a foolish thing even when quite little, and he knew how to bear trouble.... There was never a nobler soul."[55] A few days afterward, Beatrice echoed W. B. The honor of a country, if it be of any consequence at all, did not lie in the destruction of youth of purpose such as John Bateson.

> You seemed to me to complement each other and your companionship and deep rooted friendship was one of the beautiful things of my life—Now you must take heart from him dead, as you did I think often from him living. You must take inspiration from the memory and not let the bitterness of all this cruel futility overpower you. Your father and I are both thinking of you and feeling for you all the time. Each one has to bear the burden for himself and you must take comfort in our companionship and sympathy. I think of all these twenty years and the splendid promise now cut off, but you and Gregory are left to me still and you must help me back to some of the braveness that John has taken away. I hoped perhaps they would give you leave to come and see us but as that does not seem to be the case, I shall come to see you. I am going to see Gregory on Saturday. Mr. Latter has written a very kind letter and told me Gregory is sensible and steady though acutely hurt, poor child. I will come down to you on Sunday probably.[56]

Out of Martin's grief came questioning of the authority of a system of government which produced the tragedy. His pacifism resurfaced. Venting rage against the English majority and against its war, he wrote W. B. blaming the government for having entered the war in the first place. Doing so had only galvanized the German public in favor of a war which they had not, until then, supported. He expected no argument from his father, who shared his loss and ideology.

Needless to say, John's death further demoralized W. B., his mood already made bleak by the irreparable damage the war had done to English society and to the European scientific community.* But he withdrew from his son's hostile reasoning by insisting that a representative government must defend its constituency against military attack. "Those who say, 'Let us be sans patrie, like Jews,' have much to be said for their opinion," he answered Martin. "But elected governments are in honour bound to follow pretty closely to accepted courses."[57] The German autocracy, on the other hand, was not required to adhere to such courses. It was irrelevant to consider the opinion of the majority of Germans therefore. The question to ask was rather would the German government have attacked England after the collapse of France? It seemed certain to W. B. that the excuse for such an attack would have been easily trumped up.

A rift began to develop between father and son following John's death. Where Martin had anticipated support, he found pragmatic realism. W. B.'s essential fellow-feeling with him became obscured. Martin began to turn against his father, simplifying his opinions and ignoring his humor. The elder Bateson did not countenance his son's pacifism, but neither did he entirely oppose it. He did not believe that citizens must support their government uncritically when it had decided to fight a war.

> One may no doubt argue that if enough subjects refused, the war would stop. But as a matter of observation, enough do not *at that stage* refuse, and all that happens through the refusal of some is that the loyal have to take on more than their share of suffering and danger. The argument is not quite the vicious circle it at first seems to be, because in practice there are critical points and points less critical, and it is in the intervals that the objector may make his weight felt. A skipper *has* to put his ship's safety first, and during the critical moments, the only chance in the long run is for the objector to subordinate his opinions and do what he is ordered to do. Sophistry and casuistical reasoning may be used in presenting occasions as critical which are not critical, and vice verse, but in 1914 the moment as I have said, was in my judgment most certainly critical enough in every sense of the word.[58]

---

* "If posterity takes any interest in history," W. B. concluded in 1918, "they will observe that the unusual feature of the Victorian epoch was not the exceptional distinction of the notables which it produced, for perhaps that was more evident to their contemporaries than it will ever be again, but the truly extraordinary circumstance that at that time intellectual distinction was held in public estimation as a thing of great worth. How and by whose example the mass which is congenitally incapable of appreciating art, literature or science was for a brief interval cowed into doing homage to an unknown god is most difficult to explain, but so it was. The unnatural phenomenon passed quickly by, but it left its trace on the fortunes of the intellectual class, consolidating their position for the moment through inducing a false sense of security and reconciling them to concessions which they can never recall." (W. Bateson, "Common-sense in racial problems," in *William Bateson, F.R.S.*, p. 380.)

In conclusion, though, W. B. could only join Martin in feeling anger and grief.

The spirit in which we have carried on the war is enough to make anyone sick and ashamed of their country. . . . *It is always a prominent thought in my mind that strictly speaking people as we are, do not belong and are only here on sufferance. To think for oneself in most societies is a crime* [italics added]. But there it is! One has just to make the best of the situation and be thankful we are allowed our niche.[59]

VII. William and Martin Bateson

The impulse to synthesize mind and evolutionary biology was baldly manifest in Samuel Butler. For him, organisms possessed unconscious memories which were inherited, but which were shifting—won and lost in contact with surrounding environments. For William Bateson, it seems that such an impulse was near to his heart. It was only on the periphery of his expression, however.

> W. B.'s attitude towards mind and attitude towards art were not too dissimilar. He collected art, worshipped it, and regarded it as totally inaccessible to all but geniuses. He regarded science as easy and within reach of ordinary people like himself. Art was something else again. Nowadays, we might say "zen." Yes, I know he painted pictures—mostly very bad and rather like those of Winston Churchill; but when Martin switched from science to drama, his sin as W. B. saw it, was of presumption, that he, a Bateson, might contribute at that higher level. ... His preoccupation with what today is called Zen was also conspicuous on the croquet lawn. It is, of course, a self-defeating preoccupation. If you label that which you are most concerned to say as "unutterable," it never gets said. And a fortiori, if you observe a taboo on even stating that "it" is unutterable.[1]

The years of World War I had nearly halted Bateson's endeavor. His staff was reduced to a few assistants, his contacts with colleagues were restricted, and his spirits were deflated. However painfully, though, life and science proceeded. Indeed, it was W. B.'s view that his life did so because of science. After the war a few young scientists returned to the John Innes, Darlington, Haldane, Huxley, and Newton among them. But his days on center stage of British biology were ending—the newest genetics eluded him. W. B. tried to keep pace by appointing cytologists. From breeding experiments done on the vinegar fly, *Drosophila melanogaster,* the American, T. H. Morgan, had advanced the motion that heredity depended on actual particular units, called chromosomes.[2] W. B., a vitalist in a sort of visceral way, could never bear the materialism that he saw lurking beneath this conception. "The philosopher Locke," C. D. Darlington later said, "had described the soul as an 'immaterial substance,' and Bateson wanted something out of the same bottle."[3] The term "heredity" itself was unfortunate because it was based in an unwanted and, according to him, unreal analogy to property. Worse, it demanded literal representation between generations.

The view that *life* might be reduced to concrete particles was troubling. In 1923, during the spring of his youngest son's freshman year at St. John's, W. B. received from him a request for a microscope. Evidently, the purchase presented Bateson with some difficulty which was resolved by the assistance of the cytologist, W. C. F. Newton. Microscopes were foreign to him, and he maintained a teasing prejudice against them. Aware of his father's sympathies, Gregory thanked him for the gift. "I believe it was only doubtfully wise to take a microscope fiend like Newton with you. He was sure to pitch for an instrument in which genes would be subvisible, if not visible."[4] Barely concealing these preferences, in 1906 W. B. had written:

> We commonly think of animals and plants as matter, but they are really systems through which matter is continually passing. The orderly relations of their parts are as much under geometrical control as the concentric waves spreading from a splash in a pool. If we could in any real way identify or analyse the causation of growth, biology would become a branch of physics. Till then we are merely collecting diagrams which someday the physicist will interpret. He will I think work on the geometrical clue.[5]

Bateson's bias had been markedly visual, and his science was aesthetically inclined. His career had begun as a morphologist, it may be remembered, wherein form and spatial relations in "the structure and properties of the concrete and visible world" were central concerns.[6] As early as 1904, W. B. complained that chromosomes simply did not have outlines. To base heredi-tary process in invisible *things* within the cell opposed his instincts. For Bateson, the *seer,* in the visual, the prophetic, the nonconformist, and the poetic/artistic senses had his place in science. "Genetic inquiry," he said in 1908, "aims at providing knowledge that may bring, and I think will bring, certainty into a region of human affairs and concepts which might have been supposed reserved for ages to be the domain of the visionary."[7]

As W. B. had pursued a scientific career at the frontiers of knowledge, he would not now permit himself membership in an old guard. Despite the almost a priori nature of his reservations, he made a number of attempts to come to terms with chromosomes. For example, and quite characteristically, he tried to incorporate them into a larger system of his own creation, which diminished their contribution and which exhibited visible form.

> To a layman [W. B. wrote in 1920] the visible appearance of the chromosomes is scarcely suggestive of the prodigious material heterogeneity demanded, and the general course of cytological evidence seems to indicate that the role of the chromosomes is passive rather than active. ... The appearance of chromosomes is not to me suggestive of strings of extreme heterogeneity, but rather of strands of some more or less homogeneous substance; and in so far as numerical and geometrical order is exhibited by them, it would in my opinion, be more proper to compare this regularity with that seen, for example, in drying mud or in the formation of basalt than to attribute to it a more fundamental meaning.[8]

Finally, he went to the United States in the winter of 1921, in part to inspect Morgan's fly room at Columbia University. His conversion began at once, though he admitted to never having seen "the marvels of cytology, save as through a glass darkly."[9] That chromosomes were important he knew, but they were, nonetheless, beyond his ken.

In his postwar melancholy, W. B. came (mistakenly) to believe that the new conception contradicted and undermined the value of his great work on Mendelian inheritance. "The moment we most dread," he had said in 1908, "is one in which it may appear that, after all, our effort has been spent in exploring some petty tributary, or worse, a backwater of the great river."[10] Bateson felt that such a moment had now come for him. He told Gregory that in Mendelism, he had probably followed a wrong lead too far, and that his initial work on segmentation and repetition of parts was his only significant contribution. At the age of sixty, he was left old, physically depleted, demoralized, and to his way of thinking, increasingly neglected by the scientific community. He retained something of his self-mockery, however. "I had a bulldog once," he wrote a friend in 1923, "who had to sit waiting for me outside.... [St. John's] College. Street boys used to spit at him on account of his funny face, and he smirked and wagged his tail delightedly with this or any other attention. This is just how I feel."[11]

As it was said, the old order was gone; the standards that Bateson had grown up with no longer coincided with the mediocrity by which he now felt surrounded. When *The Times* of London began to include photographs, W. B. objected on the grounds that the quality of the reporting would be lowered.

Even worse, in the universities, subjects such as anthropology were introduced in the name of science. Typically, the old rigor was no longer applied, and W. B. was harsh in his condemnation of the modern situation. Everywhere he looked, science was "tolerated as a source of material gain, . . . chaos [was] acclaimed as art, and learning . . . supplanted by schools of commerce, the rarity not merely of intellectual producers but of intellectual consumers will need no further demonstration."[12] For a millenium, he wrote in 1918, the development of mankind had been arrested by the church. "It may be suspended indefinitely by the edict of the proletariat. We may have made the world safe for democracy, but we have made it unsafe for anything else."[13] Personally, he suffered inexpressibly at the loss of his son. Asked to address the Yorkshire Science Association, Bateson spoke on the potential of science for restoring world order. His gloom rang: "A great cry has gone up in all the land; and not in our land alone, but through all the earth, for is there a house where there is not one dead? Caught on the wheels of a hideous destiny the young men of the nations and the innocent boys have been torn to pieces."[14]

Politically, Bateson was neither conservative nor liberal. The myriad of scientific and political views held dogmatically in the face of stern opposition were not the result of blind acceptance of a side for the sake of consistency. W. B. was always straining for the integrative synthesis. When in 1920, for instance, the value of classical education again came under attack, and it was said that fewer needed or wanted to learn the grammar of ancient Greek, least of all men of science, W. B. naturally sided against both the detractors and defenders of classical training. He argued that learning "classical and natural, though comprising many parts, is one indivisible whole. Never was it so urgently necessary that the unity of the intellectual world should be maintained and strengthened. The natural and permanent division of society is between [intellectuals] and the rest. Instead of seeing science a competitor, the classical advocates should have welcomed natural knowledge as an indispensable and essential part of complete education."[15]

He considered nationalism to be similarly misunderstood. It was "in essence accidental and ephemeral,"[16] certainly not based in biology. Nations were arbitrary racial amalgams. Patriotism grew out of an "instinct for coherence" nothing more, ". . . and [it] is no more commendable than the instinct which compels a dog to fly at a stranger, however amiable, in imaginary defense of a master, however bad, a service he is equally ready to perform in a few weeks time for any one else who may happen to buy or steal him."[17] Therefore, instead of studying the facts of politics and military expansion which served parochial nationalisms, W. B. argued that education ought to emphasize integrative "extranational" aspects of human history.

Children should learn of the men whose contributions to the arts and sciences were so lofty that they were the property of all countries.

> Shakespeare, Beethoven, Rembrandt, Raphael and the rest, the poets and the artists who have seen the deepest into the heart of man, the makers of beauty, the creators of delight, *the pioneers of emotion* [italics added];[18] in them shall all nations of the earth be blest. Their calm and mighty works soar eternally beyond the noises of temporal, high above the plane on which the voices of the partisans are hushed. ... Who would not that his name should stand however low in this catalogue of the immortal? What honour can national pride offer that is fit to be compared with theirs?[18]

The world, however, seemed to have less time for such syncretic and perplexing points of view. Bateson blamed democracy, which he defined as "the combination of the mediocre and inferior to restrain the more able."[19] No less in his science than in mundane society did Bateson detect the hegemony of a simplifying Benthamite utilitarianism. "In the press, in the arts, and most singular of all, in learning of various kinds, the same phenomenon appears. The modern room of a picture gallery tells the same story as the pages of a scientific journal. The new generation means to go a lot more easily than the rest. Precision of language and finish are out of fashion and superfluous; as they would say, they have no use for them."[20] Though written in criticism of a faceless generation, W. B. soon saw the figure of his own son there, and upheld standards came to provoke conflict.

It was not for Gregory to arouse his father's concern, however. He was only thirteen at the time of John's death, just beginning his second year at his brother's former school, Charterhouse, where he had entered in January 1918. Except that he grew quickly, and had reached his adult height of six feet five inches by the age of fourteen, there is little to recount of his career as a schoolboy. Indeed, Beatrice badgered him constantly that he must learn to write more often. "Let your pen do it," Gregory recalled her saying. He was placed in Robbinites where he also came under the housemastership of O. H. Latter. As he had done to John, Latter encouraged Gregory's collecting. But broadly he was neither outgoing nor particularly active in school affairs. Both his closest friends opted for classics, and he remembered being lonely. "I did a lot of long-distance running" at Charterhouse, he said.[21] In his last year Gregory became a monitor, which was a middle-grade bureaucratic position. He was something of a tease, though.

> It had been announced that the state schools were having a holiday, and we [public schoolboys] had waited as long as we thought was loyal. Charterhouse

was not going to get a holiday, so we telegraphed an 80 word telegram to the Royal Household, explaining our dilemma, that we were unable to celebrate and we were anxious to do so. I bicycled up to Merton from Charterhouse, which was forty or forty-five miles, a hell of a long way to do two ways, and got [back to school] two or three hours late, and was immediately told that the housemaster wanted to see me. He wanted to know why I was late, and I explained that the journey had been a little longer than I had calculated, and I had had a flat tire. [He said] "And, oh dear! Bateson, and you a monitor. And, oh! Bateson, there's a story going around Brook Hall [the Master's Club Room] that you telegraphed the King." And I said yes sir. "It's not true, is it?" And I said yes sir. "Oh, Bateson! I can't do anything about that, you'll have to report to the Headmaster." I reported myself to the Headmaster. I waylaid him the next morning on his rounds, and he said, "Yes. I suppose you want to know whether there was an answer." I said well, it would be nice. And he said, "Well, the king did not give us orders to have a holiday. He did send a message saying he hoped it would be convenient."[22]

The intimacy which had developed between his elder brothers never took shape between Gregory and Martin, after John's death. Gregory admired Martin, but at such a distance that he hardly knew more than the barest details of his brother's life. At the time, for example, he was unaware of Martin's artistic aspirations. Throughout his brother's turbulent adolescence, they exchanged letters, whose content never admitted of the elder boy's struggles.

Many happy returns: [for Martin's birthday] I came back from the Isle of Wight on Thursday. I did not do very much collecting down there beyond sugaring and finding a few plants. A good many moths came to the sugar, but nothing of great note; *Miara bicolora* being the only one new to us. Plants I got. *Lathyrus silvestris, Orobanshe caerulia, Chlora perpliata, Anagallis tenella, Mimulus luteus, Euphorbia enigua, Lecium angustifolia.* In my sugaring this summer I found that a strong wind was the only thing that seemed to affect the number of moths, on windy nights the patches were unfrequented. I also found that moths can be used instead of rum and that cooking is only required to dissolve sugar and when there is no sugar it is unnecessary. . . . I observe from your letter that your principal occupation in Spain is swilling coffee in a cafe and hobnobbing with Spanish padres.[23]

In 1919, the year after Gregory entered Charterhouse, Martin was demobilized. He immediately entered his hereditary college, St. John's. W. B. naturally assumed that the boy would follow a scientific curriculum. "You will have seriously to consider what subjects you intend to take," he advised Martin the month before. "I incline to chemistry, physiology, and zoology and/or botany (if not both)."[24] For his part, Martin was becoming bored with the natural sciences. He returned from military service complaining about the "bullying of the inheritance"—that despite his burgeoning interest in things literary, the weight of parental pressure would push him into a scientific career. Not surprisingly, his first terms' lectures included chemistry, physiology, botany, and zoology.[25] Disregarding his indifference, initially Martin attempted to "be a humble follower of science" as he had put it during Rugby days.

Weeks after the beginning of term, he made the acquaintance of the anthropologist and psychologist, W. H. R. Rivers, then a fellow at St. John's. Martin wrote home that he found Rivers "an attractive person." Rivers had just concluded some years' wartime work as a lay psychiatrist to men suffering from "shell shock." His ear was therefore finely tuned and especially available to traumatized or troubled young men.[26] Rivers repeatedly invited Martin to his rooms for conversation, and he introduced him to elements of Freudian psychology which were then finding their way through Cambridge for the first time. Martin was fascinated. He went to Rivers' ethnology lectures, which he described as "the only scientific ones which I attend."[27] His artistic and literary interests came again to predominate in his thoughts. He wrote his mother, "I have . . . begun *Don Juan* and have nearly finished it. It has uprooted two prejudices that I was carefully nursing, 1) that long poems should not be rhymed, and 2) that defective rhymes are intolerable at any price. Simultaneously, I am reading *Dorian Grey*. The two accord well, though perhaps neither [author] would be pleased to think it."[28] St. John's did not have a literary or artistic orientation, and as such Martin's concerns did not place him in the midst of his peers. He had few friends there and was little respected in the college, where he was known as "the owl," for the size of glasses. Nonetheless, Martin resumed writing verse. He composed several poems during his first year in Cambridge, commemorating his dead brother.

GOODBYE

Oh it's not been so bad: we've rubbed along/and liked it well enough John, you and I/until the war made everything go wrong/—Try and forget me in one good old cry/Tell them I hated war and can't think why/Men are so struck with getting cash and honour!/—They'd sooner kill a man than tell a lie/And make his sweet heart weep than back a goner./But kindliness's breasts are nearly dry,/ and wisdom never stood a chance with luck,/and Belgium's rich—I mean she's our ally./And I'm knocked out, I always had the luck./I betted I should be the first to die./—You've got to pay now John—the last

Goodbye.[29]

Further, Martin began to work on a play in verse whose subject was three schoolboys' lack of courage to become conscientious objectors. And it, too, was mournful—in the course of the play, all three are killed in action.[30]

In the summer of 1919, Martin sent his favorite sonnet home. His father responded with wholehearted approval, and wrote back congratulating his son. "Your mother, in a moment of expansion, showed it to [Lawrence] Binyon who is with us, he expressed distinct interest, enough to have soothed you, had you heard it."[31] The poem was untitled at first.

> Like mighty tides which from the sea uprising,/Sweep through the ancient river in its bed./So through the common ways of man's devising/Stride they from whom man's majesty is bred./Then heave the idle waters in their wake/With tumults which though quickly they subside/Availing nothing to the stream they shake,/Yet leave the channel broader for the tide./Ah, but the moment found me out when I/Caught on a surging billow of the mind,/Rose from the drifting flood of destiny/To soar in heights too giddy for mankind/And wondered much to find such power in me,/Till I sank back—to drift towards the sea.[32]

The sonnet had built up around the line "caught on a surging billow of the mind," which captivated Martin in 1917 when he first developed it. W. B. agreed that the phrase spoke precisely of a feeling he knew well, but criticized the use of "giddy" in the third-to-last line: "I want rather the instability or the momentariness of the billow-mood, not the giddyness of the subject experiencing it. . . . I have not expressed what I mean . . . if I could suppose I would be a poet; as Browning says, 'Fancies that broke through language and escaped.'"[33]

Needless to say, the appraisal gladdened him. "Father's wonderfully complimentary letter arrived this morning," Martin acknowledged the following day. "Giddy is not self-justifying as I knew before."[34] Three months later, in November, *The Cambridge Magazine* published a slightly altered version of the sonnet. In accordance with W. B.'s criticism, Martin had changed the line from "To soar in heights too giddy for mankind" to "And saw the level of life behind." He had also dedicated the poem to Samuel Butler. Perhaps anticipating his father's criticism or expressing his own version of it, Martin wrote his parents that he "had come to dislike the verse. It is illogical and affected, but I shall leave it now. It is also inappropriate because I did not particularly intend Samuel Butler."[35] Upon seeing the poem in print, W. B. agreed that "the dedication slightly lowers it in the direction of the topical. It is, I expect a pretty safe rule in art to cut out anything that is not structural."[36]

Despite the disclaimer, Martin resumed his devotion to the writings and struggle of Samuel Butler. He reread *Erewhon*, *The Way of All Flesh*, and *The Authoress of the Odyssey*, and some time during the fall of 1920, went to Bloomsbury to study an original manuscript of *The Way of All Flesh* on deposit at the British Museum. Poring over it, he discovered a passage which R. A. Streatfield, Butler's editor, had omitted or suppressed from the published version. In the sequence, Overton, the narrator, reproduces an innocuous letter addressed "Dear Pa," sent by a boy at boarding school to Ernest Pontifex. The letter was meant to imply that Pontifex (i.e., Butler) had not been so entirely misogynist as not to have produced offspring.* Martin turned to A. T. Bartholomew, Butler's posthumous editor, who got Festing Jones to confirm the allegations. When W. H. R. Rivers invited Martin to lunch with the biographer, Jones hinted to him that the passage had been altered against his judgment. In awe, Martin followed the conversation. "One question that was put [to me] was what did Father think of Matisse? I answered that I had never heard Father mention the name. I hope that this was true. The rejoinder was that, ah, but at the first Post-Impressionist Exhibition [1922], Father had much wanted something only luckily it was too expensive. Great enthusiasm for H. G. Wells was indicated."[37]

When Martin lavishly compared Butler to Einstein, Euclid, and Newton, W. B. took issue. If Martin identified with Butler's rebelliousness, did he, W. B., then become the despicable and authoritarian father?[38] The two debated Butler's worth, in the course of which W. B. became increasingly negative. "In so big a man, perversity is a grave blemish," he wrote his son. "This perversity comes out most and worst in [Butler's] treatment of Christ. He doesn't take the trouble to distinguish between Christ and Christianity. About Christianity he may say what he likes and more power to him, but that he misses the fact that the personal Christ was 'one of us' I find hard to forgive.

---

*Martin copied from the manuscript: "When I [Overton] say that he [Ernest] never married, I mean that he never set up house, for I have often thought he is married privately and has a separate establishment on a small scale which I know nothing about: I think this because Mrs. Jupp [a maid] once picked the following letter out of his waste-paper basket, and brought it to me. Of course I ought not to publish it but he will forgive me.

"Dear Pa,

"I hope you don't mind me not putting the date but I don't know it I never do. We can't play football in our own field, I mean the first 15 can't because our cricket was rather bad last year and so they are leveling. The one we have now is a beastly one but it doesn't matter for football if it is not quite smooth. ... Thank you very much for nice letter you sent. I got my hamper quite all right it was just what I wanted, the cake was awfully good, so was the jam and plums were jolly. I liked *all* the things awfully."
(From *The Way of All Flesh*, manuscript in the British Museum, London, p. 126.)

If there was ever a 'released' spirit, one who judged for himself and suffered the same, it was Christ."[39] Beatrice, too, encouraged him. She liked Butler well enough, but advised Martin not to let him or anyone overwhelm the imagination. "I know one must go through these various schoolings, but beware of your surrendering yourself to any master absolutely. If one is any good one has to give one's own message—not another's. I see I am becoming maternal and jealous again."[40]

He went to Spain during his first summer vacation. W. B. had reservations about so far-flung a first trip, suggesting "that something less full flavoured would make a better beginning," such as a field trip or almost any scientific project. When Martin did some gambling in Santander, W. B. cautioned him: Such activities should wait until his career was under way. "The war had done us much evil. If you had your old companion, you would be using your holiday better."[41] W. B. was worried to see his boy dispirited and apparently drifting.

> You have to find a new foundation, and I still hope that you will use this change to some good purpose, and not let these frivolities find a lodgment in your makeup as they can all too easily do. I suppose this may prove a birthday letter—well, tant mieux.[42]

Lacking inspiration, his zoology, nonetheless, went well. He received high marks on his second year exams, but was not detracted from feeling that the work was not his own. On the whole, he had no passion for natural science, and complained enough to arouse his father's concern again.

> Before long you will, as I hope, feel the impulse to try to do a definite thing. I don't mean to take up a definite career, which may or may not come all at once, but to do a definite piece of real work, *some concrete task of discovery* [italics added], composition or whatever form it might take. Once begun the first task leads on to others.[43]

W. B.'s mother, Anna Bateson, died two months before John, during the summer of 1918, and in accordance with her will, Martin was to receive one thousand pounds upon reaching twenty-one. In 1920, W. B. set up a trust for his son and took the opportunity to reiterate that he must soon set himself a direction: "In making this allotment I may say I described you as a 'zoologist.' The bank objected to 'student' on the grounds that the Bank of England dislikes dealings with minors. They proposed 'gentleman,' I objected to that because we don't know how long it may be safe to be so designated."[44] But it was not simply that Martin must make a choice. "Whether it is literature, or science, or any other kind of endeavor that draws a man," W. B. advised, "you ought to resolve to aim only at the biggest thing in reach. You have very good abilities and I don't see that you should regard yourself as limited at all. You will find your limits later. But do aim high."[45] All this, though delivered with the best of intentions, must have been aggravating. The worse Martin felt about his abilities and about his usurped direction, the more W. B. affirmed the rarefied standards. "I think looking back, that what did most to pull me up was getting to feel the size of bigger things." W. B. was an assertive father, yet he did not lose sight that this was a predicament. "It is easy to give advice, but precious hard to say anything which really helps."[46]

Unfortunately, the "bigger things" were elusive. Martin continued to travel, touring Germany during the summer of 1920, with his old Rugby friend, Esmé de Peyer, and he visited Italy, the following summer. Between those times he made short trips to Wales, Ireland, and Scotland. De Peyer knew Martin well during this period, but described him as

> not the kind of person who opened up his innermost thought and feelings even to his friends.... This of course does not apply to his scientific beliefs and he introduced me to the work of Samuel Butler when at Rugby. But he never spoke to me about his brother John. He had a kind of defensive mask towards the outside world which had an element of buffoonery.[47]

One weekend in the spring of 1920, Martin took a ride to Oxford in the sidecar of a friend's motorcycle to visit De Peyer at Magdalen College. Thrilled by the speed of the machine, he wanted one for himself. Martin was not on a regular allowance, so financing the purchase required his father's approval. But to W. B., beyond being a caprice, a motorcycle meant contact with the sort of people who were not preparing to aspire to his peculiar realm of scientific endeavor. Martin must keep distance from this majority for "they accustom a man to become a hanger-on and insensibly lower the sense of personal independence."[48] Undaunted, the younger Bateson suggested that he use part of his inheritance to pay for it. W. B. thought this unwise. "The money is no doubt your own but if you do encroach on capital it should be for something that in a definite way is aiding to promote your career or development and not for an amusement."[49] Instead, he would purchase the vehicle, and accounts could be squared when the family estate was divided. In March 1923, Martin bought the motorcycle, using his father's money. "I expect it will prove an excellent investment," he wrote W. B., "and certainly I shall be glad to know how to drive one."[50]

He now began to protest that the teaching of zoology in the university was terrible. His father, ever willing to succor his son's moods, came immediately to Cambridge to inspect the situation. Martin grumbled about his future, clamored that he disliked the town, and objected to the endless round of natural science which he nevertheless continued to study. His pessimism concerned W. B. "I [do] not like to hear you speak of wanting an occupation, but in your present state of mind I should be glad to hear that you had found one."[51] Might he contact Punnett, the former colleague? "Punnett is all right," but Martin was unimpressed. "He cannot inflate the punctured tyre."[52] Approaching the close of his third and final year as an undergraduate, he thought to switch from zoology to botany, for graduate work, and he also spoke vaguely of going into the foreign service.

"That you should speak of yourself as 'punctured' at your age," W. B. told his son, "would be sad if it were not absurd."[53] Still, one should be careful to do nothing which might lower one's possible station in life.

> You have had the ball at your feet if ever a young man had; the right gifts, facility and antecedents for an intellectual career of almost any type. . . . The moment is very critical. . . . The decision made now will govern the rest of your life, and it is the first time you have had such a decision to make. You should reflect that you will not always be possessed by depression and dissatisfaction. Indeed I think the first time you can apply yourself to do a bit of real work, it will pass away like a dream.[54]

For his part, Martin had a different perception of the matter. He was not gloomy or deflated. The problem was his ambition. "I have never fallen away from the opinion that I formed in 1917 that I am no scientist, and this is the cause of all the trouble, so that working at Part II or research and Zoology or Botany, it is all the same."[55] There were also hints that the basis of his reservations about science lay elsewhere. Martin taunted W. B. to come to Cambridge for a ride on his motorcycle. "I hope you will come for an intellectual career when I am rather safer on it: there is more room in its sidecar than in any other I have sat in."[56]

Finances again became an irritation between father and son. If Martin was not to reenroll in the fall of 1921, W. B. would return his unspent stipend. Martin's idea, though, was that the scholarship was his on the basis of personal merit, to do with as he pleased. Moreover, St. John's did not yet know that he was not returning. Wanting to keep options open as long as possible, he feared that his father's sudden sense of duty would force his hand. To his friends, Martin accused W. B. of meddling in his affairs. To his father, he tried to be conciliatory. "Has my scholarship been refunded already? If not, please may I state that I am strongly against this being done! This act appears to me to partake of the nature of suicide. But apart from that it is surely the college's look-out who it gives scholarships to, and if not, then transfer it to Gregory's account, for by entering [it to] him, do you not advance the opinion of his merit?"[57] The money had already been refunded. W. B. made assurances and denials. "You remain a scholar till the expiry of your tenure," he reminded his son, "and the fact that a part of the emolument has been returned is simply a confidential transaction between the College and myself. If you had continued in the usual academic course I might have felt it somewhat less an obligation to refund but I probably should have done it in any case. I had often thought of doing so."[58]

Martin Bateson received first-class honors in the Natural Science Tripos of 1921. This success did not encourage him to do more scientific work, however. He decided to stay in Cambridge for a year to read modern languages, as preparation for a diplomatic career. "Your future," his father told him, "is a matter which you alone can determine. I thought that in our conversations this had been made clear, and that you understood that, so far as we are concerned, you are a free agent."[59] The matter settled, Martin spent the summer traveling. In July he went to Italy, and in August he toured Ireland. Away from Cambridge, his resolve to return there faltered. In Ireland, a friend, Michael Graham, arranged for him to work as a limnologist, and Martin abandoned the idea of diplomacy.

Beatrice, meanwhile, had taken Gregory on vacation to southern France. They visited family friends, Gwen and Jacques Raverat. Gregory retained an image of himself walking through the surrounding countryside with his mother, a knapsack on his back and butterfly net in hand. W. B. joined them in September, bringing the news that Martin had had yet another change of plan. Now, he would enter the Royal Academy of Dramatic Arts, intending to become a playwright. At the end of his patience, W. B. wrote him from France, "As regards your . . . plans there are only two things I wish to say. First that in whatever you do, you have our sympathy. I shall express no approval or disapproval. Secondly, you ought not forget that I cannot guarantee the continuance of the allowance of 250 pounds a year after the time my appointment at Merton comes to an end."[60] At the end of September, the three Batesons returned from vacation. Gregory went back to Charterhouse to begin his last terms. Martin, who had been staying at Merton during their absence, removed himself to his Aunt Hermia Durham's home in London. She helped him set up a flat. "I am staying these days with Aunt Hermia, who has been taking extraordinary troubles on my behalf," Martin wrote his mother. W. B. mumbled that Beatrice's sister was interfering. Martin enjoyed the drama school immensely. "Friday was my first day at the school," he told his mother, "and I came away in most cheerfulness, cast for a clergyman, a railway porter, and Shylock."[61] Yet that this was not intellectual work created some apprehension.

There was little time for disapproval though. W. B. had to prepare "Evolutionary Faith and Modern Doubts,"[62] an address he was scheduled to give at the end of the year in Toronto, to the American Association for the Advancement of Science. Martin had begun a second play which was largely autobiographical, like its predecessor. But in place of conscientious objection, it concerned the evils of fatherhood. The central character was based on a young actress at his drama school named Grace Wilson, with whom Martin had fallen in love. The play, evidently, was harsh. When Martin read it to his mother and Gregory one evening during the Christmas holiday, Beatrice became indignant. After he left that night, she told Gregory that the play was "extremely disloyal" to W. B.[63] Martin, unaware that he had been insulting, thought he was maintaining relations.

As the winter of 1921–22 passed, there were doubts about his play, and about having left the university. Martin's feelings for Grace Wilson were unrequited. He gave her presents until she said that she could accept no more. She, indeed, was engaged to marry someone else, but he would not hear it. Some months later, a friend said of them: "He was altogether too big and too exceptional for a young country girl to understand. He wooed her in a way she could not possibly appreciate without knowing him as well as his friends did. She was not nineteen yet."[64] During the first week of the new year, Martin took his motorcycle out of storage, with plans to visit her in Scotland. The play was finished and he wanted to give it and himself to her. Near Edinburgh, the motorcycle broke down. Martin proceeded by train to a small isolated farm about forty miles outside of town, where she was staying. He presented her the play and left, so that she could read it. He went to his friend Graham, who lived nearby, in Flamborough. In a few days, the play arrived at his friend's cottage, together with a letter accusing Martin of caring nothing except to make intellectual capital of her. He was horrified. Graham remembered later that Martin admitted then that "once ... he had gone out intending suicide but was prevented by circumstances. He was so amusing about it ... that although I had no doubt about the truth of his account I thought that the mood had passed and would not recur again. He assured me it would not."[65] Martin thought about what to make of Grace Wilson's response to his play. "She regards it as a familiarity, or an impertinence, or a breach of honour," he wrote De Peyer, who told him not to take her seriously because she did not understand the theater. Martin did not care what she thought of his play. He had been appealing to her as a man. "The thing is that it is *not* as a dramatic critic that I suppose my heroine to have qualifications for being taken seriously. It is as heroine."[66] After a few days, Martin burned the play in order to restore himself in her eyes. The same day he returned to London in torment.

> I hope by the end of the week to know where I am. I hope against *life* to find a modus vivendi for the play, because of course I was fearfully struck with its merits. There were merits. My ... friend [Graham] got quite excited about the third act. It is that awful second act in Spain that has been the ruination of the thing—and of me. And I don't think she likes the treatment of fathers in the third act. However my Aunts seemed to think it all right. The dreadful thing which made me burn it is not the reproof which certain passages received. I could defend that in my heart—it is the entire absence of any encouragement or approbation. Oh dear![67]

In February, Martin got himself elected to the Saville Club, a small literary and theatrical club. To soothe ragged nerves, he played bridge there almost every evening. "I am very worried about the whole business," he mentioned to a friend.[68] Grace Wilson had no interest in him, yet he persisted in his attachment, and was bothered that the attention upset her. His father returned from the United States, completely exhausted. "His energy had overtaxed his strength," Beatrice recalled.[69] Martin covered hostility with civility when he came out to Merton toward the end of the month. They agreed that the Canadian and American press had made nonsense of W. B.'s address. Headlines had appeared in Toronto papers proclaiming that "Science" no longer believed in "Evolution." Such misinterpretation was comical, but the demos was unpredictable. W. B. denied expecting to be heard publicly, but had been succinct nevertheless.

> Let us proclaim in unmistakable language that our faith in evolution is unshaken. Every line of argument converges on the inevitable conclusion; the obscurantist has nothing to suggest which is worth a moment's attention. The difficulties which weigh upon the professional biologist need not trouble the layman. Our doubts are not as to the reality of the truth of evolution, but as to the origin of *species,* a technical almost domestic problem. Any day that mystery may be solved. The discoveries of the last twenty-five years enable us for the first time to discuss these questions intelligently and on a basis of fact. Synthesis will follow analysis we do not and cannot doubt.[70]

As he was leaving Merton, Martin mentioned that his allowance needed an increase. He would itemize his current finances, but an additional hundred pounds per year would do. W. B. sent his son the money, refusing to raise his allowance, as this "would merely raise the scale of living. If you wish to incur exceptional expenditures for a definite object let me know and I will see what can be done. Meanwhile I must again remind you that our position may before long be very different from what it is now."[71] Martin was irked by what he took to be stiffness, but thanked his father. "I am sure eccentricity is an economy indulgence which should be tempered by self-restraint much more than I used to exercise at Cambridge, for example; but as to suggesting that raising my allowance from 250 pounds would really raise my scale of living—the conventional stage reply to flattery is 'Do you really think so?'"[72] Martin was unable to say that he needed the extra money to pay gambling debts—communication between them had broken down by this point. A friend described the situation a few months later to W. B.

> Although he was from time to time angry with you, he evidently had the deepest regard for you and always looked forward to the time when he would cease to regard [you] as the Butlerian father. It would have happened before . . . if it had not been for his upset state of mind about Miss Wilson.[73]

In April 1922, Gregory completed his final term at Charterhouse. Having some time to fill before entering St. John's, he was to spend a few months learning French in Switzerland, at the University of Geneva. He would stay with the family of W. B.'s colleague Fernand Chodat. To celebrate his graduation, the maternal aunts, Hermia and Florence Durham, invited the two brothers for an evening of dinner and theater. They ate at the ladies' London club, after which, Gregory recalled, he and Martin "both went off to the john before going on to the theater. He sort of sidetracked me and we talked for five minutes. I was going off to Switzerland in a few days, and he gave me a little lecture as if saying good-bye to me . . . a little bit dramatized, of which the main point, I remember, was 'keep on traveling, the thing to do is to keep on traveling.'"[74] It was an enjoyable evening, Martin had been in good spirits. They went to see Gilbert and Sullivan's *The Yeomen of the Guard*. Gregory departed for Europe without sensing that his brother was in serious difficulty. The following week, Martin saw an old friend from St. John's, M. H. A. Newman,* and appeared to be reconciled to Grace Wilson's rejection. He then went on to Lowestoft to spend Easter with his friend Graham. "He had his revolver and in fact it went off accidentally in the hotel

---

*Professor of mathematics, Cambridge University.

room," Graham recalled, "but his body and mind seemed to me to be much more healthy than before and we had a happy weekend."[75]

On 20 April, Martin received his report from the Royal Academy, in which the power of his voice and sense of humor received compliment. "With no natural aptness for the stage," the evaluation said, "he has diligently overcome many disabilities and greatly improved by the end of the term. I should not be surprised if some day by the adroit use of those very disabilities he becomes a character actor with a quaint turn."[76] When he discussed parts for the upcoming term with one of his teachers, Kenneth Barnes, Martin appeared "in excellent spirits,"[77] and an appointment was made for the first day of the new term. Later that day, he went home to Merton. During the visit, Beatrice wrote Gregory in Switzerland, Martin "seemed well and happy, and I was so pleased. I knew that he was passing through some sort of strain, I thought it was some disappointment with his progress in acting. He was not able to take us into his confidence."[78] W. B. also remarked that he was "rather distant"[79] that night, but little else.

Two days later was Saturday, 22 April 1922, John's birthday. Martin had resolved to go to Grace Wilson's flat and declare his devotion again. If she would not reciprocate, he had decided to shoot himself. The meeting must have been disturbing, for when Martin left, she wrote him never to come back. "I shall always be 'not at home.' I shall return any letter unopened. I am engaged and your persistence annoys me so much that I consider it dishonourable. You only make me wish never to see you again. I am very sorry."[80] Later in the morning, Martin met an acquaintance, Maxwell, and had a drink. "No amount of brandy can put my mind out of action today," he told his friend.[81] Returning to his flat early in the afternoon, he got his little .25 caliber automatic, and went out to the Saville Club. There, other members noticed his agitation. Oblivious, Martin scrawled a short will, dividing his possessions and repeating his love.

> It is my wish now I am about to die, as it was my wish living, since the moment I met her, that as much of my money as remains after paying debts—which should be about 1000 pounds, with the grace of God, in whom I believe in the same sense that Samuel Butler believed in him and with the grace of my friends, should go to her—and that her name should not be mentioned in connection with my death. In my most insincere mood I wrote—
> > She is the loveliest child
> > And her heart is made of gold
> > > Gold that is undefiled
> > As it was in the days of old.
> This is nevertheless true. . . . She will be lucky, she will be happy, she will be blessed, if my dying wish is of any avail.[82]

He put the letter in his pocket and then directed himself to a small café on Piccadilly Circus to have another drink. The moment-to-moment chronology has been obscured, but about three o'clock,* Martin stepped out in the traffic, to a position between Regent Street and the central fountain (beneath its statue of Eros). A taxi veered to avoid him. With final flourish, he pulled a white glove off his right hand, and reached into his coat pocket for the pistol. Pointing it behind his right ear, he pulled the trigger and collapsed to the ground. Police and passersby crowded around, and he was rushed to Charing Cross Hospital within minutes. Martin died there an hour later, without regaining consciousness and before his parents arrived.

---

*John Bateson was born at 2:30 P.M., 22 April 1898.

VIII. A Tear Is an Intellectual Thing

Gregory had grown up unnoticed. His had been a vicarious, hand-me-down sort of youth. In part, he had felt, John and Martin were more able. "I was always the stupid one," was the recollection, "or believed myself labeled so. I think I probably was. . . . W. B. was always a little embarrassed [by me]."[1] Death now made Gregory sole heir to an ambiguous intellectual heritage in the natural sciences—personified in his father—and made him a central member of his family. One of the first letters he received from his father told of Martin's inconceivable end. And though the death likely diverted Gregory's attention from it, W. B. now addressed him directly: "I could not before have thought that [Martin] would have doubts that we should be kind to him. . . . You will feel all this grievously as we must. Let us try, Gregory, never to lose each other's confidence."[2]

He returned home from Switzerland at once, but arrived after his brother's body had been cremated at Golder's Green. The house was full of mourning women, who fortified him with affection and advice. The Durham and Bateson aunts assured him of the brightest of futures. A family friend, Peggy Dimmer, spoke most succinctly of his metamorphosis: "You will have to be, in some measure, all three sons to your parents . . . and carry with you John's quiet steadfastness of purpose and Martin's refusal to compromise, as well as what is unfolding in yourself."[3] Beatrice asked for braveness. "Fix your mind on some impersonal definite interest and work hard. It is the only way to get through such a trial and to keep from smothering the great . . . kindness and gentle charity in your heart. We think of you all the time."[4] W. B. advised him to "give his natural friends a chance" when distressed. No one else was more concerned "than your mother and father." There was no one "who would hear of your troubles more leniently and with greater desire to see you through."[5]

Gregory's straightforwardness during the first days after Martin died offended his Aunt Florence. Martin, he suspected, had orchestrated the suicide long in advance. Their last conversation before going to see *The Yeoman of the Guard* now seemed oddly exaggerated, too moralistic for a mere "bon voyage" greeting. Martin, having set himself a plan, evidently had been trying to say something more permanent.* Gregory stayed at Merton for a few days, and then returned to language studies in Switzerland.

He left his father in a dismal state, investigating the development of his son's death. W. B. talked with the young woman, Grace Wilson, but fruitlessly. "She never any time had any feeling towards him," was his impression, "and I have no reason at all for supposing she ever took much notice of him."[6] He had Martin's friends, De Peyer, Newman, Graham, and Maxwell, send him relevant correspondence, and W. B. involved himself in the coroner's inquest, minutely studying Martin's last letter. At the hearing, he broke down while reading a transcript of it. Martin had been in no serious financial difficulty, and he was a young man of "clean habits," thus the coroner's verdict: "suicide while of unsound mind." W. B. concluded that Martin "formed a sudden infatuation . . . and kept it all apart from his outward and obvious life, brooding over it and moping." Parental relations had not been causal. W. B. was without recrimination, but still felt he could "have done better" for his son.[7] The death appealed to the newspapers. *The Weekly Dispatch* called it "probably the most dramatic and deliberate suicide ever witnessed in London."[8] Another published a picture of police and passersby rushing toward Martin's fallen body, and his passport photo appeared throughout the city as a poster for *The Daily Mirror*. All this was intolerable to W. B., aghast that the public eye should now invade his personal affairs. He complained bitterly that "his [son's] friends have had enough to bear without this outrage!"[9]

---

*Gregory's account of the suicide was as follows: "W. B.'s view of literature and the arts was that they were the great thing in the world but that no Bateson would ever be capable of contributing to them. Art, to him, meant the Renaissance, pretty nearly, and of course nobody in the twentieth century could make Renaissance art. But science was something one could do. It was more conscious. It didn't depend on genius, genius being some sort of daimon inside you. So Martin quarreled with W. B. about going to drama school . . . [nonetheless] he went. There he fell in love with a lady who was already engaged. And he made a tremendously dramatic fuss about it, in which he finally made a date with himself . . . that he would go to see her on John's birthday, and if she would not have him he would shoot himself. In fact, she wouldn't and he went out into the middle of Piccadilly Circus, put a revolver to his head and shot himself, under a statue of Eros." (Personal communication: 27 December 1972.)

Martin's bequests demanded attention. Rather forcefully, W. B. persuaded Grace Wilson, the main beneficiary, to agree that her one thousand pounds be donated to a charity for actors. He brushed a Bristol woman aside, who claimed that she was his son's mistress and the mother of his daughter. Returning Martin's first edition of *The Way of All Flesh* to M. H. A. Newman (whose gift it had been), he then asked De Peyer to take the motorcycle.* When De Peyer suggested that Gregory ought to have the machine, W. B. was firm that he wanted it out of his family. Finally, he informed Michael Graham that he was to receive one hundred pounds, which Graham then refused. Upon receiving W. B.'s congratulations for his decision, Graham then changed his mind. He was in financial crisis and wanted to reconsider. No, W. B. had decided not to allow him to do so, adding that "among Martin's papers was a series of your letters to him. I am not going to comment on them, beyond advising you very seriously to pull yourself together."[10] Graham answered the geneticist with irritation. "I am completely at a loss to know why you should advise me to 'pull myself together,' but since my letters are startling enough to cause an English gentleman to forsake the usual reserve as far as to give unasked for advice to a total stranger, they must be capable of being considerably misunderstood, when read by people for whom they were not intended and who are unacquainted with the writer."[11] Although he did not blame himself for Martin's death, W. B. did blame some of his son's friends for undermining his interest in science. W. B. explained his views on the matter to Gregory.

> There were influences used on him to ... keep him as far as possible separated from his wiser friends. I knew something of this was going on, but it had gone to a depth of meanness that I had not suspected.... If Martin could have found friends who shared his own better aspiration whether literary or scientific or personal, he might perhaps have been tided over his crisis, but he was surrounded by inferior people who merely worked him up and weakened his stability.[12]

Beatrice, for her part, warned of the importance of social discrimination. Gregory must learn to be careful and learn to be, unlike Martin, comfortable in the company of others.

---

*De Peyer wrote me (31 August 1976), that "Martin's death was a great shock.... I was in Brussels ... and read about it in a newspaper. When I got back to London I wrote a very inadequate letter to W. B. and subsequently went and saw him. Sometime after, W. B. invited me to lunch at the Athenaeum Club and told me he had been approached by a woman who claimed she had been his mistress. This was quite untrue and W. B. went and saw her ... in Bristol. She was trying to get some money out of him after reading about the inquest."

I am still very bad at it with a silly fear of intruding myself, and not feeling myself comfortable, but take my advice and get over these inhibitions. Other people have them ... too. Learn to take your place naturally and easily. . . . However, don't force the pace with familiarity or noisiness and leave the unclean minded alone—if you happen on them. [13]

Beatrice was also worried about W. B.'s health. Despondency now combined with an already delicate and declining physique. "Even the garden and laboratories almost failed to rouse him," [14] such was his mood. The month after the suicide, however, Bateson was made a trustee of the British Museum, an honor which exhilarated him. It was recognition of high professional achievement, but more significantly, it acknowledged his spirited devotion to great art. By contrast, when offered a knighthood a few weeks later, he declined the distinction without a second thought. His demeanor returned slowly. When one of T. H. Morgan's colleagues, the geneticist A. H. Sturtevant, came with his wife to visit the John Innes, W. B. took them to tour Westminster Abbey. "Everything had to be explained from the beginning—but there are limits to that, and when I saw they looked blank at the name of O. Cromwell and did not seem to understand why his body was carted out of the Abbey, I made no comment and added no historical footnote." [15]

Science had again resumed. Bateson turned to the phenomenon of somatic segregation and was devising experiments. In June 1922, the Genetical Society met at Merton. Morgan came from New York to show his *Drosophila* work, and A. J. Balfour chaired the meeting. More than one hundred people arrived for the occasion. "It seems that chromosomes are here to stay," Beatrice told Gregory afterward, "though I don't think it is certain at all that they will stay on a front seat! Anyway there they are, Mr. Morgan is still with us. . . . I don't like [him]. I think he is vain and silly, but that's only by the way." [16]

During the summer, mother and father joined their son in Switzerland, returning to Merton in early September slightly less beleaguered. Gregory then left for Cambridge to begin reading zoology at St. John's College. His brothers' deaths had ended an enshadowed youth. But John and Martin had been, in all, little more than hereditary emissaries for their father's pieties about the interplay between science and life which, the day after Martin's suicide, had occupied W. B.'s thoughts nakedly.

At times like this when our hearts come nearer to the surface than when all is going well [he wrote Gregory], it is possible to speak of the great things more easily than one can in ordinary life. Looking back I can see that Martin had a certain instability—not much but a little. If John had lived, possibly [it would have been] enough that the two together would have got to work and the interest which I feel sure they both genuinely had in science would have steadied Martin through trouble. What exactly had been happening to him we don't know, but it seems that he had looked for affection where it could not be returned, and in sudden melancholy he did this. He had lost faith in science and also his old confidence in us, as so often happens when a young man grows up and he has nothing to steady him through. What I want to say now is that to people like us, work, meaning the devotion to some purpose, the nobility and worth of which we cannot question, is the one and only thing that helps in time of trouble. I think that like John too, you have plenty of steadiness, and I do not fear for your force of character; but if ever there comes a moment when the horrible tempter which inhabits most human hearts raises the question whether anything is worth doing, then remember that no such doubts rise in happier times, when judgment is at best and crush those foolish doubts in your mind. *The faith in great work is the nearest to religion that I have ever got and it supplies what religious people get from superstition* [italics added]. There is also the difference, that the man of science very rarely hears the tempting voices and very seldom needs a stimulant at all, whereas the common man craves it all the time. Of course, there is great work that is not science, great art, for instance is perhaps greater still, but that is for the rarest and is scarcely in the reach of people like ourselves. Science I am certain comes next and that is well within our reach, at least I am sure it is within yours. It was just because I could never see that Martin had the real spark of art that his change of plans was alarming [to me]. The change came from weakness rather than from strength, as I thought and see more clearly now. Perhaps wrongly, I did not much try to dissuade him from the new venture, though even had I done so I believe such an attempt would have been too late. To set oneself to find out something, even a little bit, of the structure and order of the natural world is, and will be for you I dare foresee, a splendid and purifying purpose into which you can always withdraw in the periods of suffering that every man must pass through. If you keep your eyes on that, the other things of life look so poor and small and temporary that the pain they give can be forgotten in the greater emotion. . . .

Thinking over what I have written I may seem to have been wanting in sympathy for Martin. But you won't think that. I did love Martin, my dear Gregory, and I have lived long enough in the world to feel sympathy with many different ideas, and I did hope that all would go well and that Martin would be again at one with us in loving kindness.[17]

W. B. sanctified scientific enterprise. He would not question its "nobility and worth." This was his "faith," and the knowledge that despite worldly abuse, science would endure, was comforting. Yet the passionate conduct of that science, which constituted a crucial aspect of his children's upbringing, demanded the embattled independence of a pioneer. At once, Bateson offspring were exhorted to assimilate and to dissimilate. Science was birthright but it must be innovative. And confounding this, within the family culture, the creation of great art was all the more astounding. With the loss of John, the conflicting exhortations became unravelable to Martin. He ignored the stricture that artistic creation was beyond Bateson capability, that it was just "for the rarest and . . . scarcely in the reach of people like ourselves."

To Gregory then, it should, and if his brother's experience was deadly introduction, it must be sufficient to explore "the structure and order of the natural world." Only science offered religious, affective, and aesthetic resolutions to human suffering. At the age of eighteen, personal and scientific spheres coincided and the lineaments of a life's project began to appear—to make, in the words of William Blake, "a . . . tear . . . an intellectual thing."[18]

The Invisible Scientist

1922-1980

IX. As Youngest Son in Cambridge

Soon after arriving in Cambridge, Gregory Bateson made the acquaintance of Noel Teulon Porter. Lacking official position in the university, Porter was a conspicuous mystery in the community, limping around the town, dressed "in velveteen breeches."[1] Known to his friends as Baloo, after Kipling's bear,[2] he was a husky man, yet a fractured hip incurred as a child had left him crippled. Without formal education, as an adult, he had become autodidactic. Porter had his own means and lived with his wife Mus in a small house on Little St. Mary's Lane, in premises which formerly had been The Half Moon pub. Between 1912 and 1934, undergraduates and younger research people came there often. Porter offered them soup and, on Saturdays, served lunch to about thirty visitors. "He spent those years," Gregory later said, "dispensing kindness, common sense and hospitality to Half Mooners."[3] The pub became a kind of open house for those who might be under some emotional strain, but who were amenable to new ideas. To Robin Hill, the biochemist, Porter "seemed like one of the Greek satyrs, as it were, unshackling the future heroes."[4] Conversation there ranged between art and science: from the latest discoveries in genetics, to anthropology and archaeology, to impressionism, back to Freudian psychology. Porter was inclined to encourage the experimental and innovative. Gregory remembered his "very simple sort of forthright, earthy character.... He was a sort of lay psychotherapist...in an...amateur, untrained way; reaching out to the people who would drop in.... He was interested in lightening the world, if this is the way to say it, that the tragedies were not so awful, that really the world was possible."[5]

Rumor surrounded him. It was said that he collected phallic jewelry and that he had a standing order at Cameo Corner, a celebrated antique shop, for any that came in. The incidence of masturbation among undergraduates was also said to concern him. The Half Moon, under his auspices, developed a nonconformist reputation. G. Evelyn Hutchinson, then an undergraduate, recalled that it was a place to which he was not invited, "probably because living in Cambridge, with my parents there, I think that Porter . . . was afraid that they would be shocked."[6] Sometimes, it was murmured, morals in the house were lax. At one point indeed, the authorities at Newnham College put the pub off-limits to their women.

It is unlikely that Porter knew Martin Bateson personally, but through contact with W. H. R. Rivers (now dead), he had learned something of the patriarchal shape of W. B.'s family. Enough so that, when the suicide occurred, he told Arthur Tansley, the botanist and former Grantchester neighbor of the Batesons, "perhaps now we will hear something from the youngest one."[7] Gregory, however, was feeling all the more encumbered at the beginning of his undergraduate days. "I thought, acted, and believed that I was left holding a sort of bag," he said, "protecting these people [his parents] as if they were made of glass."[8] Making sense of the death was complicated by a lack of information. Other than that Martin had believed himself to be the personification of Samuel Butler, Gregory knew little about his brother's life. And after the first flurry of letters, W. B. became silent about it. Beatrice took to sighing. His friends understood that he, too, did not want to discuss the matter. Hutchinson remembered "a lack of conversation [about Martin], a kind of area that one did not approach."[9] On the first anniversary uniting John's birth and Martin's death, in the spring of 1923, Gregory deliberately returned to Cambridge, so as not to be at home. "I hope that somebody dropped in today to take your mind off John and Martin," he wrote his mother. "I would have stayed at home myself, had I not decided that it was better not to give way to that sort of thing."[10] It was evident that he was burdened. Hill thought that he seemed "to have much to live down and to live up to."[11] Gregory recalled, "feeling on the one hand, that Martin had taken a noble course and on the other, that he'd been an idiot, perhaps neither being . . . [accurate.]"[12]

The official reverberations of the suicide were minimal. Martin's former tutor, B. W. F. Armitage, to whom Gregory had also been assigned, criticized Martin for having disdained college affairs. "You need to have hobbies," was his counsel.[13] As a master's grandson, Gregory received a suite of the better rooms in St. John's and furnished them carefully. Walls were decorated with paintings by his father and mother. "My room is now, I believe, more beautiful and comfortable than those of most fellows in the college."[14] Armitage, though, was useless. "Any fool can see," Gregory wrote Beatrice, "that a tutor is not 'in loco parentis' to any serious extent."[15] Otherwise, the first months were those of a typical freshman—spent in amusement and social occasion. He was bothered not knowing how to folk-dance. He attended concerts and went to the theater. "On Saturday night, I went to *Oedipus Tyrannus* in English, . . . I went with Hutchinson. . . . The play was well produced, but it does lack some comic character to relieve the mind. I suppose the rule of unity of interest would not allow Sophocles to put in any distraction comparable to the porter in Macbeth or the fool in Lear."[16] To his own surprise—such was Bateson horror at organized athletics—Gregory began to row. "Charterhouse . . . will . . . perhaps be green with jealousy when they hear Cambridge has made me train. They used to try but it never came to much."[17]

At once, the religious believers on the staircase caught his teasing eye. "I have Powell, an ordinand . . . I do not think he will be ordained—not if he continues to be as reasonable as he is now," he wrote Beatrice in November. "There is also an older man named Harmor, a religious maniac, who holds prayer meetings 'for all' in his rooms. The ordinand despises the religious maniac very much."[18] Amid a vogue for psychical phenomena, an older undergraduate and naturalist, Joseph Omer-Cooper, tried to persuade Gregory of the possibility of séances and second sight. One evening, at the young Bateson's suggestion, the two tried psychokinetically to turn a table. "I drew up a light table and we set to work. He seemed to think it necessary to turn out the lights and the gas fire. So there we sat for twenty long minutes with our finger tips on the table. The only spirit that we felt, was that of the departed fire which came and breathed a cold breath upon us."[19]

He worked diligently in zoology, botany, organic chemistry, and physiology. Finding a sympathetic companion in science was on his mind[20] when Gregory joined the Cambridge Natural History Society and the Botany Club. "I have become a member of a mad society," he mentioned to his mother soon after the start of Michaelmas term. "The society is called the Biological Tea Club. I was present at its inaugural meeting. . . . It was something out of *Alice in Wonderland,* we met in an upper room of Thurston's Tea Shop and had tea."[21] The founder was the same Joseph Omer-Cooper, and the other undergraduates included Joyce Barrington, W. S. Bristowe, G. Evelyn Hutchinson, Ivor G. S. Montagu, E. J. Pearce, Michael Perkins, Grace E. Pickford and E. B. Worthington.*

After tea, Hutchinson gave an informal dissertation on whether individuals of

---

*Joseph Omer-Cooper, professor of zoology, University of Grahamstown, South Africa, deceased; Joyce B. Omer-Cooper, Grahamstown, South Africa; W. S. Bristowe; G. Evelyn Hutchinson, Sterling Professor of Zoology, emeritus, Yale University; the Hon. Ivor. G. S. Montagu, filmmaker; E. J. Pearce, chief rector of the Community of the Resurrection, Mirfield, Yorkshire, England, deceased; Michael Perkins, zoologist, deceased; Grace E. Pickford, professor emeritus of biology, Yale University, scientist in residence, Hiram College, Hiram, Ohio; and E. B. Worthington, scientific director, International Council of Scientific Unions, London, England.

different species are necessarily distinguishable. He said that in insects many groups of species could be distinguished only by examination of the genitalia. But in many other classes of animals no criterion equivalent to the genitalia had been found, thus in these animals, very likely, there might exist species which are distinct but indistinguishable. I thought he was rather good. His thesis was followed by slightly heated discussion in which the long haired mammalogist [Montagu] took a leading part.[22]

Among other presentations Gregory made to the Tea Club was one in which he presented contemporary views about the inheritance of acquired characteristics. Landing midway between Lamarck and mutation theory, he argued that certain cases of elaborate symbiosis required both of these two.[23] "My address was a washout," he told Beatrice, it "was followed by a little discussion in which I took very little part."[24]

His first fieldwork began that year. Thirty years before, W. B. had collected various forms of local snails, to assess their environmental adaptation. Locating the old sites involved father and son in lengthy correspondence. "I have been getting out your *Limnea peregra* from the Cambridge district. I find them very dusty and dirty but still extant. I propose to get fresh sets of Limnea from the localities which you visited and to see whether they have changed since 1890. It is possible that the conditions of life have changed considerably in many of the ponds."[25] Gregory seems to have enjoyed doing this work. "I visited the skating pond yesterday with Omer-Cooper and Miss Barrington. They caught beetles. I caught snails.... We had tea by the pond—rather chilly but good fun. The wetness and muddiness of ponds is an important part of the ritual of collecting which I would not forego for the world!"[26] He filled his college rooms with boxes of snails. "At present, I may have 1500 before I begin to understand anything about them."[27] Little came of his comparisons. Except in size, there were no appreciable differences between the 1923 snails and the 1890 ones.

In March 1923, Paul Kammerer, the Lamarckian biologist, came to Cambridge to show the nuptial pads of male midwife toads. These, he claimed, were an illustration of inherited characters which he had induced experimentally in a previous generation of male toad. After his main lecture, in which the Biological Tea Club participated, Gregory recalled Kammerer joking that at the London Zoo he had been struck by the resemblance between the face of the llama and William Bateson. "He said [he] was interrupted in this thought when the llama spat at him."[28] Detailing Kammerer's presentation to W. B., one of his sternest critics, Gregory was taken with the virtue of the man, less so with his claims.* To Beatrice, on the other hand, Gregory confessed that even though Kammerer's methods might be casual, his results were not easily dismissable. "I hope this [opinion is] not due to a weak critical sense on my part."[29] Another member of the Tea Club, Grace Pickford, mentioned similar distrusting attraction. "In respect to Kammerer, he was a charming man and completely won our hearts. I think we all wanted to believe him, even if we had lurking reservations."[30]

During the summer meetings of the Tea Club, members agreed to present nonscientific subjects. Papers were given on alchemy, dragons, railroad trains, and psychical research. Having grown up at the feet of William Blake's "Satan Exulting over Eve," which occupied prominent wall space at Merton, Gregory set to work on the poetry and mystical cosmology of this rebellious romantic.[31] "I remember the old man reading *Thel* to us, one day. But he never made any discussion at all about Blake's epistemology or philosophic position. . . . There was some chatter about 'Damn braces: Bless relaxes.' I don't think he knew his way about the prophetic books at all."[32] At the age of nineteen Gregory became captivated by Blake's radical protest against repression. Thus the poet:

> I must create a System, or be enslav'd by another Man's:
> I will not Reason and Compare: my business is to create.[33]

Beatrice cautioned that Blake was really "all symbolic, I mustn't assume that because he preached sex freedom that sex freedom was what he was talking about."[34] Gregory immersed himself, thinking that this was *his* first real research. "He somehow felt that instead of having his hands picked and put on

---

*From 1907 until his death in 1926, the Austrian biologist, Paul Kammerer, put forward numerous cases in support of the inheritance of acquired characters. A skilled experimental breeder, he studied the effects of colored surroundings on the skin color of the spotted salamander (*S. maculosa*), which he claimed produced darker or lighter colorations in progressive generations. A dark salamander in a darkly colored environment would, when artificially bred, produce offspring of even darker color. Later experiments confirmed that an individual's color would react to the color of its location, but it was never demonstrated that such effects were transmitted to descendants. Kammerer did similar experiments with midwife toads (*Alytes*) which, upon examination in 1926, were found to have been doctored with India ink. Kammerer denied knowledge of the fraud, but committed suicide at the end of the year. The affair received publicity, which brought the Lamarckian case into further disrepute. By portraying William Bateson as representing the Darwinian establishment in the controversy, Arthur Koestler, in *The Case of the Midwife Toad*, has exaggerated the importance of Bateson's role in the events which led to Kammerer's suicide.

the keys of the piano, that with Blake he was free to pick it himself."[35] The eventual notes from which he spoke to the Tea Club had "sort of thumbnail drawings in the margins, in the manner of William Blake,"[36] such was his fascination.

As an undergraduate, this last Bateson possessed a serious spirit. If his parents were looking carefully for cause, he gave them little. Save two trips to the southern coast Marine Biological Station at Plymouth, Gregory did not travel. "In zoology I am forming a small study circle for the absorption of embryology." He had stayed in Cambridge during the first long vacation. "There are some official courses on the subject but they are said to be hopeless. ... There is a good deal of physiology going on in the shape of vivisection demonstrations and lectures. ... The subject does not give much opportunity for independent lab work."[37] There was potential trouble with the Tea Club however. Members remained members as long as they stayed at Cambridge. "In time therefore the Club will consist entirely of dons and its value as a social, scientific gathering of undergraduates will disappear; it will lose its informality and happiness."[38]

In the spring of 1924, the biologist Munro Fox invited Gregory to study the exchange of fauna and flora between the Mediterranean and the Red Sea, in the Suez Canal (yet another of W. B.'s early projects). Stimulated by the opportunity, he had doubts about Fox's reputation as the "best dressed biologist" in England. Gregory decided against the venture when his father confirmed that Fox was mostly pose. "On the whole I am glad not to be going," was his fastidious relief. "The history of the connections between Red Sea–Mediterranean is really incredibly complicated. But my opinion of Fox rose somewhat when he gave a clear statement of the different factors involved, but he was unable to suggest anything of first class interest which might come out of the work."[39]

At twenty, Gregory was an outgoing character. A fellow tea drinker, Ivor Montagu, remembered that "he was extremely tall, so tall that he used to fold up in his armchair, when I called on him in his rooms at St. John's, and that ... it was a pleasure to chat and joke with him."[40] One rainy afternoon, which Robin Hill recalled, Gregory painted a coastal scene "from imagination and memory; then feeling that the sky lacked interest he inserted a very solid and small cloud and wrote [misquoting Blake]: 'Oh little cloud I charge thee tell me/Why thou complainest not/When in an hour/Thou fadest away/Then we shall seek/But not find—.' Then Gregory signed and dated it ... and presented me with what he termed 'an early Bateson.'"[41] Hutchinson also retained a playful incident. With another friend, Michael Perkins, they went out to row and picnic together on the Cam. Perkins had brought an exceptionally strong brew, known as Audit Ale. "Gregory insisted on helping himself liberally of it, and he insisted on punting the boat, standing up in the bow, instead of the stern, and using a pole alternatively on one side then the other. He could make it go along, but it was not the most efficient way of punting."[42]

His Tripos examinations in zoology went well at the end of his second year, though they included subjects about which he knew nothing and cared little. He used a Blakean strategy. "I have formed a new system of work in exams," Gregory told Beatrice, "roughly it is: Be particular and prolific of detail on general questions while Generalize on particular questions especially those treating of comparative anatomy. The zoology first paper . . . and the two botany papers were quite pleasant."[43] Trying to camouflage ignorance of comparative anatomy, he questioned the abstractions through which the subject operated. There was said to be comparability of function, when two organs have similar uses—i.e., the trunk of an elephant is said to be "analogous" to the hand of a man. There was also comparability of structure, when two organs bear similar relations to other organs—i.e., the trunk of an elephant is said to be "homologous" to the lip and nose of a man. But, Gregory asked, were these abstractions sufficiently complex?

> I argued that the bilateral fins of a fish would conventionally be regarded as homologous with the bilateral limbs of a mammal, but that the tail of a fish, a median organ, would conventionally be regarded as "different from" or at most only "analogous" to the fins. But what about the double-tailed Japanese goldfish? In this animal the factors causing an anomaly of the tail also cause the same anomaly in the bilateral fins; therefore there was here another sort of comparability, *an equivalence in terms of processes and laws of growth* [italics added].[44]

With triumph, Gregory presumed—but wrongly—that he had invented an abstraction. At the age of twenty, perhaps, the inscription of a family dedicated to the pioneering intellect was beginning to show itself. "So far as I was concerned the idea was new and I had thought of it myself. I felt I had discovered how to think."[45] Brandishing this challenge to cognitive orthodoxies against those dons whose approach seemed overly narrow, drew curious response. "The best dicta that I have extracted are a) 'Do you mean to say that you have done zoology all this time without realizing that it is all a game? If you ask questions like that you are breaking the rules!' b) 'I am afraid of you because I do not know how much you have absorbed your father's views.'"[46]

Tripos concluded, in July 1924 he returned to Merton. "I had the results of my examination sent home. I had gotten a first . . . [W. B.] hemmed and hawed and said, 'It's nice to know that you are a *little* better than the others, Gregory.'"[47] His father was then working on anomalous colors in the feathers of certain red-legged partridges *(Alectoris rufa* and *saxatilis),* having revived the morphological interests of his youth. Though the veneer was deprecating, W. B. still thought to involve his son in this project, sending him to the British Museum to check the partridges on store there. "I went and worked over in fine detail the museum birds and went to Covent Gardens in the early morning about half a dozen times and found that there was quite a lot of instability about those . . . feathers, stray striped patches turned up fairly often, not a whole patch, but one stray striped feather. I worked them in a detail which he hadn't really thought about."[48]

Further examples of aberrant partridges "had been presented to the museums of Sion and Bex, my son went to Switzerland to examine them in detail"[49] was how W. B. introduced the paper which later appeared in his *Journal of Genetics.*[50] Gregory returned to Geneva, and again spent a few weeks as the guest of the Chodats. He had not seen them since Martin's death, two years before, but had kept up correspondence with Isabelle, the daughter of the house. Now, in August 1924, they fell in love. There were proposals of marriage and acceptances. When Gregory announced the engagement to Beatrice, she answered him at once: "Isabelle must take me on, not take you away. I could not bear to have no son." She had not yet met the girl but wondered if the idea of marriage was a bit premature. "I trust that Martin's birthday [it was then 1 September] has not emotionally overstrung you, and may be a good augury that the matter was considered and not an impulse."[51] He must remember that he had no means, though there might be an inheritance, "if labour does not destroy all property," but he must try to start something independent. These reservations aside; Beatrice was ready to offer unlikely platitudes.

> One of the first rules between man and wife should be to maintain perfect candor. . . . I believe that this is the one and only way to avoid the soreness of the inevitable little griefs . . . which must fall to the lot of every couple and that is only possible with perfect confidence. If you prove as good a husband, when the time comes and it cannot be yet! as your Father has been to me and Isabelle does better than I have done, you'll be all right.[52]

At the time, W. B. was touring plant-breeding stations in Scandinavia. Upon his return, plans were made for a short holiday in Auvergne. There, while his parents painted and Gregory collected flying ants, they watched Isabelle, concluding quickly that she was not a match for their son. To find an appropriate girl within their small circle of quasi-endogamous English intellectuals would be difficult, to find a suitable "outsider" was nearly inconceivable to them. Beatrice became particularly critical. "She did not believe," Gregory remembered, "that Isabelle and I would ever achieve [being] ... internationalized, cosmopolized people.... To her Chodat was a sturdy peasant."[53] W. B. maintained an unashamed elitism such "that nobody in the world was going to be a member of the same caste. Isabelle was all right [to him] ... but they were just ordinary people—in addition to being foreigners."[54] Still feeling protective, he was left in a dilemma. "I took a day's walk all by myself, to try to sweat it all out ... [lengthy pause]. What right had they to be hurt?!!! ... I came back from that walk and told Isabelle that I didn't think it was going to work, and we broke it off."[55]

Needless to say, his change of heart was upsetting. *"Je sens qu'il faut que je vous dise que je souffre martyre,"** she wrote him.[56] Hearing of the rejection, her father and brother came to Auvergne, and Gregory had to repeat his decision to them. "There was an awful session at which I did my best to explain [it] to her dad and her brother and her before breakfast. [Pointing in opposite directions], Chodats were to sit over there and the Batesons over there. Her brother came dashing over and called me a *voyou*, a bounder, and all those things. I let it go."[57] After breakfast, Gregory wrote a letter—which her father demanded—attesting to Isabelle's virginity, and exchanged compassionate apologies with her. As the Chodats left for Geneva, he wrote her words of comfort and advice which he had heard before.

> *Pauvre petite fille. Moi aussi je suis triste de cette terrible séparation, mais je ne peux pas l'éviter. Il nous faut nous fouiller dans l'art et la science pour oublier un peu. Elles sont des choses plus grandes que nos vies et dans lesquelles on se perdre et trouver le confort que la réligion donne à des miliers de gens et qu'elle donne peut-être à vous.*[58]†

The Batesons then returned home, and Gregory went back to St. John's in early October—angry. Parental interference had scarred him. His life then

---

* "I must tell you that I am suffering terribly."
† "Poor little girl. I too am sad about this terrible separation, but I cannot avoid it. We must burrow into art and science in order to forget [each other] a little. These are the bigger things than our lives and one can lose oneself in them and find the comfort which religion provides thousands of people and perhaps provides you."

became somewhat more social. He went to concerts, had afternoons with his father's sister Margaret Heitland, and began conducting foreign visitors around Cambridge. "I did the morning's sight show [with Danes], including St. John's College silver, cellars, Wood's room, etc.—all the regular things; and then some laboratories, but the latter were too foreign to the Danes (literary and economics). They knew not what to say."[59] Part II, graduate studies in zoology began and the Swiss partridges required attention. When a porpoise appeared as the center piece in a local fish shop, Gregory purchased it and, with friends from the Tea Club, dissected it. "Gregory tried to get some porpoise steaks cooked in the college kitchen," Hutchinson remembered, "as I think Michael Perkins may have done at Trinity, but without success."[60] In general, his feeling for scientific work was shifting—souring slightly. Relative bathos followed the thrill of his Tripos examinations. Trying to collect *Pisidia* in the winter of 1924, he simply could not locate any. "I dislike them," he wrote Beatrice, "and all connected with them and with Stanley Gardiner's zoology. I am now beginning to realize what a poor faunist and oecologist I am, though I do not regret the little I have learnt of those subjects."[61] By the end of the term, he was looking forward to vacation. But when his plans collapsed, Gregory found himself at Merton, again commuting to the British Museum to complete the partridge paper.

Meanwhile, W. B. was working out an interpretation. As we have said, he preferred the outward and the visible. The variation in the feathers of these birds did not look to be the result of internal "chemical processes," distributing pigment over their body surfaces.[62] Instead, he argued that a new conceptual language was needed to describe the development and spread of "rhythmical banding" or "rhythmical barring" over an organ such as a feather. Bateson borrowed the language he wanted from the mechanics of wave motion.

> As ... in the banding of cats' skins, we may in such cases perhaps speak of these bands as "waves of pigment forming metabolic activity," and the terms "crest" and "trough" which ... [were] used in reference to the banding of a moth's wings are probably more than merely metaphorical expression. We may go further, and applying the analogy of wavelength we may speak of the pattern of Grevy's Zebra *(Equus grevyi)* as approximately the upper octave of that of *Equus zebra*. Such a terminology by familiarizing the mind with the probable nature of the process of these segmentations will prepare the way for a correct analysis, though admittedly open to abuse.[63]

In addition to being Gregory's first scientific collaboration with his father, the work in the Bird Room accidentally led to an expedition to the Galapagos

Islands. In mid-December, a telegram arrived there from Colon, Panama—the invitation of Godfrey Williams, a vacationing millionaire, asking that a naturalist join his fishing cruise between Balboa and Galapagos. "Oh! Young Bateson," it was said at the Bird Room. To Gregory, whose childhood had been so shaped by Darwinism, the opportunity to go to Galapagos was matchless. He went directly to his father. "I talked it over with W. B. He said, 'Let's see how long they're going to be there, and how long would be worthwhile.'"[64] Reminded that in 1835, Darwin himself had spent six weeks there, the elder Bateson thought that if Gregory could get that length of time, he should go. When Williams agreed, graduate studies were set aside and in January 1925, W. B. put his son aboard the R. M. S. *Cardiganshire,* bound for Panama. At the dock, looking over the ship, the crew, and the other passengers, W. B. assessed who he thought was and was not "university," and reminded Gregory to write often "for your mother's sake."[65]

Sober and wide-eyed, he spent hours staring at the water stretched out to the horizon. "Flying fish appeared . . . as we crossed the Tropic of Cancer . . . very pretty and unexpected. I should never have guessed them to be fish if I did not know. They seem able to fly closer than 45 degrees to the wind and down wind (at intermediate angles). . . . Velocity very constant so that I am led to disbelieve in the gliding theory. . . . No dolphins, porpoise or sharks and very few birds and a few Phaethon."[66] Within the *Cardiganshire,* Gregory watched the workings of a huge engine for the first time—and wondered about Paley's teleology. From a watch, Paley had insisted one could not fail to infer the design of a watchmaker. Was not the existence of a Divine Hand any less evident in nature? Was the eye less obviously designed than a telescope? To Gregory, the design of an engineer appeared in the propeller, but the engine as a whole mystified him.

> I argue "Animals are very complicated and adapted but not purposed [i.e., designed], therefore machines which are complicated and adapted are not *purposed.* And I say it shamelessly and would add that even if machines are purposed I will not worry much about their purposes, neither shall I fall down and worship 'em."[67]

At Colon, Williams' yacht, the *Surprise,* was docked for minor repairs. Gregory met its owner and his employer who seemed "a sort of big, innocent, very hefty, obese . . . man. . . . He was sure there was gold in Galapagos."[68] His job would be to identify the fish. During the first six months of the Williams' pleasure cruise, it turned out that many guests had left the *Surprise* in disgust and that many crewmen had been fired. "The job of describing life on [board] is very difficult," he wrote Beatrice. "The life is so very strange and is based on a scale of values so different from any I have experienced. The people, their manners, jokes, occupations, interests and especially raisons d'être are all mysterious."[69] Waiting for the ship's repairs, Gregory occupied himself with local insects for a few weeks. Finally the *Surprise* set sail. Passing through the canal his eye was caught by "large areas of the lakes [in which] the tops of big trees [were still] sticking up.... Very curious effect; all trees are dead, of course, but apparently decay does not proceed as quickly under water as on land."[70] Stopping at Chatham Island gave him the opportunity to see isolated natives, whose faces reminded him of "Maya's faces in the bas reliefs at the British Museum. [They are] friendly to a degree of parasitism."[71] The *Surprise* proceeded among the other islands, allowing him time to observe and collect. To the young Darwin, these blackened, cratered, slag-covered, species-dense islands eventually offered "haunting" evidence[72] which stimulated *The Origin of Species*. They only puzzled and demoralized Gregory Bateson. He concentrated on the thirteen species of Galapagos finches, whose differing beaks and differing diets had directed Darwin toward the pivotal question of species adaptation. How was it, Darwin had asked, that such extensive variation could exist in such close quarters, if evolution, as was then believed, depended on climatic or historical change? No such clarity of problem posed itself to Gregory.

> Now the excuse I've always given to myself was that the damn birds were all eating caterpillars, which indeed, was true, more or less. It rained. Rain in Galapagos is rare. When it rains, all the bushes get green and all the caterpillars eat the leaves, and all the birds eat the caterpillars.... The whole adaptive proposition that the Darwinian story was based on, that there ... are different niches, and the big beaks eat hard seeds and the little beaks eat little seeds, all sort of falls to pieces when everybody's eating caterpillars.[73]

Williams' wife, French and well-bred, finding no amusement in lizards and finches, complained loudly that she was bored. Then, after a month at sea, the ship's doctor appeared to have come down with appendicitis, and asked Gregory to operate. "I explained that I had dissected a rabbit, even a fresh rabbit. It bled. ... But I had never used such a thing as an arterial forceps."[74] The *Surprise* returned quickly to Balboa, though the doctor did not have appendicitis. Deferring to his wife, Williams gave up on Galapagos, which left Gregory feeling unable to account for himself. As it happened, the oceanographic vessel of the New York Zoological Society, the *Arcturus,* was then harbored in Balboa, radio-equipped and heavy with scientific apparatus. Due to sail for Galapagos, it was under the direction of William Beebe, the ornithological curator of the New York Zoo. There was a varied group of scientists aboard with interests in the ecology of land and marine vertebrates in neotropical regions. Gregory told Beebe of his times in Galapagos, "and we had a very merry drunken evening on board [the *Arcturus*] following which he invited me to go ... with him."[75] His hope was to make more of Galapagos fauna in this more serious atmosphere. He worked on *Pelagic coelenterates* en route and observed the eruption of a Galapagos volcano while there. But on the whole, his curiosity languished and was distracted by his distaste for Beebe. "It seemed to me very silly to be sort of romantic about what wonderful animals live in plankton, which was about where Beebe was."[76]

Gregory left Colon just after his twenty-first birthday for the New York Zoo—to deposit some of the *Arcturus'* collections there. At the behest of W. B., he went to the American Museum of Natural History to visit its president, H. F. Osborn, who momentarily confused him with his father, so closely did the two seem to resemble each other. "Your son called," Osborn later wrote W. B., "reminding me very much of yourself as you were when I first saw you as a student in Cambridge. ... I enjoyed showing him some of the salient features of our wonderful collections."[77] He also visited Morgan's *Drosophila* laboratory at Columbia University. "We greatly enjoyed seeing Gregory," Morgan said afterward. "He must come over for one year of his graduate work in this country, not because we have anything as good as what he can get in Europe, but because it is different. We are not all Beebes."[78]

Back at Merton in the summer of 1925 and dissatisfied with his future as a zoologist, he was also very critical of his Galapagos experience. "I came back feeling very restive about sitting in a lab for the rest of my life."[79] At Cambridge, resuming Part II studies only caused more frustration. "I have lately been working very badly," he wrote his parents. "When I was working on the partridges I broke off much too often to worry about it all—like a damn young fool! Indeed it was from that piece of research that I realized how little hold the work had on me—that the interest was purely intellectual and not heart felt."[80] Further, a sense of cultural awkwardness was developing. "I was born," he recalled, "with all the entrée into the ... network ... that ran British science and intellectual life. But I never could bear to be more than one foot into it. I enjoyed playing the parlor games."[81] Opportunities of which he felt undeserving came to him. "This was one of the reasons I moved out of zoology—to get into something in which I was me and not son of.... It bothered me that I was named Gregory, after Gregor Mendel."[82] Meeting often at the Half Moon, he and Noel Porter discussed current research in the human sciences. Hutchinson recalled that after Galapagos, "he had decided that the most interesting fauna was the people of the world."[83] No longer thinking of himself as a zoologist, Gregory began to grope about. "I tried psychology and that didn't make much sense and I joined the Cambridge Antiquarian Society."[84] Even the Tea Club began to pale. New concerns made it seem intellectually restrictive and he decided to quit. "Objection was taken to my bringing Noel Porter, as a guest and . . . a candidate for election was criticized for writing poetry! This last seems to me to savour so much of democracy that my interest in the club wanes."[85]

In mid-July, Gregory went to King's Lynn on an archaeological field trip with the Cambridge University Antiquarian Society. He met A. C. Haddon on the train, a fellow member, and one of the first British field anthropologists. Haddon cross-examined him about the Galapagos Islands and pressed him about natives. A few days later, Gregory described the incident.

> From Galapagos we turned to Melanesia and I began thinking of the scheme [to switch fields] again. He — not knowing who I was — invited me in joke to do a Part II in Ethnology. . . . But I do not think that Haddon had been practicing on my interest in zoology. He only casually provided an opening which I jumped at. . . . As to my fitness for the subject, I of course know little enough. All I know is that I thrive pretty well in a tropical climate and could probably get on well enough with primitive peoples—at least I have little difficulty with English peasantry.[86]

Anthropology in Cambridge was then in the hands of a small number of people, many of whom had themselves changed into it from natural science. Indeed, like W. B., A. C. Haddon—an outspoken man of working-class descent—had also been a student of F. M. Balfour. The turning point in Haddon's career had come during a visit to the Torres Strait in 1888. He went out as a marine biologist and returned to devote the rest of his life to the study of man.[87] In any case, in 1925, anthropology was becoming more social, and was emerging as a science of living relatives, rather than of speculative history. Notably for Gregory, the very status of evolutionary theory as applied to the development of society was then being challenged.

However much the new subject seemed to speak to the tensions of his family background, it did not raise his spirits immediately. Haddon's lectures were preferable to Gardiner's in zoology, but he was no less baffled. "It is terrible to find how shaky all the ground is on which the elements of anthropology ... are based and it will be so much more difficult to absorb the facts, there being no structure of theory upon which to hook them."[88]

When he announced the change to W. B. and Beatrice, Gregory was careful not to have them think that his new field might represent a rejection of them.

> I have been thinking a good deal lately about my future as a zoologist or geneticist. I feel now and have felt for a long time that such work—purely impersonal—can never give me the inspiration necessary to pull me through the difficulties of life. ... It is not that I have no interest in evolution and kindred problems. I am and shall, I imagine, always remain interested in them. *But I do not feel able to throw myself unreservedly into their study* [italics added]. ... As to the alternatives, I believe that almost the only thing is anthropology which I think would supply the personal inspiration which I believe myself to need, and indeed hope always to need. I am afraid that you will be terribly disappointed in me in this, but I could not go on as I was, and sooner or later I had to come to some sort of a break with ordinary impersonal science. ... But though this may be weakness in me I do not see any concrete reason for you to be disappointed or worry over this change. I am much more likely to get into trouble through going on as I am, as I see it, than by changing into a branch of science which is personal where I should be able to take root a bit; and if this change is to come let it be as soon as possible while I am still able to absorb training in a new subject. ... That it was in part at least this desire for a personal inspiration that made Martin leave science, I do not doubt but this does not worry me and need not worry you. I believe that one of the things which went wrong in his case was that he stuck to the impersonal thing too long and then his final reaction against it became too violent as a result. I feel that I have gone on quite long enough and it is time to straighten it all out a bit. ... This wish to change into another subject and feeling the lack of personal inspiration is not a mere after effect of my voyage to Galapagos. It started before that, and though the voyage may to some extent have precipitated matters, I doubt it. Nor is it, as far as I can analyze it, in any way connected with my broke off engagement to Isabelle Chodat, in which matter I now believe you acted rightly in saying what you thought although I felt a bit bitterly about it at the time. ... In this matter of anthropology I do not think there is any reason to worry over our relationship. I as much as I am taking up a much more honest position, instead of quietly worrying. I think we should get on better after it.[89]

But the language in which Gregory chose to explain his decision to enter anthropology revealed his rebellion. When Martin died, he had been advised that only impersonal science might resolve grief. His limnea project, his aborted trip to Suez, and his "failure" in Galapogos were all parts of the dutiful course Gregory had then pursued as an undergraduate. "The switch to anthropology was a sort of a revolt as far as I was concerned," he recalled. "I did not want to make a frontal attack, because I don't think the parents had any idea what they were doing. . . . But instead [I wanted] to use the sorts of tools that they would use to prove a new position."[90] W. B. did not make these inferences, when he answered his son's letter the next day.

> I myself understand the attraction of the "humanities," and what you mean about wanting a personal element in your work. Anthropology has become a very fine subject; and may any day turn the corner into a still newer world. That you should want to change in that direction seems to me quite natural and sound. I like your letter and am glad you wrote and that you felt you could speak of all these things to us. Only one thing in it is wrong. You have *not* been working badly. That you think this only means that you had been doing so much and learning so fast that when the pace slackens a bit, you felt to be standing still. . . . You have done very well. The partridge description is a model and sets a new standard in such work. . . . I am afraid that to me that "personal" element has been chiefly supplied by ambition—*to beat my friends at their own job. You see, I was always reckoned an outsider* [italics added]. But I know you mean something more serious by "the personal element." . . . We meet at dinner, but all this must stand over till tomorrow.[91]

At sixty-four, Bateson had been profoundly fatigued by the deaths of John and Martin. C. D. Darlington, when he joined the staff of the John Innes in late 1923, found W. B. unsure of himself. "He . . . didn't really know where he was going. . . . [He was] . . . largely occupied in painting his own portrait in oils. . . . [This] was not an indication that he was in the full stream of scientific enterprise."[92] He had also failed to establish a school, or even to locate someone to take over the directorship of the John Innes. His encroaching individualism—that he must beat his colleagues "at their own job"—which had served throughout his career to put him on the cutting edge of the newest knowledge, perhaps now entangled him. His pioneering nature, somehow, had created a problem of succession. "There are fashions in all things, especially in research," Bateson explained to Sir David Prain, the chairman of the John Innes Council. "And just now those who. . .would have been zoologists or botanists are bio-chemists, almost every one. Having been so long disappointed I am not sanguine that in the short time that remains I can succeed, but I shall make the question of a successor more and more my first preoccupation."[93] That the last of his sons should, when the search for a scientific heir was in W. B.'s thoughts, take up some sort of humanities, was difficult. But in contrast to the disapproval and endless suggestions of disapproval, by which W. B. had surrounded Martin's predicaments, his response to Gregory's decision to go into anthropology was mild. The taboo which Martin broke by turning to drama only forbade artistic creation. W. B. did not know quite what to make of anthropology. He tried to read Malinowski's recently published *Argonauts of the Western Pacific,* "and got to a mention in the text ... that the Trobrianders had roasted an opposum alive. ... He was so horrified he would read no further. He did not see patterns in the manners and customs of primitive people."[94] But a paper Gregory wrote on secret societies did catch his interest.

> I wonder whether anyone with powers of observation and expression has ever written on the huge development of these institutions in the U. S.... The Universities, especially Yale, are riddled with them.... What one would like to know is the feelings with which these societies are really regarded, to what extent their power rests on primary basic emotion as they must ... among savages, or whether the whole thing is derivative. ... One thing I do know, when I, of malice, brought up the topic in a mix of company at Yale, a feeling of genuine horror was "registered."[95]

In September 1925, together with two colleagues, Henry Meirs and D'Arcy W. Thompson, W. B. received permission to attend the bicentennial meeting of the Russian Academy of Science. The long negotiations—Bateson had originally applied in 1924—had been facilitated by N. I. Vavilov, a former student.* Fascinated by the revolution, he worked all the while to resurrect his dormant knowledge of the Russian language.

---

*The noted plant geneticst, N. I. Vavilov, studied at the John Innes with W.B. in 1913-14. In Russia, he initiated a broad investigation of plant pathology, hoping to create disease-resistant varieties of cultivated plants. With Lenin's encouragement, he proposed, in the early twenties, to collect "foundation material" throughout the world from which he might hybridize more effective breeds. Vavilov traveled widely with this purpose. However, his career was curtailed in 1939, when he came under attack by T. D. Lysenko. At a meeting of the Lenin All-Union Academy of Agricultural Sciences, they had the following exchange:

Lysenko: I understood from what you wrote that you came to agree with your teacher, Bateson, that evolution must be viewed as a process of simplification. Yet in Chapter Four of the history of the party it says evolution is increase in complexitiy....

Vavilov: In short, there is also reduction. When I studied with Bateson—

L: An anti-Darwinist.

V: No. Some day I'll tell you about Bateson, a most fascinating, most interesting man.

L: Couldn't you learn from Marx?

Vavilov was incarcerated in 1940, and died of pneumonia in prison three years later. (R. Medvedev, *The Rise and Fall of T. D. Lysenko,* p. 62.)

The two weeks in Leningrad and Moscow provoked a shocked note in *Nature*.[96] It was jarring to hear that the first duty of the state was to foster science. "We ought perhaps not to inquire too closely whether they and we mean the same thing by the term science. Zinovieff, for example, speaks in the same breath of the 'discovery' of Karl Marx, and the 'discovery' of Charles Darwin."[97] Distressed by the poverty, W. B. thought himself conspicuously well dressed, for the first time in his life.

> Of liberty we saw no sign. We here are accustomed to think of science and learning as flourishing best in quiet places, where they may come to slow perfection, under systems providing a reasonable measure of personal independence and security. Present conditions in Russia have brought about the very contrary, and among the grave indications of disharmony, which every visitor observes, the want of freedom is by far the most serious.[98]

He spent the rest of 1925 at Merton in poor health. In January he contracted acute bronchitis, but felt, by the end of the month, up to going out again. On the evening of 2 February 1926, he visited the Athenaeum for dinner and chess. As was typical, W. B. plied himself with a heavy meal and a long evening. On the way home, he collapsed in a train station, having suffered a second heart attack. He lingered for a few days at home, and Beatrice wrote Gregory that his father was in very serious condition. This turn confused him. "You had told me that he had had trouble with his heart but I thought that this was all finished.... Please tell me as soon as anything definite is known and if I can help at all, call me in, I could read Anthropology by a bed side just as easily as in Cambridge."[99] When he did arrive, Gregory found W. B. delirious, "muttering, muttering, muttering mainly about Mendelian ratios, counting peas or something. And in the middle of all this, 'Haldane, coming for tea, a most undesirable ingredient in an afternoon's entertainment.' The nurses were so puzzled about what on earth he was going on about, these ratios of counts and calculations of linkages."[100] He died on 8 February 1926. Gregory saw his father's dead body, and for the first time touching it, wiped the corpse's running nose.[101]

The family gathered to grieve again, as they had for Martin and John: Gregory and Beatrice; W. B.'s brother and sisters, Edward, Anna, Edith, and Margaret Heitland; and Beatrice's sisters, Florence and Hermia Durham. Cremation at Golder's Green took place a few days later. In Cambridge, groups of mourners assembled at St. John's College. Obituaries appeared, the most telling of which was in *The Eagle*, the college publication. W. B. was described as "a man of intuitions" that ran sympathetically with the working of the natural universe, and of enthusiasms which were for clear-cut, new ideas.

> Bateson was a born leader. He loved to lead a cause and win, and was at his best in attracting young men to the good scientific causes he had at heart. Never for half-measures or compromises, it sometimes happened that when he was against men of older generations, whose views were inflexible, he could make no progress but only camp out against them in stubborn opposition. This is a situation that does not make for personal happiness in a scientific community, and Bateson certainly sacrificed something for his faiths.[102]

Beatrice hurried to corroborate that her husband had been a pioneer of science. The month following W. B.'s death, she set to work on a glowing memoir that introduced him as a "rare personality."[103] Then in the summer of 1926, Gregory added a son's thoughts about the man. Family friends, the economist Claude Guillebaud and his wife Pauline, asked him to officiate as godfather at the baptism of their first child, Philomena. Participating in this ritual bothered him. Why affirm ritual renunciations of the devil and of the flesh? Why involve an infant in beliefs that sanctioned repression? Why begin her life by conceding behavior to empty orthodoxy? On the other hand, he remembered W. B. arguing that a little hypocrisy—what he called a "stiff front"—greased the wheels of social life. Within the family, Gregory imagined, this attitude had fatally obscured his father's essential sympathy for both Martin and himself. But in retrospect he understood that it could have been solicited, had they only made the advances.

> I have decided instead of a Bible to get Philomena a copy of Butler's *The Way of All Flesh,* to be kept by you until she's able to understand about half of it, i.e., about three or four years before, I suppose, you think she's firmly enough rooted to bear it, and before she has ceased to talk freely with her parents, then she should be recommended to read it. It contains a lot that is a propos in the present instance, e.g., about infant baptism, and the comparison of the four accounts of the resurrection. Also, of course, the parent vs. offspring wrangling is the way of *all* flesh, and the sooner both sides accept that, you stand a fair chance of avoiding the bitterness which must otherwise accompany it. Also you may avoid the hateful reticence and lack of candor, which had made such a mess of our family. I suppose I'm giving advice in your affairs where not wanted, but you did ask me to Godfather her, and I feel rather strongly on a number of these religious, ethical questions, having got into a bad enough state myself. As for the baptism, if it is to take place in St. John's Chapel, of course, many present will know *that I have never been baptized myself* [italics added], and that alone should serve as a label for Philomena. . . . If you say, come and officiate, I will.[104]

To suggest something of what W. B. thought about himself by the end, w
may turn to one of his final publications—a review of the Iltis life of Grego
Mendel.[105] Approving of the book, he disagreed with its representation of the
monk's religious beliefs. To Bateson, Mendel was simply an honest man who
took the world as he found it, untroubled by questions of faith or doubt.

> I imagine Mendel as a man full of practical good sense, with exceedingly clea:
> head, thinking in well-divided compartments, rarely disturbed by the eccen-
> tricities of genius. We are told that he was not given to brooding or
> sentimentality, that he was devoid of music and cared nothing for "Belle:
> Lettres." But when roused he showed nevertheless, that he had in him a strong
> element of the martyr, as appears very plainly from the protracted resistance to
> authority which embittered the last ten years of his life.[106]

X. As Anthropologist

Gregory Bateson described the state of social anthropology circa 1925, when, as a gangling twenty-one year old, he first knew the subject.

> Anthropology in England consisted mainly of Malinowski and Radcliffe-Brown. In America, Boas was a brooming operation. [He was also] proving that there were no simple causal relations in culture. There was no trade-off between English and Americans. The Americans did the American Indian, and the English tended to focus on the South Pacific and West Africa. The continental sociologists, Durkheim and Mauss, were not in my anthropological picture. They would have been, if I had been under Radcliffe-Brown, because he knew them. [But] nobody, around Cambridge, was looking at that. . . . It was all rather gentlemanly, rather scholarly. It didn't have much to do with anything. . . . Anthropology was, on the whole, pretty thin, which I suppose, was, in one way, lucky.[1]

Perhaps it is characteristic of newly founded, or recently invigorated, professional disciplines that they seem to abound with central ideas and central figures—the doctrinaire theoretician or the charismatic pedagogue. But curiously, because a subject is embryonic, these are as yet few in number. Youthful disciplines have few adherents. The kinship of the generations is thereby reduced and sharpened. In a sense, all this is doubly true of modern social anthropology, for it has been a field organized around the apical ancestor in two ways—both in terms of its research concerns and in terms of its internal arrangement. J. O. Brew, a historian of the subject, has noted that "the first two decades of the twentieth century in American anthropology . . . might be called the Age of Boas, so completely did that giant dominate the field."[2] Although in England, social anthropology was more multicentered than in the

United States, it is still fair to say that in both countries the discipline has been prepossessed by the central figure, and that practitioners strongly identify themselves with their intellectual forebears by paying homage to them freely. This being the case, it will do us well to look briefly at the modern history of the subject.

Gregory Bateson's antecedents were the so-called historical reconstructionists, Herbert Spencer, Lewis Henry Morgan, E. B. Tylor, and others in the sway of the Darwinian revolution, who attempted to fabricate the evolutionary development of all cultures. Theoretically, there were two views of this process. There were those classical evolutionists who believed in a temporal ordering of cross-cultural data, and who saw all culture as unfolding according to certain laws, from the simple to the complex, culminating in the institutions of Western European society. There were also diffusionists who stressed the role of geography and migration in cultural development. Data, for both groups, were secondhand and were furnished by missionaries and travelers.

In England, systematic field research began in 1898, when A. C. Haddon led a group of six Cambridge scientists (among them, W. H. R. Rivers) to the Torres Strait, located between the southern coast of New Guinea and Cape York, the northernmost tip of Australia. Haddon, trained initially in zoology, was a diffusionist, and he later became Gregory Bateson's Cambridge mentor. The Torres Strait experience had led him to concern students with fieldwork methodology. Still, in the 1920s, formal training in anthropology was rudimentary. Bateson recalled that he learned how to measure skull sizes with calipers, techniques for interviewing, elementary phonetics, and how to collect genealogies.

> The latter has to be done . . . step by step and . . . done through the bellies of the women. Given an informant [the question to ask was] what was your mother's name in whose belly you were born? . . . And who was the husband who begot you . . . ? I was told always to lead the interview away from the direction in which I thought it would go. If [you] think there is nobody in the village who has birds as totems, you ask who has birds as totems? That is, the question which leads should always lead in what you think is the improbable direction. . . . One learned to handle things concretely . . . you did not say, do you respect your parents? You say what happened yesterday when papa came home from work?[3]

By 1920, Bronislaw Malinowski and A. R. Radcliffe-Brown had begun a critical reaction against evolutionary anthropology. They harangued against unscientific, speculative reconstructions of cultural prehistory in whose place they proposed substituting an ahistoric, or synchronic, approach to ethnographic fieldwork. Malinowski, in particular, became a successful, penetrating observer of native life, so that unique and intimate details of his subject's lives appeared in his monographs.* With Radcliffe-Brown, Malinowski began "functional" explanation, and attempts were made to elucidate the social structure of societies. Although both men had been influenced by A. C. Haddon, divergent perspectives developed between them. Malinowski, in his famous seminar at the London School of Economics,[4] centered on the holistic notion of the tribal microcosm which he called culture and on the functioning of institutions, which were oriented around mostly biological, immutable needs of the individual. To become a social anthropologist meant in part to have contact with Malinowski's teaching. The discipline was very small in 1925, enlarging the influence of this man, who was, in any case, a passionate personality. A young American woman, Hortense Powdermaker, who was in London then to study anthropology, recalled that Malinowski, though marvelous at encouraging students to think, was also something of an antagonistic prima donna who "delighted in shocking people . . . [whom] he considered bourgeois and conventional."[5] Gregory Bateson's impression of Malinowski, or rather his memory of it, showed the beginnings of his heterodoxy.

> The conventional view of Malinowski was that he was a horrible, detestable man, but a genius as an anthropologist. My view was that he was rather an amusing man, but a lousy anthropologist, a lousy theorist. . . . [He proposed] the simple teleological explanation. I mean that natives plant X to eat them. . . . The whole [Malinowskian] functional theory of human needs, that if you make a list of human needs, and then you dissect the culture on how it satisfies them—this seem[ed] to be to me absolute balls. It being true, of course, that if the culture does not provide the people any food, the people die. But that is not the same as saying that the food is provided to keep them alive; the food can be provided to give them social status, to ornament festivals, or any number of things.[6]

---

*Reo F. Fortune, who was then getting part of his field training in London, recalled the sort of techniques which were current then. "Malinowski used to grab them [natives] by the collar so they couldn't get away. . . . As they become independent you can't do this. This bullying technique is part of imperialism. [You're saying that Malinowski was an imperialist bully?] When it comes to natives he was. Not because he was imperious, and not entirely because he was a bully, but because this technique was taught as a method." (Personal communication: 14 December 1975.)

Radcliffe-Brown, who had been trained by W. H. R. Rivers in psychology before becoming a social anthropologist under Haddon, joined Malinowski in attacking evolutionary speculation. The synchronic study of society was more scientific, he would argue,[7] using an analogy from biology to assert his view of the new science. "I conceive of social anthropology as the theoretical natural science of human society, that is, the investigation of social phenomena by methods essentially similar to those used in the physical and biological sciences."[8] More specifically, he had a Spencerian conception of the internal organization of an organism through which he proposed to view the organization of society.

> An animal organism is an agglomeration of cells and interstitial fluids arranged in relation to one another not as an aggregate but as an integrated living whole. ... The system of relations by which these units are related is the organic structure.... Over a period its constituent cells do not remain the same, but the structural arrangement of the constituent cells does remain. The process by which this structural continuity of the organism is maintained is called life.[9]

The analogy suggested that the social structure of a society, by which he meant the system of subgroups, clans, moieties, age-grades, factions, was comparable in organization to the structure of an organism. Both remained constant over time—internal relations persisted even though constituents were changing. Ironically, despite vendettas against conjectural history, Radcliffe-Brown found the ultimate verification of his social system in history. He could visit a stable community, then return to it ten years later and find that many people had died, while others had been born. Survivors, of course, were "now ten years older and their relations to one another may have changed in many ways. Yet I may find that the kinds of relations that I can observe are very little different from those observed ten years before. The structural form has changed very little."[10] Perhaps as a by–product of his use of a biological analogy—organisms not possessing beliefs—Radcliffe-Brown distinguished the study of social structure from the study of culture, and denied the existence of the latter. To him, culture was a vacuous, nebulous concept, denoting "not any concrete reality, but an abstraction ... a vague abstraction."[11] Social structure, on the other hand, was an "actually existing" network, or system of relations.[12]

The activity of the social organism was said to be the functioning of its structure. There was unity to this functioning. Constituent parts might work together without producing persistent or irreconcilable conflict. Cohesion was the essence of this social vision. Radcliffe-Brown believed that the "function of any recurrent activity, such as the punishment of a crime or a funeral ceremony, is the part it plays in the social life as a whole, and therefore the contribution it makes to the maintenance of structural continuity."[13] Following Durkheim, the French sociologist, Radcliffe-Brown deduced individual behavior from social structure. Observable social phenomena, he would say, "are not the immediate result of the nature of individual human beings, but are the result of the social structure by which they are united."[14] As such, the psychology of individuals was irrelevant to the study of society. Marriage became an arrangement by which offspring were made legitimate members of society. Etiquette and kinship terminology integrated the social structure. And religion, by implanting a sense of interdependence among people, became a sort of social glue. For example, the people of the Andaman Islands, among whom Radcliffe-Brown had done research, wept at conventionalized times and not at others. They cried when they met friends or relatives after long separation, at peace-making rituals, after concluding mourning, after a death, at a marriage, and during initiation ceremonies. In characteristic fashion, Radcliffe-Brown construed even this intimate sentiment to be a public expression of collectivity. He argued that the thread underlying this crying was the reaffirmation of their social structure in settings "in which social relations that have been interrupted are about to be renewed."[15]

A little less than a year after his father's death, in January 1927, Gregory Bateson sailed south, financed by Anthony Wilkin and by Strathcoma studentships, with plans to do fieldwork in New Guinea. His objectives, handed on to him by A. C. Haddon, were to investigate the effects of contact between natives and whites.

> It has been recognized for many years [wrote Haddon] that the natives of the Sepik river, in what is now Mandated New Guinea, possess a remarkably rich culture for a savage community, and some fifteen years ago I suggested that various cultures of the south coast of New Guinea had their origin in that river. Although the material culture of the Sepik peoples has been sufficiently well described, we know absolutely nothing about their institutions, or their religion. Not only is the area one of the most promising fields for ethnological research in the world, but the need for immediate investigation is extremely urgent; as the river has for some years been subject to alien influences and I understand that it is soon to be the scene of missionary enterprise. We therefore may be justifiably gratified that it has fallen to a Cambridge man to undertake this important research.[16]

In addition to Haddon's sense of urgency, Gregory recalled the feelings which propelled him into fieldwork: "I fled from my mother."[17] In the months following W. B.'s death, Beatrice had become somewhat possessive about the activities of her last son. After one of his visits, she confessed to Nora Barlow of feeling "restless and distressed. I used to laugh at jealousy as an impossible passion and now I believe my malady is jealousy, helpless and maddening."[18] Gregory remembered that Beatrice began mimicking W. B. "The two of them together kind of neutralized each other somewhat. But after he died, she took on the worst of his mannerisms with the rigidity of a convert. She had the whole thing rigged in which I was to become the precise reincarnation of the old man."[19] None of this aspect of his life was Haddon's affair however. To him, Gregory spoke only of goals. His research would divulge significant illustration of the processes of "social evolution."[20]

Bateson described his voyage to New Guinea in some detail to Beatrice, and, among other things, the correspondence shows that en route, the issue of contacting groups was on his mind. "I was awfully priggish," he judged himself in retrospect, "guilty, obsessive-compulsive, virtuous, [and] painstaking in a humorous sort of way."[21] By choice, he traveled third class. The guarded conversation between passengers in different classes struck him as a "peculiar sort of nervous camaraderie and class consciousness." The improvement of shipboard life, Gregory concluded to his mother, lay in candor.

> If only they [passengers in different classes] could accept the fact that when such unnatural meetings take place the only subject for interesting conversation is that of class distinctions and that before they can discuss anything else they must get the class thing settled and accepted on both sides. If they would take it as a free subject for conversation instead of carefully repressing it and shivering whenever the complex is tapped—we should get on much better together. . . . By the way I have won a prize for Fancy Dress. I appeared as a naturalist under the title of "myself" and got the prize by realistic acting the part. . . . I have been asked to preach next Sunday's sermon. Of course accepted, but I am not sure what I shall give them—probably black-white culture contact.[22]

In Melbourne, Bateson met E. W. P. Chinnery, the colonial anthropologist for the New Britain/New Guinea area. Despite Haddon's hopes, Chinnery pointed out that for someone without experience in the bush, it would likely be unsafe to do research along the Sepik River, where large head-hunting raids had been recently reported. Bateson opted to work and live among the Baining, a group of migrating cultivators of the Gazelle Peninsula in northern New Britain, because he understood that they did "nothing about their corpses."[23] He assured Beatrice that the Baining were also "most accessible, most primitive and fairly healthy."[24] By virtue of their "sulky reticence and stupidity," missionaries had been unable to convert them. "But I don't think I need to worry about failure."[25] Leaving Melbourne, to spend a few days in Sydney before beginning his research, Bateson met A. R. Radcliffe-Brown, who, like Chinnery, was also in Haddon's sphere. Brown, as he was known then, was solicitous, at once offering him Rockefeller grant support, which he controlled, and a theoretical view of society. Gregory was jubilant when he wrote his mother.

> This ten days will modify considerably my aims and object in work on Baining. He is the only real "sociologist" I have come across full of real criticism of the rot that is written and with a good many sane ideas on social physiology and organization to take rot's place. He has put me on to reading Durkheim of whom he is a great admirer. D[urkheim] has quite a new point of view for me, unfortunately all his arguments are based on fallacious axioms about Totemism, the meaning of [the] word "primitive." But the point of view and conclusions rest pretty solid. In any case, Radcliffe-Brown will soon have here the only school of anthropology with any sane inspiration in it.[26]

In early April 1927, a ten-month period in the Baining village of Latramat began. At first glance, the place seemed "beautiful and obviously healthy ... and the people [are] friendly and jolly—the native women unattractive!"[27] He described enchantment with the morning dew to Beatrice. It is "very much like walking in English woodland after a summer shower, but far richer in smell and color and all the time prodigious variety of plants and insects. I fear I shall get to love the tropics too much."[28] Unfortunately, his research floundered. Upon arrival, Bateson began measuring heads with calipers until one of the Baining asked why he was doing it. This so confused him that he was unable to explain himself, much less formulate a response in his then meager pidgin English. The termination of this part of his research did not clarify what he ought to do instead. In addition, the Baining language was difficult and the people were secretive. Trying to participate fully in their lives—eating their food,* sleeping in their houses, and rehearsing their ceremonies—made him feel awkward. "I am a creature whose intrusion they resent," he wrote Beatrice.[29] After a half year's work, Bateson felt that the

---

* "Dear Mother, One of the things which I still remember from Grantchester days is the eating of caterpillars in the wood behind the house, with J[ohn] and M[artin]. I remember that we held the more hairy species to be unfit for human food and that of the rest, some were unpleasantly gritty and these we avoided. But try as I will I cannot [recall] what any of them tasted like. This searching of the brain was instigated by an opportunity of eating MA SARON. A friend of mine had collected some and told me. All that I knew of them was that they were beetles which lived in wood. Hearing he had some, I at once asked that a few be brought for me to try. Then followed the effort to recall the taste of caterpillars ... [a comparison of cooked beetles to paté de foie gras follows]." (G. Bateson [hereafter cited as GB] to C. B. Bateson, 24 July 1927.)

research was simply not progressing. "I cannot even find out for certain whether my own Baining have any totemism, nor can I get a decent genealogy, owing to difficulties with name taboos."[30]

His cook boy deserted him. Often, he was tricked out of the village, later to discover that some significant collective activity had occurred in his absence. Religion they refused to discuss with him until, it was said, he knew their language. What was more, Bateson found himself indifferent to the little of their mythology which he was able to elicit. After watching a group of men dancing he wrote home, "I understand now what Malinowski meant when he said ethnologists must be able to withstand boredom!"[31] Bateson did become interested in informal, relatively inconspicuous, behavioral detail which Malinowski had called "the imponderabilia of actual life."[32] In Latramat he read Doughty's *Arabia Deserta*,[33] whose intricate and masterful portrayal of Bedouin life led him to think about recording and representing everyday minutiae. Bateson began to experiment with fieldwork technique.

> Often I have wanted to put down in my notebook a note, say, on a bit of "horseplay" or a gathering of men for some purpose or other, say for a native trial. The thing defies any sort of cold analysis. Of course there is the literary-artistic method but that is not what I am here for! ... It is now possible to some extent at least, to describe a coconut palm botanically and all the technical terms in that description could be reduced to simple almost Biblical English. The description would not give any *impression* of the beauty or monotony, etc., of coconut palms but it would give something in the way of knowledge of the organization of nature. The same sort of description of anthropological things should be possible. But I cannot see it coming. ... I begin to think Malinowski and R[adcliffe]-Brown, etc., may be right that our main need is for knowledge of "physiology" of society. Funny! I have scarcely thought in terms of "anatomy" and "physiology" of society, "structure" and "function," etc., since I have been here. The academic stuff does not seem very real when one is in the presence of natives. I wonder if I made notes on all the measures and reactions that I use to secure my own position and get native confidence, etc.—that might give something. But terribly difficult. It should improve my methods anyway.[34]

In March 1928, Bateson left the Baining and returned to Sydney.* Beatrice

---

*At Cambridge, Haddon was pleased with this development. He wrote Mrs. Bateson, "To tell the truth, I am very relieved that G[regory] is leaving the Baining for a spell. He has had a rough time of it! I suppose he knows what he is about living on native food—but he must not get run-down. ... The Sydney visit will ... refresh and stimulate him. ... He can talk over his problems with A. R. Brown ... and ... be better able to tackle his refractory Baining" (4 December 1927).

was planning to meet him there in April, and he arranged to teach a term of Pacific languages under Radcliffe-Brown.* In addition to himself, Bateson found three other anthropologists there, visiting from fieldwork: W. Lloyd Warner, Reo F. Fortune, and H. Ian Hogbin. With Camilla Wedgwood, Brown's assistant, they discussed current research. Although his colleagues spoke of their progress, while Gregory had only frustration to report, by fall he was optimistic. Instead of returning to the Baining, he "deserted" them, as he wrote his mother, for a neighboring coastal people, the Sulka. They provided a contrast in anthropologist-native relations. Among the Baining, information had to be "dragged out of them a sentence at a time. Here I can say to a man, 'What is such and such a ceremony like?' and he will sit and give me a long coherent account of it in pidgin—of course omitting such aspects as he wishes me not to know about but still what he says is true as far as it goes.... My difficulty is to keep informants quiet while I catch up with writing notes."[35] The Sulka piqued his curiosity. Their political organization, marriage system, mythology, and even their art were all comparatively visible and compelling. "Sulkas are a *painting* people, many pigments and all geometrical patterns—no careful representations. I gather all the patterns are symbolic in some way but I don't know yet. I have a couple of artists who shall instruct me."[36] He continued to be bothered by his inability to describe native life.

> We went down to the beach with lamps and ... little lads carried my line out to sea. It was all very amateurishly done—Sulkas are not sea people. They never enter the sea for pleasure. I am the only regular bather in the village. While we waited optimistically we heard shouts and a mun (native plank boat without outrigger) came up in the night. It had come from Mope where there are still many Sulkas. Now the village is full of visitors and excitement—but without language I can do nothing with incidents of this kind. I still don't know why they came nor how long they will stay. Tomorrow I shall be told these things if informants think fit. Now I write to you till the excitement shall have died.[37]

Again, frustration mounted. Gregory contracted malaria. The quality of his research suffered, and Sulka culture began to appear decaying. Their civiliza-

---

*In London, Beatrice had missed her son terribly; visiting with him in 1928, she was in little better humor. Sydney seemed to her "a sad exhibition. I think the perpetual strike is merely the expression of the spiritual discomfort of grossly material ambition. There is literally nothing. The very landscape of this great harbour seems trite and commonplace. The speech, the papers, the cinema, the advertisements, the shops all aim low to establish the equality of inferiority, which is perhaps all that equality means in the mouths of its advocates. A certain interest in front gardens seems the only hobby or desire for doing or thinking." (C. B. Bateson to N. Barlow, May 1928.)

tion was dying, he wrote Beatrice. Noticing a certain apathy throughout their lives, he said he felt a sort of sympathetic anxiety. In December 1928, on the occasion of his mother's sixtieth birthday, the future of his own generation seemed hopeless.

> I wonder whether there will be found of my generation to take the places of such as my father and you. I know of none among my Cambridge friends or acquaintances who could ever fall into that category. I remember in one of father's letters to you he describes his own father as "a gentleman of the old school"—now I forget the phrase, so I suppose he had the same feeling! But there is a more violent change of sentiment and culture in the time of our "ripening" than there has ever been before in the ripening time of other generations, though they, too, thought themselves rebels. That "complete break with the past" has us young ones well washed off our feet at present and I doubt if we shall ever develop a civilization in which to put trust. You often say you know not the sentiment of religion, probably because it is too deep in you. But consider how much of father's greatness lay in his feeling that the tradition of past great men was in him—that is one of the sentiments which religion implants in people.[38]

Bateson's experience among the Baining now appeared to have been a total failure and waste of time, "they ate up a lot of good enthusiasm."[39] He considered returning immediately to England. "My belly is full with this travelling and poking my nose into the affairs of other races."[40] After nearly five months with the Sulka, Bateson returned to Rabaul in the worst of spirits. "I have been too depressed to think properly," he answered Beatrice after she had written to ask for his advice about which of the cherished Old Master drawings to sell.[41]

In the middle of February 1929, at the invitation of a ship captain whom he knew slightly, Gregory took a cruise to visit both Manus in the Admiralty Islands and the Sepik River region of New Guinea. His hopes were minimal. The trip might improve his mood, and in Manus he might meet Reo F. Fortune, the New Zealand anthropologist who was working there with his wife, the American anthropologist Margaret Mead.

Bateson narrowly missed them. But when the schooner stopped along the middle Sepik River, he "began collecting genealogies from force of habit," as he informed his tutor at St. John's. "I found the Sepik systems odd and dropped off the schooner to get four days in a village while [the] schooner went up stream."[42] Again, a community of natives—this time the Iatmul—fascinated him. He spent a few exhausting days in the village of Tambunam, "a wonderful place about three quarters of a mile in length and with a population of about one thousand—great big houses all set on high floors six feet from [the] ground."[43] Hectically, as he tried to collect their kinship and to make sense out of their "sweetly complicated" marriage systems, he made doubting plans to extend this research. "I want to do a bit of work on the Sepik—say six months," he wrote Beatrice. "But what would happen? I may quite likely get disgruntled with the whole thing and come home. In any case I will write up my Sepik notes and send a copy to A. R. Radcliffe-Brown."[44]

The twenty-five-year-old ethnographer was working in Mindimbit, a month or so later, finding local histrionics congenial. "The brutality of the culture is shocking, but there is a certain fineness and pride in it all."[45] Iatmul religious behavior seemed "beastly." He was told that in initiation ceremonies "each novice does a kill—kills a child or old person brought for the purpose from a neighboring village. Just think of this as the central event in the education of every young man.... These people take their religion seriously and in big doses."[46] The general tenor of life in Mindimbit was "a continual smouldering irritation," expressed in charges and counter-charges, boasting, threats of revenge and punitive expeditions bent on hunting heads. He understood that it was believed "everything that goes wrong is attributed to lack of homicide."[47] The vitality with which informants discussed their feuds perhaps influenced his mood. "Since I have been here," he observed, "I have been [a] little rougher in my methods. I don't mind losing my temper a bit now and then when I have a touch of tropical fever. The other day I shot a pig—in anger."[48] Of all things, the act seemed to have won him prestige in the village.

> After all, these people are savages—their ways are savage, to a certain extent savagery is here a virtue—and its absence a weakness. Since I have been here [many informants] ... have all boiled over with temper—once or twice—and as for women—they have a brawl about one every 3 or 4 days. ... Beasts. During one of these women's "scenes" I asked a man what the quarrel was about. "They're cross about a penis—that's their fashion." So I said, "What do men quarrel about then?" "Oh! They quarrel about vaginas,"—such is life.... In this country we express these things more directly than in England, but yet with a certain amused detachment.[49]

Although the Iatmul marriage system perplexed him, the outline of a system of classification by age-grades was quickly visible. Bateson was relieved when he wrote Haddon and Radcliffe-Brown asking them to send him a partner to work with. He was still stung by the isolation of his Baining and Sulka experiences. "The Sepik shall be my magnum opus, here I have exactly the type of local cultural variation which I originally set out to study. I have an easy language of wide distribution. Transport is easy by canoe. The natives are friendly and intelligent. . . . For the present I feel to have got through the worst of my troubles and to have a good subject of research at last."[50] After six months, however, the initial euphoria had worn thin. His fieldwork among the Iatmul was halting, in his view ineffectual and haphazard. "I am just going on collecting material blindly as heretofore. I don't believe in any sort of questionnaire, etc."[51] He set about gathering totemic songs. Listening to these at night was especially moving. "I don't know—it's odd but I still am affected . . . [by] nocturnal firelight incidents. I lose for a moment the feeling that they are all the time toadying to the white man and get a sort of picture of old days."[52] He collected stories about the origin of dry ground, an event which seemed to be the source of much cosmological meaning to the Iatmul. He was straining to fill gaps in his field notes. Yet when an old woman died, and he missed observing her funeral, Gregory was strangely shy. "I hate all that side of my work and I always feel that I am intruding when I try to learn about such things. . . . I suppose the perfect anthropologist is as cynical as a newpaper reporter."[53]

Answering his mother's questions, Gregory admitted that after three years in New Guinea he was almost ready to return home.

> All I see is that I can't go on like this much further. Physically I am as well as can be, but psychologically I fancy I ought to see my own odd species again, I don't see any further ahead than that—I feel I could scarcely face another anthrop. expedition—not without a partner. Perhaps I shall feel otherwise when I see the fogs of England. I want badly to shake some dust of this country off my feet. But not as simply as that. I am very fond of it too.[54]

By spring of 1930, Bateson—now twenty-six—was back in Cambridge, looking for lodgings. In St. John's College, where his grandfather had been master, there happened to be no rooms available. He went to Noel Porter's Half Moon, and stayed there briefly while planning to develop his Iatmul notes into a fellowship thesis and some articles. Evidently, he found upper-middle class academic self-satisfaction and formality irritating.* After years of

---

*He had anticipated appearing rude. Before leaving for home, Bateson wrote Haddon: "I have noticed . . . that I now despise that hallmark of a gentleman, the university accent. Of old I used only to hear it in the mouths of Oxford young men. But now I hear it in mouths of almost all university people (except my own mouth) and detest it. I wonder what a return to Cambridge will feel like. Certainly not all beer and skittles. For one thing, there are many stories and vulgar expressions to [be] rubbed out of my repertoire" (21 November 1930).

participant-observation of ongoing social situations, it seemed his bent to watch and to analyze jarred with what he thought of as an anti-introspectionist quality in English intellectual life.

> I came to Cambridge feeling that my Iatmul were very noble. And at the high table* of St. John's college, I was terribly shocked at the unreality of [the etiquette. It was] a sort of elegant intellectual weaving of quasi-scholarship and quasi-wit which ... terrified and shocked me deeply. So I went off to the country and established myself as a paying guest on a farm in Yorkshire."

Bateson spent a year there preparing his master's dissertation, which then appeared in Raymond Firth's journal *Oceania,* entitled "Social Structure of the Iatmul People of the Sepik River."[56] In it, he presented an individual's career advancing through the network of their kinship systems, as well as descriptions of various marriage systems, clans, totems, and shamans. Attention was paid to Iatmul initiation ceremonies which he found peculiar, but whose symbolisms he wrote "are to me obscure."[57] The paper was little more than the descriptive sort of ethnography that was being done in 1931. It stood apart in that Bateson spiced his text with confessions of the inadequacy and incompleteness of his field research. "I was never able to understand natives," he admitted, "when they conversed among themselves."[58] And though Bateson had only witnessed a minor version of the naven ceremony, he still considered the event of enough significance to describe and to discuss. This sort of candor evidently pleased A. C. Haddon, who wrote, in recommending his thesis, that "this frank acknowledgment of the imperfections in his studies which gives one great confidence in accepting the definite statements that he makes."[59] makes."[59]

Bateson's account of Iatmul social structure was largely without theory, except for a short conclusion in which he broached the general problem of how to conceptualize social phenomena. In his view, the science of anthropology diverged from that of the physical scientist, because the fieldworker was much less in control of—and much less focused upon—a single body of data. Although the word did not yet exist, Bateson was advocating an interdisciplinary approach. The anthropologist, in short, "must be at one and the same time, anatomist, and physiologist and geneticist."[60] Bateson joined Radcliffe-Brown in believing that the organization of a society was analogous to that of an organism: both were internally organized and externally adapted to their

---

*A regular, but semiexclusive—because restricted to fellows—formal meal in the college dining hall.

environments. "So perhaps influenced by early biological training I have taken a hint from the biologists and have grouped my material under the two great headings of Structure and Function."[61] However, he dispensed with the concept of "social structure" to designate the static and normative rules of descent, moieties, clans, and age grades. Instead, Bateson substituted the vaguer term "series of formulations," so as to specify that native description of their social groupings might vary widely from the constant flux of actual native practice. He proposed to return to New Guinea to expand his research, especially to disentangle this conflicting variation which he had identified there.*

Beatrice suffered quietly throughout the year her son spent writing in Yorkshire, as she thought, aloof and avoiding her. But when, in the summer of 1931, Gregory was granted funds to return to his Iatmul and began to set plans to do so,† Beatrice could no longer contain herself. There was an outburst between them, during which she accused him of insulting and ignoring his inheritance. When Gregory said he would take no more of the family money, Beatrice became remorseful. "If you do not accept the allowance I shall know it is the end," she wrote him in October. "I don't think my anxiety for your happiness and well-being merits such harshness. I am only a rather mild and timid old woman solitary and staring into solitude. . . . I vaguely think of shutting down here and burying myself in the anonymity of continental boarding houses or steamships."[62] Nonetheless, the second round of Iatmul research, which was to last fifteen months, began in January 1932.

Working alone in the villages of Palimbai and Kankanamun, by summer he was again yearning for a co-worker. Little had been resolved about Beatrice, and that Gregory did not write upset her deeply. "I feel as though this August will be horrible and painful as last," she wrote him after long silence.

> But I suppose it is just fate and try to think that you would help it if you could—but I don't even know that. . . . I garden, I strain, I read, sleep and eat and try not to imagine you in difficulties. Anxious and sad I am. If only you had never gone with that Welshman to Galapagos, you might never have got the travel fever nor been caught by old Haddon, nor been embraced by Melanesia. I admire more and more the wisdom of firm, strict, even harsh parents of former days.[63]

He continued through the fall until discouraged and, as he later said, "hopelessly sick of field work."[64] Part of the problem was that, having

---

*"In studying variations Bateson is following in the steps of his father, but he is attacking the more complex field of human nature," Haddon wrote in his report to the St. John's electors. (A. C. Haddon, "Report to the Electors to a Fellowship at St. John's College," unpublished, n.d.)

†The Percy Sladen Memorial Fund, Royal Society Government Grants Committee, and St. John's College all supported him.

dismissed the accepted theoretical foci of his day—historical reconstructions, material culture, economics, and functionalism—Bateson was left collecting disconnected scraps of data to which he could attach no unifying significance. "I did not clearly see any reason why I should enquire into one matter rather than another ... this not so much from lack of training as from excess of skepticism."[65]

Off a tributary of the lower Sepik meanwhile, Reo F. Fortune and Margaret Mead were struggling as badly. The playful competition which characterized their early marriage and research in Manus had turned serious in New Guinea (in New York, where Mead's developing celebrity dwarfed Fortune, their relations were already problematic). During the first half of 1932, among the Mountain Arapesh, Margaret had experienced an imprisoning depression, that in retrospect, she considered to have been the worst—and the only—one of her life. Then during the last few months, among the Mundugumor of the Yuat River, she was continually feverish. Throughout her illness, Reo Fortune—in accordance with his own stoic nature—had left her alone and silently craving to be taken care of. The day before Christmas, they left Mundugumor to holiday at the government station at Ambunti and to look for a new research setting. On their way up the Sepik, the Fortunes stopped in Kankanamun, where Gregory was camped. Margaret was then exhausted from the travel and in pain from an accidental injury to her hands the night before. Her eye was immediately caught by a screened room which had a tree growing through its roof, allowing Bateson's cat (and the mosquitoes) to come and go freely.

At first, the three were delighted to be together. "As anthropologists do, we began talking—and kept it up for 30 hours on end. The result has been a very odd party. Three garrulous anthropologists talking shop as hard as they could go, in the midst of tipsy New Guinea whites."[66] Mead's recollection was essentially the same. Bateson and Fortune had sat up their first night together, while she felt compelled to make conversation with the colonial officer who was with them. Himself hungry for companionship, and having looked forward to their visit for a month, Gregory attended to his visitors compassionately. His tenderness so soothed Margaret that forty years later, she described the ensuing three months as "an extraordinary concatenation of events that no notions of serendipity provide an explanation."[67] Rivalry, however, was incipient between Bateson and Fortune, who had known each other slightly in Cambridge, when they both had been in contact with A. C. Haddon. Then professionally envious, Fortune suspected that Bateson was favored there for hereditary reasons. "Haddon is very kind to me," he had written Margaret, "but he gave Gregory Bateson his mosquito net."[68] Fortune had also been highly critical of Bateson's first Iatmul articles in *Oceania*, and demanded to know why he had not been given the opportunity to work in the most splendid culture along the Sepik River.

With Bateson's guidance, Fortune and Mead soon moved to start investigating the nearby Tchambuli (now Chambri), but this did not interfere with their intense exchange of ideas and observations.

> I was at first shocked [Gregory wrote Beatrice]. They bully and chivvy their informants and interpreters and *hurry* them till they don't know whether they are on head or heels. But in the end I was converted and I am going to do some bullying too. I feel on this subject something like Samuel Butler's calf that knew it was eating mulch, but didn't realize it till its mother told it. I spend hours feeling my way and getting into *rapport* with natives and it is all quite unnecessary. Also they *plan* their work while I very gingerly pick up what comes.[69]

As Bateson found their fieldwork techniques useful, Mead was fascinated by his knowledge of natural science and by his Iatmul data. "Gregory was floundering methodologically and we were feeling starved for theoretical relevance."[70] She had been trying to assess the contribution of culture to development of sex roles. Apart from innate biology, how did cultural patterning differentiate masculine and feminine personalities? But this question drew no answer in Arapesh and Mundugumor. Though the expected norms contrasted between the two cultures, within each, men and women displayed similar behavior. Arapesh were uniformly cherishing (and to Fortune uncongenial), where Mundugumor were uniformly fierce (and to Mead unbearable). Tchambuli and Iatmul, however, possessed just the vivid differentiation of roles that Mead had hoped to study. Among the Tchambuli, the women were austere and hardworking while the men were narcissistic and involved in aesthetic pursuits. Among Bateson's Iatmul, there was a ceremony, called naven, which dramatized the everyday roles—by reversing them. Father's sisters and mother's brothers would exchange clothes; the men dressing in filthy skirts while the women adorned themselves in male finery, and strutted as they grated their husband's serrated lime sticks in and out of lime gourds. By contrasting these data, they worked out some ideas about the relations between sex roles and individual temperament—which they understood to be the raw material of personality that culture shaped and selected. Mead was especially concerned to develop a view of personality which was free of biology. She thought that temperament overrode the biological differences between the sexes. There were rather male and female versions of a range of types of temperament from which cultures might draw so as to differentiate between the sex roles or maintain them uniform.

To a large extent, accommodating this problem turned their discussions in sociological and psychoanalytic directions and focused their thinking upon their own personalities and cultures. Gregory and Margaret came to identify their temperaments, agreeing that they both deviated from expected norms. Bateson found the aggressiveness appropriate to an Englishman distasteful. Mead felt she departed from stereotypes of the possessive American mother and the unmaternal career woman. By contrast, Fortune's temperament appeared to fit the male role acceptable in New Zealand. "It was exciting to strip off the layers of culturally attributed expected behavior," Margaret remembered, "and to feel that one knew at least who one was. However, Reo did not have as great a sense of revelation about himself."[71]

Week after week, they were "cooped up together in the tiny eight-foot-by-eight-foot mosquito room ... mov[ing] back and forth between analyzing ourselves and each other, as individuals and the cultures that we knew and were studying, as anthropologists must."[72] Their conversation was enriched by the arrival of a manuscript draft of Ruth Benedict's *Patterns of Culture,* which at least Bateson and Mead greeted enthusiastically.* Its urgency was increased by "the triangular situation"[73]† which was emerging among the three of them— on a theoretical level at first. Gregory's thinking came into clearer articulation as a result of this contact with the American anthropology of Ruth Benedict and Margaret Mead. Both these women had been students of Franz Boas. As George W. Stocking has pointed out, Boasians were immured not with analogies borrowed from the natural sciences which suggested unitary notions of "system," but rather with the "psychological, aesthetic and humanistic" premise of "pattern," in which the idea of cultural integration was a problem and not a given. "Boasians did not start, like Radcliffe-Brown, with the Durkheimian assumption of system," they vaguely intuited the unity of a culture and, in retrospect, appreciated its beauty.[74] Partly because of these differing premises, and because of his background in biology, Mead admired Bateson for possessing a surer grasp of science than herself. Reciprocally, she

---

*On the other hand, Reo Fortune recalled that "a manuscript of *Patterns of Culture* reached me when I was on the Sepik, but I never saw the galley proofs. [Did you read it?] Well, Ruth Benedict asked me to read it and make any corrections on points of fact, but not on points of interpretation. As it was all interpretation, I didn't correct it at all. I was left no option but to send it back to her or to drop it in the Sepik River. I didn't drop it in the Sepik ... so I sent it back. I didn't agree with the interpretation at all. Also it was wrong on points of fact." (Personal communication: 14 December 1975.)

†Margaret Mead remarked that she had been aided at times in her career by being female. In organizations for example, "I am always being made president when there are two men who are fighting each other, or more; then they make me president because it usually isn't a woman who is rival." (M. Mead quoted in *The Visible Scientists,* R. Goodell, p. 153.)

introduced him to the study of the person—to the new problems of personality in relation to culture, and to explanations in terms of Gestalt psychology, psychoanalysis, and learning theory. Mead herself had already conducted studies of individual childhood and adolescent development,[75] and Ruth Benedict had taken to psychological characterizations of cultural configurations. To Benedict, society was analogous, not to an organism, but to a person. Both were organized in consistent patterns of thought and feeling. "Within each culture," she wrote, "there comes into being characteristic purposes not necessarily shared by other types of society.... Taken up by a well integrated culture, the most ill-assorted acts become characteristic of its particular goals.... The form that these acts take, we can understand by understanding first the emotional and intellectual mainsprings of that society."[76]

The concatenation of events spoken of by Mead included the strain between Gregory and his mother, the troubled marriage of Margaret and Reo, the chronic desperation of three lonely fieldworkers, Margaret's enfeebled state, which exaggerated Gregory's warmth and Reo's reserve, and it involved the past rivalry between Fortune and Bateson. Together with all this, Gregory and Margaret shared a curious predilection for the sort of science which each brought to the middle Sepik. With the stimulus of Benedict's *Patterns of Culture,* Bateson began to learn more about the *personal* sciences, which he had been after since leaving zoology for anthropology. Mead, on the other hand, was learning notions of system and theoretical natural science which were new to her. As ideas interacted and cross-fertilized so did affections and antipathies. Theoretical exchange had passionate human correlate. "Gregory and I were falling in love," Margaret remembered, "but this was kept firmly under control while all three of us tried to translate the intensity of our feelings into better and more perceptive fieldwork."[77] However, by the spring of 1933, the tension of the situation had become insurmountable. Amid anxiety about Mead's health and well-being, she and Fortune hurried away from the mid-Sepik, and from each other. Their marriage over, she returned to New York while he went back to England. Bateson took a slow freighter home to Cambridge. In all, their last months of research had been unique. "When we came out of the field," Margaret later wrote, "we ... saw the world with eyes that seemed freshly opened to every slightest act and gesture; our friends all seemed to have become more intelligible to us!"[78]

Gregory was silent to his mother about the personal side of his field experience. Nonetheless at the age of twenty-nine, the idea was coalescing that temperamentally and professionally, he was unsuited for the life of a Cambridge don. With even less patience and tact, he reexperienced difficulties with the conventions of an academic society within which he was thought to be somewhat elusive, self-satisfied, overprivileged, and rather casual in a Bohemian sort of way. Of course, there were more intimate misgivings. "There's a dream which I had in the early thirties somewhere, in which Freeman, which was Martin, was climbing a ladder into some sort of garden, some sort of other territory. And . . . my father, by then dead, helps him by lifting the ladder, pushing the ladder upwards, as a result of which it falls over backwards and he [Martin] is killed."[79]

Deepening these estrangements, Bateson was not compelled by the utopian revivalism which had resurfaced during the early 1930s, among some progressive and politically disgruntled natural scientists of his generation. Men such as J. D. Bernal, J. B. S. Haldane, Lancelot Hogbin, Hyman Levy, and Joseph Needham sought to foster application of science to the public welfare. They were "rooted in . . . scientific rationalist tradition as well as in communist theory, the movement captured the imaginations of scientists of varied social and political outlook; liberals, socialists, Marxists and 'scientific humanists.'"[80] Underlying their position was the activist and materialist premise that scientific enterprise, at least, grew out of—or at most was determined by—man's imperious struggle to control nature. They opposed the perspective that science and its technological application were separable, inasmuch as the true purpose of science was the passive, pure, and reverent understanding of nature. As the Hungarian physicist and chemist Michael Polanyi succinctly put this view, "science exists only to that extent to which the search for truth is not socially controlled."[81] Bateson seemed to have no involvement for or against. However, his close friend, the geneticist C. H. Waddington, loudly denounced liberal science and what he took to be its necessary concomitant, democratic politics. Though Waddington conceded that the Russian experience contained flaws and excesses, the deliberateness of communist forms of social control seemed to him most congenial to the sort of manipulation which scientific experimentation required.[82]

Finally, Bateson infused these various disaffections with the notion that his newly Americanized theoretical interests were not compatible with what he construed to be consensus within the tiny circles of British social anthropology. "I got together with Malinowski's students," he recalled. "No communication occurred. They hadn't the faintest idea what I was at. It was exceedingly difficult to say what I was at in those days."[83] And in Cambridge, where Gregory spent three years until 1936, formulating his criticisms of functional theory into *Naven*, his first book, there was similar isolation.* Edmund R. Leach, the English social anthropologist, suggested that,

---

*Except for productive contact with the psychologist F. C. Bartlett who was working on problems concerning human memory. (F. C. Bartlett, *Remembering*.)

generally, this ought to have been the case because, "in the working situation in social anthropology in Cambridge at that time . . . there was no one who really understood what Gregory was talking about. . . . Then, it was a purely ethnographic field—the taking of notes and the collecting of objects. The notion of psychology and sociology that runs all through *Naven* was very much something that was not done around [here then]."[84]

Following Radcliffe-Brown, Bateson assumed that society was an organic whole. He also thought by analogy to the natural sciences. Aesthetic inclinations, however, broadened his approach. Bateson argued that scientific presentations of cultures had ignored informal material that novelists were able to convey almost implicitly. Specifically, the emotional tone, which he called the "ethos" of a culture, was missing from recent ethnographies. To Bateson, this was a matter of language.

> The artist . . . can leave a great many of the most fundamental aspects of culture to be picked up not from his actual words, but from his emphasis. He can choose words whose very sound is more significant than their dictionary meaning and he can group and stress them so that the reader almost unconsciously receives information which is not explicit in the sentences and which the artist would find it hard—almost impossible—to express in analytic terms. This impressionistic technique is utterly foreign to the methods of science, and the Functional School . . . [has] scarcely attempted the delineation of those aspects of culture which the artist is able to express.[85]

This appeal for wider, more inclusive social anthropology was only whispering of a radical divergence from British peers and predecessors. What essentially distinguished Bateson then was a preoccupation with theoretical abstraction and with the problem of explanation itself. By contrast, Malinowski's leading students—Raymond Firth, Audrey I. Richards—did ethnographies in which critical premises were left unarticulated, contained within descriptions of concrete activities.[86] *Naven,* on the other hand, was "not primarily an ethnographic study." In retrospect, Bateson wrote that he "was trying not only to explain by fitting data together but also to use the explanatory process as an example within which the principles of explanation could be seen and studied."[87]

The book took its title from the name of a Iatmul congratulatory ritual which occurred in order to laud a sister's child for having performed some specified adult deed for the first time. At its most ornate, the ceremony involved transvestitism and ritualized homosexuality. The mother's brother of the initiate, dressed in bedraggled skirts, would offer his buttocks to the sister's son, and would also simulate the female role in mock copulation with his wife. This, in any case, is a bit of the seemingly bizarre ethnographic background to Bateson's goal of presenting "a study in the nature of explanation."[88] The naven ceremony was held to be a subsidiary part of a larger analytical configuration which included manifestations of personality, such as emotion and cognition, as well as social structure. The full title of the book reflects the complexity and confusion of its aims: *Naven* (ethnography of a ceremony): *A Survey of the Problems* (epistemology) *suggested by a Composite Picture* (holistic configuration) *of a New Guinea Tribe drawn from Three Points of View* (affective, cognitive, and social structural).

If a wider view demanded new analytical language, Bateson was willing to offer his own. To describe displays of emotion in culture, there was its "ethos" (a term to which he had been introduced by Radcliffe-Brown). He defined the concept as "the expression of a culturally standardized system of organization of the instincts and emotions of the individual."[89] The ethos of Iatmul men, for instance, demanded "pride, self-assertion, harshness, and spectacular display; the tendency to histrionic behavior continually diverts the harshness into irony, which in its turn degenerates into buffooning."[90] The ethos of a group seemed to possess a normative component as well. In Cambridge, Bateson had observed that

> the dons of St. John's College drink water, beer, claret, sherry and port—but not cocktails; and in their choice they are guided both by tradition and by the ethos of the group. These two factors work together and we may say that the dons drink as they do both because generations of dons have drunk on the same sound system in the past and because actually in the present that system seems to them appropriate to the ethos of their society.[91]

To describe cultural styles of thought, Bateson introduced the word *eidos*, which he defined as the standardization and expression of the cognitive aspects of the personality of the individuals. Iatmul men were again his illustration—they possessed agonistic minds which cultivated vast and detailed erudition. They possessed a keenness for memorizing totemic names of four to five syllables, and a learned man could carry as many as twenty thousand around in his head. Further, this feat was not accomplished by rote but rather by processes of imagery or word association. Bateson noted other characteristics of Iatmul eidos, such as a sense of paradox, a sense of direct dualism—that everything has a sibling—and a sense of diagonal dualism—that everything has a symmetrical counterpart.

Another subject which is matter for this characteristic intellectual inquiry is the nature of ripples and waves on the surface of water. It is said secretly that men, pigs, trees, grass—all the objects in the world—are only patterns of waves. Indeed there seems to be some agreement about this, although it perhaps conflicts with the theory of reincarnation, according to which the ghost of the dead is blown as mist by the East Wind up the river and into the womb of the deceased's son's wife. Be that as it may—there is still the question of how ripples and waves are caused. The clan which claims the East Wind as a totem is clear enough about this: the Wind with her mosquito fan causes the waves. But other clans have personified the waves and say that they are a person (Kontum-mali) independent of the wind. Other clans, again, have other theories. On one occasion I took some Iatmul natives down to the coast and found one of them sitting by himself gazing with rapt attention at the sea. It was a windless day, but a slow swell was breaking on the beach. Among the totemic ancestors of his clan he counted a personified slit gong who had floated down the river to the sea and who was believed to cause the waves. He was gazing at the waves which were heaving and breaking when no wind was blowing demonstrating the truth of his clan myth.[92]

Unlike Radcliffe-Brown, Bateson's causal scheme did not deduce individual behavior from social structure. Neither did it induce social structure from individual behavior. Rather, both these processes were invoked. The pervading themes of individual behavior not only resulted from processes of standardization but also effected them. He posited a circular, interdependent, bidirectional system of causation, "If it could be shown that Iatmul culture stressed man's gregarious tendencies, we should be justified in regarding the gregarious sentiment or instinct as important in the moulding of the culture. As a matter of fact, however, this facet of human nature is not specifically stressed in Iatmul culture and this explanation must therefore be disgarded."[93] The circularity of this process was imposed upon him, he believed, by the organization of the phenomena themselves. Just as he envisioned culture in terms of a reticulate series of cause and effect,* so his own epistemology was based in the notion that the relationship between observer and observed might reflect both. He argued, for example, that "in my own conscious mental

---

*Though conversations with C. H. Waddington were not inspiring ideologically, through them, Bateson was introduced to the ideas of the philosopher A. N. Whitehead. "A further and more compelling argument in favour of the circular . . . view of functional systems is to be found in the fact that any other view would drive us to belief either in a 'first cause' or in some sort of teleology—in fact we should have to accept some fundamental dualism in nature which is philosophically inadmissable." (GB, *Naven*, p. 117.)

processes, the structural and logical aspects of behavior are more clearly seen than the emotional, and I believe that the same is true of Iatmul men."[94] His fieldwork methods, such as they were, attempted to let the culture "speak" for itself as much as possible, so that the ethnographer became a stenographer. Data were forced upon rather than contrived by the anthropologist. "I know, for example, how great a value the natives set upon their enormous system of totemic names; and I know this, not from some colourless statement, but from the curious experience of writing down thousands, literally, of names at my informant's bidding."[95]

Bateson's theoretical emphasis was on processes and dynamics of social equilibrium—on the potential for change inherent in society and on the checks by which a status quo is maintained. "The tightrope walker," he later wrote, "with a balancing pole will not be able to maintain his balance except by varying the forces which he exerts upon the pole."[96] Yet this dicussion was to be constrained within a synchronic perspective. Increased or decreased differentiation—e.g., change—would occur not for any chain of historical circumstances but rather because groups of people react to the reactions of others, and tend to maximize held values. The key was *interaction*. "We have got to consider, not only A's reaction to B's behavior, but we must go on to consider how these affect B's later behavior and the effect of this on A."[97] Among the Iatmul, women watched

> for the spectacular performances of the men, and there can be no reasonable doubt that the presence of an audience is a very important factor in shaping the men's behavior. In fact, it is probable that the men are more exhibitionistic because the women admire their performances. Conversely, there can be no doubt that the spectacular behavior is a stimulus which summons the audience together, promoting in the women the appropriate . . . behavior.[98]

If functional analysis stressed the unity of societies, Bateson was interested in creating a language for the analysis of dynamic—yet synchronic—processes of sustained differentiation. In the illustration above, men exaggerate their exhibitionism in response to women's spectatorship, which in turn creates more intense spectatorship on the women's part. Bateson's was a view of observable social relations oscillating or perhaps vibrating, during which a process of intensification of role occurs. To describe the process of degenerative change in norms of behavior (the "vicious circle"), Bateson coined the word "schismogenesis." This term stood for processes of disintegration and of increased differentiation. He further distinguished between two fundamental patterns of schismogenesis: *complementary* patterns in which two roles differ but coincide, as in dominance-submission, exhibitionism-spectatorship, feeble-ness-succorance, master-apprentice, and various classes of feudal hierarchy; and *symmetrical* patterns in which both sides exhibit competitively similar behavior, as in boasting, armaments races, and wars.* In the complementary case, a dominant group or person in an interacting pair will become more assertive while the submissive one becomes more passive. The submission enhances the dominance and the enhanced dominance encourages more submission. In the symmetrical case, progressive change will occur as each actor reacts identically but increases the degree of reaction. Among the Iatmul, for example, rival moieties compete against each other during initiation rites by bullying the novices. The men of each group taunt the men of their rival group, which prompts the latter to taunt back with more ferocity; obviously the consequence of this symmetrical schismogenesis will be painful for the novices. Bateson advised that he also expected to find these two patterns in intimate dyadic relations, in cases of "psychodeviance," in culture contact, as well as in political rivalries. Schismogenesis, then, designated interactive collapse of relations. "The inverse process," Bateson noted wryly, "differs from schismogenesis in the direction of change. Instead of leading to an increase in mutual hostility, the inverse process leads rather in the direction of mutual love . . . and on theoretical grounds we must expect that if the course of true love ever ran smooth, it would follow an exponential curve."[99]†

Bateson freely acknowledged that Malinowski and Radcliffe-Brown had influenced him so deeply that he could not "point to any ideas and say that they are truly mine . . . though perhaps the begetters might be unable or

---

*The difference between complementary and symmetrical schismogenesis," Bateson suggested, "is closely analogous to that between schism and heresy—where heresy is the term used for the splitting of a religious sect in which the divergent groups have doctrines antagonistic to those of the parent group, while schism is the term used for the splitting of a sect in which two resulting groups have the same doctrine, but separate and competing politics." (GB, *Naven*, p. 173.)

†Malinowski had little sympathy for Bateson's new concept. When Raymond Firth's *We, The Tikopia* appeared ready for press (1936), he wrote a sharply toned preface noting that in some corners native life was being plundered by wild theorizing. "New standards are being hoisted every few months, and the reality of human life is being submitted to some queer and alarming manipulations. . . . [A]ttempts are made to analyze cultures in terms of Schismogenesis, or to define the individual and singular 'genius' of each particular society as Apollonian, Dionysiac, or Paranoid and the like. Under the deft touch of another writer the women of one tribe appear masculine, while in another males develop feminine qualities almost to the verge of parturition. By contrast the present book is an unaffected piece of genuine scholarship, based on real experience of a culture and not on a few hypostasized impressions. The anthropologist who still believes that his work can be scientific will therefore breathe a sigh of relief and gratitude." (B. Malinowski, Preface to *We, The Tikopia*, 3rd rev. ed., R. Firth, pp. vii-viii.)

unwilling to recognize their progeny."[100] Radcliffe-Brown, it is true, briefly alluded to many of the points he stressed, such as balanced opposition, a more relativized sense of function, and interactive dynamics. He also admitted to the limited scope of a sociological approach. Upon seeing Bateson's *Oceania* articles in manuscript, Radcliffe-Brown informed him of what he considered to be the crucial difference between their perspectives.

> In reference to your discussion on theory there is one point I should like to mention to avoid possible misunderstanding. When I speak of morphology and structure I am referring to *social* structure, i.e., to the integration of human individuals into groups. ... You, on the other hand, are referring to the morphology of culture, I think this idea ... to be an excellent one.[101]

Both men held that the analysis of human relations was the central concern of social anthropology. Bateson viewed them as interaction. Relations were construed as exchanges of behavior: B reacts to A and A reacts back to B. Implicit was a more dynamic sense of equilibrium than Radcliffe-Brown proposed, of a system which could erupt but for internal controls. For example, though Iatmul culture emphasized pride and harshness, "if a man specialized too far in his violence, his wives will run away from his house, his brothers-in-law will turn against him, and he will live under a threat of perhaps violent death, but certainly sorcery."[102] Whereas Radcliffe-Brown's conception of social organization was static—stressing structural relations that were harmonious—and Bateson's view was potentially dynamic, it should be understood that, ultimately, both were conservative views of society. The dynamism which came of interaction might result in destructive change (schismogenesis), but did not because of immanent compensatory devices.

Both men agreed that evolutionary conjectures had no place in anthropological explanation. To Bateson, this meant that historical evidence was scientifically inadequate and should be consigned to lawyers for evaluation. At base, cultures and societies were ordered if the scientist could build, out of his own interactions with his data, a system that contained repetition, i.e., that reiterated similar premises in assorted behavioral contexts. This was a purely synchronic approach. To Radcliffe-Brown, on the other hand, opposition to evolutionary reconstructions did not totally exclude history. To him, societies evidenced structure because they continued. Despite the passage of time, standardized social relations were maintained. He addressed this divergence in his review of *Naven*.

> We read that "the culture in some way affects the psychology of the individual, causing whole groups of individuals to think and feel alike," and "a culture may

standardize the affective make-up of individuals." Thus the culture of a society, as the standardization of modes of acting, thinking, and feeling, is conceived as producing that standardization which it actually is. This is, of course, true, but is unfortunately expressed. A culture continues, and may be said to reproduce itself, by the fact that the standardization of behavior ... produces a very similar standardization *in succeeding generations* [italics added].[103]

Bateson derived from, yet exaggerated, Radcliffe-Brown, by taking a sort of fundamentalist synchronic position. "In a synchronic study of a fire I would say that the fire burns because there is oxygen in the room, etc., but I should not enquire how the fire was first ignited."[104] This point of view, he admitted, was based not entirely in the logic of analysis. "I myself have so little appreciation of time that I omitted ... to enquire" into Iatmul calendric beliefs.[105]

Together with these magnifications of functionalist theory, Bateson's disarming candor and his precocious metatheoretical introspection, flagrantly separated his work from all of British social anthropology. Indeed, Radcliffe-Brown called *Naven* an "intellectual autobiography."[106] In part, Bateson's honesty had the purpose of excusing the inadequacy of his empirical base.

> It is clear that I have contributed but little to our store of anthropological facts and that the information about Iatmul culture which I have used ... does no more than illustrate my methods. Even for the purposes of illustration my supply of facts is meagre, and I certainly cannot claim that my facts have demonstrated the truth of any theory. ... This would be a serious confession of weakness, and indeed the book would have no value, were it not for another shortcoming which in a sense cancels out the first. ... [I]t so happens that none of my theories is ... new or strange. They are all to some extent platitudes which novelists, philosophers, religious leaders, lawyers, the man in the street, and even anthropologists, have reiterated in various forms probably since language was invented.[107]

In a sense, the book was as concerned with its own conceptual development as it was with the Iatmul. Throughout, the reader is advised of modifications in the explanatory framework. This led one reviewer, Kurt H. Wolff, to rebuke him for reworking his stance publicly. "Bateson's theory ... includes too many personal elements to be called, without qualification, scientific."[108] It might be said that the ebb and flow of theory in *Naven* is evidence that the interaction which Bateson attributed to relations in the phenomenal world were occurring within his own habits of thought. We follow *him* reacting to his own reactions.

While composing the last chapter of the book, Bateson noticed that in the course of developing his abstractions, they had become overconcretized in his mind. He had construed them as *actual* interacting entities. "I thought that there was one sort of phenomenon which I could call 'eidos' and another sort which I could call 'culture structure' and that these worked together—had mutual effect on the other."[109] The difficulty was to maintain distinct categories, all the while acknowledging that these were merely interpretive abstractions that were independent of the data itself.* Bateson settled this confusion for himself by concluding that no category excluded any other. "This meant that I had only to keep clearly before me the conviction that ethos, structure, etc. were merely points of view or aspects of the culture, and to look for each aspect in every piece of behaviour and in every native statement."[110] When in 1936, the Social Science Reasearch Council enlisted the anthropologists Robert Redfield, Ralph J. Linton, and Melville J. Herskovits to develop a memorandum on methods for the study of acculturation,[111] Bateson repeated this conclusion. He opposed both generalized, programmatic formulations, and monochromatic analytic categories. Culture must not be divided up according to any rigid set of functions. Barter was not just a matter of economics, just as prayer was not only a matter of conformity.

> From this it follows that our categories ... are not *real* subdivisions which are present in the cultures which we study, but are merely *abstractions* which we make for our own convenience when we set out to describe cultures in words. ... In handling such abstractions we must be careful to avoid Whitehead's "fallacy of misplaced concreteness," a fallacy into which, for example, the Marxian historians fall when they maintain that economic "phenomena" are "primary."[112]

In all, the data seemed to accumulate in an accordion-like way: (1.) The observations which were made to maximize the self-expression of phenomena were accompanied by (2.) the conceptual development of the scientist trying to make sense of them, and this latter gave rise to (3.) self-conscious scrutiny of that development which, Bateson audaciously believed, might reveal something of the process of scientific thought itself. Four years after *Naven* reached publication, Bateson discussed his view of the personal and general advance of science. A holistic ideal and an organic analogy were canonical in British social anthropology of 1936. For Bateson, however, the general use of

---

* "There is an error; but it is merely the accidental error mistaking the abstract for the concrete. It is an example of what I call the 'Fallacy of Misplaced Concreteness.'"[122] (A. N. Whitehead, *Science and the Modern World*, p. 51.)

analogies was based in a pervasive sense of the unity of all scientific thought such that training in one field was applicable to another.[113] Bateson believed that he had acquired "a vague mystical feeling" from the overtones of his father's conversation, that "we must look for the same sort of processes in all fields of natural phenomena—that we might expect to find the same sort of laws at work in the structure of a crystal as in the structure of society, or that the segmentation of an earth worm might really be comparable to the process by which basalt pillars are formed."[114] His own thought process and that of science in general were a combination of "loose" and "strict" thinking.* Loose thinking was what he called his intuitive hunch relating the supposed structure of a set of data by analogy to the organization of some possibly relevant phenomenon. The loose hunch would then give way to strict or rigorous exploration "against the rigid formulations which have been devised in the field from which . . . the analogy" has been borrowed.[115] The limitations of the analogy were then perceptible, as were new research directions, and new descriptive language.

> I want to emphasize that whenever we pride ourselves upon finding a newer, stricter way of thought or exposition; whenever we start insisting too hard upon "operationalism" or symbolic logic or any other of these very essential systems of tramlines, we lose something of the very ability to think new thoughts. And equally, of course, whenever we rebel against the sterile rigidity of formal thought and exposition and let our ideas run wild, we likewise lose. As I see it, the advances in scientific thought came from *a combination of loose and strict thinking,* and this combination is the most precious tool of science.[116]

Bateson's identification of subject and object, and his belief in the unity of scientific thought—expressions of his holism—also created a tension. That is, how could the integrity of phenomena—their wholeness—be preserved in the face of scientific reductionism, whose bent was to isolate categories and hold them separate for analysis? How could phenomena be described critically such

---

* "In my case, which is a small one and comparatively insignificant in the whole advance of science, you can see both elements of the alternating process—first the loose thinking and the building up of a structure on unsound foundations and then the correction to stricter thinking and the substitution of a new underpinning beneath the already constructed mass. And that, I believe, is a pretty fair picture of how science advances, with this exception, that usually the edifice is larger and the individuals who finally contribute the new underpinning are different people from those who did the initial loose thinking. Sometimes, as in physics, we find centuries between the first building of the edifice and the later correction of the foundations— but the process is basically the same." (GB, "Experiments in thinking about observed ethnological material," in *Steps to an Ecology of Mind,* p. 86.)

that their natural unity was maintained? Literary or artistic solutions were not acceptable. And more difficult, if a culture was conceived as a unitary "reticulum of interlocking cause and effect,"[117] how could one portray it with words in a linear series?

> When I stated that the "tone" of the men's behaviour in the initiation ceremonies was expressive of harshness and irresponsibility rather than of asceticism, I meant that the actions performed by them, the washing of the novices, etc., were *accompanied* by other details of behaviour so that the whole picture was one of harshness. Until we devise techniques for the proper recording and analysis of human posture, gesture, intonation, laughter, etc., we shall have to be content with journalistic sketches of the "tone" of behaviour.[118]

In January 1936, with the problem of representing behavior in mind, but before the manuscript of *Naven* was settled at the Cambridge University Press, Gregory sailed to meet and marry Margaret Mead, since divorced from Reo Fortune. They had seen each other twice during the years Bateson was preparing *Naven*. In 1934, Margaret had come to spend the summer in Ireland, where Gregory was vacationing with his friends C. H. Waddington and the architect Justin Blanco-White.* The following spring, Bateson returned her visit, while he was lecturing at Columbia and the University of Chicago. Mead recalled, "Working together with Radcliffe-Brown, we made further attempt to define what is meant by society, culture, and cultural character."[119] They also were making plans to embark upon cooperative research in Bali, which they had selected in hopes of enlarging hypotheses about universally prevalent temperaments.

The two anthropologists were married in Singapore so as to be legally wed in England. Although they were in love, Gregory, then thirty-one, did not think Beatrice would receive this news sympathetically, anticipating that she would see rejection in it and be hurt. Margaret, at thirty-four, was older than he and unalterably foreign. Appealing to the ultimate value of science, still incontrovertible to his mother, was the solution. Their marriage, he wrote her, had been the result of anthropological—not romantic—motives. As they were committed to cooperative research which would require at least four years

---

*"When Gregory and Waddington talked," Mead recalled, "I learned . . . about the way English biologists think, by listening to the two of them. They would pick their illustrations right across the field. One minute from embryology, the next from geology, the next from anthropology, back and forth, very freely, so that the illustrations from one spot illuminated, corrected, and expanded the one from another." (GB, M. Mead, "For God's Sake, Margaret," *CoEvolution Quarterly*, Summer 1976, p. 38.)

of work together, getting married seemed the simplest thing to do. He admitted to Beatrice that they both had doubts about their new partnership. Margaret was pessimistic, because of her failure with Fortune, that science and family could be combined successfully. Gregory worried about the strain romantic involvements with others might put upon their ability to work together.

> My chief feeling about the whole thing is one of relief. Partly relief at not having to go into the field alone—that so far as the immediate future is concerned. But there is deeper relief too. As far as I can see my past difficulties—in attempts at marriage and awkwardnesses in my relations with you—have been largely a result of inarticulacy, some internal clumsiness which makes me not see my own personal relationships frankly and sanely. And now the relief comes from having gone into this business openly looking along every avenue—and M[argaret] and I have been pretty brutally frank about it.... Poor mother, I know you have had a pretty dismal life so far as I have been concerned, with ... occasional good hours that we have together and long intervening inarticulate periods. And now I wonder what you will make of this unconventional solution. My own feeling is very clearly that it will do a good deal to ease us.[120]

En route to Bali, with Margaret's exacting assistance, Gregory continued to work on *Naven*. While preparing a glossary of the book's conceptual and native vocabulary, he realized that his analysis was overconcretized. "As a result of marriage, I composed a lot of corrections and then sent them off," he informed his friend and Cambridge colleague, the anthropologist E. J. Lindgren, who had volunteered to herd the book through press.[121] Beatrice, he knew, would be more concerned with his bride than with his book.

> I imagine you have a considerable series of questions to ask about the lady. She is the daughter of an economics professor in University of Pennsylvania. ... Her mother, a little rosy cheeked old lady, is very much alive and formerly a sociologist.... M[argaret] herself is small, very businesslike and very quick intellectually. What are the points that you will want to know? Is she a lady? Yes, if you will ever allow that term to be applied to an American! As a hostess she is smooth, and cosy, unfussy, gracious even. English of course she is not, but she is an anthropologist and a good enough one to be able to learn the points of English culture. No doubt—and she insists on this—you will have to give her lessons in English cultural norms.... Her family are, she says, "rationalistic, agnostic, Spencer-reading, New England Puritans" and when I boasted of my five generations of atheism, she capped the tale with a statement that her great grandmother was "read out" of the Unitarian Church for heresy.... She has just

brought up a photograph ... so that saves me an exercise in description of her face—as you see a good sound plain intelligent—almost female-Darwin face.[122]

Despite the Batesons' efforts to announce and to explain their marriage and Mead's divorce as being of professional convenience, anthropologists in England and America were gossiping about the news. With this as a background, Bateson was involved in the first of three somewhat half-hearted applications to Cambridge University for jobs in social anthropology. "I should try," he wrote from Bali, "to build up a team of students who should see the problems of social anthropology, psychology, and economics against the theoretical background provided by the theory of cultural standardization."[123] Haddon supported him, but unsuccessfully. Instead, he was awarded the William Wyse Studentship—essentially an unfettered research grant.* Beatrice wanted her son settled in Cambridge, but was not displeased by this outcome. Occupying a chair would have required him to administer subjects for which he had no interest. "You can only ride a Bateson on the snaffle," she later concluded, "they can't brook curbs."[124]

Gleefully married and entranced by the vividness of Balinese life, Gregory and Margaret began their research in March 1936. "The day we arrived was new year according to one of the overlapping Balinese calendars, and it was taboo for anybody to take any sort of vehicle, the hotel bus was about the only thing on the roads [that day] and the village deserted, padi fields empty—it all gave an effect of dream under influence of some drug."[125]

The first two months were spent practicing technique by making a film, *Trance and Dance in Bali.* They then moved to an impoverished mountain village, Bajoeng Gede, and worked there intermittently for almost two years, until February 1938. By contrast to past Balinese studies which had stressed the culture's amalgamation of a variety of Asiatic diffusion, they selected this village of five hundred people, because it seemed to have been isolated from historical influences. It was also ceremonially and artistically modest in comparison to baroque life throughout rice-raising Bali. Ritual, in Bajoeng Gede, was at "a meager and skeletal minimum."[126] The Balinese there suffered from hypothyroidism and "the whole population was markedly slow both in

*From America, the Balinese research was originally funded by the American Museum of Natural History. The preparation of the resulting monograph was funded by the Committee for Research in Dementia Praecox, supported by the Thirty-third Degree Scottish Rite, Northern Masonic Jurisdiction, and by the Social Science Research Council.

intellectual response and in speed of bodily movement."[127] If the beauty of the island pleased Bateson, the people evidently did not. By contrast to Iatmul bravado, Balinese formality was uncomfortable and too reminiscent of England. "The most striking thing about these people," he felt after two months among them, "is their nervousness—always expecting that something is going to bite them when they are in any sort of uncultural situation (e.g., in their contacts with us). This leads to the appearance ... of impenetrable dullness."[128] At least the loneliness of his Iatmul fieldwork did not recur. It had been supplanted, to an extent, by Mead's endless enthusiasm and by a frenetic immersion in research. "Most of the time as we worked together far into the night," she recalled, "[we] went to bed after washing our faces in the remaining pint of water when the last films had been developed, or after we had labeled the last film or had worked out a new theoretical point—we felt we were working in harmony."[129] Bateson, after seven months of work, gave similar impression, "I wish there were some means of preventing field-work, which god knows is hectic enough in the first months, from becoming more and more hectic as the worker knows more and more about the culture he is studying and his people become more and more forthcoming and anxious that he shall attend every ceremonial in the place."[130]

For the first time in the short history of ethnographic fieldwork, film was used both on a large scale and as the primary research tool. Gregory did the photography and cinematography, while Margaret annotated behavior.* In keeping with Bateson's concern for preserving the integrity of observed phenomena, they "tried to shoot what happened normally and spontaneously, rather than to decide upon the norms and then get Balinese to go through these behaviors in suitable lighting."[131] At Mead's insistence, their cooperation was very methodical. They recorded such details as the angle from which pictures were taken and with which machine Bateson worked. "Whenever a new roll of film was inserted in the camera, the data and the time of insertion were scribbled on the leader, and when the film was removed, the data and time were again recorded, so that the film could be accurately fitted to the notes."[132] Mead, in her autobiography, *Blackberry Winter,* has called their collaboration "the perfect intellectual and emotional partnership in which there was no pulling and hauling resulting from competing temperamental views of the world."[133] Together, they photographed manifestations of village

---

*They worked in concert with an interesting group of Western artists in residence there: Jane Belo, Colin McPhee, Katharane Mershon, Walter Spies, and Beryl de Zoete.

organization, rites de passage, calendrical ceremonies, the gestures in dance, daily life,* and cockfighting, woodcarving, painting, death and marriage rituals, but most of all, they focused on parent-child† and sibling interaction. The organization of their work is evident in Bateson's description of their efforts to elicit as wide a frame of behavior as possible.

> The photographer [i.e., Bateson himself], with his eye glued to a view finder and moving about, gets a very imperfect view of what is actually happening, and Margaret Mead (who is able to write with only an occasional glance at her notebook) had a much fuller view of the scene than Gregory Bateson. She was able to do some very necessary directing of the photography, calling the photographer's attention to one or another child or to some special play which was beginning on the other side of the yard. Occasionally, when we were working on family scenes, we were accompanied by our native secretary, I Made Kaler. He would engage in ethnographic interviews with the parents, or take verbatim notes on the conversations.[134]

The photography of daily life became so routine that Bateson ceased to be aware of doing it. "It is impossible to maintain camera consciousness," he said later, "after the first dozen shots."[135] Much of the business of this work was mundane—cutting and developing film, keeping track of tripods and filters. When it came to the actual shooting, however, Bateson immersed himself

---

* "At a very simple postural level, we may observe that, in our own culture, people tend to leave their fingers, when at rest, in regular positions. If the fingers are flexed, they will either be all flexed to the same extent, or, if differentially flexed, the differences will follow some regular system of progression, commonly each flexed a little more than its neighbor on the radial side. The Balinese, very much more often, leave their fingers in what appear to us to be distorted positions, as though each finger were a separate entity or a separate sense organ. True, in our culture, it is polite in certain sections, to extend the little finger when holding a teacup, but in Bali this sort of thing is enormously developed, and photographic records show that the tendency to disharmonic finger postures, *increases* in the extreme excitement of rioting over the body at funerals." (GB, "Cultural determinants of personality," in *Personality and the Behavior Disorders*, vol. 2, ed. J. McVicker Hunt, p. 731.)

† "A small boy learns to stand and walk. His father has set up for him in the household a horizontal bamboo supported on two posts.... The boy learns to walk by using this as a support.... The topology of this arrangement is the precise opposite of that of the play-pen of Western culture. The Western child is confined within restricting limits and would like to escape from them; the Balinese child is supported within a central area and is frightened of departure from this support." (GB, M. Mead, *Balinese Character: A Photographic Analysis*, p. 88.)

zestfully and, if those anthropologists who still model their work on his are any indication, with considerable skill.

> This afternoon [he wrote a colleague, we observed] an astonishing exhibition by two children and their parents—this started with a little quiet photographing of the children—and the parents took so little notice that I went on photographing—and got a series of about sixty Leica pictures of acts and postures and relationships between the children and the parents—weaned child flirting with the mother's breast and finally succumbing to temptation and being pushed off—stupidly I took the photograph at the moment of suckling instead of doing it at the moment that he was pushed off. And pushed too hard too but without animus ... M[argaret Mead] was all the time working with one of the fathers and prompting on the conversation between him and our native secretary—so that nobody regarded my activities seriously—and so the situation lasted for nearly an hour and a half—till the light was too bad to get any more.[136]

In the middle of this intense research schedule, Beatrice Bateson arrived to spend Christmas 1936 in Bali—having accepted her son's invitation to come and study his ménage. In preparation, she bought a copy of Mencken's *American Language*. Nora Barlow, hearing that Beatrice was set on going to Bali, offered to accompany her friend. "Nora came along to see that Beatrice didn't spoil Gregory's marriage," Margaret Mead recalled. "She felt that Beatrice was a dominating person. She had seen something of her dominating-ness in the past. [Nora] insisted ... that Beatrice must now ask me to call her Beatrice, which I detested. I would have been perfectly happy to call her mother."[137] Before the two ladies arrived, in fear of his mother's well-known horror of modernism, Gregory went about the Bajoeng Gede house removing from the walls all the reproductions of expressionist art. After a brief sojourn in the mountains, the whole party moved down to Bangli where Gregory and Margaret had rented the former summer palace of the Rajah of Bangli in order to house their guests properly. Mead remembered a suggestive incident during the visit.

> We took [Beatrice] to see a dance, and we didn't like the way it was being handled. We thought it was being over secularized, so we had very beautiful offerings made. . . . We went into the cave [in Bangli], where you had the hobby horse dance, and presented the offerings. We knelt and Beatrice knelt for the first time in her life. It was her son's scientific work and she knelt. . . . Then you go back to the dinner party that the Whiteheads told us about where somebody said grace, and Beatrice looked at W. B., who didn't bow his head, and she didn't either. But ... she respected scientific work.[138]

They stayed for about six weeks, and outwardly at least, Beatrice seemed to accept her new daughter-in-law, undeniably American as she was.

In the spring of 1938, as World War II became a conspicuous probability, the Batesons left Bali to return to New Guinea.* For comparative purposes, their intentions were to film a variety of Iatmul behavior. They would then return to England, via New York, to begin a life together in Cambridge, where Gregory had been awarded a fellowship at Trinity College. Margaret wrote Beatrice that her son was "looking forward so happily to the Iatmul whom he likes so much better than the Balinese. He has a little of the attitude of a man who comes in expecting a good stiff drink and finds himself put off with a coca-cola—the Balinese were so incurably mild and unexciting."[139] In fact, Gregory was disappointed. "The Bali show was a great success—as far as anthropology is concerned, but they left us and we left them without either side very much attached," he wrote then. "It's like trying to make friends with beautiful gazelles. They are beautiful and move beautifully. And they are gay in a light gentle way. But human personal contact with them ends there, and their contact with each other ends there. And the landscape rather in the same way. I think it is physically the most lovely place I have been in—but, somehow, what of it?"[140] However, once back in Tambunum, they struggled for eight months. For one, Gregory was again malarial. For another, it was dry season and the men were occupied with crocodile hunting. Village life was minimal—except for arguments over dividing meat. Still, they were able to collect some material on Iatmul child rearing and theatricals. Enough to allow contrast between "the way the Balinese confined drama and action to the theater and maintained their everyday relationships placidly and evenly, never allowing children to contend even for a toy, whereas the Iatmul, who struggled and screamed and quarreled in real life, used their artistic performances to introduce moments of static beauty into their more violent lives."[141]

Upon reaching New York in the spring of 1939, Margaret was pregnant. Since earlier she had miscarried in Bali, she decided to follow Dr. Benjamin Spock's personal advice not to continue on to England until after the birth. "I

---

*Beatrice was horrified by the collapsing political situation. "I feel terribly depressed and trembly—longing to hit out somehow and set the world right [she wrote Gregory on 15 March 1938]. Hitler is terribly crazy and altogether amoral—but there's terrible method in his madness. The wretched Jews in Austria are already, though the whole business is not a week old, 'for it.' ... Public uncertainties and political crudenesses rather smother private bothers— take my advice and stick to the Sepik—unless the Germans suddenly swarm over and bomb you. Europe is no place for intelligent young men. And all because Clemenceau and Lloyd George made such an infamous peace treaty."

had never cared about particular professional status," she has said of their plans to settle in Cambridge. "I expected to have the baby to care for, and there was plenty of work to do."[142] World War II confounded the Batesons' future together. In September, a few days after Germany attacked Poland, Gregory sailed for England, expecting to be used for some national purpose. Before his departure, Margaret recalled, they had discussed what to name the infant.

> We had already decided that if the baby were a boy, we would make our home in England, because the English did a better job of bringing up a boy; but if it were a girl, we would live in the United States where girls are better off. But in any event, the child's surname would be Bateson, and so we considered Bateson names. We decided that we should name a girl Mary, after the most distinguished of Gregory's paternal aunts, a pioneer historian, who had died young, much loved and deeply regretted.... [W]hen I suggested that a boy should be named William, Gregory dissented. "Too hard on librarians," he commented.[143]

Yet at this early stage of the war, before the evacuation of Dunkirk in May, complete mobilization had not occurred, and the services of academics were going unsolicited. Bateson had anticipated this difficulty en route: "After about twenty-four hours on the ship I realized that it was most unlikely that England would find any use for social sciences."[144] And indeed Bateson could find nothing of consequence to do there. In Cambridge, where he had submitted himself for a pair of jobs, no likely employment emerged. At the same time, psychologist F. C. Bartlett, at Trinity, prodded him to get on with the analysis of his Balinese material, on the basis of which he had been granted a fellowship. After nearly three months of frustration, Gregory cabled Margaret—on 7 December 1939—that he had applied for a permit to return to New York. As he did, or rather the next day after he did, she gave birth to a girl, who was named Mary Catherine and called Cathy. Hearing that he had become a father, Gregory cabled Margaret again—the infant must not be christened. Although there is no record of Beatrice's reaction to her new granddaughter, evidently Nora Barlow was quite delighted and "began to plan all over again for a Darwin-Bateson marriage as she visualized Cathy as a prospective bride for her [new] grandson Jeremy."[145] One month later, Gregory departed his native ground, feeling bittersweet about the course of events. Once in New York, six weeks after his daughter's birth, he went directly to Philadelphia, where he found Margaret in the throes of demand breast-feeding Cathy, and with her mother's help, taking careful notes about the experience.

At once, they "let the nurse go and took care of [Cathy] for a whole weekend during which she had a bad episode of colic. This was the only time [Gregory] took much physical care of her. But it was enough to establish a very close relationship between Gregory and Cathy."[146]

Bateson and Mead quickly turned to the complex problem of selecting and organizing their Balinese data, which had amounted, by the end of their fieldwork, to 25,000 stills, and to 22,000 feet of 16mm film. Countering criticism that his *Naven* had been merely literary, and self-criticism that the integrity of naturally occurring behavior was violated when represented verbally, Bateson did not invoke the concepts of ethos, eidos, and schismogenesis which he had developed in New Guinea. "Margaret Mead and I," he explained, "were engaged in devising other tools—photographic methods of record and description—and partly...I was learning the techniques of applying genetic psychology to cultural data, but . . . [also] at some inarticulate level I felt that the [Iatmul] tool[s] were unsuitable for this new task."[147] Instead, they chose 759 stills and arranged them into 100 plates such that "the wholeness of each piece of behavior" was preserved.[148] The outcome of this work was their uniquely innovative ethnography, *Balinese Character: A Photographic Analysis.*

> In this monograph we are attempting a new method of stating the intangible relationships among different types of culturally standardized behavior by placing side by side mutually relevant photographs. Pieces of behavior, spatially and contextually separated—a trance dancer being carried in a procession, a man looking up at an airplane, a servant greeting his master in a play, the painting of a dream—may all be relevant to a single discussion; the same emotional thread may run through them.[149]

In one sequence of photographs, depicting a mother-child interaction, they suggested that Balinese mothers seemed to arouse their children's expectations for affection and then, when approached, would either spurn them by suddenly becoming uninterested, or by turning to play with someone else's baby. "The child responds to [a mother's] advances either with affection or temper, but the response falls into a vacuum. In Western cultures, such sequences lead to small climaxes of love or anger, but not so in Bali. At the moment when the child throws its arms around the mother's neck or bursts into tears, the mother's attention wanders."[150] They detected this pattern of arousal and frustration in courtship, or djoget, dancing, in which pairs of dancers continually separate from each other "pirouetting off in opposite directions, until they arrive at another momentary face-to-face encounter."[151] Indeed, they reproduced a picture of a dancer simultaneously "coquetting while fending off her partner with her hand."[152]*

They also observed that the Balinese taught dance by relying solely upon visual and kinaesthetic cues. Total physical pliancy was expected from a youth learning to dance. "A Balinese hand, if you hold it and manipulate the fingers, is perfectly limp like the hand of a monkey or of a corpse."[153] An adult teacher employed methods that Bateson and Mead called "muscular rote,"[154] either guiding the child-pupil by example, or else by having him marionette the choreography while holding and moving the child's limp limbs.[155] Out of this repeated experience and out of numerous others like it, they concluded that Balinese children were led to construe their position in the world as deeply passive. Approaching a sort of naturalist's behaviorism, Bateson abstracted the wider notion that "an individual's character structure, his attitude toward himself and his interpretations of experience are conditioned not only by what he learns, but also by the methods of learning. If he is brought up in habits of rote learning, his character will be profoundly different from what would result from habits of learning by insight."[156]

In a festschrift for Radcliffe-Brown ten years later, Bateson explained why stasis, and not schismogenesis, typified human relations in Balinese society.[157] Infants' emotions were regularly aroused there but were then frustrated by their parental figures. This pattern also appeared in numerous contexts throughout the culture and it shaped a social system in which schismogenic interaction was muted so as to support these child-rearing patterns. Balinese only rarely engaged in escalating combat or rivalry. They avoided escalating domination or submission. In many ways, life there inverted Iatmul and Western rationality in which held values—money, affect, prestige—were maximized. In Bali, men lived frugally but not acquisitively. They avoided climaxes in sequences of love and hate and tended to withdraw into vacancy—to be "away" —especially after some definite activity.[158] Even death was celebrated without a strong sense of finality. "A system of ends and purposes," in which values were maximized and opposed, would be unnatural to a Balinese, just as their passivity seemed to be life without "punctuation," to a Westerner.[159] The premise which underpinned dynamic social theory,

---

* "This photograph," Bateson noted, "was obtained by entering the stage and dancing to the djoget [preadolescent dancer], camera in hand, as if photographing were a courtship act." (GB, M. Mead, *Balinese Character*, p. 172.)

namely that men everywhere possess a "tendency to involve themselves in cumulative interaction," was not disconfirmed by the Balinese case. [160] Balinese babies were ready to do so until they learned appropriate cultural restraint. Rather, as a counterinstance of nonschismogenic society, Bali was evidence that escalating processes would occur but for the modification or inhibition exerted by culturally integrated childhood training.

XI. Deus ex Machina: Cybernetics

After the Reichstag fire in February 1933, Leo Szilard, the Hungarian nuclear physicist and biologist, realized the hopelessness of his situation. Leaving Germany, eventually to settle in the United States, he took "a train from Berlin to Vienna . . . close to the first of April . . . [which] was empty. The same train, in the next day, was overcrowded, [and] was stopped at the frontier. The people had to get out and everybody was interrogated by the Nazis."[1] Szilard's reminiscence is only a hint of the dramatic circumstances under which scores of European academics abandoned their native countries. Many intellectuals came to America and flourished, having been "saved" from destruction. In a sense, it was as if a sort of salvation or rebirth occurred—some minds were liberated, and there ensued a surging of innovative thinking and activity. But as the American historians Donald Fleming and Bernard Bailyn have noted, the matter of successful adjustment to the new society involved more than a sea change. Even before they were forced from homes and universities, many transplanted continentals were already on the fringes of society and were prepared to continue this way in a new country. Indeed, some attributed their emergent creativity to a flexibility bestowed on members of the periphery. Whatever the case, once they had arrived, their problems of identity—personal and professional—became crucial. The Austrian sociologist, Paul F. Lazarsfeld, for instance, has discussed his own role in establishing the Bureau of Applied Social Research at Columbia University, in terms of having been a "marginal man who [was] part of two cultures." Referring to himself, Lazarsfeld described the intellectual immigrant as living "under cross-pressures that move[d] him in a number of directions. According to his gifts and external circumstances he [could] become a revolutionary, a surrealist, a criminal."[2]

There were exceptions, of course, who were incapable or unwilling to adjust—like the German sociologist T. W. Adorno, who was offended by commercialism in the society and by vacuous empiricism in the thought. But even Adorno, who returned to Germany after the war, said he felt enriched by American sensibilities, of which he wrote in retrospect.

> In spite of all social criticism and all consciousness of the primacy of economic factors, the fundamental importance of the mind—Geist—was ... a dogma, self-evident to me from the very beginning. The fact that this was not a foregone conclusion, I learned in America, where no reverential silence in the presence of everything intellectual prevailed, as it did in Central and Western Europe ... inclined the intellect toward critical self-scrutiny. This particularly affected the European presupposition of musical cultivation in which I was immersed.[3]

If the emigrés were experienced visitors, American intellectuals were willing hosts. One need only cite the hungry greeting that met Continental psychoanalysts and physicists in this country,[4] to indicate the readiness American colleagues demonstrated for European knowledge. More concretely, efforts were made to endow positions, to found new institutes and universities, to establish fellowships and, as if recapitulating the dispersal and reconvergence that was occurring on a larger transcontinental scale, interdisciplinary communication was established in the form of conferences which were widely attended.

Surveying prewar immigration to the United States, Laura Fermi, the physicist's wife, has stated the truism that British emigrés differed from their European counterparts.[5] Emigration from Europe developed from political and racial persecution, whereas expatriation from England occurred largely according to individual, peacetime preference. British intellectuals never suffered mass dismissals and had less difficulty in finding employment at home. Without gross language problems and with common traditions, they were confronted by a different, more subtle, sort of adjustment. Resettlement in the United States came more easily for them and was more likely to end in repatriation if the opportunity arose. Still, both the continental immigrant and the British expatriate shared the daily promptings of life in a new place—promptings which demanded a myriad of new definitions.

During July 1940, two teenage girls, Philomena Guillebaud and her sister Florence, arrived from Cambridge, England, to join Greogry and Margaret at their summer residence near Holderness, New Hampshire. This was during the first of a number of wartime summers which the Batesons spent together with the family of the psychologist Lawrence K. Frank, whose big house on Perry Street in Greenwich Village they all shared during the winters. At Holderness, the two families were often joined by neighboring vacationers and their children—the sociologists Robert and Helen Lynd, the psychologists Gardiner and Lois Murphy—and there were visitors such as the psychoanalyst Erik H. Erikson and his wife Joan, and the anthropologist Ruth Benedict. The two Guillebaud girls had now come to stay. A combination of past wartime experience and current political anxieties had led their parents, the Cambridge economist Claude Guillebaud and his wife Pauline, to entrust the children to the care of Philomena's expatriate, anthropologist godfather for the duration of the war.* Philomena Guillebaud remembered that their household consisted of Gregory, Margaret, and Cathy, who was then eight months, their English nanny, who doubled as cook, and [her teenage] daughter. "It was a weird house. It had seventeen rocking chairs in the living room. The whole family was always going around with bruises on shins from the rocking chairs. The house was beautifully located on the edge of a lake."[6] Idyllic recollections accumulated of these summers. While gamboling children amused themselves, parents pursued interdisciplinary research which, increasingly, was war-related. Writing to Beatrice after seven months in the United States, Gregory was clearly enjoying this community.

> The worries of parenthood swirl around us.... So far everybody is mixed happily enough with everybody else. The Guillebaud children are very popular with the other children around in the four neighboring households of psychologists, etc., and are a source of amazement to the parents. Nobody in America had ever dreamt that children could be so nicely mannered. Yes, but that has its drawbacks. If the Guillebauds appear so "butter-wouldn't-melt-in-the-mouthy" to the neighboring children, what will be the effect of the neighboring children on the Guillebauds? Will all the beautiful manners disappear? Or will [they] simply turn up their noses at the foolish neighbors, with the inevitable loss of friends their own age? The only answer to the difficulty seems to be constant rubbing of cultural and national differences, with the general implication that there are other ways of living, and that each way has its beauties and awkwardnesses. And fortunately the Guillebauds have seen enough of Europe for this lesson to take root.[7]

---

*Philomena Guillebaud recalled how her family had gotten to know the Batesons: "My parents were pretty well midway between Gregory's parents and Gregory [in age]. I don't know how they met. But my mother talked about her recollections of Gregory as a gangly thirteen year old. Margaret has told me that Gregory's father was very much attracted to my mother in an entirely Platonic way. This did not please Gregory's mother.... [W.B.], who was an amateur painter, and quite a good one, did a portrait of my mother at one point. The way I got the story initially was that Beatrice resented this whole thing so much that she tore it up when Gregory's father died. But that isn't the whole story. Apparently, the painting was offered to my mother by Beatrice and my mother in a peculiarly obtuse act said, "No, thank you." Anyhow, they were friends for a long time, certainly." (Personal communication: 13 January 1976.)

Margaret also puzzled about and was somewhat concerned by the behavior of their young guests. Gregory, she assumed, would be of no help understanding them because having grown up without sisters, he could know nothing about the conventions of British child rearing as they applied to girls.

> They were very inexplicable to me. My notion was I'd give them materials to fix up their rooms. All they did was take things out of the room they didn't want and put them in the hall. They had no idea of the kind of initiative that American children do. It worried me what we were developing them into. They had this trivial type of conversation, schoolgirl, giggly, funny type of conversation, that I found unbearable. They had no idea of what to do at a dinner table with adults. I made a rule that if we mentioned anything they didn't understand and they didn't ask, they paid a fine, and if we challenged [them] and they knew, we paid a fine.[8]

Philomena Guillebaud also recalled these methods which were meant to draw the two of them if not into the thought, at least into the language of the adults.

> We behaved as we had been brought up to behave in a good, quiet "children-should-be-seen-and-not-heard" fashion, and [they] got exasperated by this tendency of ours to tune out of adult conversation. . . . Margaret and Gregory, I don't recall which one, instituted a system of fining us a nickel if a word was used in conversation of which we didn't know the meaning and hadn't asked. I remember asking what [was] "anal neurosis," and what [was] "schismogenesis." Well . . . we only got a quarter a week in the way of allowance, so the nickels mounted up. We began to pay attention and listen. It was a marvelous idea. But one of the things I noticed was that Margaret and Gregory were observing us. This was partly Margaret's fascination with seeing, you know, she hadn't had much exposure to the English, she was learning things about Gregory, about the way children were brought up in England, from watching us. There were many, many cases when I would catch Margaret and Gregory sort of cocking an eyebrow at each other because one of us had said something which was interesting. We were sort of subjects.[9]

Subjects, and colleagues too. Margaret and Gregory included these children in their anthropology. Through the summer of 1942, the Balinese material was being analyzed and Philomena remembered, "that every evening after supper, we children set up the projector and got out whatever the next series of films was. We loved it. There was no question, I think, if we had been bored, nobody would have cussed if we'd come away. As far as I was concerned, it was very difficult to believe that I had never been to Bajoeng Gede."[10] There were also evenings of play—charades, amateur theatricals (Gregory played Hamlet one summer), word and mathematical games—in which children were made to feel involved with adults on as equal a footing as possible. Gregory particularly took time to invent mathematical conundrums and to enthrall children with his knowledge of the local ecology.[11] "The life of the young in this country, and somewhat too, in England seems rather empty," he wrote his mother. "My own picture of what one does in childhood is so much colored by collecting insects, etc., etc., that I find a difficulty in believing that life can be filled in any other way. And perhaps 'all play and no work may make Jack a dull boy.'"[12] Anatol W. Holt, a systems theorist and mathematician, recalled Bateson's attention to him as a boy of sixteen. They spoke regularly during the winter of 1942–43 "about the whole range of Gregory's subjects—biology, mathematics. . . . Mainly what happened was Gregory was partly witness to and partly midwife to, one might say, my beginning to think earnestly. . . . He shoved a lot of books into my head, and a lot of conversation, too."[13]

Child-rearing patterns comprised both their science and their lives, Margaret Mead seems to have said in her autobiography. "Bringing up Cathy was an intellectual as well as an emotionally exciting adventure."[14] When their daughter celebrated her first birthday in December 1940, Gregory conveyed to his mother something of the side of their love for the child which was expressed in observation and analysis.

> Still she shows no sign of being able to speak—she understands a fair number of words and is, in general, well oriented to life—but still has used no single word. If you say, "Where is the ball?" she will stop what she is doing and look at you fixedly for a moment—then patter off into the next room and get the ball and bring it to you. . . . I imagine that walking and talking always conflict with each other to some extent—that whichever is learned first will delay learning of the other. Since when you can walk there is less need to be able to talk—and vice versa.[15]

One month later, there was further progress.

> Your grandchild—is gradually beginning to accept certain limitations of the "life-space" —she hardly ever now takes a book off the shelves, and only hesitantly grabs for packets of cigarettes. And this is nearly as basic a change in attitude as that implied in learning to walk—still she has no words in her mouth—but recognitions of words increases. Also recognition of voice. And use of gesture for purposes of communication.[16]

Gregory became disturbed "almost immediately" about how the grammar of the Appalachian nurse would affect their infant.[17] As a result, Margaret remembered feeling compelled to "find a trained English nanny, who would fit [his] . . . picture of how a child should be brought up."[18] When she did begin to speak, Gregory catalogued the accomplishment:

> Your granddaughter begins to talk—definitely to use words meaningfully; though not very consistently— "baby" means any sort of representation of human beings, from her own image in mirror via dolls to photographs of President Roosevelt in newspaper. Other words— "pretty," "all gone," "daddy" (meaning still obscure), "book," "duck," "bye-bye." And a constant flow of imitation talk—and she is definitely puzzled when she does not understand something that is said to her.[19]

He sent his mother photographs, of course. There was one of mother and daughter, which evidently caused Beatrice to remark that she liked Cathy's hands. They were like her father's, the alcoholic surgeon, the beauty of whose hands had so charmed students. Margaret had nice hands too, "though small."[20]

By the end of Beatrice Bateson's life, which came in the spring of 1941, the spirit of the woman had succumbed neither to solitude nor to the world situation. From the birth of British genetics on through the decline of that discipline's founding member, she embroidered especially ornate tapestries. After W. B.'s death, Beatrice continued to weave and was again composing short stories, the delight of her youth. On the whole, without her husband, she led an active life of avocation. She did some parish work—that ancestor of social service—visited with friends, and traveled extensively. About a year before World War II began, she asked an interned German couple, who were professional musicians, to live with her.

In June 1940, soon after the fall of France and the surrender of Belgium, Gregory and Margaret invited Beatrice to come over to New York and live with them. "She said, 'Quite well! May be useful! Will not behave like those Belgians!'[21] Her refusal meant that Beatrice never met her granddaughter." In February 1941, she suffered a stroke which weakened her corpulent and by now elderly body. At the time, though, Nora Barlow informed Gregory that his mother was recovering her strength and was not expecting to see him. Beatrice spent the rest of the winter bedridden, apparently regaining her health. But this was momentary—a second stroke occurred, and she died in the middle of April. According to Margaret Mead, Gregory's response to the news of his mother's death "was gentle and compassionate. He said, 'She tried so hard to be good.'"[22] The war limited international travel and for the first time since his immigration, more than a year before, Bateson was gainfully and enthusiastically employed. He did not attend his mother's funeral.

Bateson undertook several short-term projects during the first years of the war. With Mead and other social scientists such as Geoffrey Gorer, Ruth Benedict, and Lawrence K. Frank, he volunteered to devise methods for safeguarding Allied domestic morale, under the auspices of Arthur Upham Pope's Committee for National Morale.[23] Just before Beatrice died, Margaret had given her a glimpse of her son's immersion in this group's work.

> Gregory has been working fifteen hours a day, really giving all that his training and experience and mind and values could give to something which we feel may have a definitive connection with the outcome of the war. The task of mobilizing attitudes in this country so as to retain full vigor and avoid the paralyzing apathy producing effects of propaganda is an enormous one. He has been in the center of the planning. Everything that he hoped he would have a chance to do when he came back has worked out as if by magic. Right now he is dead tired out, living on a thin frayed edge of excitement for he has had very little experience of big heavy pressure offices and lots of tiring conferences and deliberations.[24]

Part of the committee's analytic effort concerned the general problems of applying science to society. Mead had asked the question "Could deliberate social planning be reconciled with the democratic ideal of individual autonomy?" Historically, it had been a recurrent issue, Bateson wrote, in "Social planning and the concept of deutero-learning," which was a paper given to the Second Symposium of the Conference on Science, Philosophy, and Religion. But in 1942, the quality of mind which was ready to use the social sciences freely in order to achieve a planned blueprint of society seemed, in essence, to be totalitarian. The implication followed that the war itself opposed, inter alia, conceptions about the use of knowledge in determining human order.

> It is hardly an exaggeration to say that this war is ideologically about just this— the role of the social sciences. Are we to reserve the techniques of a few planning, goal-oriented, and power-hungry individuals, to whom the instrumentality of science makes a natural appeal? Now that we have the techniques, are we, in cold blood, going to treat people as things? ... The problem is one of very great difficulty because we, as scientists, are deeply soaked in habits of instrumental thought—those of us, at least, for whom science is a part of life, as well as a beautiful and dignified abstraction.[25]

Bateson's caution expressed one side of a more far reaching ambivalence in his life. As he participated in the application of anthropology and science in general to society, he condemned it as peripheral to research and dangerous to the human spirit. The communist politics of natural scientists in England had not attracted him during the 1930s. In the early war years, though, he was committed to making direct policy contributions. At one point, indeed, there was hope that a Morale Service might be instituted at the federal level, and the prospect of working in Washington excited him. Nonetheless, conception was the more stimulating task; and despite avowals that he meant to do so, Bateson's work on national character said little about safeguarding the morale of wartime American society.

Instead he debated the pertinence of the concept of national character to modern nations. It was argued that no uniformity of experience existed in such politically contrived states. Such countries were rather diversities of sex, ethnic, and occupational differentiation which had considerable deviance from norms and cultural flux. Bateson dismissed all challenges to the validity of the idea of national character by referring to a familiar holistic assumption. Both individuals and communities were necessarily organized units "such that all [their] 'parts' or 'aspects' [were] mutually modifiable and mutually interacting."[26] The knotted varieties of differentiation in contemporary and traditional societies could be unraveled into holistic and systemic interrelations. Although individuals or groups who were engaged in on-going contact might display different behavior, they still had to be organized in some mutually relevant manner. "The boy on whom English public-school education does not take," Bateson noted, "even though the original roots of his deviance were laid in some 'accidental' traumatic incident, is reacting to the public school system."[27] Iatmul males, although they might behave gaudily and loudly, did so especially in front of attentive, restrained Iatmul females. "The significant point is that the habit system of each sex cogs into the habit system of the other; that the behavior of each promotes the habits of the other."[28] A sense of unitary differentiation was the crux of this view. Even the seemingly infinite heterogeneity of modern, urban society had presumed integration. Bateson ventured that Ripley's "Believe-It-or-Not," was an expression of a holistic "world made up of ... disconnected quiz-bits."[29] This was evidence that heterogeneity itself might contribute to character formation and maintenance.

As long as sufficient time was permitted to elapse so that habits of behavior could form between groups, the ethnically synthetic quality of modern nations would not hinder national character analysis. "The motifs of relationship"[30] between individuals and groups, however opposed, were to be rendered as a binary unit. "We have to think of the individual ... as trained [for example] in dominance-submission, not in either dominance or submission."[31] This sort of integration, Bateson added, need not be binary. Three-tiered patterns of relationship were possible in which, for example, an intermediary executes discipline and instruction to a subordinate on behalf of the superordinate. An "instance of this threefold pattern occurs in some great public schools (as in Charterhouse), where the authority is divided between the quieter, more polished, intellectual leaders (monitors) and the rougher, louder, athletic leaders (captain of football, head of long room, etc.), who have the duty of seeing to it that the 'fags' run when the monitor calls."[32] Similarly, nannies in English upper-middle-class families were responsible for issuing parental sanctions to children. "This means that the patterns of dominance and submission are, in some measure, seen, not as interpersonal but rather as being in accord with an impersonal external structure of the universe."[33]

Bateson contrasted complementary roles (in his usage of the term) in English and American family relations to suggest generalized themes of national character. In upper- and middle-class English families, dominant parents preside over submissive children* (modified by a nurse). They succor their dependent young until they send them off to boarding school. At meals, children are expected to listen quietly. Adults are exhibitionist to their offsprings' spectatorship. By contrast, in the American middle class, parental dominance and their children's submission are comparatively minimized. Parents succor their dependent offspring. But instead of performing in front of them, American parents have their young do the entertaining. "This pattern differs from the English not only in the reversal of the spectatorship-exhibitionism roles, but also the content of what is exhibited. The American child is encouraged by his parents *to show off his independence*."[34] While the English child will be weaned from without by being sent away to boarding school, his American counterpart is continuously weaned from within the family by the help of his parents' spectatorship.† Bateson suggested that the tangle of accusation and cross-cultural misinterpretation between allies— Englishmen thought that Americans tended to swagger boastfully while Americans viewed Englishmen as haughty and aloof—was based in these

---

*"Children kneele to aske blessing of Parents in England," said John Donne, "but where else?" (J. Donne quoted in "Marriage among the English nobility," L. Stone, in *The Family, Its Structures and Functions*, ed. R. Coser., p. 176.)

†Mead recently wrote that this "specific formulation grew out of observations of our two-year-old daughter, the behavior of her English nurse, parallel observations of two English children who came to live with us during the war, and discussions between Geoffrey Gorer, Gregory Bateson and myself in the winter of 1941–42 about Anglo-American differences." (M. Mead, "End-linkage: a tool for cross-cultural analysis," in *About Bateson*, ed. J. Brockman, p. 141.)

reversals and differences in family relations. Exhibitionism in England, that is, was "end-linked" to dominance, whereas in the United States, it was "end-linked" to submission. Bateson, abstracting from autobiography, viewed the confusion this way.

> The Englishman in a performing role (the parent at breakfast, the newspaper editor, the political spokesman, the lecturer, or what not) assumes that he is also in a dominant role—that he can decide in accordance with vague, abstract standards what sort of performance to give—and the audience can "take it or leave it." His own arrogance he sees either as "natural" or mitigated by his humility in the face of abstract standards. Quite unaware that his behavior could conceivably be regarded as a comment upon his audience, he is, on the contrary, aware only of behaving in the performer's role, as he understands that role. But the American does not see it thus. To him, the "arrogant" behavior of the Englishman appears to be directed *against* the audience, in which case the implicit invocation of some abstract standard appears only to add insult to injury.[35]

Conversely, what seemed like swagger to English eyes was a child's appeal to a parental audience, ex hypothesi, a crucial source of esteem to Americans. "The American, when he boasts, is looking for approval of his upstanding independence; but the naive Englishman interprets this behavior as a bid for some sort of dominance or superiority."[36]*

---

*When, in the summer of 1943, Margaret Mead went to lecture in England on behalf of the American government's Office of War Information, she used Bateson's analysis. "By a little careful interviewing in each new area in Britain, I could get verbatim, and therefore acceptable, statements of British objections [to American character]. 'The trouble with the Americans is that when they are good at something they say so.' 'The trouble with Americans is that they talk so much about what they are going to do; we don't talk, we just do it' (from the Scots). I could then rely upon the lecture situation, itself one in which the exhibitionistic role of the lecturer and the spectatorship role of the audience was defined, to provide me with additional illustrative material. I could quote from the chairman who, in presenting me, putatively in the paternal role on a British stage to a great tired audience who had come out in the black out on a freezing Sunday in Scotland, said, 'Be as kind to the audience as you can Dr. Mead'; or I could refer to the whole institution of the 'vote of thanks,' in which the British audience, after sitting docile and respectful while the lecturer plays Father, re-establishes the balance by the paternalistic tone in which the proposer of the vote of thanks addresses the now seated lecturer."

The formulation was again in extensive use between 1947 and 1951 by anthropologists working in the Columbia University project, Research in Contemporary Cultures, which was financed by the Navy and employed some 120 people working on seven cultures (China, Czechoslovakia, the East European Jewish shtetl, France, Poland, pre-Soviet Great Russia, and Syria). (M. Mead, "Applications of end-linkage formulations to Anglo-American relations in World War II," in *The Study of Culture at a Distance*, ed., M. Mead and R. Metraux, p. 381.)

Underlying the few suggestions for influencing national morale Bateson did make was the naturalist's premise that intentional application of knowledge ought to be scrupulously consistent with freely evolved patterns of character. "It is not sensible," he wrote at the time, "to encourage a donkey to go up hill by offering him raw meat, nor will a lion respond to grass."[37] If American children display independence before their parents, then Bateson thought that "a certain bubbling up of self-appreciation is ... perhaps an essential ingredient of American ... strength."[38] In accordance with Americans' tendency to dualize the world, enemies ought to be represented in terms of a single, hostile entity. Further, as both Englishmen and Americans respond most energetically to symmetrical stimulation (tit for tat), Allied military defeat ought to be widely publicized, so as to activate reciprocal belligerence and vitality.

In conjunction with Margaret Mead, Lawrence K. Frank, and the anthropologist Edwin Embree, the Institute for Intercultural Studies was established early in the war, to combine a policy orientation with national character research. As Mead put it, their group was trying to relate "cultural regularities in the behavior of members of nation-states" to indigenous child-rearing patterns.[39] The point, in part, was to produce ethnography of enemy life. They inaugurated studies of "culture-at-a-distance," in which techniques were developed to yield data normally available at first hand to the resident fieldworker. In one project, highly educated German and Austrian immigrants "played a double-role [as informants], relating parts of [their] own life history and then commenting upon it from the standpoint of [their] own scientific discipline."[40] In another, methods were improvised for eliciting data from fictional films. Funded by the New York Museum of Modern Art, Bateson developed an analysis of the Nazi propaganda movie, *Hitlerjunge Quex* (1933), which was, according to Mead, one of the first efforts "by a cultural anthropologist to apply anthropological techniques to the examination of ... film."[41]

Like myth, a film was the production of a native group made with an eye to popular appeal, and could be therefore a revealing datum of national character. The analysis Bateson called for would be a two-step operation. After identifying themes of behavior from a film, these had to be confirmed or disconfirmed as culturally typical, from material gathered in interviews. "As usual in such research, the peculiarities of daily life and daydream are referred back to the family setting and especially to the position of the child in that setting."[42] From a meticulous study of *Hitlerjunge Quex,* Bateson developed a series of generalizations—about time perspectives and climax structure, about relations between Nazis and Communists, about family interaction, about the symbolisms of death and the knife—and related each to the film as a whole.

> There is clearly a rather close relationship between the hypnotic fascination that comes from staring at waves and that which comes from looking at spinning objects, and this relationship is probably another facet of the relationship we have already noted between Nazism and Nazi characterization of Communism. There is, however, an important difference between waves and spinning objects. Waves contain an illusion of progress, of forward movement, but spinning objects evidently get nowhere. It is possible that the waves used to characterize Nazism are related to the endless marching that has such great fascination for Nazis and which appears in almost every Nazi film. Only in its endlessness does this marching resemble the spinning of the symbols associated with Communism.[43]

Although the wartime situation somewhat obscured the internal organization of the social sciences, minimally it should still be said that the subdiscipline of "culture-and-personality" comprised the contemporary milieu within which Bateson was developing his thought. This was a group of American anthropologists, predominantly, who were infused with psychoanalytic insights and emphases—to the point that some critics took to calling the subject diaperology. During the 1930s and 1940s, students in this field attempted to tie symbolic aspects of culture (e.g., mythology, religion, etc.) to intrapsychic processes by the study of family life and socialization. Leading contributions came from Mead and Benedict, of course, and from Cora Dubois, Erik H. Erikson, Geoffrey Gorer, A. I. Hallowell, Abram Kardiner, Clyde Kluckhohn, and Eric Fromm.[44] Bateson firmly adhered to one of the premises underlying much of the work in this field, and recited it often during these years. "To the cultural anthropologist, man appears *not* mainly as a physiological mechanism, nor yet as a creature endowed with instinctive urges and innate patterns of response. He appears to us, above all, as a creature which *learns.* The face of human flexibility under environmental experience determines the main focus of our scientific attention."[45] In denying the role of instinct, Bateson disclosed something of his diffidence about Freudian psychoanalysis, however. The terminology of the theory seemed scientistic, given to false concreteness, and the somatic analogies of mental "energy," which had been derived from nineteenth-century physics, were to him inapplicable to mental process. "We may joke about the way misplaced concreteness abounds in every word of psychoanalytic writing," he wrote in 1940, "but in spite of all the muddled thinking that Freud started, psychoanalysis remains *the* outstanding contribution . . . to our understanding of the family—a monument to the importance and value of loose thinking."[46]*

To Bateson, the problem was rather to relate simple notions borrowed from elementary learning experiments to the conditioning of human world view. What sequences of stimulus and response distinguished learning by insight from Pavlovian learning? And, what sorts of assumptions were engendered in the experimental subject who undergoes the differing sequences?

> We are asking "how does the dog acquire a habit of punctuating or apperceiving the infinitely complex stream of events (including his own behavior) so that this stream appears to be made up of one type of short sequences rather than another?" Or, substituting the scientist for the dog, we might ask, "What circumstances determine that a given scientist will punctuate the stream of events so as to conclude that all is predetermined, while another will see the stream of events as so regular as to be susceptible of control?" Or again, on the same level of abstraction let us ask—and this question is very relevant to the promotion of democracy—"What circumstances promote that specific habitual phrasing of the universe which we call 'responsibility,' 'constructiveness,' 'energy,' 'passivity,' 'dominance,' and the rest?"[47]

Margaret Mead had introduced him to behaviorism during their fieldwork in Bali, and Bateson "reviewed a textbook by Hilgard and Marquis on learning theory in 1941."[48] But a conversation sparked him. Lawrence Frank mentioned a commonplace in the psychological laboratory—that an experimental subject will become a more efficient problem solver, in effect a "better" subject, in the course of undergoing repeated experiments. Bateson called this by-product process *learning to learn,* that is "the subject has acquired a habit of looking for contexts and sequences of one type rather than another."[49] He called any successfully completed task (such as pulling a lever) *proto-learning,* whereas *deutero-learning* designated progressively increasing facility in solving a series of experimental problems. The signs of disturbance a subject will display in cases of "experimental neurosis,"[50] when a previously rewarded behavior is then

---

*The psychoanalyst, Erik H. Erikson, who consulted with Mead and Bateson during the early 1940s about their work on children's play in Bali, recalled experiencing these attitudes. "I must say that I always felt very inferior to him, to Gregory. I have absolutely no solid training in logic, in natural science. And he is an excellently trained person. So when he was a little contemptuous of the whole psychoanalytic approach I felt of course, that I wasn't even much prepared as a psychoanalyst.... But, you know, it was bearable ... I envied Gregory very much." (Personal communication: 16 April 1976.)

punished or not rewarded when performed, was indication of the occurrence and force of deutero-learning. An animal, for example, may be trained to discriminate between some specified X and some specified Y. When the task is slowly made more difficult—the X and the Y are altered so that they resemble each other—the animal will appear unsettled. When discrimination becomes impossible, it will appear distressed, having deutero-learned to "expect" one sequence of stimulus and response which the experimenter has made irrelevant. The shaping of expectation about future learning which occurs simultaneous to any learning experience also seemed to occur in human settings. In psychoanalytic therapy, Bateson noted, a patient will have feelings and beliefs about his therapist (transference), which have been learned in sequences of relations with some significant other (usually a parent).

Experimental psychologists had distinguished at least four classes of learning context which would give rise to differences at the deutero-level: (1.) *Pavlovian* sequences in which an animal responds with behavior (e.g., salivation) to an unalterable conditioning stimulus (e.g., a bell) and is then rewarded; (2.) sequences of *instrumental reward* in which the conditioning response occurs after successful solution of the task (e.g., a maze); (3.) sequences of *instrumental avoidance* which are instigated by a definite stimulus (e.g., a bell) in response to which the animal must perform some preselected behavior or else be punished (e.g., shocked); and (4.) sequences of *serial* and *rote* learning in which the stimulus is the previous act of the subject. The issue was to encompass thematic human beliefs and attitudes in these formalized phrasings of the learning process. "I went to Frank Beach at the National Institute of Mental Health to ask for experiments of deutero-learning—after a lengthy explanation, Beach's conclusion was that they would be too difficult to construct and too risky for graduate students."[51]

The problem was that only spare indications of these relations were visible. If a child's training approximated Pavlovian methods, as in the Trobriand Islands, he might be limited to fatalistic interpretations and submissive behavior. "He would see all events as preordained and he would see himself as fated only to search for omens, not able to influence the course of events—able, at most, from his reading of the omens, to put himself in a properly receptive state, e.g., by salivation, before the inevitable happened."[52] By contrast, typical Balinese learning might be translated in terms of a combination of s-r sequences. Balinese child rearing utilized rote sequences of instrumental avoidance. "They see the world as dangerous, and themselves as avoiding by the endless rote behavior of ritual and courtesy, the ever-present risk of faux pas."[53] In Bali the means-end causation was therefore altered. Instead of expecting reward for the accomplishment of a task, they are rewarded by properly rehearsing the sequence itself. A Balinese child will learn to dance not for a future performance, but for an immediate satisfaction of eluding punishment by carrying out the sequence exactly. "It is the acrobat's enjoyment both of the thrill and of his virtuosity in avoiding disaster,"[54] was Bateson's sense of these feelings.

Professionally, the ideas into which Bateson dipped during the early war years were of only indirect relevance to immediate application. They were marginal to—although created in the midst of—policy concerns. That men were exquisitely capable of learning, and that the ways of learning seemed to affect their general attitudes suggested that society at large might be changed—were it based in a particular childhood experience. In Bali, for example, motivation had a means rather than a goal orientation which was instilled punitively. Gregory admired the attitude but withdrew at the source. In an atmosphere of applied anthropology, opinions such as these had an audience. "If the Balinese is kept busy and happy by a nameless, shapeless fear, not located in space or time, we might be kept on our toes by a nameless, shapeless, unlocated hope of enormous achievement."[55] This modification of instrumental reward would depend not upon actual accomplishment but upon hopeful anticipation of it.

> We have got to be like those few artists and scientists who work with this urgent sort of inspiration, the urgency that comes from feeling that great discovery, the answer to all our problems, or great creation, the perfect sonnet, is always only just beyond our reach, or like the mother of a child who feels that, provided she pay constant attention, there is a real hope that her child may be that infinitely rare phenomenon, a great and happy person.[56]

In the summer of 1943, like many anthropologists, Bateson went to work in Washington, D.C., for the Office of Strategic Services (O.S.S.) as a "psychological planner."[57] That office dispatched him to Southeast Asia, where he spent twenty months in Ceylon, India, Burma, and China. By his own accounts, he accomplished very little. The one activity which caught his interest, however, was operating a radio station aimed at undermining Japanese propaganda in Burma and Thailand. Studying its content, Bateson had translators engaging in small-scale symmetrical schismogenesis. "We listened to the enemy's nonsense and we professed to be a Japanese official station. Everyday we simply *exaggerated* what the enemy was telling people."[58] Upon his return to New York he gave Geoffrey Gorer the impression of being "very disturbed with the O.S.S. treatment of the natives. I think he felt that he was associated with a dishonest outfit."[59] Gregory described something of his experience to his mother's sisters, Hermia and Florence Durham.

Two years dully wasted in India and Ceylon, trying to introduce a few anthropological ideas into the U.S. intelligence service, relieved by a period of fieldwork in the Arakan [lower Burma, on the Bay of Bengal], getting native reactions to the Japanese occupation and returning British raj. Really this was my first considerable contact with highly educated native individuals in the British empire. The tops of Arakan society were all in retirement in a little village and I spent ten days with them—but oh dear—what a mess it is. Native supernaturalism all shot to pieces by materialism gathered from Oxford and Cambridge educations, and in its place a longing for some sort of supernatural structure. My old host brought me one morning two books— "perhaps there might be something in them—perhaps I would be interested—he did not know—but perhaps." One book was on astronomy, the other a collection of M. R. James ghost stories. The latter was sidelined to stress all those little paragraphs that the author puts into such stories to try to make them sound more "scientific."[60]

Throughout the United States during the war years, applied science and national service had taken precedence over family ties. Margaret and Gregory were separated intermittently since 1942, when she began to commute to Washington, D.C., with Ruth Benedict, to investigate American eating habits for the National Research Council. Their marriage, whose alias, it may be recalled, had been professional convenience, had slowly given way to just that—which is not to imply that it substituted in productivity what it lacked in feeling. Still Mead's inexorable fecundity and force of character no longer bolstered Bateson's intellectual and personal sprawl, as it had when they were both focused in the same research.* Gregory returned from Asia during the winter of 1945, to live with Margaret and Cathy in Lawrence Frank's Perry

---

*In response to a question about the different levels of intensity at which he and his wife worked, Gregory said: "My procedure for analyzing fictional films [is one] in which you go to the film and you go as if you were going to the flics on a Saturday evening and you either enjoy it or don't enjoy it, without any intention of analysis at all. You do not analyze film for three days. Then you sit down and make a genealogical diagram, so to speak, of the plot. You go back to the theatre and arrange to come in in the middle—so you see the back end of the film before the front. Having seen the back end you go off quietly and start to consider what in the back end has determined the front because causation in the film goes both ways. Then you go back and see the front half. But the point I'm making now, is that you do not start to analyze it until after you've enjoyed it—let it sink in. Now Margaret is much more eager than that. She doesn't forget anything—a total recall. I am, on the whole, inclined to think it is a good thing to forget most of what one says, because it is an automatic way of deciding what is important. You don't have to work at finding what is important. Let the unconscious decide for you—or the forgetting mechanism, whatever it is. Is that part of the unconscious?" (Personal communication: 27 December 1972.)

Street household. But this arrangement did not last long. A year later, he established himself independently on Staten Island and was divorced (by Mead) in 1950. Their marriage, Mead has said in retrospect, was an incomparable model "of what anthropological fieldwork can be like, even if the model includes the kind of extra intensity in which a lifetime is condensed into a few short years."[61]

Compounding the collapse of his marriage and the depression which followed O.S.S. service, Bateson had "no idea of what he wanted to do next."[62]* At the age of forty-two, he initiated and underwent face-to-face psychotherapy in order "to sort of have a look at things."[63] He found these sessions pleasant and informative. When I asked how his view of English exhibitionism-spectatorship applied to an English anthropologist's relations with his subjects, Bateson answered that he did not know, but he realized that this particular relationship was an important one in his life.

> When I was undergoing what was vaguely called my psychoanalysis, I had a dream, which was a very important dream in the analysis, as important as the one with my father pushing Martin up the ladder. Now that was an old one—it was ten years before I was in analysis. But I'd written it down at the time and used it in analysis. The dream [was that] I have committed a sin, [and have] some Kafkaesque unidentified guilt. I am guilty. And because I am guilty I am condemned and taken to the place of my execution where I may speech [sic] to my assembled friends and fans and relatives, in a sort of Renaissance manner of speech, you know, on the way to the guillotine. And it's a very noble speech. None of it probably even in words at all in the dream—but the fact that it is a noble speech. And at the end of the speech, I bow, and I say, "Excuse me, if I dramatize myself a little," and wake up roaring with laughter.[64]

By contrast to his anthropological colleagues in England—Evans-Pritchard, Firth, Fortes, Shapera, and others—who were achieving professorial rank in the postwar years, Bateson held only temporary, interstitial posts. Neither

---

*He was involved in the postwar efforts of atomic physicists to instill awareness in the American public of the dangers of the bomb. Bateson was also concerned with enlisting their contributions to the social sciences. Pressing social problems of the globe "created by the wholesale application of the sciences," however compelling and chronic, found the social scientist ignorant and inadequate, in need of cross-fertilization. The physicist was especially prepared to help, for epistemological reasons. Like the field anthropologist, he knew to include the observer "within the sphere of relevance of the observation," in systems of reciprocal causation. Further, the problem of purpose in behavior, with which social scientists had long struggled, recently had been clarified by electronic physicists in discussion of circular feedback systems. (GB, "Physical thinking and social problems," *Science* 103 [1946]:717.)

Naven nor *Balinese Character* had stimulated great interest within American anthropology. He was awarded a Guggenheim Fellowship. Then, in 1947, while a book on theory of schismogenesis did not get written, he taught anthropology courses as a visiting professor at the New School for Social Research. At the New School in New York, John H. Weakland, a young chemical engineer and sinologist by avocation, introduced himself to Bateson, mentioning that he was interested in the possibility of changing careers. Weakland remembered that Bateson received this idea quite cordially.

> I brought up the subject rather gingerly, since most people felt "My God! Why the hell you going to get out of engineering and go into social science!?" He was very pleased to talk to me ... I found out later that he'd got the mistaken idea that as an engineer I was a lot more mathematical than I was and I might be able to clarify a few things he was hearing about through his connections with the cybernetic movement.[65]

As a teacher, Weakland recalled that Bateson tended toward both the dramatic and the abstract.

> We had a sample [in class] of an anthropologist's interviewing a live informant to attempt to gather data of the culture from which he came, to try to attempt to make something out of it. The informant's name was Gregory Bateson and the culture he represented was Cambridge University, a very peculiar culture. The whole class was interviewing. ... I remember he played the role essentially of an ordinary Cambridge student of the time, not helping us, by doing any of the analysis himself, but just giving responses. ... So that curiously the whole thing was an interesting combination of, and typical for Gregory, down to the ground matters of observation on the one hand, and very general high level ideas, on the other.[66]

The following academic year through June 1948, he held a visiting professorship in anthropology at Harvard. Evidently, Bateson did little, as it were, to institutionalize himself there. Mead mentioned that he had spent too much time with students, "goldbricking."[67] He sensed that colleagues thought his courses were inappropriate. On the other hand, he enjoyed them. "A damn good exam, I set those kids. ... The lectures were on Bali and Iatmul—and the differences between them. The exam contained three parts. ... You had to so design your answers to all three parts to make a single thesis. Part one was three factual questions about Bali; part two was three factual questions about Iatmul; part three was four theoretical questions. You had to use the facts you had adduced in parts one and two to support a position in part three. That was all. You should have seen how the goats and the sheep fell apart when faced with that one!"[68]

Amid rumors that he advocated psychoanalysis for all anthropologists, Bateson was not rehired at Harvard. He is fond of denying the story: "I did not say this, and I don't think I ever believed it, but if they thought this was a good reason for dropping me, then I was lucky to be dropped."[69] The anthropologist Alfred L. Kroeber, then a visiting professor in Cambridge, had his office next to Bateson's in the Peabody Museum. Seeing that he needed a job, Kroeber contacted the Swiss psychiatrist Jurgen Ruesch, M.D., of the Langley Porter Neuropsychiatric Clinic in San Francisco, California. Ruesch was initiating a study of psychiatric communication and had a lectureship available in medical anthropology. He hired Bateson to fill this position for the beginning of 1949.

In Cambridge, Massachusetts, during the 1930s, the Mexican physiologist Arturo Rosenblueth conducted an informal interdisciplinary seminar on methodology with a group of young scientists from Massachusetts Institute of Technology and the Harvard Medical School. Norbert Wiener, the American mathematician who participated, recalled the conviction which he shared with Rosenblueth "that the most fruitful areas for the growth of the sciences were those which had been neglected as a no-man's-land between the various established fields."[70] Little came of their hope until World War II, when Wiener, in collaboration with the American computer engineer Julian Bigelow, began investigating the mathematics of self-regulation in antiaircraft missiles (servomechanisms). This machinery contained internal controls, or governors. By measurement of the angle between the occurring direction and that of the target sought, the projectile used the margin of error to adjust its path. "When we desire a motion to follow a given pattern," Wiener wrote some years afterward, "the difference between this pattern and the actually performed motion is used as a new input to cause the part regulated to move in such a way as to bring its motion closer to that given by the pattern."[71] The study of guided (purposive) missiles suggested the possibility that both machines and organisms might be subsumed within a single mathematical theory of "behavior." In 1943, together with the physiologist Rosenblueth, Wiener and Bigelow published a small paper, "Behavior, purpose and teleology,"[72] announcing their consensus that mutual communication of *error* between the ideal and the actual, called "feedback," was pivotal to the theoretical understanding of all voluntary or purposeful behavior.

At this point, approximately, other scientists, attracted by the overarching quality of the framework and by the new conception of purpose, expressed interest in self-regulatory mechanisms: the Hungarian mathematician John von Neumann, the Mexican physiologist Lorenté de No, the American mathematical logician Walter Pitts, the American neurophysiologist Warren S. McCulloch, M.D., the anthropologists Gregory Bateson and Margaret Mead, the American psychologist Lawrence K. Frank, and the American psychoanalyst Lawrence S. Kubie. They all gathered initially in May 1942, when the Josiah Macy, Jr., Foundation* sponsored a two-day conference entitled Cerebral Inhibition. They were convened by the American neurologist and psychiatrist, Frank Fremont-Smith, M.D., who represented the Macy Foundation. Official accounts described the participants as sharing "an interest in the physiological mechanism underlying the phenomena of conditioned reflex."[73] Bateson recalled, however, that the brunt of the meeting was "on hypnosis. 'Cerebral Inhibition' was a respectable word for hypnosis!" Nonetheless, there was informal discussion of the Wiener-Bigelow-Rosenblueth paper. "Most of what was said about 'feedback' was said over lunch."[74] Bateson left for Asia soon afterward, much taken with what he had heard. "While I was overseas. . .bored and frustrated, I occasionally comforted myself by thinking about the properties of closed self-corrective circuits."[75]

At Princeton in 1944, a second meeting was held, attended by engineers, physiologists, and mathematicians. The excitement felt by the members of this diverse group led one of them, Warren McCulloch, to arrange another conference for the spring of 1946. The original conferees were primarily concerned with feedback processes "in" the human nervous system, but now McCulloch and Fremont-Smith beckoned others of wider interests: the English ecologist G. Evelyn Hutchinson, the German biologist Heinrich Kluever, the German psychologist Kurt Lewin, the American philosopher F. S. C. Northrup, the American information theorist Claude E. Shannon, the American learning theorist Donald G. Marquis, and the German engineer Heinz von Foerster. "The idea ... [was] to get together a group of modest size," Wiener recalled in 1948, which would include some twenty participants from various disciplines, "and to hold them together for successive days in all-day series of informal papers, discussions, and meals together, until they had the opportunity to thrash out their differences and to make progress in thinking along the same lines."[76] This group met biannually in New York

---

*The Josiah Macy, Jr., Foundation was endowed by the shipping and oil fortunes of a Quaker family of colonial Britons, who emigrated to the United States in the seventeenth century, establishing ties with Standard Oil in the nineteenth. Herself in ill-health, Kate Macy Ladd became a medical philanthropist. She endowed the Macy Foundation in 1930, specifying that it be oriented around knowledge relevant "to such special problems in medical sciences, medical arts, and medical education as require for their solution studies and efforts in correlated fields ... such as biology and the social sciences." (The Josiah Macy, Jr., Foundation, *A Review of Activities: 1930–55*, p. 5.)

until 1949, and then on an annual basis, concluding in 1953. Except for the second conference, called Teleological Mechanisms and Circular Causal Systems, all the rest retained the name of the original meeting, Feedback Mechanisms and Circular Causal Systems in Biological and Social Systems.

The participants felt that historically significant theoretical innovation was occurring in these conferences. It was the impression of Lawrence Frank, for instance, that they were creating nothing less than "a new conceptual frame of reference for scientific investigation of the life sciences."[77] Evelyn Hutchinson called the Macy meetings "extraordinary."[78] Margaret Mead was equally enthusiastic. "In a sense it was the most interesting conference I've ever been in because nobody knew how to manage th[o]se things yet."[79] And Gregory Bateson has flatly stated that "membership in those conferences, with Norbert Wiener, John von Neumann, McCulloch and the rest, was one of the great events of my life."[80]

The March 1946 meeting was rich with didactic summary of a variety of concepts originating in mathematics and engineering. Wiener and Von Neumann led the way, differentiating between "analogical" and "digital" coding, discussing circuits, servomechanisms, positive and negative feedback, the measurement of information and its relation to the idea of entropy, binary systems, Von Neumann's theory of games, Bertrand Russell's theory of logical types, "pathological" oscillations (yes-no-yes-no-yes, etc.) in a computer confronted by a Russellian paradox, and the notion that communication systems depend upon "information" and not "energy."[81] The cybernetic model—around which the Macy conferees suspended personal and professional parochialisms—had been named by Norbert Wiener.

Historically, the word had three diverse sets of reference: to automated control mechanisms, to men controlling vehicles such as ships, and to political control in society. Writing in 1948, as if he was widening the implication of the word, Wiener attributed his use of the term solely to the Greek, κυβερνήτης for "steersman." Yet in Plato, this word was already used to refer both to nautical and to social control. The Latin words *gubernare*, "to steer or pilot," *gubernaculum*, or "helm," and *gubernator*, "helmsman," all derive from the Greek, and in French *gouvernail* means "rudder," although as in English, the majority of its derivatives are politically related. In 1790, the word "governor" in English returned to a mechanical meaning, when James Watt invoked it to designate a device he had invented to stabilize the rotation speed of a steam engine. Finally, in 1834, the French physicist and mathematician André Marie Ampère, for whom the unit of electrical current is named, attempting to classify all knowledge, during this project he translated the Greek κυβερνᾶν into *cybernétique* to signify the study of government.

The Armorial Bearings which were granted by Patent, 22 June 1809, to Richard Bateson of the town of Liverpool, Merchant.

W. H. Bateson, Master of St. John's College (1854-81), and his wife Anna Aiken.

Arthur F. Durham, senior surgeon of Guy's Hospital, London, and father of Beatrice Bateson.

Martin (1899-1922) and
Beatrice Bateson, behind Merton
House, Grantchester (1900).

Gregory Bateson was two years
old in 1906.

The two early Mendelians, R. C. Punnett and
W. B., his mentor (July 1907).

Above left: John Bateson, age ten (1908).

Above right: Martin Bateson, age ten (1909).

During the summer of 1910, John, Martin, and Gregory stayed with their father's sister, Anna Bateson, and collected beetles together in the·New Forest.

W. B., in the gardens of the John Innes Horticultural Institute (Merton Park, Surrey).

John Bateson graduated from Charterhouse in 1916.

*Gregory, age sixteen, is standing in the third row, second from the right.
O. H. Latter, housemaster of his dormitory Robbinites, is sitting in the
middle of the second row (Charterhouse School, 1920).*

*W. B. (in fez) standing above his wife, Beatrice, who is flanked by two of
her husband's assistants: Miss Cayley on the left, and Miss Pellew on the right (1919).*

Above left: Martin Bateson, age twenty-two. Above right: Gregory Bateson, age seventeen, bowling on the lawn of the John Innes (May 1921).

Wilhelm Johannsen, the Danish geneticist who coined the term "gene," and W. B. (Merton Park, 1923).

The anthropologist, at the age of
23, in New Britain.

*Above and above right: From April 1927
through March 1928, the Baining
people of New Britain frustrated Bateson's
ethnographic interests. Still, his experience
among them provided a first opportunity to
take photographs.* Credit: Gregory Bateson.

*Gregory Bateson and Margaret
Mead in Ireland (Summer, 1934).*
Credit: C. H. Waddington

In June 1938, after their Balinese research, Mead and Bateson returned to the Iatmul in New Guinea to collect comparative photographic data.
Credit: Gregory Bateson.

Mead and Bateson working in the mosquito room Gregory built (Tambunam, 1938). Credit: Gregory Bateson.

In Bali, between 1936-38, Bateson photographed daily and ritual life, while Mead annotated the behavior. The result of this research was their remarkable Balinese Character (1942). This plate of photographs, entitled "Balance," illustrates themes of body movement exhibited by children and supernaturals.
Credit: The New York Academy of Sciences.

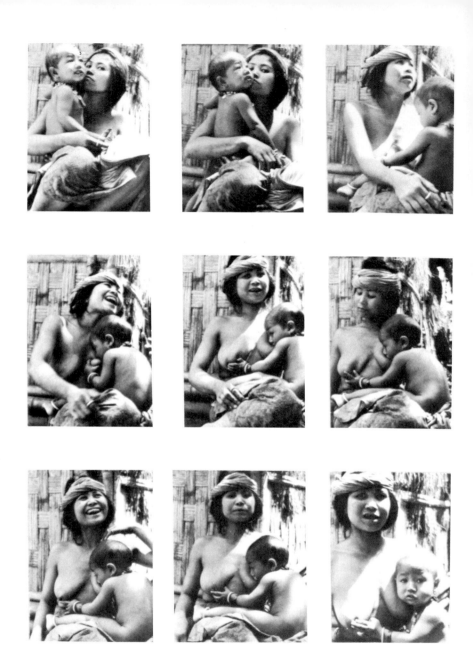

This plate, called "Stimulation and frustration," identifies a two-minute sequence of characteristic interaction. It is meant to illustrate how a Balinese child's responsiveness is frustrated by his mother. When he responds to her attentions, she loses interest and never allows the flirtation to climax in any sort of concentrated emotion. Thirteen years later, Bateson termed this pattern "double bind." Credit: The New York Academy of Sciences.

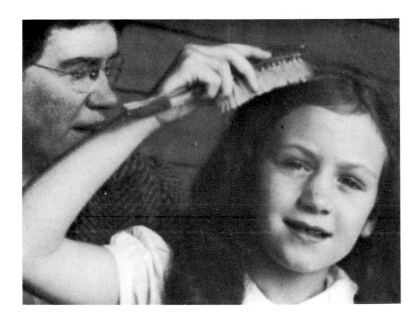

Margaret and Cathy, at the age of eight (circa 1947).
Credit: Gregory Bateson.

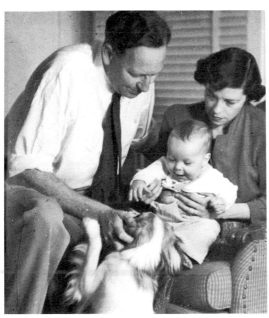

Gregory; his son John, born in April 1951; his new wife, Betty Sumner; and their dog, Rusty (Woodside, California, 1951).

The original members of Bateson's Rockefeller Foundation research project, "The paradoxes of abstraction in communication": William F. Fry, M.D., John H. Weakland, Bateson, and Jay Haley, Don D. Jackson, M.D., is absent. Credit: Jack Fields.

Gregory and John Bateson, age ten (1961). Credit: Paul Byers.

Bateson at 58. Credit: Imogen Cunningham
Trust, Berkeley, California.

*Mary Catherine Bateson and her father walking
away from her wedding to Barkev Kasarjian (1961).*
Credit: Paul Byers.

In 1961, Bateson married Lois Cammack (above). During the summer of 1963, they moved to the Virgin Islands to work on dolphin and octopus communication. Credit: Frank Essapian, Communication Research Institute.

Listening to and taping notes about dolphins (Oceanic Institute, Waimanalo, Hawaii, 1965). Credit: Life photo by Henry Groshinsky.

Gregory Bateson, at the age of 63 (1967).
Credit: Roger Coryell.

In April 1969, Nora was born. Credit Roger Coryell

Credit, Gregory Bateson.

The members of Bateson's second Wenner-Gren conference, "The moral and aesthetic structure of human adaptation," which was held in July 1969 at Burg Wartenstein, Austria. Front row: Taylor A. Pryor, Geoffrey Vickers, Lita Osmundsen, Ted Schwartz, Mary Catherine Bateson, Gordon Pask, Horst Mittelstaedt, Anatol Holt, Peter H. Klopfer. Back row: Warren S. McCulloch, Shepard Ginandes, Bert Kaplan, Stephen A. Erickson, Guy S. Brenton, Barry Commoner, Roy A. Rappaport, and Gregory Bateson.
Credit: Wenner-Gren Foundation.

During the academic year 1971-72, Bateson led a group of American undergraduates on an anthropological tour of Asia. In February, he returned to Bajoeng Gede, the small Balinese village in which he and Margaret Mead had worked. He met I Karba who, as an infant, had been the subject of his photographs in 1936-38.

Lois and Gregory Bateson (1973, Gorda, California).

Gregory Bateson, Margaret Mead, Lois Bateson, and Barkev Kasarjian (August 1978, Carmel, California). Credit: G. Frederick Roll.

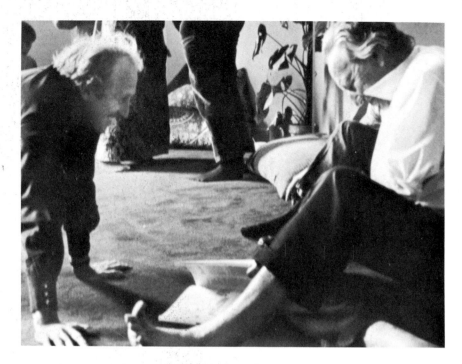

Stewart Brand, the editor of The CoEvolution Quarterly, *and Bateson (circa 1975).*
Credit: Stewart Brand.

Between 1974 and 1978, Bateson taught at Kresge College in the University of California, Santa Cruz.
Credit: Richard Gordon.

At the Esalen Institute (1979).

Contemporary editions of Larousse admitted the new word, although it is unlikely that it gained currency.[82]

Thus in 1948, when Wiener supposed that he was forming "cybernetics" from the Greek, specifying intellectual debt only to Watt and to Clerk Maxwell's classic 1868 paper, "On Governors,"[83] the etymology he omitted was in line with his current research—self-regulatory machinery. The development of cybernetics struck Lawrence Frank as somewhat ironic. "We have leaned so heavily upon the models of man-made machines, guided missiles, and other complicated electronic devices. We have accepted these as models or clues to an understanding of the living organism provided by nature, learning to see organisms in terms of what man himself has first fabricated."[84]

An accessible, albeit hackneyed, example of a cybernetic circuit is the thermostatically controlled heating system. The whole unit, weather-house-heater-thermostat, is said to be *a system of communication.* The thermostat will respond to transforms of messages of difference—that is to *information*—between a specified ideal and the actual changes in room temperature. When too warm or too cold, the thermostat will respond to its own codification of the change—and not to physical energy transfer—by equilibrating to conserve the specified ideal temperature. This process, which features interactive oscillation between messages communicating the real to the ideal and the ideal to the real, is called a *steady state,* or *homeostasis* in Cannon's term. Messages of temperature change, called *positive feedback,* are counteracted, in this case thermostatically, by messages of control, called *negative feedback,* which activate or deactivate the heating element so as to maintain an ideal temperature.

The cybernetic model prescribes explanation in terms of serial and reciprocal chains of cause and effect. "If ... we consider a circular system containing elements A, B, C, and D, so related that an activity of A affects an activity of B, B affects C, C affects D, and D has an effect back upon A—we find that such a system has properties totally different from anything which can occur in lineal chains."[85] If, somehow, the thermostat's codifier is reversed so that it responds to positive feedback with positive feedback—increased room temperature triggers the heating element which raises room tempera-ture, which again triggers the thermostat to trigger the element, etc.—the system would exponentially self-destruct. This process is called *regenerative feedback.* The potentiality of systemic self-destruction, or *entropy,* is central to the model. It is assumed that self-regulating systems tend toward the randomization of themselves. Therefore "the study of ... effective messages of control," Wiener wrote, "constitutes the science of cybernetics."[86] Explana-tion, in addition to being circular, is formulated in terms of *negative entropy* c information. "When under a varying load, we shall look for restraints—e.g for a circuit which will be activated by changes in rate and which, when activated, will operate upon some variable (e.g., the fuel supply) in such a way as to diminish the change in rate."[87]

In 1947, Wiener lectured in Europe about the cybernetic ideas, proclaiming them, and the automata from which they derived, to be the second Industrial Revolution. The following year, his introduction to the subject appeared, which presented the mathematics of feedback, controlled oscillation, and information.[88] Wiener then made only brief reference to the study of society. Like individuals, social systems were "bound together" by communication in which circular feedback processes played important roles.

> On this basis, Drs. Gregory Bateson and Margaret Mead have urged me, in view of the present age of confusion, to devote a large part of my energies to the discussion of this side of cybernetics. . . . Much as I sympathize with their sense of urgency of the situation. . . . I can neither share their feeling that this field has the first claim on my attention, nor their hopefulness that sufficient progress can be registered in this direction to have an appreciably therapeutic effect on the present diseases of society.[89]

Despite Wiener's misgivings, the new theoretical framework was intoxicating to Bateson and came to dominate his scientific imagination. The parallels between the cybernetic model and his own approach to social and cultural systems were commanding. Both stressed *units* in which dynamic sequences of circular interaction were internally regulated. What was more, where Bateson's theoretical notions of symmetrical schismogenesis, end-linkage, and deutero-learning were "ad hoc and awkward,"[90] cybernetics seemed to offer the promise of a unified structure of abstractions for the whole of behavioral science—a disciplinary utopia of virtually unrestricted use.[91] Taking his turn to speak during the March 1946 meeting, Bateson alluded to the difficulty of avoiding teleological accounts of stability in social organization, and to his search for new concepts which he felt the mathematicians and communications engineers might lend to social scientists. Now at the age of forty-two, he had a new set of conceptual tools and a new task, which was to glean what he could from them, although without the mathematics in which they were based, and to use them empirically. Sharing with Norbert Wiener an intuitive yearning for scientific synthesis and a love for metaphor, Bateson "made Wiener his . . . mentor in the concepts and vocabulary of computers, communication theory and formal logic."[92]

The effects of his theoretical conversion—in a postwar world—were ~ible instantly. The process of schismogenesis became regenerative feedback in a 1946 paper on self-perpetuating interaction between nations engaged in arms competition.[93] He also became familiar with Von Neumann's game theory which he criticized for the world view its assumption seemed to affirm, that relations between individuals and nations must be competitive and paranoid.[94] Further, in September 1946, Bateson organized a Macy meeting to introduce social scientists to Wiener and Von Neumann, and to advocate homogenous revision of behavioral data from multiple disciplines. Even ten years later, his hopes for cybernetic theory were unguarded. It was the beginning "of a general theory of process and change, of adaptation and pathology; and, in terms of the general theory, we have to reexamine all that we thought we knew about organisms, societies, families, personal relationships, ecological systems, servomechanisms, and the like."[95]

XII. As Communications Theorist

In late 1948, Bateson reassembled himself in San Francisco, and began a two-year appointment at the University of California Medical School. The western city enchanted him but did not settle his life. There were brief run-ins with shadows of British social anthropology—meeting former colleagues—which angered him, stimulating as they did doubts or regrets about what had been abandoned. There was revulsion at having participated in the crude manipulations of wartime applied anthropology. Discussing his malaise, a psychiatric colleague recalled that he expressed something of it in a reluctance about the possibilities of the world, based not in timidity, but rather in irrevocable pain.[1] In 1973, responding to some notes I had sent him, Bateson wrote of feelings which had contributed to "enormous inefficiency" in his life. "I mean the amount of whole man hours and whole man days that simply get squandered on endogenous depression."[2] Similarly, Cathy Bateson recalled her adolescence, when she berated her father for his rancor "that the universities and the political and economic structures of the world were ... steeped in folly."[3] In the summer of 1949, after three quarters of a year in San Francisco, Bateson was again reading T. S. Eliot's "The Wasteland," when he wrote Margaret Mead that he had little loyalty remaining for the human species.

> Perhaps I would feel happier ... if I read the newspapers and got myself properly propagandized. But that's difficult. Something went wrong at the deutero-level and all I get out of a newspaper is the "writer seems to think it would be a 'good thing' to damn the Russians." I never get the simple reassurance that "The Russians are bad people." Perhaps if I had had more intimate contact with your culture cracking projects, I should by now have sounder opinions.[4]

The Swiss psychiatrist Jurgen Ruesch, M.D., had invited Bateson to join his study of human communication in psychotherapy.* He introduced the somewhat discouraged anthropologist to psychiatric medicine, to the activities of a psychiatric institute, and to the thinking of medical students, residents, and psychiatrists.[5] As a doctor, Ruesch recalled the patience which their collaboration demanded of him. Bateson was far too idiosyncratic for hospital schedules. His capacity for imaginative conceptualization, however, was exceptional and rewarding.

> He had difficulty with timing. It was difficult to have him show up in time for a lecture. And then, often, he didn't stick to the title of the lecture. He had to improvise to speak. He wasn't, in a sense, a compulsive character, who sat down and prepared himself to deliver a lecture. That wasn't Gregory's mode of operation. He came ... and hopefully somebody would ride herd on him ... then, he would talk. But very often he would talk about something else [which was] always interesting and fascinating. .... That was almost standard etiquette for him.[6]

Hoping that she would be able to manage Bateson, in 1949 Ruesch hired one of his former patients, Elizabeth (Betty) Sumner, then in her early thirties, to work as their research secretary. Her bosses "were both prima donnas," she remembered. "There was nothing intrinsically wrong with their relationship. They both wanted to be up stage and ... couldn't get anything done."[7]

At times, the two men argued. On the one hand was Bateson's restless agnosticism about psychological theories—the skepticisms of a research scientist, made inviolable by the sanctity of autonomous intellectual inquiry in a democratic society. On the other was Ruesch's clinical responsibility for the welfare of his patients, which took priority, whether or not the intervention was fully grounded in theory.† Once, when such confrontation occurred, Bateson attempted to clarify and to mitigate these contrasts which he felt lay beneath the tension. "Yesterday, you said more drastically than ever before that you feel an antipathy between the freedoms and elbow room of therapy and the compulsive questioning of science. .... [In this sense my] ideas

---

*Ruesch was a fellow at the Harvard Medical School during Wiener's years under Rosenbleuth. He had participated in interdisciplinary studies throughout the Boston area, becoming interested in communication.

†The problems arising between basic and applied scientists were elaborated by Ruesch, in a paper, "Creation of a multidisciplinary team" (*Psychosomatic Medicine* 18 {1956}: 105-12). Then, some twenty-five years later, he worked out the differences between knowledge in general, the position that Bateson represented, and knowledge in action, the position that Ruesch represented, in *Knowledge in Action: Communication, Social Operations and Management.*

are, for you, a threat to that which you love above everything."[8] Similarly, their responses to everyday administrative affairs differed. Such tasks challenged Ruesch's creativity, and he seemed to draw a kind of support in methodically working them out. By contrast, Bateson regarded this "reality with terror and hatred and contempt and . . . as the destructive thing leading only to muddle, frustration, lies and war."[9] When threatened by administration, he would rather immerse himself in the abstract realm of ideas and science. At the time, he made this point to Ruesch with an odd set of faunal and somatic metaphors.

> If ideas are, for me, a network of fortifications, but for you first a threat and then something to be assimilated, it would follow that I would naturally want the network intact—compulsively, testing every link in it, and often jumping from one part of the net to another to make sure it is all OK. Deriving my reassurance and joy from keeping the whole set up in the air at the same moment and all the time. But, if your problem is one of assimilation—then you want to deal with the ideas one by one. The image that comes to mind is of a turtle trying to eat a network of rather wiry worms—he cannot swallow unless he can somehow chew off a separable piece. But, to me, when you succeed in chewing off a separate piece, that piece, ipso facto, becomes completely tasteless and uninteresting.[10]

Their collaboration was composed of more than this sort of negotiation. It also produced fruitful theoretical discussion. At one point, they were addressing the problem of how to define a behavioral "message." Could there be actions which were not messages? If these existed, what distinguished them from explicit ones? The moment of clarification, Bateson has since said, occurred "not in [Ruesch's] little office but over on my side,"[11] when the psychiatrist imagined a silly variation upon a classical question. "Suppose a man is peeing in the woods," Ruesch asked, "and he thinks nobody is looking at him. Is his act of peeing against a tree all by himself a message?"[12] Pursuing this fancy, they raised more detailed questions. What sort of message is exchanged if there is someone watching a man who does not know it? What sort of message is it if the man urinating is aware that someone is watching him but the observer does not know that he knows? And, what sort of message is it, in the case of mutual knowledge, when both the actor and the observer know of each other's presence? According to Bateson's recollection, the conversation then digressed to the behavior of the jackdaw; the two had been reading Konrad Lorenz's new book, *King Solomon's Ring*.[13] Did that bird, when it chirped *kiaw*, and then flew home, recognize its *kiaw* as a message to another jackdaw which would cause the second to fly home also? Can the one, for example, modulate sound to correct volume if the second fails to respond to the call? "Though we did not know it, we were asking about the epistemology of jackdaws, and the word 'epistemology' had suddenly jumped out of philosophy to become a cross-cultural word."[14]

Simultaneously, they were looking into the nature of communication among "a tribe called psychiatrists."[15] At Ruesch's behest, Bateson carried out ethnographic interviews and observations of these professionals, wanting to detail transactions of messages in the course of successful, change-inducing psychotherapy. The mental health professions, they argued, were based on communication, as in group therapy and psychoanalysis, yet psychiatrists "just talked about personality," Ruesch recalled, "which was after all only a nice . . . construct."[16] The goals of the study Bateson introduced to prospective informants were to elicit the underlying premises and overt goals of psychotherapy. "I am interested in the general principles and criteria that you use in recognizing mental health, and the ideas implicit and explicit, which frame and determine the therapeutic situation."[17] Bateson busied himself among San Francisco Bay Area psychiatrists, taping interviews and jotting notes. His casual and somewhat unfastened ethnographic style evidently disconcerted not a few of his subjects. At the time, he noted that one of them was particularly bothered "by the amount of freedom I gave him during the interview and felt that there must be a trick somewhere. . . . In reply, I said I used minimally directive techniques because in the end one gets there better by going there sideways, and the direct attack does not pay."[18] Others, however, especially the Jungian analysts Joseph Henderson, M.D., and Joseph B. Wheelwright, M.D., became willing informants and close friends.

None of Bateson's interviews fully came to publication.* But a short survey of psychiatric epistemological beliefs did appear in a theoretical book on which he and Ruesch collaborated, *Communication: The Social Matrix of Psychiatry.*[19] Bateson reviewed predominant attitudes about a series of topics, some of which by now were not unfamiliar to him: the tendency of psychiatrists to reify abstractions, their definitions of reality and pathology, their increasing self-reflexiveness, and the implications of their beliefs in

---

*Indeed, more generally, as Margaret Mead (possibly insinuating her absence from his life) aptly pointed out, Bateson never did any more conventional anthropological fieldwork after the war. According to her, he preferred rather "to generate small stretches of data . . . not in themselves priceless or timelessly valuable . . . that can be discarded when the thinking they were meant to underpin [was] done." (M. Mead, *Blackberry Winter,* p. 219.) Or, as Ruesch said, "Gregory's thinking runs differently—most people make observations and then devise a theory. He doesn't work that way at all. He proposes a theory and then descends to observations." (Personal communication: 24 February 1976.)

Freudian energy theories, which he caricatured, "if we rigorously restrict ourselves to seeing man only in terms of energy conservation, our picture of his situation will resemble that of a billiard ball, the prototype of fatalistic 19th century materialism."[20] More significantly for future work, the psychiatrist and the anthropologist were extending Norbert Wiener's embryonic views about the pertinence of formal notions of information exchange to human communication. In his chapters, Bateson continued to express conversion to the new model. The book appeared in 1951, when cybernetics was still in its first flush.* Ruesch and Bateson were in the forefront, tentatively introducing behavioral scientists to the conceptual organization of information in circular causal systems. As Steve Heims, a historian of science, has pointed out, Wiener admired their attempt. After reading a draft of the book, he wrote Lawrence Frank of Bateson's "valiant work in attempting to bring psychoanalytic processes under the heading of cybernetics," although he admitted that it was "and must be sketchy" because of the partial nature of knowledge of even elementary psychological processes.[21]

The cybernetic model drew upon the communication theory of Claude E. Shannon and Warren Weaver[22] in which the crucial idea was codification, or the transformation of events in the world into symbolic information. The process by which perceived events become messages was said to depend upon the systematic preservation of the formal relations obtaining among the events in themselves. Bateson noted that this was observable phenomenally. In order to clarify codification of an object, a person will alter the relationships between himself and that object. "To judge the weight of an object, we heft it in the hand, and to inspect a seen object with care, we move our eyes in such a way that the image of the object moves across the fovea."[23] To expand the analysis of information processing, Bateson used vocabulary from a Macy Conference analogy. Communications engineers had then distinguished three types of computer codification systems. 1. *Digital* codifiers, such as desk calculators, that require input—numbers—which sharply differ from the external events they represent. 2. *Analogic* codifiers, such as wind tunnels, that translate input into recognizable models which can symbolically represent changes in the external environment. 3. Codifiers that identify formal relations between external events and classify groups of such events into categories (e.g., that

---

*Y. Bar-Hillel has recalled that this was the time "when Cybernetics and Information Theory reached their common heydays and created among many of us the feeling that the new synthesis heralded in them was destined to open new vistas on everything human and to help solve many of the disturbing . . . problems concerning man and humanity." (S. P. Heims, "Gregory Bateson and the mathematicians: from interdisciplinary interaction to societal functions," *Journal of the History of the Behavioral Sciences,* 13(1977):158.)

"read"). Bateson argued that humans and a few other mammals had a system of linguistic codification which corresponded to "digital" codification because it also bore little or no relation to represented objects. They also had a system of non-verbal codification which was "analogic" by being more closely related to its subject matter. The content of language, not required to resemble that for which it stands, was obviously unlimited. The content of gesture and tone, being tied to its referents, was not. Specifically, nonverbal messages conveyed information about the immediate relations of the communicators and about their habits of codification, however partially shared. In the language of the analogy, men were said to emit and codify along both channels—digital and analogic messages, that is, were exchanged simultaneously.

Out of the wealth of model and metaphor that had been placed before the cybernetics conferences, Bateson took another heuristic analogy. He sought to apply the theory of logical types to the relations between the two different channels of communication.[24] As A. N. Whitehead and Bertrand Russell came to admit, logico-mathematical systems are necessarily unable to found or base themselves in axioms for which they, themselves, may account. There is always a discontinuity, in other words, between a class and its members. They described this gap in hierarchical terms: the class of machinery, for instance, is of a higher logical type, or level of abstraction, than the class of typewriters or the class of record players. The totality of objects sharing properties shall itself not be part of that totality. This was the pivotal prohibition of the theory of logical types. When breached—when a class is mistaken for a thing—a paradox, that is a logical contradiction following consistent deductions from correct premises, may develop.

Russell offered his famous example. A person divides entities into classes such that every class which he establishes defines then a class of nonmembers. The class of bananas, to be sure, is itself not a banana. But the class of nonbananas is itself a member of that class—the *class* of nonbananas is not a banana. The person observes that there seem to be two classes of classes: those which include themselves among their members and those which exclude themselves. Of the second class, the question is then posed: Does the class of classes which exclude themselves include itself as a member? The class of bananas is a member of the class of classes which excludes itself, but what about this second class? If it is said, yes, that the class of classes which excludes itself, does include itself, then the class no longer accords with its own definition. It does not exclude itself and must be a member of the class of classes which includes itself. If it is said, no, that the class of classes which excludes itself does exclude itself, then it follows that the class must be a member of the class of classes which includes itself. If it excludes itself, it must then include itself. If it includes itself, it must then exclude itself. Epimenides the Cretan, when he stated that "All Cretans are liars," had presented another paradox of essentially the same organization. Was he telling the truth? If he was, then he was lying. Dissected, paradox reveals ambiguity, a single statement is made which refers negatively to itself. When both the statement and the concomitant statement are not distinguished as occupying different levels of abstraction, that is being of different logical type, paradox ensues. In order to resolve the infinite oscillating regression, Whitehead and Russell forbade the conflation of the hierarchy. Distinction was to be maintained between a class and a class of classes. To do so, logical type markers— subscripts, quotation marks, italics—were to be employed to emphasize that the name of a class is of a higher level of abstraction than a member.

To Bateson, the central notion was "that a class cannot be a member of itself. The class of elephants has not got a trunk and is not an elephant. . . . . This truism must evidently apply with equal force when the members of the class are not things but names or signals. The class of commands is not itself a command and cannot tell you what to do."[25] It appears he was among the first to argue that communication might be usefully construed in terms of a hierarchy of levels of abstraction or logical types. "Corresponding to this hierarchy of names, classes, and classes of classes, there is also a hierarchy of propositions and messages, and within this latter hierarchy the Russellian discontinuity between types must also obtain. We speak of messages, metamessages and meta-meta-messages."[26] Analogic message, all the nonverbal aspects of communication which express the on-going relations of the participants, he called *metamessage* or *metacommunication*. Following the analogy to logical types, Bateson deduced that these would classify, or order, digital— verbal—messages from a higher, or logically distinct, level of abstraction. "There is a gulf between . . . metamessage and message . . . which is of the same nature as the gulf between a thing and the word or the sign which stands for it, or between members of a class and the name of the class. The. . . metamessage *classifies* the message, but can never meet it on equal terms."[27] Analogic message, emitted unisolably upon the stream of digital communication, consisted of overtone, of facial and physical gesture, and of the situational context of the exchange. Riding an elevator, for instance, strangers may eye each other and make awkward conversation in order to convey digitally what they are communicating analogically. The other's very physical presence is a metamessage that relationship is occurring. But if two strangers exchange such a message, yet do not talk, what are they communicating? Their silence is the peculiar message that relationship is *not* occurring, while being together is the metamessage that relationship *is* occurring. In this sense, all observable behavior were interactive sequences of communication.*

Simple analogic messages possessed normative claims over their digital counterparts. In an elevator, talk brings the one into congruence with the other, defusing a situation which would otherwise be "explosive" with paradox.[28] Consistent use of the two channels and mutually qualifying levels of communication was neither voluntary nor particularly valuable. In many cases and fields, when this hierarchy was abused, humor, play, pathology, therapy, and even creativity might develop.

> It is not merely bad natural history [Bateson said in 1955] to suggest that people might or should obey the Theory of Logical Types in their communications; their failure to do this is not due to mere carelessness or ignorance. Rather, we believe the paradoxes of abstraction must make their appearance in all communication more complex than that of mood signals, and that without these paradoxes the evolution of communication would be at an end. Life would be an endless interchange of stylized messages, a game with rigid rules, unrelieved by change or humor.[29]

During their collaboration, Bateson and Ruesch had speculated about the evolution of communication by making the observation that human ability to exchange messages far surpasses other species. They posed the question of whether this contrast had evolved gradually or in sudden dramatic steps. "In this conversation we developed the idea that one such dramatic step must have been the moment when creatures—be they animal or human—discovered that their messages were messages."[30] In January 1952, skeptical about the conventional notion that animal communication lacked such awareness, Bateson went to the Fleishhacker Zoo in San Francisco. He had prepared a list of criteria which might indicate that nonhuman animals possessed the sort of awareness he was looking for. Could, for example, an animal send a message

---

*Bateson even viewed inner speech in terms of interaction, "i.e., as addressed to someone and as a response to the message of that someone. I know that a great deal of my own thought is in words and that a great many of these words I would not address to anybody. (Perhaps not even to myself if I were attending.) But still insofar as the inner stream is accessible to study it is, ipso facto, addressed to somebody. And this goes for dream, schizophrenic utterance, and all the rest of primary process stuff. And the stuff which is inaccessible is so, I think, for good interpersonal reasons. Its very accessibility is contrived, as I see it, to prevent the access of others.... We might say that the schizophrenic is the individual who feels safe in pouring out his inner speech because he knows that it is so masked and that mamma can't invade." (Gregory Bateson, hereafter cited as GB, to L. Frank, 3 October 1956.)

about a message? Could an animal correct or falsify a message? Were there messages made to insure message exchange? Observing some monkeys at play gave him pause. Play seemed so close to combat, yet the animals were able to discriminate between the two classes of message. Bateson believed that this distinction "could only occur if the participant organisms were capable of some degree of metacommunication, i.e., of exchanging signals which would carry the message, 'This is play.'"[31] Given the proper context, the playful slap was a composite signal. It was both a message and a negative message about a message, "Don't believe this. It is unreal, we are friends." Play was paradoxical. Animals were able to make signals about signals, along Russellian or Epimendian lines, such that a negative statement contained an implicit self-negating, self-asserting, metastatement. Bateson construed the message of playful, pseudoantagonism as follows: "These actions, in which we now engage, do not denote what would be denoted by those actions which these actions denote. The playful nip denotes the bite, but it does not denote what would be denoted by the bite."[32] This convolution echoed Charles Darwin's 1872 articulation of metacommunicative phenomena. "When my terrier bites my hand in play, often snarling at the same time, if he bites and I say *gently, gently,* he goes on biting, but answers me by a few wags of the tail, which seems to say, 'Never mind, it was fun.'"[33]

When animals began playing, an important step in the evolution of digital communication occurred. Signals standing for other events were exchanged. Of course, without words, the discourse of preverbal mammals was primarily analogic, that is almost entirely concerned with the rules of immediate face-to-face social relations. A cat may not signal "milk," but instead may communicate sounds and movements typical of those a kitten makes to her mother. In words, Bateson supposed that it was saying something like "Mama!" or "Dependency! Dependency!"

In the spring of 1952, Bateson turned his attention to that notoriously playful creature, the otter. With Weldon Kees, an accomplished poet, he observed and filmed a pair of zoo otters, intermittently over a two-year period.[34] During the first year, the otters disgruntled the poet and the naturalist-anthropologist. Bateson told a 1955 Macy conference, called Group Processes,[35] that they interacted minimally, rarely groomed each other, and seemed lethargic. Then, in March 1953, being frustrated and bored, Bateson lowered a piece of paper at the end of a string into their compound, jiggling it as he did. The otters had just eaten and ran toward the object. They began to compete for the "toy" seemingly, an interaction which began to resemble combat, but which was not fighting. Bateson then lowered a fish the same way to "explore," as he put it, "the contrast between behavior vis à vis a toy and behavior vis à vis food."[36] Evidently the otters lost their enthusiasm at this point. In subsequent days, Bateson and Kees observed the resumption of active play. The otters dived and swam briskly, spinning over and over. Grooming each other, their coats, once dull, began to shine. This sort of rejuvenation continued until the season changed, when the two animals returned to the listlessness which characterized their state, as Bateson said, "before our interference."[37]

These data were of wide significance. Although the change was only temporary—possibly seasonal or hormonal—Bateson still presumed "that the presentation of a toy which was *not* food created a context for interaction which was *not* combat, and that the dramatic change in behavior of the otters might be a result of this 'psychotherapeutic' experience."[38] The dangling paper had served to crisscross the logical typing of their communication such that a flip or a bite could be reclassified as "in play." Although this conception was set in the contrast between play and what it was not—not combat, not courtship, not feeding—Bateson wanted to phrase the matter formally. The specific behaviors which the metamessage "this is play" negated were irrelevant. Play was to stand symbolically for other codes of behavior which it was not. It was "a class of behavior defined by means of a negative without commonly identifying what the negative negates."[39] Human children play not as a way to practice the content of specific behavioral roles, but as indication that like roles exist flexibly, to be crossed according to "the frame and context of behavior."[40] For children, play was learning to distinguish the relations between whole categories of behavior. From play, said Bateson, came human conception, healing, and imagination.

> My personal interest in the abstract problem of play is a desire to know about those processes whereby organisms pull themselves up by their bootstraps. And they do it, as far as I can see, by loosening up on the rules of communication— the onionskin structures within which they are operating. They play with these structures or rules and thereby move forward to new rules, new philosophies, etc.[41]

For the otters, play might be mildly restorative, but a conception which did not admit some fixed teleology could not be used to cure. For a doctor to try to prescribe play therapeutically, Bateson noted, would be "as if he were prescribing an act of discovery, but unable to define what the patient is to discover."[42] He was loath to nominate a dominant or single purpose or function of play. Human laughter merely provided an indirect clue to mutual premises about a range of implicit elements in communication. It was an opening in the hierarchical codes of discourse through which men might pass, and change their communication.

This sort of formal analysis was part of a more general attack upon atomistic teleology in the social sciences. Bateson wanted a more extensive view. At a Macy Conference in 1955, when asked to define how he did think play functioned for his otters and if it would be important to investigate this experimentally, Bateson denounced simplistic determinism.

> Our whole thinking about the nature of purpose and related ideas is culturally biased towards the identifiable purpose, and I suspect that this is very often too narrow a way of looking at what an organism does. For example, I can say that I have a socially mobile upward purpose of convincing you of the importance of my discoveries in regard to otter's play. This would be my narrowly defined purpose. Or I could mention a whole range of other narrowly definable purposes that might bring me here. But actually, as an organism, I am here for much wider purposes including a sense of well-being.[43]

He had shown his film *The Nature of Play: River Otters* to this Macy Conference, and then had worked out his ideas. Throughout the meeting, Bateson recoiled from the push and pull of his audience. They wanted to know what play was not, and what the precise circumstances of his otter data were. Erik H. Erikson asked a series of detailed questions, at one point in the discussion, and then expressed his hesitations, "because I don't have their life history and a description of their environment."[44] Similarly hesitant, the child psychologist Fritz Redl thought Bateson might be reading his feelings into the otters' behavior, being too ready to attribute symbolic function to their play. "Just because the piece of paper you dangled in front of your otters' noses was not a fish, that does not mean that it had to become a symbol for the animal, or that it had to be perceived by the animals as a substitute for something else at all times."[45] As if to sum the exchange, the group's secretary, the psychoanalyst Bertram Schaffner, M.D., was doubtful. For him, play was more a freedom from responsibility and consequences. "I wonder if this isn't a little more accurate way of looking at play than to define it all simply as a 'not something.'"[46]

However ultimately distinct they are, crucial to both poetic and scientific thought is a readiness to draw resemblances. In making his metaphors, the poet juxtaposes images or ideas and identifies them ("O that this too, too sullied flesh would melt, Thaw, and resolve itself into a dew,..."[47]), but leaves the sense he intends the comparison relatively undefined. The scientist, too, juxtaposes notions by making analogies (i.e., thinking is like formal logic), yet he employs them with more closure, escalating the precision of his intended meaning empirically. Between this polarity, Bateson's thinking seemed to involve both definition and open-endedness. There was his habit of exposing the weaknesses of analogies, but equally he believed that knowledge always existed surrounded by an unknown which was penetrable to the ambitious investigator. His pleasure in telling and retelling of Bertrand Russell lecturing at Harvard on quantum theory was then that of both the poet and the scientist.

> It is reported that Russell labored to make the quantum theory intelligible, and quantum theory was then a novelty and even more difficult than it is today. But Russell did his best and at the end of the lecture [the philosopher A. N.] Whitehead rose to thank the lecturer. In his excited almost falsetto voice, Whitehead expressed the appropriate gratitude for Russell's efforts, "and especially on leaving ... *unobscured* ... the vast darkness of the subject."[48]

Bateson's use of the otter data—of an empirical base—during the Macy Conference had been deliberately vague, almost metaphoric, in the sense that he wanted to pose questions and to open discussion. He feared and opposed the closure of some fixed teleology—i.e., play releases tension—and in particular he wanted to stimulate the play of ideas during the conference itself. He knew that his data were inadequate. "My film serves only as an illustration or a problem-setter. I don't think ... [it] gives answers to the nature of play by any means."[49] Still, he clung to the formalist conception for which it stood as an exemplar.

> The point is that we are playing with an example, a metaphor, a bit of play, in which there was a piece of paper, which itself is metaphoric to otters, but I don't know whether or not it is food that the paper stands for. I have, on the whole, set up the discussion with that assumption. The correctness of that interpretation is not what I am concerned with, but rather the notion that the paper is somehow *skewed* against other parts of an otter's life which may be fish or crayfish or other otters or huntable objects or edible objects. The paper is *not* one of the objects, and that sets up some vaguely analogous skewing in the relationship of the otters. As a result, what they engage in, is something which is *not* courtship. Again, I don't know what it is not, because I can't fill in that gap.[50]

His play research developed in the area of Palo Alto, California, where Bateson had moved in the fall of 1949. There, he was a visiting professor of anthropology at Stanford University for a number of years, but his central institutional tie was to the local Veterans Administration (V.A.) Hospital in Menlo Park. Holding the title of ethnologist, he was given "singular freedom to study whatever . . . [he] thought interesting . . . [and] was protected from outside demands . . . by the director of the hospital, Dr. John J. Prusmack."[51] Bateson did some minor work on alcoholism, continued to ponder psychotherapy,* and to have casual and formal contact with psychiatric residents.

He hosted—as Noel Porter had done for him—a regular weekly seminar in his home for residents, hospital staff, and various interested people from the Palo Alto area. These were unstructured evenings, although occasionally, he might pose a particular subject. "Usually it would be . . . ad lib. There wasn't any presentation. People would come in and sit down on the floor, chairs, couches."[52] Bateson would guide conversation provocatively. In the recollections of one of those present, the psychiatrist William F. Fry, M.D., the ideas discussed—about religion, abortion, euthanasia—were avant-garde for the early 1950s. "There were a lot of fairly strong and sometimes rather unconventional points of view expressed. There were some people that were disturbed by those meetings."[53]

Filling a more traditional didactic role, Bateson also lectured to residents. The sudden appearance of an anthropologist, amid a medical-psychiatric education, otherwise clinically oriented, seemed peculiar to his students. That he was discussing the Iatmul and the Balinese, animal behavior, and culturally contrasting student-teacher relations confused many of them. Now and then, a few felt enriched by his discourse. Fry said that Bateson's classes were anomalous for their content as well as for their stimulating quality. But evidently, his was the atypical case. Most of the psychiatric residents did not understand him. Bateson knew it and was concerned. Indeed, this professional difficulty in communicating probably supported his scientific interest in the theoretical structure of communication. Repeatedly, students asked him a disarming question, "What are you talking about?" He remembered that "almost every year a vague complaint . . . came to me as a rumor. It was alleged that 'Bateson knows something which he does not tell you,' or 'There is something behind what Bateson says, but he never

---

*In a 1952 letter to Norbert Wiener, Bateson wondered whether administering to a "defective" computer might shed light on strategies for psychotherapy. Was it conceivable that posing appropriately diagnosed paradoxes to men and machines might be an effective form of treatment? What would happen if the machine or the patient responded in kind? (S. P. Heims, "Gregory Bateson and the mathematicians," pp. 150-51.)

says what it is.'"[54] After an introductory lecture comparing Balinese and American families, a perplexed resident overcame the natural diffidence one feels before large, imposing intellectuals and approached him, wanting to know how much of the material he expected them to learn.

> *Bateson:* I don't know. Obviously you are not going to treat any Balinese.
> *Resident.* Or is it meant to be a kind of example?
> *Bateson:* [excitedly] Yes, that is it, some kind of example. There is a principle involved.[55]

Oddly though, at this point in his life, Bateson was not yet able to articulate it.

At the age of forty-six, this obliqueness did not extend into his emotional life. In Reno, Nevada, during the winter of 1951, Gregory married again. "I think the devil in him was attracted to me," joked Betty Sumner, his former secretary and then new wife, "because I was the daughter of the Episcopal bishop of Portland, Oregon."[56] They were married for seven years until 1958.

> I fell very much in love with him. . . . But I couldn't stay married to him. It was just too much and I was terribly depressed. I had lost three sets of twins, after I was thirty-six, and the doctor said I would probably go on twinning or even have triplets. It was an organic thing. But Greg adored babies and children and wanted more. . . . I think one of the things that went wrong with our relationship was that he was overprotective, if you can imagine it. I never had a relationship with anyone that wasn't on a strictly sibling basis. But with Greg, he was both mamma and poppa! And he is that way with his children. He plays a marvelous mamma role with his children. So I felt overwhelmed toward the end because I was so depressed and I said I think we better get a divorce. So we did. It was amicable and I took no alimony.[57]

Their life as a family began in April 1951 with the birth of a son, John, named after Gregory's dead brother. "As an infant John had terrible colic," his mother remembered. "Gregory spent every dinner with him, wrapped up in a diaper over his lap, for three months."[58] The three of them spent two years in suburban tract houses, living hospitably. Colleagues came daily for lunch, residents visited on a weekly basis. The Batesons picnicked often.

Betty B., as Gregory called her, gave birth to twins in December 1953, William and Anne. They lived for one month and died. "After the first set of twins, Greg was depressed about the house. That was when everything came from England. He said, 'I'm going to find a new house for us,' and he went out and found a very nice two-story house on Colby Street in Menlo Park."[59] At this location for the rest of their marriage, family life abounded with innumerable animals which Gregory gave his young son.

> John had everything under the sun living in the house on Colby Street. Snakes of all kinds, and an armadillo brought from Texas one time in a special cage, and alligators, of course. One arrived with an eggshell still on its back. John was fascinated by this. He and Greg share that. They spent a lot of time together when John was growing up, in the woods hiking and fishing, and Gregory was always interested, always inquisitive, always asking of nature, what is going on here? Instead of turning against it, which a lot of people would have done, John took it even further. He now [1978] spends all his time up a tree, cutting down, or supervising men cutting down trees.[60]

As a father, Gregory was rarely angry. According to his mother, John only once remembered being physically frightened by him. "Greg would often pull up rocks and look at little insects and everything, and John said [they were looking under a rock], 'I let the rock fall on Greg's head and boy, did he let me have it. That was the only time I remember ever being punished by him.'"[61]

When John was almost three years old, in early 1954, Alan and Nora Barlow, having taken responsibility for the Bateson family estate after Beatrice died, suggested that W. B.'s papers, books, paintings, Old Master drawings, Japanese prints, and furniture be taken out of storage and sent to California. Needless to say, Gregory was of two minds about the arrival of his father's property. He felt both a "love for some of the objects and what they stood for—and therefore still stand for; and ... an aching horror or fear of the old pressures which tried to mould me into that for which all the beautiful objects stood."[62] He worried about the "coercive" presence of these ancestral remnants in the American life of his young son. "It's the problem of a link with the past and the problem of a certain sort of discipline. ... The discipline is that of aesthetics, of that which is not kitsch and TV and vulgarity; of the craftsman; of the hand. ... And the products of such a discipline in an eighteenth century craftsman are frightening to a child who has not yet the inner knowledge of his own potential discipline and love."[63] When the books, artwork, and furniture all arrived and were unpacked, little overt respect was given it. Gregory, indeed, was a permissive father about domestic order. When the psychiatrist, R. D. Laing, M.D., visited Bateson at the Colby Street house in 1962, he observed the "collection of original paintings and drawings by William Blake, one of which ['Satan exulting over Eve'] was up on the mantelpiece, where the kids were playing ball beside it."[64]

Usually in the summer, Cathy Bateson, by now an adolescent, came to visit from New York City. Betty B. could not remember conversation about Cathy's mother, Margaret Mead, during these visits. Instead Gregory and Cathy talked about the knowledge of his father's culture. If there was residual reticence about the things of that culture, it is evident, perhaps from the order of his daughter's recollection, that he was more than willing to transmit its science. They "used to go camping in the California state parks," Cathy has written, "and in between efforts to get me to master the multiplication tables, he would respond to my demand, 'Teach me something!' with an account of how amoebae divide or Mendel's experiments with beans [sic], Mobius strips, or an explanation of the dark symbolisms of William Blake, or he would translate ideas he was working on."[65]* Reciprocally, during his appearances in New York, father and daughter saw one another. Gregory was constantly teaching. "I remember once picnicking with him in Central Park when I was about thirteen," Cathy said in 1971. "Then he talked about the Theory of Logical Types. . . . He took a pen and pointed out that it was a member of the class of all pens—but that the class of all pens was not itself a pen; you couldn't write with it or put it in your pocket, or compute with it. . . . Similarly, he said, the class of pens was a member of the class of classes which could not be a member of itself."[66]

Perhaps this picnic had occurred in the late summer of 1952, because

---

*Bateson developed their talks into a series of what he called "metalogues." These were partly imagined theoretical exchanges about a variety of very general topics, in which the "structure of the conversation as a whole is also relevant to the same subject." (GB, in *Steps to an Ecology of Mind*, p. 1.) For example:

Daughter: Daddy, what is an instinct?

Father: An instinct, my dear, is an explanatory principle.

D. But what does it explain?

F: Anything—almost anything at all. Anything you want to explain.

D: Don't be silly. It doesn't explain gravity.

F: No. But that is because nobody wants "instinct" to explain gravity. If they did, it would explain it. We could simply say that the moon has an instinct whose strength varies inversely as the square of the distance. . . .

D: But that's nonsense, Daddy.

F: Yes, surely. But it was you who mentioned "instinct," not I.

D: All right—but what does explain gravity?

F: Nothing, my dear, because gravity is an explanatory principle.

D: Oh. (GB, "Metalogue: What is an instinct?" in *Steps,* p. 38.)

Bateson was in New York to approach Chester Barnard—then president of the Rockefeller Foundation—about grant support. He had intended to sell and explain a research project, the Paradoxes of Abstraction in Communication, but found this difficult to do. At the time, the prestige of science in the United States was very high and, in any case, Barnard had long been devoted to *Naven*. He was immediately willing to become Bateson's patron. "I tried to put into words my dream and my puzzlement. Finally he said, 'I do not know what you are going to do. Nor what you will find. If we knew that, there would be no sense in giving you money. Would there? ... How much do you need?"[67] While in New York, Bateson was the guest of his former student John H. Weakland, who also remembered that successful day. "He came home one afternoon and said, 'I've got a research grant!' I said, 'That's nice.' And he said, 'How would you like to come out to the West Coast and work for me?' Under the circumstances, I said, 'Great!' We all went out and had dinner and celebrated."[68]

By the following winter, when the project began, Bateson had completed his research team, hiring two other young men to join himself and Weakland.* The first, Jay Haley, a graduate student at Stanford, had contacted Bateson about his work on fictional films. Impressed by the postwar movie boom in which Americans were immersed, Haley was exploring why people were going. "I went over to talk to Gregory about it, to get an adviser. We had a big argument and he hired me on the project."[69] The second man was William F. Fry, M.D., a former psychiatric resident and student at the V.A.

---

*Part of the discourse among sociologists of science is, for present purposes, a suggestive analysis of career development in science. The assumption made is that scientists are rational men acting to improve their places in the prestige hierarchy of their disciplines. They design "research strategies," by choosing which ideas to promote and which to discard. They do so according to the balance of costs and benefits, measured in professional recognition and made in the significant contribution. Sociologists holding these premises look for the emergence of innovative thinking from men at various extremes of the prestige hierarchy, from youth who seek a reputation and from eminence who seek to maintain one. But the latter must protect their intellectual investments and therefore may resist reconceptualization of their field of origin. "It seems likely," according to the sociologist of science, M. J. Mulkay, "that scientific revolutions will usually be led by relative newcomers to research or by entrants from other networks." Intellectually mobile, scientists from other disciplines apply their reputations, preconceptions, and techniques in another field. Introducing new ideas may be resisted by scientists defending the status of their knowledge. There are appropriate strategic responses to this problem, however. "When the cognitive structure of the receiving community is relatively imprecise, it is possible for the newcomers to stress their intellectual uniqueness and to reduce conflict by forming a distinct network." (M. J. Mulkay, *The Social Process of Innovation*, pp. 53 and 46.)

Hospital in Menlo Park. In January 1953, Fry was starting private practice. Bateson invited him to join the project to "try to collect material demonstrating the role played by the Russellian paradoxes in psychotherapy."[70] Fry did so on a part-time basis until a year later, when he was inducted into the Navy. Fry later returned to the project in 1956, but in the meantime, Bateson had hired Don D. Jackson, M.D., to fill in as a psychiatric consultant, and to provide them with supervision of therapy with schizophrenics. Jackson was already thinking about family behavior in terms of closed information systems, and indeed, the two men had met after a lecture Jackson gave on the subject. In addition to the fit of his theoretical orientation, Jackson was a man of independent mind and ambitious, almost entrepreneurial character.[71]

The belief that applying formal logic to different settings of human communication would produce a set of nontrivial problems lent an air of expectation to the first grapplings of Bateson's project. Ideas and data were not to be drawn from the phenomenal domain of any single discipline, for Bateson "respected the mystic's approach to life as much as the scientist's."[72] His worldwide intellectual ties brought a stream of interested colleagues into contact with the project. Both Norbert Wiener, the mathematician, and Alan Watts, the student and theologian of oriental mysticism, were involved in the early work. Housed in the Menlo Park Veterans Administration Hospital, the project began its collaborative life when Bateson proposed a list of contexts in which multiple classes of messages might be visible.* He did not exert pressure, but afforded them "full freedom to investigate whatever [they] wished as long as [it] dealt somehow with the paradoxes that arise in the communicative process."[73] Fry initiated a study of humor. Bateson, Weakland, and Haley observed that in the training of guide dogs for the blind messages were simultaneously emitted either by voice and harness, or through two harnesses. Bateson observed the messages exchanged between a ventriloquist and his puppet. A film was made of communication among mongoloid children. Haley continued his fictional film analysis, while Bateson was in the middle of his observations of otters. Weakland and Haley examined the practice of hypnosis with the psychiatrist Milton H. Erickson, M.D., whom Bateson and Mead had consulted during their work on Balinese trance. Haley, in his brief history of their project, has recalled that "in 1953, Gregory Bateson arranged that I take a seminar on hypnosis, although he was not an enthusiast

---

*Bateson wrote Wiener: "I am about to start on a piece of research or better, an exploration of data. . . . If at the end of the work I achieve some idea of how to think about matters of this sort, I shall be satisfied—it is a matter not of investigation by studying how investigation might be achieved—later, and probably by others." (Circa 1953.)

about that subject."[74] The whole group also began to review the varieties of psychotherapy. For one, they interviewed and observed the dramatic methods of John Rosen, M.D.* Finally, later in the year, a resident suggested to Haley that it might be fruitful, in light of his group's interest in classifying messages, to study a schizophrenic patient he knew from "Mars," who called himself Margaret Stalin. This was convenient and striking communication. They all started collecting film and tape recordings of such patients.

Their initial attitude toward schizophrenia was descriptive—natural historical—rather than diagnostic. Working within Bateson's anthropological biases, they focused the observable interaction of a small population. Within his theoretical orientations, they ignored intrapsychic explanation in favor of sequences of interaction in which hierarchically organized digital and analogical messages were exchanged. Bateson also sanctioned a fresh view, with a sort of intellectual effrontery to the theory of others, past or present. The prejudice he encouraged, Weakland recalled, was that previous literature on the subject would only draw their attention away from watching behavior occur.

> Most people who were interested in schizophrenic language weren't really interested in things observable. . . . They were taking samples out of context and their main aim was to leap from this bit of crazy talk to [ask] "What are the deep processes that explain it?" . . . They didn't look at the thing itself very thoroughly before they got off of it, into the brain or into symbolism . . . as soon as possible.[75]

They shared the notion that research among madmen approximated anthropological fieldwork. The language and behavior of patients, however

---

*Rosen employed a kind of intense empathy, which he called "direct psychoanalysis," for a patient's psychosis. Attempts were made to enter the patient's psychotic "reality," as he said, often by orchestrating it, using the patient's family as actors, or as follows: "The patient's mouth is pulled and distorted as with pain. As sick as his mind is, he has still not lost the faculty of expressing his thoughts with speech. He says it isn't a pain; he says it's an ache. He has been going to the dentist with it, pain or ache, for fifteen years but to no avail. He has been to the hospital and has had many shock treatments, but still he has that awful torture in his mouth. One day I pictured this patient as an infant injuring his mouth on a stony breast. I told him about it, and he was able to reflect. He wondered that he had never thought of that before. The pain stopped, a long time has passed, and there is no more talk of pain in the mouth, no grimacing, no need for a dentist. . . . I tried to find the words to describe what this patient went through and what I did to help him, but there are no words for this experience. (J. Rosen, *Direct Analysis*, preface.)

bizarre, were presumed to be as thick with systematic meaning, to be as orderable, as that of any ethnographic data. They played each others tapes and films, trying simply to make sense of schizophrenic utterance. In one case, Bateson presented a tape in which a patient made oblique references to the characters whom he called Frude and Littleton. "Gregory presumed ... that [he] was Frude, that is Freud, and Littleton was this little, short guy, about half Gregory's height, himself. Haley and I had two patients who were both named Earl. So we would refer to them as 'the two Earls,' and at least mine kept referring to himself as a nobleman, as a sort of play on his own name."[76]

Their collaboration at this point had a miscellaneous quality. "We dabbled around," Weakland said, "in all sorts of communicative situations."[77] Partly, they were preoccupied with grasping the central ideas of their project. Bateson rehearsed his views on the structure of communication, with varied success. Strolling together one day, he and Fry watched the operation of a circling-arm lawn sprinkler. Reminded of the oscillating character of paradox, Bateson asked the psychiatrist to specify the direction in which the arm was rotating.

> As we were far enough from the sprinkler for the mechanisms in optical illusion to operate, I found it necessary to tell Bateson first "Clockwise," then "Counterclockwise," and then "It's alternating with each half turn between clockwise and counterclockwise." Finally I was forced by the evidence of my apparent vision to state that the sprinkler did not appear to be rotating at all, and that the two arms from which the two streams of water spouted were crossing back and forth, apparently through each other, so that one arm was first on the left and then the right, while the other arm occupied the opposite pole— all of this in a two dimensional plane. After I reached this peak of confusion, we walked up closer and found that the sprinkler was, in truth, consistently and without hesitation, rotating in the clockwise direction. Although I was not actually visualizing a material operation of, say the Epimenides paradox, what I did see made it infinitely easier to comprehend paradox thereafter.[78]

But in general, Fry, Haley, and Weakland found the theory of logical types obscure and troublesome to assimilate. In their informal weekly meetings, according to Weakland, "the main topic of conversation was, 'What is this project about?'"[79] Haley has put it more firmly: "The first difficulty within the group centered on whether the paradoxes of abstraction were relevant to anything important in human life."[80]

The idea that messages occurred in simultaneous combination with other messages that can qualify them was clarified by S. I. Hayakawa's paradox:

> All statements within this frame are untrue.

They began to say that the metamessage frames the message, i.e., tone frames speech. The unusual behavior of the schizophrenic then seemed to be an inability or an unwillingness to codify conventional "framing" messages. A pathological otter might answer a playful slap with brutality—misframing the message "this is play." Schizophrenics seemed to do similarly. They "confused" metaphor with literal statement and failed to discriminate fantasy from reality, the jocular from the serious, or the sincere from the histrionic. They generally abused, and were abused by, the implicit and involuntary signals which immediately classify the human relations and feelings going on within the exchange. A schizophrenic patient in the hospital canteen, the story went, is asked by a counter girl, "What can I do for you?" He does not refer to the context and loses her meaning. Is it a sexual advance, a threat, or an offer of coffee?

Haley advanced their understanding by pointing out the analogy to the hierarchy of logical types. Schizophrenic "word salad" was a failure to keep classes separate from members. Flattening the discontinuities between levels of abstraction resulted in metaphoric speech that took itself literally. There was no classifying metamessage—a smile perhaps, or a wink—by the patient who called himself Margaret Stalin to communicate anything about his communication. Another man, one of Bateson's patients, revealed himself to be a "mailman" one Monday morning. "In a few minutes it appeared that 'mailman' was a metaphor referring to the fact that he had been pacing the ward over, throughout the weekend and had walked as far as a mailman. Further discussion disclosed that 'mail' was also a pun. Bitter and with tears in his eyes, he described his former wife as a 'mailbag'—a double pun."[81]

By April 1954, although Bateson and Haley continually disputed definitions of terminology, the project members had achieved a modicum of consensus.* They shared common research problems, but their theoretical concepts lacked precision. They agreed to think in terms of exchanges of potentially paradoxical levels of messages, demonstrated in animal play and human laughter, in fictional films, in psychotherapy, and increasingly in

---

* "Gregory had some alcoholics he was working with," Haley recalled "and I was disagreeing with the way he was handling them. But I didn't know anything about it either. . . . They were too easily able to turn Gregory on, and then he'd give them some lecture, and I could see that nothing was going to change." (Personal communication: 14 January 1976.)

schizophrenia. As a two-year-old research group, though, they had published nothing. In science, of course, private consensus is rarely supported. To make the situation worse, at the Rockefeller Foundation, Chester Barnard had retired. Haley remembered Bateson's pessimism before returning to New York City to apply for the grant renewal. "He said he was sure that they were going to say no. And he went back there, and they said no."[82] No one left the project despite the crisis. Bateson recalled, "My team loyally stayed with me without pay."[83]

For a second time, he was in panic for his professional life. Among others to whom Gregory turned—at the age of fifty—was Norbert Wiener. "Can you suggest any persons or foundations who you think might be interested in the study of the natural history of human communication?"[84] During Bateson's trip east, they speculated that a telephone system might be termed schizophrenic "if it mistook numbers mentioned in the conversation between subscribers for those numbers which are the names of subscribers."[85] A telephone system might be programmed—and might learn—not to discriminate between its reactions to numbers, and react to all numbers as if they identified the callers. Bateson had discussed his analysis of play with Wiener, in which this kind of type confusion occurred. The message "this is play" qualified itself and the behaviors to which it referred. A class and a member of a class were collapsed, creating something like the Cretan's paradox. Amid his anxieties about the death of his research project, Bateson recalled this conversation when he dictated a letter to the mathematician. With Haley acting as secretary, he constructed an ugly scene in which the ability to confuse logical types might be conditioned. He assumed that punishment was the reinforcement involved because avoiding it was also rewarding, and because behavior conditioned by punishment tended to persist long after the cessation of the reinforcement.

As I understand it, type confusion leads to paradox when both message and metamessage contain negatives. On this principle we can *imagine* [italics added] the generation of paradox in the deutero-learning system when an organism experiences punishment following some failure and learns that it must not learn that punishment follows failure. This would be approximately the picture of a man who, having been punished for failure, later is punished for showing his expectation of punishment after, e.g., is punished for cringing. ... It thus seems to me that the Epiminedes paradox latent in the message "this is play" becomes almost the same as the paradox generated by unlearning to unlearn. But of this last step I am unsure.[86]

In his desperation, Bateson had worked out a rough expression of hypothetical learning context, the project's slang for which soon became "double bind."*

For financial reasons, the nominal focus of the project turned to the investigation of logical typing in schizophrenic communication and to the learning of these habits. Six months later, by the winter of 1954, on the basis of his little documented conception, another two-year grant was obtained through Frank Fremont-Smith of the Josiah Macy, Jr., Foundation. Bateson reiterated his hypothesis, in the application, in terms of mother-infant learning. Could an unwitting child be trained to be schizophrenic?

> It is suggested that the base for later psychosis may be laid in infancy by the experience of dealing with a mother who both punishes the child for certain actions and punishes the child for learning that punishment will follow certain actions, i.e., she generates paradox in the child by combining negative learning with negative deutero-learning. That such an experience would be traumatic for a child is easy to imagine. But we are not concerned here with the mere matter of pain. Our hypothesis concentrates upon the formal structure of the pain-producing context.[87]

Curiously, at the time when the Macy Foundation was willing to support the future of these ideas, Bateson's student-colleagues did not know what to make of them. Since he had arrived at the hypothesis deductively—almost intuitively—there was no data to offer them. When Haley and Weakland took him for a secluded weekend in the mountains, to plan the upcoming round of research, not least of their intentions was to clarify the new notion for themselves. Haley recalled the situation:

> We all sat up there in this cabin.... Actually we were trying to find out what on earth Gregory was talking about. And he couldn't tell us.... We were asking, "How do you know that a schizophrenic is so because he is punished for being punished?" It took about six or eight hours, and finally he said, "Well that's *the sort of thing* that must be happening." Then we knew what he was talking about.... He never had any data. It was a hypothesis really, that Gregory pulled out of the sky, on the basis of looking at the way people communicated.[88]

---

*Gregory later felt obliged to Wiener. "It was because I was writing you that I could think those thoughts on that day. Life is not so simple that we can say that this man contributes this idea and that man that idea. There is also the mass of thoughts that are generated by interaction." (GB to N. Wiener, circa April 1954.)

Perhaps, in illustrating the notion of double bind communication, Bateson was reminded of the stark cruelty in the Pontifex family, so damned in *The Way of All Flesh*. Perhaps he alluded to this book's place within the deadly paradoxes of his family of origin. And perhaps there was reference made to the spate of double deaths in Bateson's current family life. One can only speculate without memory or document. More likely, the mountain discussion among the three men began with the suggestive movies Gregory had made of schizophrenic families. Most likely it roamed widely within his career: touching upon the observations made with Margaret Mead of Balinese mothers' titillating frustration of their children, upon deutero-learning and experimentally induced neurosis, upon computers oscillating as if caught in Russellian paradoxes, and upon the self-negating message "this is play," exchanged by otters. At the age of fifty-one, Bateson was trying to express a remarkable amount of his cultural background and current thinking. It remained for the idea to make its way outward—among psychiatrists at first, and then throughout Europe and America of the middle twentieth century.

In 1955, as the Bateson project shifted toward schizophrenia, the psychiatrist Jackson, in any case an enterprising man, began to play a larger role. He prodded them to record, to transcribe, to publish, and to credit priority. Both Haley and Weakland agreed that the group's first paper on the double bind hypothesis was the outcome of Jackson's organizational nature. Bateson had misgivings about publishing prematurely. Continuing observations of schizophrenics and their therapists, they prepared the classic article, "Toward a Theory of Schizophrenia," though the ideas were still skeletal.[89] In 1956, an overview of their research appeared in the first issue of the journal *Behavioral Science,* which outlined the place they gave to a hierarchy of levels of abstraction in their conception of communication and learning, and affirmed that breaches of the hierarchy had significance for schizophrenics and therapists.

> According to our hypothesis, the term "ego function" (as this term is used when a schizophrenic is described as having a "weak ego function") is precisely *the process of discriminating communicational modes either within the self or between the self and others.* The schizophrenic exhibits weakness in three areas of such function: a) He has difficulty in assigning the correct communicational mode to the messages he receives from other persons. b) He has difficulty in assigning the correct communicational mode to those messages which he himself utters or emits nonverbally. c) He has difficulty in assigning the correct communicational mode to his own thoughts, sensations, and percepts.[90]

Assuming the view that in communication, there are primary messages which are verbal and classifying messages which express the on-going relationship of the actors, they proposed that the discourse of schizophrenics especially distorts or omits the signals about relationship. Haley's analogy was that this sort of communication bore resemblence to an unaddressed telegram: I (the sender) am sending something (the message) to you (the receiver) in this situation (the context). A schizophrenic might avoid defining the implicit messages of relationship by mislabeling any one of these four elements. Calling himself somebody else, he could deny his own involvement with the message (and often, schizophrenics do not use the first or second pronoun). By creating obscure metaphor, or by emphasizing the playful aspect of the communication, he could camouflage the message or deny its personal import. By refusing to acknowledge the receiver's existence, he could converse as if to his own imagination when the other person "happened" to be there. Simply by denying the context, he could make a hospital into a gas station. Haley contributed an illustration of this communication to the 1956 paper.

> A patient may wish to criticize his therapist for being late for an appointment, but he may be unsure of what sort of message that act of being late was—particularly if the therapist has anticipated the patient's reaction and apologized for the event. The patient can not say, "Why were you late? Is it because you don't want to see me today?" This would be accusation, and so he shifts to a metaphorical statement. He may then say, "I knew a fellow once who missed a boat, his name was Sam, and the boat almost sunk.". . . . The indication that it is a metaphorical statement lies in the fantastic aspect of this metaphor, not in the signals which usually accompany metaphors to tell the listener that a metaphor is being used.[91]

Corresponding to these patterns of sending messages, schizophrenic *codification* of them was altered. The ability to discriminate the various contextual cues which specify both the semantic and personal meaning of a message seemed to be impaired. Human communication was construed in terms of multiple levels of reference, which they called an onionskin structure. The schizophrenic then did not hold the levels in check. Instead of codifying the whole package of messages and disentangling from them the appropriate one, he appeared to respond as if to all of them at once. Bateson pointed to the difficulty such people commonly have interpreting proverbs—themselves resonant with implication—as evidence of the breakdown in their capacity to distinguish levels of meaning.

Proverbs are, in general, very much like schizophrenic utterance and it is, perhaps, the schizoid personalities who contribute these items to our culture. A proverb commonly has multiple levels of reference. "Don't cry over spilt milk" carries a multitude of meanings which may be enumerated:

1. The past cannot be changed.
2. Emotional and autonomic outbursts do not serve pragmatic purpose.
3. The second law of thermodynamics is supreme, and when any organism or organic product has been randomized, "all the king's horses and all the king's men" cannot sort it out again.
4. You have been weaned and it's time to be a man. . . . To the schizophrenic, it is as if all these meanings are present simultaneously but in such a way that no one of them can be brought separately upon the screen of consciousness. When offered an interpretation even of his own utterance, he will commonly accept it even if he had really scarcely entertained that particular aspect of the matter in his mind before.[92]

The problem which they posed for the schizophrenic was *how* does a simple statement mean if it is not pinned down by normal metamessages.* Bateson translated conventional Kraepelinian diagnostic categories into communicational terms. (1.) The paranoid patient will assume that behind every statement lurks a concealed meaning detrimental to his welfare. (2.) The hebephrenic patient will ignore the levels of message and laugh them all off. (3.) The catatonic patient will entirely give up receiving all messages.

While granting that the symptomatology of the disease could be based in an as yet unidentified genetics, Bateson and his group were more concerned to explain the observable side of schizophrenia. More personally, Gregory's empathy with their pain and the way he appreciated their sense of humor sustained his interest in the human matrix within which "the confused loneliness" of the schizophrenic made a "sort of sense."[93] Genes or combinations of genes, Bateson said in 1959, "will . . . only alter patterns and potentialities in the learning process, and . . . certain of the resultant patterns when confronted by appropriate forms of environmental stress, will lead to overt schizophrenia."[94] The atavism was ironic, although expectable perhaps, for

---

*But the two sides of the schizophrenic's communicational difficulties were not seen to be an isolated phenomenon. "We all make errors of [cue interpretation] at various times," Bateson wrote. "I'm not sure that I've ever met anybody that doesn't suffer from 'schizophrenia' . . . more or less. We all have some difficulty in deciding whether a dream was a dream and it would not be very easy for most of us to say *how* we know that a piece of our own fantasy is fantasy and not experience. The ability to place an experience in time is one of the important clues and referring it to a sense-organ is another." (GB, "Epidemiology of schizophrenia," in *Steps*, p. 197.)

Bateson's interest in learning theory had developed from his strong ambivalence about the genetics of his youth. The double bind theory of schizophrenia then provided him with a complicated arena in which he could argue about the priority of nature and nurture for the rest of his life.

> These [genetic] theories seem to me of little interest until the proponents try to specify what components of the complex process of determining "schizophrenia" are provided by the hypothetical gene. To identify these components must be a subtractive process. Where the contribution of environment is large the genetics cannot be investigated until the environmental effect has been identified and can be controlled.[95]

The 1956 double bind paper explained that the schizophrenic had deutero-learned to "live in a universe where the sequences of events are such that his unconventional habits of communication will be ... appropriate."[96] Rather than emphasize the impact of single traumatic events, the Bateson project looked to on-going sequential patterns of interaction that included the entire family.[97] Bateson had tried to describe this point of view the year before during a conference sponsored by the University of Utah department of psychiatry and psychology.

> I am not talking at all about the content of ... traumatic sequences whether they be sexual or oral. Nor am I talking about the age of the subject at the time of trauma nor about which parent is involved. I'm only building up toward the statement that the trauma must have had formal structure in the sense that multiple logical types were played against each other to generate this particular pathology in this individual.[98]

The problem had two parts: what was the pattern of communication within families of schizophrenics? and how were such patterns learned? To answer the second question, they proposed a general formulation. "The hypothesis we offer is that sequences of this kind [message confusion] in the external experience of the patient *are responsible for* [italics added] the inner conflicts of Logical Typing. For such unresolvable sequences of experience we use the term 'double bind.'"[99] This communication was said to require two or more people *in intense and vitally important relationship,* who repeatedly engage in contradiction and conflation so that this pattern comes to possess the preschizophrenic's expectations of all interaction. The double bind experience was defined as a triadic constellation of conflicting messages at different levels of abstraction. (1.) The "binder," usually the mother, makes a primary negative injunction, something like, "If you do not do such and such, I will punish you severely." (2.) This is accompanied *simultaneously* by a secondary injunction inconsistent with the primary one. Possibly nonverbal, it is of a higher level of abstraction disqualifying the primary one, although like the first it is extremely threatening. The verbal expression might be "But do not see this as a punishment," or "Do not think of what you must not do," or "Do not question my love," of which the primary injunction is, or is not, an example. (3.) There is finally, a tertiary negative injunction, which prohibits the bound child from escaping the relationship. This message is usually implicit in the context of the nuclear family and in the terror of parental rejection. Jackson proposed a clinical illustration of the paradoxical pattern.

> A young man who had fairly well recovered from an acute schizophrenic episode was visited in the hospital by his mother. He was glad to see her and impulsively put his arm around her shoulders, whereupon she stiffened. He withdrew his arm and she asked, "Don't you love me any more?" He then blushed, and she said, "Dear, you must not be so easily embarrassed and afraid of your feelings." The patient was able to stay with her only a few minutes more and following her departure he assaulted an aide and was put in the tubs.[100]

The primary injunction here, "Show me affection," was stipulated by the mother's presence. In response to her son's warmth, she stiffened, communicating the secondary injunction, "I don't like it when you do." Finally, the tertiary injunction denied both their awkwardness: "Talk to me, be open and comfortable. I'm your mother."

Recurring communication in the schizophrenic family was said to consist of a child whose mother becomes anxious when he responds to her as a loving mother; of a mother who cannot express this anxiety and hostility, and forces loving behavior to persuade the child to respond to her as if she were a loving mother, but withdraws from him if he does not; and of the absence of a strong curtailing force, e.g., a father, to support the child. He is caught in experience similar in structure to the infinite regress of Russell's paradox. The mother, hostile or withdrawing when the child approaches, tries to counteract her hostility by sending loving messages just as the child loses interest or is hurt. The child must look for a way out. If he interprets his mother's communications for what they seem to be, and responds in kind to her loving messages, she will withdraw, and if he withdraws, she will respond lovingly, and when he responds to that, she will withdraw, ad nauseum. "The important point is that her loving behavior is then a comment on (since it is compensatory for) her hostile behavior and consequently it is of a different *order* of message than the hostile behavior—it is a message about a sequence of messages. Yet by its nature it denies the existence of those messages which it is about, i.e., the hostile withdrawal."[101]

To continue the relationship, the child will learn to distort his processes of codification. If his mother says, "Go to bed, you're tired," in a cranky voice, metacommunicating "Get out of my sight," the child may not correctly interpret the message. If he does, he suffers the punishment of the hateful metamessage that his mother has sent. He may prefer to accept deception. To survive he must falsely discriminate the messages of others.[102] Even this is not a solution, for if he accepts his mother's message-codification system, he is loving her, which she cannot tolerate. Thus *the child is punished for discriminating accurately what she is expressing and he is punished for discriminating inaccurately, he is caught in a double bind."[103]* Jay Haley suggested that certain practices of Zen Buddhism were analogous.

> The goal is to achieve enlightenment. The Zen master attempts to bring about enlightenment in his pupil in various ways. One of the things he does is to hold a stick over the pupil's head and say fiercely, "If you say this stick is real, I will strike you with it. If you say the stick is not real, I will strike you with it. If you don't say anything, I will strike you with it." We feel that the schizophrenic finds himself continually in the same situation as the pupil, but he achieves something like disorientation rather than enlightenment.[104]

Bateson filmed a number of schizophrenic children, one of whom had a woolly animal which he treated as a safe and healthy surrogate for himself. He tried to use his animal as a recipient of his mother's affection, saying, "Jocko wants to kiss you, Mommy." The animal could ask to do what the child could not quite dare to do. Touched, the mother still responded outwardly as if this were an attack. She accused her child of using devious tricks to get attention. Were the child able to question his mother about the meaning of her messages, the double bind might be broken. Yet to make such a remark would be interpreted as reproach, prompting punishment for distorting the mother's intent. In this way, all exits are blocked. In normal relations, on the other hand, metacommunication goes on constantly. In order to assure accurate message discrimination, people make direct comments, or ask questions like "What do you mean?" "Why did you do that?" or "Are you kidding?" The schizophrenic child was unable to use this level of metacommunication. He had grown up "unskilled in his ability to communicate about communications and, as a result, unskilled in determining what people really mean, and unskilled in expressing what he really means."[105]

Bateson's favorite illustration of the double bind sequence, a scene in the children's story *Mary Poppins,* appeared in a later paper. In the scene, the English nanny, Mary Poppins, has taken her charges, Jane and Michael Banks, to get something to eat at a gingerbread shop. They there find two large and sad young women, the Misses Annie and Fannie, whose mother, Mrs. Corry, comes out from the back of the store.

> "I suppose you've all come for some gingerbread?"
> "That's right, Mrs. Corry," said Mary Poppins politely.
> "Good. Have Fannie and Annie given you any?" She looked at Jane and Michael as she said this.
> Jane shook her head. Two hushed voices came from behind the counter.
> "No, mother," said Miss Fannie meekly.
> "We were just going to, Mother—" began Miss Annie in a frightened whisper.
> At that Mrs. Corry drew herself up to her full height and regarded her gigantic daughters furiously. Then she said in a soft, fierce, terrifying voice:
> "Just going to. Oh, *indeed*! That is *very* interesting. And who may I ask, Annie, gave you permission to give away *my* gingerbread—?"
> "Nobody, Mother. And I didn't give it away. I only thought—"
> "You only thought! That is *very* kind of you. But I will thank you not to think. I can do all the thinking that is necessary here!" said Mrs. Corry in her soft, terrible voice. Then she burst into a harsh cackle of laughter.
> "Look at her! Just look at her! Cowardy-custard! Cry-baby!" she shrieked, pointing her knotty finger at her daughter.
> Jane and Michael turned and saw a large tear coursing down Miss Annie's huge, sad face, but they did not like to say anything for in spite of her tininess, Mrs. Corry made them feel rather small and frightened.[106]

Mrs. Corry's double binding question to her daughters, "Have Annie and Fannie given you any" is ambiguous. Are they being encouraged or criticized? She puts the girls in suspense—before humiliating them completely. Even before this turnabout though, Miss Annie speaks in terror, almost asking for her mother's sadism. "The two young women have been caught in similar traps before," Bateson pointed out, "but even so they get caught again."[107] However, the active role of the child in the sequence, as well as the contribution of the father, only gained emphasis in later years. The 1956 paper stressed the mother. The view only later developed that the bound offspring participated by provoking and expecting paradox. By 1962, the source of the contradiction was shifted away from the mother so as to include the "victim" and the father.[108]

The most useful way to phrase double bind description is *not* in terms of a binder and a victim, but in terms of people caught up in an on-going system which produces conflicting definitions of relationship and consequent subjective distress. In its attempts to deal with the complexities of multi-level patterns of human communication systems, the research group prefers an emphasis upon circular systems of interpersonal relations to a more conventional emphasis on the behavior of individuals alone or single sequences in the interaction.[109]

The double bind sequence contributed not only to psychopathology but was applicable to psychotherapy as well. Project members had conferred with the psychiatrist Freida Fromm-Reichmann, when she was in Palo Alto, at the Ford Center for Advanced Study in the Behavioral Sciences.* Fromm-Reichmann's therapeutic techniques, they noticed, made conspicuous and benevolent use of paradoxical messages. Not part of the deadly struggle between parent and child, she could both accept and deny a patient's fantasy. As Fromm-Reichman told her celebrated case, "I'm willing to talk with you in terms of [your]

---

*Bateson admired Fromm-Reichmann. After her death in 1957, he delivered a lecture in her honor, recounting their contact the previous year. She had come to Palo Alto at age sixty-seven, to enrich her psychiatric skills with the fields of semantics, linguistics, and communications. "She already had extraordinary senstivity to the overtones and nuances of human behavior, but she said she felt insufficiently conscious of the actual nonverbal cues from which she arrived at her conclusions." (GB, "Language and psychotherapy," *Psychiatry* 21 [1958]: 97.) She collected two linguists, Norman N. A. McQuown and Charles F. Hockett, the anthropologist Ray L. Birdwhistell, and another psychiatrist, Henry W. Brosin, to study paralinguistic—nonverbal—phenomena in the psychiatric interview. While waiting for a film of such interaction to be prepared, they analyzed one of Bateson's films of a schizophrenic family, as a result of which he joined Fromm-Reichmann's project, The Natural History of an Interview. (GB, H. W. Brosin, R. L. Birdwhistell, et al., *The Natural History of an Interview* [Chicago: University of Chicago Library Microfilm Collection of Manuscripts in Cultural Anthroplogy] 15[1971]: 95-98.)

Later, when they worked on a film of Bateson with a patient, he was especially impressed by Fromm-Reichman's ability to maintain a productive group of individualists and to support him in particular, in "moments of considerable pain when the others were interpreting my actions and I was forced to see those actions on the screen." (GB, "Language and psychotherapy," p. 99.) Not only did she seem to possess a wider view than he of interpersonal process in family pathology, but also she seemed to have a firmer grasp on the conceptual unity of subject and object, and of self and other, which Bateson aspired to elaborate into a new personal and theoretical synthesis. "The universe of humanity does not have the objective character which has been a source of reassurance to the natural scientists since the days of Locke and Newton. . . . For everybody who would work in the sciences of man, every new discovery and every new advance is an exploration of the self. When the investigator starts to probe unknown areas of the universe, the back end of the probe is always driven into his own vital parts." (Ibid., p. 96.)

world, if only you know that I do it so that we have understanding that it doesn't exist for me."[110]

Together with their survey of the practices of psychotherapists, each man was treating individual patients, with varying degrees of enthusiasm. Haley, and later Weakland, began part-time family practices. Jackson became director of psychiatry at the Palo Alto Clinic, and Fry continued his psychiatric career. By contrast to his colleagues, Bateson was less eager to apply his thinking therapeutically. He had led them into clinical waters, having treated patients from the time of his entry into the psychiatric profession in 1948. Even as early as 1935, he was thinking about psychotherapeutic strategies. Psychoanalytic therapy stressed an individual's intrapsychic processes and oedipal history. In *Naven*, Bateson had already asked, "Might psychotherapy find success by drawing a patient's attention to his immediate behavior?" For patients who were preoccupied with notions of inevitable destiny, the historical orientation of psychoanalysis might be inappropriate treatment. Such patients might be better assisted by insights into on-going escalating relations. "A sense of contemporary process," Bateson had then imagined, "is perhaps a necessary corrective to an overdeveloped sense of personal history."[111]

As a therapist, Bateson again maintained reservations about the invasive enterprise of applied social science. He believed that seeing patients was secondary to the matter of theoretical exploration. "While I have cared for several schizophrenic patients," he asserted in 1962, "I have never been intellectually interested in *them*. The same is true of my work with native peoples in New Guinea and Bali. Always my intellectual focus has been on general principles which were illustrated or exemplified in the data."[112] His conduct toward them was patrician, rather casual, but friendly and warm. Bateson drank coffee with patients and played golf. Weakland confirmed this, and Haley held that, "Gregory used to bust his ass for patients, in terms of making himself available. He would see them all the time. . . . He spent hours with them, walking around. . . . Gregory really extended himself. He'd stay up all night with alcoholics, to get them through. . . . He felt that being human with people was good for them."[113]

Bateson treated a number of patients between 1948 and 1963, when he left psychiatry. However there was one focal individual who was a short, Catholic-raised, thirty-five-year-old, ex-Air Force machinist. Despite his psychosis, the man possessed considerable, even rhythmic, verbal skills. During the second week of treatment, they had the following exchange, which Bateson taped.

Patient. When you have to send a shirt back to the factory, it becomes awfully incriminoiding. So those who force a man to have to smoke to take him out of a bank building, and do things like that to him become overintoxicated when they have gray au-to-mo-biles. Understand?

Bateson. No.

P. That's perfect.

B. I wasn't meant to anyway, so what the hell?

P. It wasn't meant to have movement in it.

B. One half of this whole competition or war—or call it whatever you like—is [you] trying to make it difficult for Gregory Bateson to understand what [you] want to say. But [you] still want to say it, like hell.

P. Listen, some of us weren't using ... if you ever confuse an eye, you'll never get a man to write his name. (Patient stands up and starts to orate, pacing the floor.) No-doze tablets are reasonable. They always say "Awake!" "Awake!" "Awake!"[114]

Already hospitalized for twelve years when they met, the patient spoke in terms of a rich, although opaque metaphoric language—word salad—which Bateson spent weeks and months translating. The man died of leukemia in 1957, but in the course of their activity together, Bateson several times watched and possibly helped him out of his madness. One day he was "52318," which Bateson identified as a code. Each number corresponded to a letter of the alphabet, except that the last number was one less than the initial of the man's real surname, because he refused to use *I*, the ninth letter of the alphabet. Another day, he was the abdicated "King Edward," testing the "British Admiralty." After a succession of the patient's identities hinted about wanting to stop the therapy. Bateson was firm in his refusal to that day's persona, adding, "When I talk, I talk to all of them." It happened over a cup of coffee, that the patient said his real name. Bateson thought this was an enormous achievement, a momentary assimilation of the man's vast diversities. On another occasion, after thoroughly confusing his therapist, he blurted, "Bateson, you want me to come and live in your world. I have lived in it from 1920 to 1943, and I don't like it."[115] Unprepared for the sudden candor, Gregory could offer no reply.

While they were playing golf, Bateson was again surprised that his patient could talk a normal game, and act like an ordinary sportsman.* They

---

*"I took him out to the golf course. He was obviously frightened. He wanted me to hit my ball first, which I did. I didn't dare pull my stroke deliberately because I was sure that he would be aware if I did, but I was fortunate and only hit a hole in the grass." (GB, "The message 'This is play,'" in *Group Processes: 1955,* ed. B. Schaffner [New York: Josiah Macy, Jr., Foundation, 1956], p. 149.)

were a typical twosome for a number of holes until the patient duffed a shot and slipped back into his unintelligible schizophrenic speech. Temporarily, the game had provided a play frame for this man, in which he could behave normally. "But when the frame was modified by competition and when he started to fail, it became a little harder."[116] The first time they had played spontaneously. The second time, Bateson tried to manipulate their play. The two of them were walking on the hospital grounds toward the golf course when the therapist suggested that they "try" another game. The patient at once "turned around and said nothing. He walked in the opposite direction, his back to the golf course."[117] They walked for some time, Bateson wondering what had happened. Finally on the hunch that his patient had taken his phrasing of the invitation literally, Gregory said, "I was a fool to say, 'Let's *try* a game of golf.' Why should we do that? Let's *play* a game of golf."[118] Evidently they then went off and had a pleasant afternoon's stroll around the links.

Patient and therapist developed a convoluted confidence in each other; the one would signal the other when ready to give up some aspect of his self-concealment. The patient was, in this instance, anorexic and threatened by the possibility of intravenous feeding. Although the wood was unusable for furniture, the man began to complain that that he was an end table of manzanita wood. Early one morning, as a ruse to eat in a different context, Bateson took his patient out of the hospital to visit his parents. On the way back, they stopped at a roadside restaurant to have a meal. Both ordered and ate well. After they finished, the patient willingly relinquished the meaning of his pun.

> He ... sat back in his chair and said, "Manzanita" (man's an eater). If the circumstances were resolved, he wood (would) [eat]. From then on, except for occasional references to a woman named "Anita," this "Manzanita" symbolism [was] not ... used. He used it initially as a *barrier* between himself and me.... "Manzanita" between us is now a statement, not that "I know how to mystify you, Mr. Bateson," but rather "This is something which we now mutually understand."[119]

Earlier that day, Bateson had gone home with the man to meet his mother. The two arrived before they were expected and no one was home. It was a tract house. A newspaper rested on the neatly trimmed lawn. The patient trembled when he walked on it to pick up the paper. The inside did not look like "a house furnished to live in, but rather [it was] furnished to look like a furnished house."[120] In the middle of the mantel stood a perfectly centered bunch of artificial flowers. When the patient's mother arrived, Bateson, the therapist, began to feel "a little uncomfortable and intruding."[121] Mother and son seemed to be getting along well, though they had not seen each other for some years. Bateson decided to leave them alone together.

> That gave me an hour in the streets with absolutely nothing to do, and I began to think what I would like to do with this setup. What and how should I communicate? I decided that I would like to put into it something that was both beautiful and untidy. . . . I decided flowers were the answer, so I bought some gladioluses. . . . When I went to get him I presented them to the mother with a speech that I wanted her to have in her house something that was "both beautiful and untidy." "Oh!" she said, "Those are not untidy flowers. As each one withers you can snip it off."[122]

If the patient mystified Bateson, his mother's answer astonished him. She felt threatened presumably and was flexing domestic muscles, reassuring *him* as if he had apologized for the quality of his gift. For Bateson, in May 1955, her distortion and his disorientation were instructive. The incident was experience of the swirl of duplicity demanded of a child growing up amid the relentless reclassifications of the schizophrenogenic mother.[123]

At that time he omitted analysis of his side of that interaction, although the gift was chosen deliberately to have an ambiguous message.[124] It was to be both "beautiful and untidy." Bateson had meant it as adornment and as critical challenge to the mother's domestic style. But for her, replying rudely would have been ungracious, while meekly accepting the gift would have acceded to the rebuke of her son's therapist of whom, perhaps, she was already suspicious. Caught in such a tangle, switching Bateson's abuse into a deferential apology was, in a sense, a shrewd parry. Repeatedly, *mutual* interaction had been a central feature of Bateson's world, among Iatmul, among Balinese, and even within his own theoretical development. Yet describing the interaction between himself and his patient's mother, he was unilateral and partial.* He later balanced this view a bit by judging the child to be "an accomplice in the parent's unconscious hypocrisy."[125] However, circa 1956, Bateson thought that

---

* "In passing, it is interesting to note that the metaphoric language of dreams is intermediate between the relational language of the cat and the objective language which human beings think they would be able to use if only it were possible to stop dreaming. In dream, we define relationships with an utter disregard for the relata. I perceive [in a dream] the contingencies of relationship between myself and my mother as being comparable to the contingencies which would obtain between a little man in a desert and a spring on top of a granite mountain. The mountain appears in a dream and the 'interpretation' of the dream becomes possible when we see that the mountain is the analogue of one of the relata in the original perception." (GB, "A social scientist views the emotions," in *Expressions of Emotions in Man*, ed. P. H. Knapp [New York: International Universities Press, 1963], pp. 233-34.)

the schizophrenic was a victim. He stated this clearly to one of the Macy Foundation's Group Processes meetings in October of that year.

> At the previous conference I introduced myself by trying to convince those present that zoology, anthropology and psychiatry are really all one and that it is perfectly natural to slide gently from one to the other via an interest in patterns. I might introduce myself this time as, on the whole, an angry man who believes that what happens to people oughtn't to happen to dogs. That at once suggests an obvious connection between psychiatry and zoology. Seriously though, I suppose the thing I hold sacred is something in the nature of patterns, and that which makes me angry is the violation of patterns in some form or other. So I find myself today trying to help them to find valuable patterns in their lives; and, on the other side of the same picture, I find myself angry at the distortions of pattern that happen to them as children. [126]

As an inadvertent outgrowth of his project's work with individual psychotics, a pioneering approach to therapy with their families developed. This turn derived from their basis in "culture-and-personality" anthropology, from Bateson's abiding stress on observable interaction and interest in learning; and it derived from Jackson's precocious view that families of schizophrenics self-corrected homeostatically in order to preserve a pernicious status quo (e.g., the improvement of one member might coincide with a disturbance in another). Early in 1956, hoping to collect data which would confirm the double bind hypothesis, they brought a sick son together with his parents to investigate the stress that this interaction seemed to arouse in the patient. "It was an information-gathering session, not a family treatment interview," Haley has written. [127] The project then gathered a sample of twenty-five middle-class families, residents of the San Francisco Bay area, which included both parents, and the identified patient was an offspring. They interviewed and observed a group of "normal" families for comparative purposes. As each worked individually with a number of families, Bateson filmed schizophrenic children interacting in their families. Despite this research, the double bind sequence remained unquantified, only anecdotes mounted up: of a mother who encouraged her child to be critical and who would condemn him for it, and of a son who elicited paradox, by sending his mother a commercial Mother's Day card, with the message "You've always been like a mother to me." [128]

Fry said Bateson's manner with these families seemed like that of "an anthropologist. . . . He was not there as a clinician or as a therapist, but as an . . . observer. [He would] switch between that role and the role of sort of a friendly mother's brother . . . raising tantalizing and significant issues. . . . They were very intuitive and hit the nail on the head, and would do all sorts of terrible things ... creating insights and stirring family patterns up."[129] The psychiatrist R. D. Laing, who came to Palo Alto toward the end of the project in 1962, recalled watching Bateson conduct a family interview.

> I don't think he ever regarded himself as a therapist, but then some of the best therapists might not do so.... If I was the patient in the session, I certainly wouldn't have felt there was anything to be frightened of. I think that's the main thing. He wasn't trying to spring people out of ... these on-going family constellations.... I don't think he ... [ever] said anything to me which indicated that he thought in terms of actually actively adopting strategic, practical means to use to pry people out of the entanglement they were in—which, in a way, you've got to be a small scale political activist to do. ... I mean you actively play off power against power. Bateson was never involved with that.[130]

Haley remembered that he worked with one family at length. "The son had a lifelong problem and Gregory succeeded in ... getting him to go to a normal school."[131] During the first interview with this family, Bateson introduced himself, stating only that he would insist on one rule: that they all be present during the sessions. There ensued a half-hour's stuttery exchange during which Bateson elicited aspects of the family's history. The son had been expelled from a long roster of schools. In addition, though, the family had moved repeatedly throughout the boy's childhood. Bateson commented at this point that gypsies lived in caravans, wandered continuously, but seemed to enjoy their lives. When he questioned why the family moved so often, the mother began to attack psychiatry in general for inventing trouble. Moving was wrong, she said, because it made it impossible to tend to a garden and to become involved with community activities.

> *Bateson.* I agree with much of what you say.
> *Mother.* Moving is just for the birds.
> *B.* Having been an old—
> *Father.* (laughing)
> *M.* And even birds stay in the same nest (laughs).
> *B.* —been an old mover myself. I spent time in New Guinea, in the Dutch Indies, and God knows what else.
> *M.* Well—
> *B.* But—
> *M.* It's all right if you're built that way. I mean each person has to do—
> *F.* No.
> *B.* I don't know.
> *M.* The reasons have to be voluntary. Mine are involuntary, I know—

B. I was frankly running away from all sorts of things.

M. Well, that's all right. (unvoiced laugh)

M. If you're running away with your own consent, but just to have to go anyway is no good, which is—

B. What's your occupation, sir?[132]

At Haley's insistence, authority relations in the schizophrenic family drew the project's attention. Bateson observed that his family regularly arrived between fifteen and twenty minutes late. His recollection gives a further picture of the heuristic quality of Bateson's therapy.

> I briefly investigated the mechanics of this regularity in the course of a conversation in which I was trying to find generalizations that could be regarded as "rules" for this family. It became evident that it was inconceivable for them to operate by a regular rule that would ensure their arrival for a family session at any specified time. The regularity of their lateness was, in fact, achieved by complex family interaction and interpersonal struggle which lasted about the same length of time every week. The father—an intermittently authoritarian figure—claimed that he tried to lay down rules, but the mother acted on the premise that no rule that he laid down could have validity because she was sure he would not maintain his own rule.[133]

In this family, exerting control and admitting it were not located in the same person. The mother persistently pestered her husband to act—e.g., to arrange their schizophrenic son's education with school officials. Losing patience when he procrastinated, she went to school and offended the administrators. The conflict had been her own fault, but she denied it because, she said, her husband should have gone in the first place. The pattern seemed to be that when he decided to act, she would undermine him anyway. For fifteen years, she blamed him for refusing to allow her to control the family finances. He admitted that he ought to have done so but felt certain that now, the situation was in hand.

> *Father.* My reasons for thinking it was a mistake are entirely different from yours, but I admit that it was a very serious mistake on my part.
>
> *Mother.* Now, you're just being facetious.
>
> *F.* No. I'm not being facetious.
>
> *M.* Well, anyway I don't care because when you come right down to it the debts were incurred, still there is no reason why a person would not be told of them. I think the women should be told.

F. It may be the same reason why when Joe [their psychotic son] comes home from school and he has had trouble, he doesn't tell you.
M. Well, that's a good dodge.[134]

The hostility in this marriage was continuous yet concealed. The wife, a keen gardener, once spent a singularly pleasant Sunday afternoon with her husband planting roses. The following morning, to her complete surprise, a taxi arrived which deposited a stranger who asked when they were vacating the house. "She did not know that from her husband's point of view the messages of shared work on the rose garden were framed within the larger context of his having agreed during the previous week to sell the house."[135] Extending the mutual disqualification to their roles as parents, they spread a contradictory web of punishments and rewards over their nearly hebephrenic seventeen-year-old son.

> He . . . had two important treats [every] week. On Sunday he went to church with his father and on Friday he went to a teen-age dance club which was a treat arranged for him by his mother; when he offended his mother, she punished him by saying he could not go to church; when he offended his father, he was forbidden to go to the teen club. His mother would say that going to the teen club was *so* good for him, and she would then comfort him by taking him to the movies that night.[136]

In 1958, Bateson began to puzzle over first principles of family organization. If schizophrenic communication was learned in the family, the problem was how to account for the "normal" abilities of unafflicted members? Irregular beach pebbles, when subjected to the beating of breaking waves, would come to resemble each other. Many would turn spherical, while others retained more distinct shapes. Bateson's notion was that the development of human groups was similar. They developed either uniformity, or systematic differentiation such that "the achievement is a sharing of premises regarding the meaning and appropriateness of messages and other acts in the context of relationship."[137] In the families of identified schizophrenics, it was as if a group had formed of relatively uniform human pebbles which contained and maintained one member, who was distinct. "As in many organizations, there is room only for one boss," he noted, "in spite of the fact that the organization operates upon those premises which would induce administrative skill and ambition in its members; so also in the schizophrenic family there may be room for only one schizophrenic."[138] If the family was an organization based in learning, Bateson then asked:

Can the peculiarities of the ... patient be seen as *appropriate*, i.e., as either homogeneous with, or complementary to, the characteristics of the other members of the group? We do not doubt that a large part of schizophrenic symptomatology is, in some sense, learned or determined by experience, but an organism can learn only that which it is taught by the circumstances of living and the experience of exchanging messages with those around him. He cannot learn at random, but only to be like or unlike those around him.[139]

To become schizophrenic was a "sacrificial" learning, internalized amid a tyranny of good intentions. In order to be close to his parents, the patient would adhere to the "sacred illusion" that family transactions were making sense, despite the metacommunicative incongruities.[140] Overt schizophrenia[141] in an offspring was viewed as a more conspicuous version, as "almost a caricature"[142] of parental obscurantism and identity loss. "They are all of them chronically afraid to entrust themselves and their emotions to the quicksand of human relationship within the family."[143]

In order to build a theoretical model of this sort of family organization, Bateson returned to that exquisite expression of Western rationality, the theory of games of Von Neumann and Morgenstern.[144] This was a mathematical study of the formal conditions, or rules, which would compel robots (armed with total intelligence and a preference for gain) to collude at the expense of excluded players. These coalitions were imagined to occur in something like a game which required at least three participants. When formed, an alliance between any two players would give rise to supplemental conventions to insure its stability. However, a game would become more provisional if five played. The difficulty in maintaining alliances would increase in proportion to the increase in the number of possible alliances. The premise of self-maximization would require that players perpetually oscillate between subcoalitions. "There will always be a circular list of alternative solutions so that the system will never cease from passing on from solution to solution, always selecting another solution which is preferable to that which preceded it."[145] Given such instability, and their total knowledge of the game, players become unable to select and carry out a single tactic.

This was the crucial correspondence. The schizophrenic family was typified not by successive purposive alliances, but rather by a rigid system of whole group indecision.

No two members seem able to get together in a coalition stable enough to be decisive at the given moment. Some other member or members of the family will always intervene. Or, lacking such intervention, the two members who contemplate a coalition will feel guilty vis à vis what the third might do or say, and will draw back from the coalition.[146]

Instead of total awareness, family members held myopic views of their interaction. Indeed, the information that each individual did possess about the goals of others served only to stimulate more subterfuge. In such a group, each player's "moves"—and beliefs about them—were invalidated in perpetual sequences of double bind experiences.

> One is surprised when one meets the members separately to find that there is strong affection between them and this, in spite of the fact that when they are together they are almost continuously hurting each other or letting each other down. They are all trapped in a system, such that any move any one of them may make to alter the current styles of behavior is penalized by the others.[147]

By contrast to the intractable premises of game theory, those of the schizophrenic family, being based upon learning, were said to be emergent. Humans adapt themselves to their experience and become emotionally committed to those adaptations. "It is this ... commitment that makes it possible for them to be hurt in the way members of a schizophrenic family are hurt."[148] The premise organizing schizophrenic families inverted the rationality of colluding Von Neumannian robots. Whereas the machines played in order to maximize "themselves," the people lived in order to negate themselves.

But how could so perverse a system maintain itself? In part, this question stemmed from their sample, which had been designed only to include intact families. The problem was that despite disruptiveness on the part of its conspicuous member, despite hospitalizations or improvements, despite maturation or parental senescence, established patterns of communication persisted unabated. Bateson looked to cybernetics for a conceptual clue. In a thermostatic heating system, two processes operated to maintain room temperature: calibration and feedback. On the basis of feedback, a furnace would shut down or would activate around a calibrated setting. Calibration then, was like human habit. They were both more economic solutions to problems than feedback, which was similar to the indefinite process of trial-and-error. There was little calibration of rules within schizophrenic families except, internally, that the psychotic offspring continue in his role and, externally, that appearances be maintained. These two rules immured each member in convoluted feedback processes which no one member could control.

The nature of unilateral dominance in their description of dyadic or family relations was an ongoing dispute between Bateson, on the one hand, and Haley and Jackson on the other. "This issue of power and control," Haley has since written, "was always a problem within the project. It seemed to me that how much power one person would allow another to have over him was a central issue in human life. It was also a particular issue in our special fields of investigation—hypnosis, therapy, and processes within the family, particularly families of the mad."[149] Bateson's reciprocal view was that Haley "believed in the validity of the metaphor of 'power' in human relations, I believed . . . that the myth of power always corrupts because it proposes a false (though conventional) epistemology."[150] At the theoretical level, they agreed that a homeostatic model was appropriate to the problem of family organization, but Haley opposed Bateson's use of game theory. Robots did not learn, he argued, and their interaction occurred within an overly defined set of choices which was expressed in terms of "decision" and not in terms of "messages." Instead Haley favored a two-level homeostatic model which was focused on family members' attempts to control the behavior of each other.[151] The one wanted to stress the struggle over who was to "set the range of behavior" in the family,[152] whereas the other preferred a view in which the behavior of the individual and the family as a whole was set by "calibrations of habit."[153]

Although based in a hospital setting, originally their study of family organization was not oriented toward psychotherapy. The revolution which conjoint family therapy brought to psychiatry,[154] according to Weakland and Jackson, had holistic and serendipitous origins. They had simply "wished to view the schizophrenic patient communicating . . . in his natural habitat which was not the hospital."[155] But as each of them became involved with these families, pressures mounted which made it difficult to keep observation separate from treatment. Their interest in clinical communication joined with these exigencies. Following the 1956 paper, Jackson, Haley, Weakland, and Fry began intensive publication of papers on the subject: distinguishing family from individual therapy, discussing the homeopathic idea of using double bind tactics therapeutically, exploring brief therapy, and developing interpretations of the role of communications paradoxes both in psychoanalysis and as a basis for a formal explanation of psychotherapeutic change.[156]

Bateson, for his part, edited an autobiography written by John Perceval, the son of an early nineteenth-century English prime minister.[157] He had bought the two-volume work—which was a narrative of Perceval's four-year psychosis—after returning from his second New Guinea field trip, and then had rediscovered owning it when the whole of his family estate arrived in California. Among a number of intentions, reissuing *Perceval's Narrative* was meant to serve as a premodern example of a double binding family, of double binding in mental institutions, and of double binding in the accusatory voices of the schizophrenic himself. Thus Perceval:

I was tormented by the commands of what I imagined was the Holy Spirit, to say other things, which as often as I attempted, I was fearfully rebuked for beginning in my own voice, and not in a voice given to me. These contradictory commands were the cause, now, as before, of the incoherency of my behaviour, and these imaginations formed the chief causes of my ultimate total derangement. For I was commanded to speak, on pain of dreadful torments, of provoking the wrath of the Holy Spirit, and of incurring the guilt of the grossest ingratitude; and at the same moment, whenever I attempted to speak, I was harshly and contumeliously rebuked for not using the utterance of a spirit sent to me; and when again I attempted, I still went wrong, and when I pleaded internally that I knew not what I was to do, I was accused of falsehood and deceit; and of being really unwilling to do what I was commanded. I then lost patience, and proceeded to say what I was desired pell-mell, determined to show that it was not fear or want of will that prevented me. But when I did this, I felt as formerly the pain in the nerves of my palate and throat on speaking, which convinced me that I was not only rebelling against God, but against nature; and I relapsed into an agonizing sense of hopelessness and of ingratitude.[158]

To introduce the book, Bateson took the opportunity to question conventional assumptions about psychosis. For Perceval the madness had ultimately cured itself. Might psychosis be comparable to "some vast and painful initiatory ceremony conducted by the self?"[159]

Gradually, in the wake of the very considerable disciplinary and public reception of the 1956 paper, psychotherapy came to dominate the project. Tension arose as this happened. At issue, Haley thought, was that Bateson

didn't like power. He didn't even like the word.... If I said that a therapist should take power, he didn't like that. If I said a therapist shouldn't take power, he didn't like that either. [laughs] ... He'd take something I said and turn it into a power issue, when I didn't mean it that way at all. He was so oversensitive to the whole issue ... and yet, he was not that way ... about Bali or Iatmul. [Do you think he'd have this conflict with anybody?] Anybody who said, "I'm going to change this person." If they said, "I will offer this person some ideas, and if they change, it's up to them," then Gregory would have no trouble with them. But if you take the responsibility for changing people, then you would have a problem. ... Any influence outside the person's range is odious to him. Any indirect manipulation is [also] out of the question. ... About ten years [after the project ended], I met Bateson at a party in New York, and ... we got into an argument that we'd had in 1959—exactly the same issues and the same positions.[160]

Bateson's growing distaste for psychiatry was one aspect of the problem. Haley suggested another which he attributed to Margaret Mead. Bateson's talent was for "the extraordinary broad concepts and . . . [the] minor little . . . details. But the middle ground, he's not so good at. She thought that she and I filled in that middle ground [for him]. . . . One of the reasons it is hard to grasp the connections . . . [Gregory makes is] because he jumps the middle. He goes to the extraordinarily broad from very small observations."[161] Bateson had little interest in experimenting with schizophrenic families or in studying treatment of them. Yet these were the grounds for which, in 1959, grants had been won from two mainstream psychiatric sources of funding. The National Institute of Mental Health had finally give them support to continue investigating family therapy, and the Foundations Fund for Research in Psychiatry had subsidized their proposal to investigate systematically double bind communication in schizophrenic and normal families.* At the time Jackson, being anxious to expand the new field of family therapy, began to establish an institute in Palo Alto. A number of consultants were more or less involved in these projects: the family counselor Virginia M. Satir, the psychologists Alex Bavelas, Charles Fulweiler, and Paul Watzlawick, and a variety of psychiatrists, Jules Riskin, M.D., and Frank Rosman, M.D., to name two. Fry recalled Bateson's uneasy questioning, when Bavelas joined the five project members in Monterey, California, to plan the new research: "What was he going to do with this Frankenstein that had been created?"[162] Weakland and Haley "didn't question what was going on. I was . . . so involved in getting my book[163] finished that I wasn't concerned. . . . Jackson was quite satisfied. He was riding his professional crest,"[164] and suggested that they subsume the Bateson project within his new Mental Research Institute (M.R.I.), itself to operate within the Palo Alto Medical Research Foundation. Gregory declined obstinately. "He didn't want to have his consultant over him as director," Haley said. "Jackson was going to be the director at M.R.I., and he wanted Gregory under him. [How did he object to that?] He said so. They had a big battle about it. Bateson wanted to know what the restrictions would be on his work and interests."[165]

The research they developed in Monterey added emphasis to family studies. Besides administering interview schedules to normal families and to

---

*The enumeration of sources of funding, along with publications in professional journals, attendance at conventions, and the like, convey to sociologists of science the degree of membership in a disciplinary community. The point is simply that the project's constituency within psychiatry was made explicit by these grants.

ones with schizophrenic members, they designed experiments during which they could watch families performing simple tasks together. The hope at the outset was "so far as . . . possible [to] engage in rough counting of double bind sequences in family interaction."[166] No double bind count emerged from this study. No firm statistical verification. Their failure was vaguely prefigured in the grant application, in which it was noted that isolated characteristics of family constellations necessarily diverted attention from "the larger patterns, and the particular variables . . . are perhaps only pathogenic when they occur in conjunction with the rest of the pathogenic pattern."[167]

Instead of counting particular responses, they attempted to distinguish categories of family according to their performances in the experimental setting. Again the peculiar complexity of their theoretical approach intervened. Collecting and measuring differences between types of relationship in natural groups, rather than differences between individual responses, required sampling categories for relationships which they could not devise. They succeeded in developing an experiment to test coalition behavior in families, however, where members scored points by pressing buttons which signaled to other members that they were willing—or willing to accept—to form an alliance. The findings Haley reported were inconclusive.[168] But it did appear that normal families could plan a game's outcome, e.g., "Let's have mother win," whereas members of schizophrenic families were prone to fatalistic predictions which they then would not fulfill, e.g., "Well, Dad won before so he will probably win again." During the game itself, which consisted of members sitting individually behind barriers, pressing buttons, schizophrenic families formed fewer coalitions, and the ones that they did achieve were likely to consist of parents without their child, rather than the equal sharing of coalitions which occurred in normal families. During the few cross-generation alliances which did form, the schizophrenic child was observed more often together with his father than with his mother.

In 1959, Bateson's interests were branching away from those of the other members of his project. The politics of this dissonance formed part of a major lecture he gave that year to the Institute for Psychosomatic and Psychiatric Research and Therapy, at the Michael Reese Hospital in Chicago. In "Minimal requirements for a theory of schizophrenia,"[169] he discussed the bearing double bind theory might have "upon evolutionary theory and biological epistemology."[170]

Theoretically, he believed that learning was organized in terms of an expanding, discontinuous hierarchy of contexts. Stimulus and response could occur in a variety of contexts, each with differing formal characteristics and with differing consequences. But however structured, specific learning always existed within a wider context—a metacontext—which in turn could be part of an infinite series of more embracing or more abstract frames. Relations between contexts were such that a metacontext could contradict a context—an appropriate response within a context of Pavlovian conditioning that occurred within an incongruous metacontext might be punished. "The organism is then faced with dilemma either of being wrong in the primary context or of being right for the wrong reasons or in a wrong way."[171] Bateson offered a human example. An interned schizophrenic, who is offered cigarettes to reinforce some conformist behavior—by a hospital staff of whom he is afraid—may prefer to resist, although this behavior may be punished. That is, the setting can skew the message. What the experimenter may see as a reward, the subject construes to be indignity.

The stress on the metaorganization of learning in communication systems—the emphasis upon relations between contexts—distinguished this new science from the realm of nineteenth-century materialism on two counts: (1.) in such systems no energy is exchanged; and (2.) in Newtonian physics the movement of a free-falling object is uninfluenced by wider context. Indeed, communication systems did not contain "objects" at all, only exchanges of transforms of messages in hierarchies of contexts. The individual was not to be bound by his body, given such a view, but rather by channels of message. "It is not communicationally meaningful to ask whether the blind man's stick or the scientist's microscope are 'parts' of the man who uses them."[172] An idealist epistemology was thus emerging.

> This world, of communication, is a Berkeleyan world, but the good bishop was guilty of understatement. Relevance or reality must be denied not only to the sound of the tree which falls unheard in the forest but also to this chair which I can see and on which I am sitting. My perception of the chair is communicationally real, and that on which I sit is, for me, only an idea, a message in which I put my trust.[173]

Following Darwin, Bateson noted that theorists of evolution assumed that learning was essentially a stochastic, or probabilistic, process in which accidental physiological changes were reinforced, or extinguished, according to their survival value. Learning was said to give "direction to the accumulation of random changes of the neural systems, just as natural selection is seen as giving direction to the accumulation of random changes of variation."[174] In C. H. Waddington's work on phenocopies of *Drosophila*, however, the changes in the phenotype under environmental stress appeared to contribute to the maintenance of a hereditary line amid stress and competition. Bateson proposed to construe the process by which such changes occur in terms of a parsimonious hierarchy of adaptation. A given problem is solved by trial and error in learned behavior until, in the course of successful solutions, habitual or automatic technique develops. "It would appear that in learning when the solution of a given problem has been passed on to habit, the stochastic or exploratory mechanisms are set free for the solution of other problems, and it is quite conceivable that a similar advantage is achieved by a passing on the business of determining a somatic characteristic to the gene-script."[175] Was there an analogy, as Samuel Butler had thought, between the formation of habit and evolutionary adaptation?[176] It would seem, Bateson suggested, that two stochastic systems—somatic and chromosomal—would be compelled by selective conditions to operate on a parallel basis, although no message originating in somatic change might pass to the germ plasm. As far as the relationship between genetics and schizophrenic communication, there was to be no reductive solution. "We cannot simply assume that the hospitalized [patient] carries a gene for schizophrenia and that the others do not."[177] If schizophrenia was viewed as a modification or distortion of the learning process, then the problem was one of identifying the degree of genetic preparation for this sort of learning that an identified patient—or covertly schizophrenic family—might possess.

Bateson argued that any science, once it makes normative claims to the unique accuracy of its findings, has moral implications. "In breaking away from the premise that contexts are always conceptually isolable, I have let the notion of a universe much more unified—and in that sense much more mystical—than the conventional universe of nonmoral materialism."[178] Did this view of messages interacting within an infinite regress of contexts propose an ethical position? Bateson addressed the psychiatric audience specifically by considering the nature "of 'control' and the whole related complex suggested by words such as manipulation, spontaneity, free will, and technique."[179] If individuals were composed of their relations with others, then they possessed only a limited command over any whole system in which they participate. "Just as in logic a proposition can never determine the metaproposition, so also in matters of control the smaller context can never determine the larger."[180] To control life, with its complicated chains of causation, would be as difficult as trying to back up a truck that is pulling a number of linked trailers. The range of angles within which the trailers are lined up straight is very small, and the potentiality for jackknifing is proportionately large. Control required the skill of a delicate hand. The problems of manipulating other men resembled creating art. Both were unpredictable and mistakes in both could result in ugliness. The moral Bateson drew took the form of a stricture and an aspiration.

> We social scientists would do well to hold back our eagerness to control that world which we so imperfectly understand. The fact of our imperfect understanding should not be allowed to feed our anxiety and so increase the need to control. Rather, our studies could be inspired by more ancient, but today less honored, motive: a curiosity about the world of which we are a part. *The rewards of such work are not power but beauty* [italics added]. ... It is a strange fact that every great scientific advance—not least of the advances which Newton achieved—has been elegant.[181]

According to Warren O. Hagstrom, a sociologist of science, entire disciplines contain scientists who participate in communities of colleagues.[182] Internally, these communities are said to be arranged in status hierarchies within which researchers make reciprocal but noncontractual "gift" like exchanges of original information. Scientists make "contributions" to (their community of) knowledge. They "give" papers to symposia, and "acknowledge" one another in them. Crudely stated, what enlivens this system is recognition—incentives—from within the discipline. Recognition facilitates access to funding, but the primary currency in science is said to be social and intellectual rather than financial. In fact, herein money is "granted." Scientists are favored with honors and awards which are emblematic affirmations and increments of status within their specialities. Of these, as Robert K. Merton has luminously written, eponymy—i.e., the designation, in this sense, of an entire science or a particular innovation by reference to the discoverer's name—is the most enduring, the most distinguished, and therefore the most coveted form of recognition. To name a few, there is eponymy of epoch as in the Darwinian era, eponymy of the founding father as in Freud and psychoanalysis, eponymy of disciplinary shape as in Euclidean geometry, eponymy of law as in Planck's constant, and eponymy of instrument as in the Rorschach inkblot. "Eponymity not anonymity is the standard," at least for Merton's sociology of science. "Anonymous givers have no place in this scheme of things."[183]

This is a lofty view, to say the least, of scientists seeking to bask at the tops of their trees, but it has a relevance to the size of Bateson's intellectual resolve. As an adult scientist, he was recognized in two fields. Although *Balinese Character* was regarded somewhat quizzically, social and cultural anthropologists considered his *Naven* among the classic theoretical ethnographies of its generation.* After some twenty years in one printing, Stanford University reissued the book in 1958. In the mental-health community, he had achieved no eponymity, yet the double bind concept was entering a variety of vocabularities. Indeed, Bateson and Jackson each received the 1961 Frieda Fromm-Reichmann Award from the American Academy of Psychoanalysis in recognition of their research in schizophrenia.†

According to a sociological view, the degree of a scientist's integration within his specialist community should be augmented in proportion to the attention which greets his contribution. The dynamic of this relationship may be more complicated, however, in the case of the cross-disciplinary innovator. Despite acclaim in two fields, Bateson's membership in both was somewhat questionable. First, he was marginal to the Anglo-American anthropological community. He considered himself as such; and though former colleagues had shifted emphasis in directions which *Naven* prefigured, Bateson, maintaining very little productivity in the discipline, was more commemorated as an interesting but peripheral ancestor.[184] Secondly, his foray into psychiatry was nearing completion at the very time when its recognition of him was mounting. Other hospitals were offering clinical research opportunities when Bateson appealed to J. Robert Oppenheimer—then director of the Princeton Institute for Advanced Study—for a three-year fellowship there. "At present, I spend too much time talking to applied science people, especially psychiatric audiences whose basic scientific orientation is either uncritical or unsophisticated. I need some tougher sparring partners."[185] If this meant the company of psychologists, logicians, and information theorists, Oppenheimer was doubtful that the institute could accommodate him. "I sometimes think," Bateson noted, thanking the physicist, "that the ideal sparring partners died off like the dinosaurs at the end of the eighteenth century."[186] Disenchanted and somewhat embittered, he was withdrawing from clinical matters into the theoretical realms of learning and evolution, and into the ethologist's realm of freely interacting animals.

Eight years earlier, at the ninth Macy cybernetics conference in 1952, when Bateson presented views on humor in human communication, J. Z.

---

*Edmund R. Leach evaluated the place of *Naven* in the history of British social anthropology: "Gregory, of course, maintains that the book fell flat on its face. But really, this isn't true. I think the anthropologists who became influential in anthropology read it rather carefully, and many times, and . . . tried to get to the bottom of it. I should have thought it was not a book which was reprinted for undergraduates. It was a book which the donnerie tried to digest and tried to get hold of." (Personal communication: 17 December 1975.)

†Given to an individual in recognition of original research in the etiology, nature, or therapy of schizophrenia. (P. Wasserman and J. Mclean, eds., *Awards, Honors and Prizes*, vol. I, p. 16.)

Young, the English anatomist, had discussed simple stimulus-response experiments done with an individual octopus.[187] In a film Young then showed, Bateson noticed the "despair" of an octopus—its vertical lobe surgically removed—who was unable to solve the experimental problem. In 1960, as he prepared an essay, "The role of somatic change in evolution," for the journal *Evolution*,[188] he was still chilled by this observation, and applied to the National Science Foundation for a grant to study octopus communication. The aim was to investigate the coding of analogic—nonverbal—signals, given the assumption that their content and structure of those signals were distinct from the syntax and content of digital language. Among mammals, analogic communication possessed no negatives or logical type markers. Learned in childhood experience, it expressed the definitions of on-going relations. To wean a puppy, an adult wolf will crush the puppy down, by pressing its open mouth on the back of the infant's neck. A sort of metaphorical use of this behavior then recurs between adults. When a pack leader affirms his status, he will press down the head of an insurgent male, as if to say, "I am your senior adult male, you puppy!"[189] If the metacommunication of all vertebrate mammals seemed to derive in this fashion, from their infantile or maternal experience, then to devise a sweeping theoretical view of communication would require data from a contrasting invertebrate species. Lacking a period of maternal nurturance, yet exhibiting patterns of mammallike communication, octopus was to serve as the contrasting case. Among these creatures, a mother will attend to her eggs only until they hatch. The little octopuses then become free swimming, and settle at the sea bottom after a period of planctonic life.

> Octopus was deliberately chosen as being both complex and maximally different from the human species, both in a phylogenetic sense and in the degree to which its normal environment contrasts with that of man. . . . It was hoped that from a study of such an animal and comparison of the findings with what we know of mammals and the human species, it might be possible to add to those generalizations which can be regarded as universally true for all communication whatsoever. The notion was that if some general proposition be true both of man and octopus, then this proposition at least stands a chance of being universally true.[190]

The research committee of the Veterans Hospital was rather puzzled, Haley recalled, when Bateson applied to them for permission to set up tanks of octopus in the morgue. For a time, after an agreement was reached, he was there at all hours, observing pairs of *Octopus bimaculatus* and *Octopus bimaculoides,* until, inconvenienced by the location, he moved the tanks into the living room of his Colby Street home. Obtaining fresh seawater and maintaining tank temperatures constant were always a problem. However, there was help, in 1959, from Lois Cammack, a psychiatric social worker from North Carolina, who met Gregory when she came to Palo Alto from the Langley Porter Clinic, where she worked, to watch him do family therapy. Lois remembered her pleasure in finding that they shared an appreciation for the penetrating sensitivity and humor of schizophrenic people. Becoming first an enthusiastic participant in Gregory's current research interests, Lois then became Lois Bateson in 1961.

> Some of our early courting was done during [octopus] runs. . . . We would pack up the kids—his John and my Eric—and the camping gear. We'd take off in his jeep, and go down to La Jolla camping along the way. We would collect octopuses and bring them up to the hotel room, where we had all these little bubblers and plastic bags to keep them in, until we were ready to go back. After we'd got all the octopuses we wanted, we would put everybody in the car and then marathon back to Menlo Park, so that the octopuses wouldn't die, and we could get them in the tanks. . . . Gregory was interested in how the relationships were, which nobody had ever done before. We had them in threes. We had them in twos. We had them in different combinations in tanks all over the house—just to sort of watch the kinds of relationships and cues and messages . . . that would happen. . . . It was a big family project, octopus watching.[191]

They observed two male octopuses of equal size threaten each other when newly placed together in a tank, large enough to contain several lairs. One octopus would displace the other from his spot. This was followed, in two instances, by an entire day during which both hid close together if not in actual contact, beneath the base of a sand filter. In the first case, Bateson noted, "I disturbed this arrangement by lifting the filter and the animals never returned to it."[192] The second time, the two persisted together until one left to get food. Upon return, the slightly larger one, who had remained, denied its partner entry back into the lair. "The smaller octopus came back, felt under the filter, and was driven out by threat."[193] After two to six weeks of minimal contact, the larger octopus began to steal food from the smaller one, and they fought. An hour later, the larger animal bodily "enclosed" his companion and carried off a prawn which the smaller one had been eating. Exposing its vulnerable abdomen, the smaller octopus presented itself backward, and pushed the now passive larger octopus out of its lair. "From this point on there seemed to be a mutual understanding between the two animals."[194] The Batesons observed no more combat, noting that the two octopuses often sat together with their arms interlocked, or sat one above the other so that a head nearly touched a posterior end of an abdomen. These relations persisted until both animals died of unknown causes within two days of each other.

Although these data were collected unreliably in primitive conditions, and the N.S.F. had turned down his grant application, Bateson was anticipating an extensive and systematic investigation when, in the summer of 1962, his project disbanded. He had accepted a position in the dolphin communication laboratory of John C. Lilly, M.D., in the Virgin Islands.

> What landed me in porpoise research originally was a piece in a scientific magazine, that said that the big-brained animals were not so bright. The elephants had never invented matchboxes. . . . The big brain was all a fad. I got a little angry with this and wrote a letter to John Lilly, whom I hardly knew, who was in the West Indies then. I said, "Look, let's twist this guy's tail. Am I not right that the personal relationships among these fellows, the porpoises, are where the complications come in, where they use their big brains?"[195]

Lois Bateson recalled that friends in Palo Alto saw temerity in their prospective move. "I think Gregory was ready to have some fun, to do some of the stuff that maybe he didn't do when he was younger, chasing after octopus and dolphins, all these animals that play so beautifully."[196]

In the spring of 1963, while arranging to leave for the Virgin Islands, Bateson and his friend Joseph B. Wheelwright, M.D., drove to Berkeley to attend a meeting on senescence. During the discussion, evidently, Freudian psychoanalysts characterized old age as impoverished—as the instincts subsided so did the possibility of ego development. For Gregory, however, at the age of fifty-nine, expanding scientific horizons and remarriage were then giving a new shape to his life. Put negatively, the intellectual, personal, and physical* disjointedness which had vexed the past years seemed to be diminishing. In challenging the Freudian view, Bateson expressed both sides of his anticipation.

> Joe [Wheelwright] and I are approximately the same age, and of course, we both think about death. At the moment, I am not particularly ready to die because I am just preparing to start some new research on dolphins. Six months ago I was reasonably ready—this schizophrenia stuff had sort of fallen into a pattern and other people would carry it on. . . . Now, there is a certain amount of unrolling of the scroll, if you like, and there are punctuation points in this scroll which

---

*Bateson had nearly died in 1960, when a major operation was unsuccessfully performed to counteract a diaphragmatic hernia.

are in some sense completion points. I think the completion points get further apart, as one goes on. The embarking on work on schizophrenia involved something of the area of ten years before something that I felt was a completion point was reached; whether other people would think it is a completion point is another question and irrelevant. The dolphin stuff may be that difficult or worse—I don't know. [197]

If Bateson's career was veering, those of his project colleagues were developing also. Jackson was pushing ahead with the Mental Research Institute, while Fry and Weakland had individual and family practices which they conducted in addition to research. Haley would quit private practice to devote full time to experimenting with and classifying families, independently of changing them.

Relations within the project, at its outset, were as those between mentor and students who were focused from a communications perspective, on the role of paradoxes of abstraction in observable phenomena. By the conclusion, a sort of unity still prevailed, although labor had been divided. An outline of what transpired among them appears, however crudely, by enumerating their 1962 collective bibliography which was published in *Family Process*. [198]

Topic	# of papers	GB	WF	JH	DJ	JW	% of total papers
Descriptions of schizophrenia	3	1	—	1	1	—	6
The family/etiology	17	2	2	3	8	2	27
Theory/misc.	16	13	1	—	—	2	24
Therapy/hypnosis	27	2	2	12	9	2	43
# of papers	63	18	5	16	18	6	
% of total papers		28	3	25	28	4	
Collaborations	15						19

They listed sixty-three publications in which there were fifteen coauthorships (Jackson was involved in two thirds of these). As a group, however, only two collective papers were published—their first and their last. As of 1962, Bateson's, Haley's, and Jackson's contributions evenly made up 90 percent of their total product. The greater part of the content of the articles were on therapy (43 percent), and the family (27 percent), as seen from communications theory (24 percent). Bateson, not surprisingly, accounted for most of the theoretical pieces (80 percent), whereas Haley (44 percent) and Jackson (35 percent) were responsible for a large proportion of their papers on both individual and family therapy. Jackson wrote nearly half of the papers on the family and on its role in the etiology of schizophrenia. In 1964, Bateson stated the bald essence of these numbers: "There is a fundamental difference between my position and that of Lidz, Wynn, and even Haley and Jackson. They are clinicians. I am a theorist. They are all the time looking for examples of generalized narrative. I am only looking for examples of formal relations, which will illustrate a theory."[199]

The unity of the group, expressed in a last formulation of the double bind hypothesis, was a three-page note tersely rehearsing their consensus that the core of their work was the approach, rather than any of the phenomena to which it had been applied.

> We are always concerned when examining the activity of people (or other organisms) to consider how this behavior may be in response to observable communications from others, and how it in turn itself is communicative. Especially, we have been concerned with the importance of attending adequately to the complexity of communication. That is, there is never "a message" singly, but in actual communication always two or more related messages, of different levels and often conveyed by different channels—voice, tone, movement, context, and so on. These messages may be widely incongruent and thus exert very different and conflicting influences.[200]

Double bind communication was still at the heart of their explanation of schizophrenia, but only as "a necessary . . . [and] not sufficient condition in explaining etiology."[201] Notably, they had changed to a less specified, less concrete phrasing of the causality. Rather than mother, father, and victim, the whole schizophrenic family was invoked, enmeshed, as it was said to be, in an interactional, circular system of conflicting definitions of relationship.

They also agreed upon the value of research autonomy. Although the project's interstitial position between disciplines and between institutions had meant a degree of financial insecurity, Bateson often remarked that he protected his scientific freedom in this way, sheltering it under "three umbrellas." His project was housed in a hospital, was funded by grants from independent agencies, and these were administered through the Anthropology Department at Stanford University. "When you have three bosses," he was fond of saying, "you have none."[202] Each institution maintained that the other was supervising. Or as Haley said, "Nobody knew what the hell he was doing."[203]

After ten years of very productive work together, their original anticipation had given way not to anger, but to tedium. "I think we had had enough of each other by 1962," was Haley's opinion.[204] Something of this overfamiliarity, perhaps, was evident to R. D. Laing, who attended one of their last meetings.

> The first time I met the group was in the morning ... in Palo Alto. I met Bateson first. As I got out of the car, he was ambling, shuffling along.... I think he was the only one on time for the meeting. Then the others started coming. Practically none of them said anything to each other or looked at each other. Haley took a chair and turned his back on the whole meeting, and put his feet on the window sill. Weakland stuck himself somewhere. Bateson took a sort of unobtrusive but central position from the side. Somewhat later, Jackson came in. No one gave him any [recognition]. The thing just sort of went on.[205]

Fifteen years later, Weakland and Haley would not deny that "difficult and intense debate" had taken place during the project's collaboration. Yet both still felt enriched and indebted, as the latter has firmly acknowledged.

> Few men were ever given the opportunity that John Weakland and I had in that decade. We not only enjoyed each other's company, but we were able to do full-time research on whatever we thought important with Bateson as a teacher and guide. When we were struggling in the dark with unformed thoughts, Bateson offered us an expectation that we would work at our maximum ability, a confident attitude that a problem could be solved, and often an idea to solve it. What more could one ask of a research director?[206]

XIII. As Ethologist

In 1963, John Lilly's more rigorous study of vocal exchanges among dolphins—conducted in laboratories in Miami, Florida, and in the Virgin Islands—also involved an element of Shaw's Henry Higgins. He was experimenting in the training of dolphins to speak or mimic a few words of English.[1] Bateson found such a line of investigation to be a perversion of spontaneous behavior, which was scientifically and morally unacceptable. "The point," he told an international symposium of cetacean ethologists, meeting during the summer of 1963, "is not either to discover that dolphins have complex language or to teach them English, but to close gaps in our theoretical knowledge of *communication*."[2] That is, sequences of interaction from the cultures of Cambridge, England, the Baining, the Sulka, the Iatmul, the Balinese, and schizophrenic Americans were not to be supplemented by further human data, but by data from the culture, as it were, of a different species of actors. To the enduring naturalist in Bateson, the word "universal" meant generalizations that were true across species. Given a theory which claimed such scope, even after only a few weeks of observing dolphin interaction, hypotheses about investigating their communication came easily.[3]

To begin, he would continue to assume that the content of messages exchanged among all preverbal mammals involved "matters of relationship— love, hate, respect, fear, dependency, etc., between self and others and between self and environment."[4] Humans hide this emotional component in communication behind digital language. Men express their relationships unwittingly, in kinesic and paralinguistic signals.* In terms of evolution,

---

*At a Wenner-Gren Conference on animal communication in June 1965, Bateson elaborated two implications of the involuntary nature of analogic message. (1.) Blindness is uncomfortable to humans, he noted, not because we empathize with the blind man, but because of the absence of an important source of information from which we can gauge relations. (2.) Deliberate attempts to falsify or camouflage such signals—to take one sort of control of natural reflex—

however, Bateson thought it would be a mistake to presume that these were a crude precursor of human language. Nonverbal signals should have fallen into disuse and decay, if anachronized by a more effective adaptation. "If what dogs and cats do had evolved into 'language,'" he expected that "men would do *less* of what dogs and cats do."[5] Instead, the assortment and quantity of human signals far exceed those among preverbal mammals. Men have even embellished such messages artistically into music, poetry, and dance. Bateson believed that there were two "coding devices" which had evolved independently, each responsible for a separate content.[6] Investigating analogic signals, therefore, would reveal little about the evolution of human language.

As Charles Darwin noticed, animals send and receive messages of relationship through their ears, eyes, and noses.[7] The case was different for dolphins; adapting to the visual opacity of oceanic life had left them largely to abandon the kinesics which used their sense organs in favor of the voice. Thirty million years ago, when terrestrial, dolphins may have been four-footed, stumpy legged, hairy, even-toed ungulates. Their heads, it is thought, then resembled those of pigs, and, likely, slight humps protruded from their backs. If so, they possessed the visual cues common to landed mammals, and could use their external ears, the hair on their backs, the direction of their eyes, and their faces to communicate with each other. In the water, however, all these expressive devices gave way to whistles and creaks.

Bateson discounted the possibility that this vocalization might be comparable in structure to human language. "I personally do not believe that the dolphins have anything that a human linguist would call a 'language.' I do not think that any mammal without hands would be stupid enough to arrive at so outlandish a mode of communication."[8] In digital language a name only has arbitrary or conventional coordinance with the thing named, which theoretically was why, at first hearing, it was impossible to understand foreign languages. On the other hand, analogic messages, being more directly expressive of their subject matter, were immediately comprehensible cross-culturally. Dolphins appeared to communicate using their voices, but the strangeness of their tones suggested that they might possess a digital language whose primary content was social relationships. If this was an accurate

---

could be pathogenic. "For ... people who can lie with kinesics, the special usefulness of nonverbal communication is reduced. It is a little more difficult for them to be sincere and still more difficult for them to be believed to be sincere. They are caught in a process of diminishing returns such that, when distrusted they try to improve their skill in simulating paralinguistic and kinesic sincerity. But this is the very skill which led others to distrust them." (GB, "Redundancy and coding," in *Steps to an Ecology of Mind*, p. 418.)

formulation, then dolphin communication seemed inconceivable to Bateson. "This system is something we terrestrial mammals cannot imagine and for which we have no empathy."[9]

The goal of his research would be to crack the code of dolphin messages which Bateson conjectured might more resemble music than English. In order to do this, attenton to on-going relations—dominance hierarchies, sleep formations, mating behavior, and the like—would constitute the first ethological activity.* These would be construed as interactive sequences of stimulus and response, which were integrated in terms of a more abstract knowledge of the modes and contingencies of contexts—deutero-learning— such that an animal's behavior would reflect its proximate social environment. Bateson said he would start by listing individual dolphin's kinesic signals with reference to the contexts in which they occurred and possibly relate them, metaphorically, to earlier childhood experience. He hoped in this way "to form a picture" of how these contexts "fit together piece by piece."[10]

In animal-communication studies, evidently, it is standard that conception contrasts accomplishment.[11] During the early summer of 1963, Gregory, Lois, and their two boys arrived in St. Thomas, Virgin Islands. The Communication Research Institute, which was Lilly's laboratory at Nazareth Bay, had been founded in 1958 for the investigation of interspecies communication.† Assigned to the position of associate director of research, Bateson was hired, in part, to administrate the operation and construction of the facility.

---

*In addition, investigating the animal's use of sonar was another requirement to complete their ethology. "One of the things we must . . . acquire is a knowledge of what one animal knows and can read from another animal's use of sonar. I suspect the presence of all sorts of courtesy rules in this business; it probably isn't polite to sonar scan your friends too much, just as among human beings it is not polite, really, to look at another's feet in detail. We have many taboos on observing one another's kinesics, because too much information can be got that way." (GB, "Problems in cetacean and other mammalian communication," in *Steps,* pp. 377-78.) Contrasting Bateson's speculation is that of John Stuphen, an American physician who has been involved in the study of the biological capabilities of cetaceans. He has noted that the dolphins' sonar effectively permits it to receive echo messages not only from the surface of, but also from within, the bodies of their conspecifics. "To cetaceans then, there would be another order of magnitude of visualizable information and another cultural experience to bring to bear on their meanings. What sort of candor might exist between individuals where feelings are instantly and constantly bared? It would be irrelevant to hide, to lie, or to deny one's feelings." (J. Stuphen, "Body state communication among cetaceans," in *Mind in the Waters,* ed. J. McIntyre, pp. 141-42.) Curiously, where Bateson expected to find dolphin etiquette, Stuphen spoke of a limitless candor.

†The Communication Research Institute was funded by private contributions and by the Air Force, National Aeronautics and Space Administration, National Institute of Mental Health, National Institute of Neurological Diseases and Blindness, Public Health Service, National Science Foundation, and the United States Navy.

Lois recalled that then Gregory "just wanted to go off quietly in a corner and think, or, if somebody was going to build him a viewing mirror, he was willing to sit in front of it."[12] Instead, there were personality frictions leading to dismissal of the staff photographer cum aquarium manager. There were also plenty of chores: keeping the tanks clean, arranging for fish to feed the bottle-nosed dolphins (Tursiops), and meeting newly arrived equipment. The first addition to the tide-fed holding tank which housed the animals was to be an underwater viewing station. Native labor was uncooperative, and when the tank was completed, the visibility was poor. "The animals are back in the pool today," he wrote Lilly the following July. "The walls and bottom of the pool are spotlessly clean and the water is filthy. The war against silt shall go on."[13] Seven years later, thinking back on the whole of his experience, Bateson said that maintaining "a laboratory dubiously funded in a place where the logistics [were] intolerably difficult"[14] was neither his gift nor part of his ambition.

The octopus research went haltingly. "The electricity would go off," Lois recalled, "and the bubbling system would stop."[15] In captivity, the local Atlantic species, O. vulgaris, died quickly and were not so very interesting. "Frankly," Bateson wrote Karl Pribram* in the winter of 1964, "I find these animals much duller and perhaps more stupid than the O. bimaculatus that we played with in California."[16] Dolphins, by contrast, were stimulating intellectually but the work with them was slow. Their vocalizations were totally incomprehensible. They did not seem to have either the affective expression of cats and dogs, or anything that hinted of the character of language. "A priori, [dolphins] are highly specialized as sound producing mechanisms and their brains seem highly specialized for analyzing auditory material. If their sounds are not parts of a digital language and are not emotional signals ... what in hell are they?"[17]

If the research floundered, being in transition across disciplines added some imposition to that frustration. In Bateson's mind, the psychiatric community had been disowned, yet this was not immediately apparent to those who knew of him in terms of double bind theory and family therapy. He was still on call to them. The Veterans Administration Hospital in Menlo Park offered Bateson the opportunity to return there—with a raise. "It would be tough to confess defeat [with dolphins] and return to schizophrenics," he responded, requesting that the job be held available as long as possible, "even though world wisdom and financial caution tell me that this is the thing to do."[18] Invitations to psychiatric conferences were declined on the grounds that "at present and for the future [he was] devoting [him]self to problems of

*Professor of psychiatry and psychology, Stanford University.

animal communication."[19] Similarly, those who requested reprints and bibliography were told that their interests no longer coincided with his own. "I have just taken on a job in a new location studying dolphins and octopuses," he repeated over and over "in order to fill some theoretical gaps."[20]

Renewed ties, of course, were established with ethologists and geneticists,. There was correspondence with the former about the characteristics of Caribbean species of octopus. But not many geneticists had been aroused by the 1963 appearance of a paper entitled "The role of somatic change in evolution,"[21] the work on which, Gregory noted to J. B. S. Haldane, "was a piece of filial piety."[22] Arguing that somatic change in an organism was necessary for survival, Bateson stressed that it was also necessary to cope with genetic changes. Soma and gene, however, were independent,' being of the same relation that pertained between analogic and digital coding, i.e., serving different functions. Genotypic messages were coded digitally, whereas the soma was said to be an analogic system of finite flexibility. Both environmental and genetic change drew upon the organism's limited flexibility. If evolution was to be continuous, then genotypic change must confer an increase in the available range of somatic flexibility so that it can respond to other demands.

> It appears then, that the process of biological evolution could be continuous if there were a class of mutations or other genotypic changes which would simulate Lamarckian inheritance. The function of these changes would be to achieve by genotypic fiat those characteristics which the organism at that given time is already achieving by the uneconomical method of somatic change.[23]*

---

*Bateson compared this view of genotypic change to the legislative change of a human society. A "wise legislator" would merely certify changes that had already become custom among a people, because to initiate social change would stimulate other compensatory changes, and "perhaps overload...a large number of homeostatic circuits in the society." (GB, "The role of somatic change in evolution," in *Steps to an Ecology of Mind*, p. 354.) In responding to a reprint of this article Bateson had sent, Haldane disapproved of its political views. "Social changes can be initiated by governments. Thus infant marriage is disappearing in India, partly because it was made a crime punishable by a small fine. The law was passed before independence, but the social change, as shown by statistics, came later. And I happen to believe that the Soviet Government has done a good job. So do the people in the Pentagon, though they mayn't say so. ... I see you are interested in schizophrenia. In my opinion W. Blake was a schizophrenic, as shown by the Prophetical Books. But he retained enough grip on the real world to earn his living and even organize the escape of radicals. A lot of Indian schizophrenics have founded religious sects. A schizophrenic who keeps some touch with reality can be quite valuable." (J.B.S. Haldane to GB, 10 April 1963.) Bateson's retort tried to clarify what he felt was the geneticist's misinterpretation. "I did not say or suggest that [deliberate social change] is impossible—only that it is difficult and subject to the price of precipitating often unpredictable changes which may be needed to adapt the society to the legislative innovation. ... The whole

If natural science was replacing social science as the center of Bateson's interests, he continued to find no place in any conventional academy. Answering a Cambridge University undergraduate, who was interested in studying his sort of psychology, brought forth straightforward assessment of this institutional and intellectual isolation. "There is no academic setting," he informed the young man, "in which you can get a degree in my . . . stuff. . . . In the long run your best bet would be a Cambridge degree* but I suggest that on the side you spend time at Madingley with the bird behavior people and cut your teeth on the introduction to Whitehead's and Russell's 'Principia Mathematica!'" [24] Before Bateson attached himself to Lilly, the possibility had arisen of starting a research group in La Jolla, California, at the Scripps Institution of Oceanography. Describing his research utopia, he then outlined conditions essentially similar to the ones which had evolved in the Menlo Park V.A. Hospital, in terms of forming a small team of scientists concentrating on problems of communicational behavior. His research was exploratory, and his daily habits enough of a disaster so that those working with him should be independent. Bateson did not like, in any case, to tell people in detail what to do next. "What I do . . . is live with a flow of data passing under my attention and scratch at this data with various sorts of theoretical orientation." The overall view, which he then advocated, saw cross-fertilization between humanists and natural scientists on the one side, and engineers on the other. "When I am teaching, I have a strong tendency to preach a mathematical approach if the class consists preponderantly of humanists—and vice versa for classes of natural scientists." [25]

After one year in the Virgin Islands, during the summer of 1964, Bateson's longtime friend, the geneticist C. H. Waddington, offered him a position at the University of Edinburgh, oriented toward the analysis of applied science in industrial society. Though this was the most appealing of the few chairs then in reach, Bateson declined it nonetheless.

---

question of major metamorphoses as in the pupae of insects and in Soviet Russia is beyond my power to think about. . . . I have long since given up using the word 'schizophrenic' as a term of abuse and have pretty nearly given up using it as a diagnostic category. If the word means anything, certainly Blake was one. . . . There are questions about the scale upon which we might measure schizophrenia. I take it that a human individual with 'zero schizophrenia' would lack poetry, dreams, religion, humour, aesthetic appreciation—in fact would be a rather dull dog, indistinguishable from a well-oiled computer." (GB to Haldane, 16 April 1963.)

*In 1965, Bateson made inquiries about enrolling his son, John, in St. John's College, Cambridge. It would seem that the lack of conventional academies involved in his sort of science did not preclude his affection for conventional academies, or at least for hereditary ones. "It would give me great pleasure," he wrote the senior tutor then, "to continue the family tradition." (GB to senior tutor, St. John's College, circa 1965.)

I do not think I am the man for it. ... I have set my hand to the plow of trying to make sense of dolphin behavior and do not want so soon to give up this effort. ... And ... I suspect that my opinions about the rule of science in human life are as obsolete as the adaptations of the dinosaur. I can hardly think of a piece of applied science since the invention of cheese which has not turned out to be destructive—either of human ecology or of the larger ecology within which the people live. ... I do not think this is what the Edinburgh faculty would want me to teach. I do not even think if I taught it many of the students would learn it.[26]

In the months before Waddington's offer, Bateson had affiliated himself with the National Institute of Mental Health (N.I.M.H.), as the recipient of a five-year institutional grant, the Career Development Award. The solicitation of the award aside, it was as much citation for past achievement as it was endorsement of emerging research. In order to scrutinize the latter, N.I.M.H. seconded a small group of behavioral scientists to St. Thomas for a site visit. At issue, explicitly in the resulting discussion, was what measure of scientific license would N.I.M.H., as patron, permit a theoretical innovator. Part of Bateson's inability to ally himself permanently to an institution involved the deeply interdisciplinary nature of his science, but part of the matter involved his suspicion that all such settings necessarily restricted freedom of research and discovery, and this, above all, Bateson guarded jealously. "We spent most of the day," he recalled, "arguing about what knowledge a man can have about what he's going to do."[27] Afterward, regretting his frankness, he was genuinely astonished at their verdict, which came as Bateson was turning sixty. "The Career Award is more recognition than I ever hoped to get in my lifetime and evokes strange feelings," he conceded at that time. "My public image of myself is still that of 'Ethnologist' scratching my head in a quiet backwater of the Veterans Administration [Hospital]."[28] In gratitude, he turned to his former boss in Menlo Park, John Prusmack, finalizing his resignation there: "Especially, I recall your patience as an administrator with a rather unpredictable research man who brought in octopuses, strange human characters, and whose desk was not always cleared by the end of the day's work. I received from the V.A. freedom to spend twelve years (or was it more) of gestating the problems that interested me."[29]

The question of Bateson's institutional base did not quite resolve itself with the N.I.M.H. award. The grants supporting the Communication Research Institute were not renewed for 1965, the upcoming year, which meant that the laboratory could not continue its operation. John Lilly evidently took it upon himself to find his colleague another situation, contacting Taylor A. Pryor, a young marine biologist in Hawaii who had just opened a cetacean research center at Waimanalo. "Lilly felt strongly," Pryor's wife, Karen, has remembered, "that Bateson was important and that his work was important—strongly enough to travel to Hawaii to try to convince us to shelter this man. We agreed to do so."[30] They invited Gregory and Lois to come meet them and to inspect their facilities, which were a singular combination of public oceanarium and scientific-research institute. The new conditions of work were then themselves new. The oceanarium, Sea Life Park, and the research wing, the Oceanic Institute, had been open less than one year. The two performance arenas had suitable observation portholes, however, and a number of species of Hawaiian *Cetacea* already stocked the holding tanks. Both the society and intellectual concerns of young dolphin trainers were amiable, as was the attitude of moral conservationism which clothed their zest and sympathy for animal behavior. With some relief, Bateson left the Virgin Islands, having consented to become associate director of research at the Oceanic Institute.*

In the fall of 1964, they chartered an airplane to take all their gear, Lois remembered, "and [we] stored it . . . and then Gregory and I took off in a couple of suitcases to Hawaii and stayed [seven] years."[31] The Batesons' domesticity, during these years, was supple: a number of residences, constant visitors, two boys growing up, animals—two gibbon apes, dogs, and cats— and, in 1968, Lois gave birth to Nora, named for Nora Barlow. They gave up the gibbons for the baby, but Gregory's science was the irrepressible center of their life together.

> Patient as he is with students who want to learn from him, if he's got [them], they take priority over his being with the family. His work has always come first. He has said as much and been very clear about this from the very beginning. I think it . . . follows from . . . that part of him which does not value himself as a person. . . . It's denied [us] . . . a lot of time with him that would have been nice. As it is we have kind of lived around him, holding court at the dining room table. Family life has just circulated and modified itself around that because . . . he wasn't going to change. I mean he's a good Taurus, he doesn't change. . . . His idea-making is the most important thing in his life. . . . [It is] what he sees as his reason for being. . . . To do that, he has to let other things go. In one sense he does pay a price in not having other things people enjoy having, more of a family life and vacations.[32]

---

*The new situation did not indispose N.I.M.H. either. Bateson's Career Development Award was renewed in the name of the Oceanic Institute one year later.

Unlike John Lilly, who was then making rather visionary claims about dolphin intelligence, the Sea Life Park trainers did not glamorize the extent of this animal's abilities.* Under the direction of Karen Pryor, they were taught that the key to the operant conditioning of any animal was patience and not punishment.† There was a weekly class, for example, in which Pryor had her apprentices play a game, in order to make vivid the perplexing experience— for the subject—of the learning process. When a subject was sent out of the room, a complicated behavior would be chosen for her to perform, and a trainer was selected to administer the reinforcements. Upon return, the subject would act freely until she did something that approximated the selected behavior. When this happened, the trainer blew a whistle, and onlookers cheered. The subject would then return to her starting point to begin the next round. The game was useful, Pryor felt, because when a person failed to identify and enact a certain behavior, players learned the sense that it was the trainer's technique at fault, rather than the subject. Indeed, generally, the ideal was espoused that there could be collaboration between trainer and subject. "When you have good stimulus control," she believed, "you have, in effect, a sort of language between yourself and the animal, and not entirely a one-way language. Your actions and his reactions begin to add up to mutual communication."[33]

---

*After six years of working with dolphins, Pryor said she heard nothing to suggest the presence of an abstract dolphin language. On the other hand, she noted that John Lilly had the unique ability—which he belittled—so closely to mimic dolphin whistles, that they would respond in terror. Pryor's group of trainers could only hear barks of anger and distress signals, "a rising and falling whistle from middle C to high C and back to C." (K. Pryor, *Lads Before the Wind*, p. 155) †Except with the otter. Amusing and frisky animals, at first the Sea Life Park community was charmed. Over time, a pair of otters—which had arrived as a donation from a fancier—exposed themselves as unpredictable, irascible creatures, and as sly and manipulative. They might wriggle affectionately, for example, in a trainer's arms—but only when wet. "Humans were just mobile bath towels to the otters," Pryor has recalled. Of high intelligence, they were relentlessly independent and difficult to confine. Conversely, "they didn't want permanent freedom. They came back . . . willingly. They just wanted the liberty to do as they pleased and go where they wished." Otters were demanding to train. "Life for an otter is a constant search for novelty. It's amusing to watch, but it is not a trait that lends itself to five trained shows a day, six days a week, or even to one sensible training session." (K. Pryor, *Lads Before the Wind*, pp. 136-137.) Pryor once attempted to train one to stand on a box. Upon reward, the animal caught on immediately, but then would not repeat the behavior precisely. "For twenty minutes [the otter] offered me everything imaginable except just getting on the box and standing there." (Ibid., p. 157.) The otter's variations made judging what to reward a fatiguing and irritating problem. "Otters," it was her conclusion, "are natural experimenters." (Ibid., p. 138.) And she sent them away, in the end, to conduct their experiments in a zoo.

Despite the evident goodwill in all of this, Bateson abhorred the deliberate manipulation involved in operant conditioning, which he damned as "applied behavior."[34]* Karen Pryor thought this was peculiar. Bateson "always hated the thought of bending creatures to one's will, especially if the creatures happened to be human (in spite of the fact that [he] goes around bending people to his will all the time)."[35] Disapproving so vehemently, still he consulted with the trainers, devising suggestions of more complex interdolphin behavior to have the animals perform. "The keepers and staff," Lois Bateson recalled, "would come and see him . . . as their philosopher guide, family or marriage counselor, or as anything that came up."[36] He also taught, by "example and by conundrum,"[37] an instance of which Pryor has reconstructed.

> *Karen.* (carrying a bucket of fish) Good morning, Gregory.
>
> *Gregory.* (He is a huge elderly man in old trousers, a faded shirt and the world's oldest sneakers. He stoops, squints and smiles with an air of surprise at running into a friend) Good morning, Karen.
>
> *K.* (sets down bucket)
>
> *G.* You know, I've been thinking. . . .
>
> *K.* (attentive and silent)
>
> *G.* If you had been born with two left hands on your left arm, would both of them be left hands? Or would one of them be a right hand?
>
> *K.* (after a pause for consideration of a brand-new puzzle) I don't know.
>
> *G.* Hmm . . . (nods, smiles and ambles on)[38]†

---

* "Around here," he wrote a student, "everybody follows Skinnerian theory and Skinnerian training is used for all sorts of purposes. You train an animal to bump a disk in the tanks and then take him out to sea to see how deep he will dive to go bump his disk." (GB to B. Gilbert, 6 October 1964.)

†Bateson was then reconsidering the problem of bilateral symmetry in reduplicated limbs, about which his father, when surveying regularities in biological monstrosities, (see W. Bateson, *Materials for the Study of Variation*) had asserted a generalization, yet mysterious, called Bateson's Rule. William Bateson had noticed that when an appendage—a hand—is reduplicated, the morphology of each extra limb is as a mirror image of its double. The son applied cybernetic explanation to his father's discovery, developing a new hypothesis to account for it. "In 1894, it appeared that the problem centered around the question: What causes the development of bilateral symmetry in a context where it does not belong? . . . But modern theory has turned all such questions upside down. Information, in the technical sense, is that which *excludes* certain alternatives. The machine with a governor does not elect the steady state; it *prevents* itself from staying in any alternative state. . . . Let us therefore invert the question about the symmetry of the total reduplicated appendage: Why is this double appendage not asymmetrical like the corresponding appendages of normal organisms?" (GB, "A re-examination of Bateson's rule," in *Steps*, pp. 381-82.)

On one occasion, Pryor's first lieutenant, a Swede, Ingrid Kang, persuaded Bateson to be the "animal" in the training game. His task was simple: to sit in a chair. Quickly realizing that the reinforcement somehow related to the chair, he began to offer a range of behavior, except the one of precisely sitting on it. "After twenty minutes Ingrid gave up in disgust, and Gregory, who . . . had not been trying to flummox her on purpose, continued to despise and [to] disbelieve in operant conditioning."[39] In the fall of 1966, B. F. Skinner visited Sea Life Park (his daughter had been working there as a trainer). Skinner and Bateson exchanged views at this time, and there seems to have been a note of discord. Pryor saw the two learning theorists as personifying opposition between the disciplines of experimental psychology and ethology, and she felt "like a British barmaid with a fight on her hands."[40]

During the first year of operation, the Sea Life Park trainers, Pryor and Kang, became uncomfortable with the monotony of their shows, which had become predictable and, to them, increasingly lackluster. To relieve this boredom, they experimented with demonstrating the process of operant conditioning in front of audiences by rewarding behavior which the dolphins enacted spontaneously or accidentally. Characteristically, during a performance, an animal entered the holding tank, expecting a cue in response to which it would comply with a conditioned behavior. But now, no cues were given. They worked with a female *Steno* who, after waiting for a cue, began to slap her tail on the surface of the water—as if, in Pryor's view, annoyed. Kang rewarded this behavior and waited for the dolphin's response. She repeated the tail slap and was fed fish after she did. This sort of conditioning succeeded. The dolphin began to swim quickly about the pool, repeatedly smashing the water with her tail. In the performances that followed, the same animal was again presented with this kind of antistimulation. When she "offered" a behavior which had been previously reinforced, she was not rewarded. When she initiated unconditioned response, she was given fish. At a rate of five shows a day, by the third day the animal had exhausted her repertoire of "free" behavior. All the actions in which she typically engaged had been well conditioned by this point, and therefore none were rewarded. During the fifteenth show of the third day, the dolphin—still without cues—did something unforeseen. After gathering velocity swimming normally, she turned over on her back and coasted, her tail protruding out of the water.

Pryor went to Bateson with a description of the day's events, "and he got very excited and wanted to see for himself."[41] The next morning, he watched the dolphin, after repeating her tail-out coasting for a time, throw herself out of the water backward, making an arching upside-down leap back into the water. "Gregory was delighted," Pryor recalled, "Ingrid was delighted, and so was I. Malia [the dolphin] had again done what I suspected she might: invented a novel behavior."[42] This went on routinely in succeeding days. More often than not, the animal displayed previously unobserved actions. To Bateson, who was enthralled, it seemed that the dolphin had abstracted complicated generalization: "Only things which have not been previously reinforced are reinforced."[43] Here was an instance of deutero-learning in which coercive—double bind—training techniques had given rise to creative change. He prodded Pryor to repeat the process more rigorously and to publish an account of it.[44] She secured funding from the U.S. Navy and filmed their work with a second dolphin. With more difficulty, a second animal learned what she must not do to merit a fish and began to exhibit a radical variety of unseen activity. And oddly, her trainers noticed that she metamorphosed in the process, changing from a somewhat docile, insipid creature into one who was wildly imaginative. The behavior of the first animal was similarly emboldened. She developed the ability to leave the water and slide about on the cement borders of her tank, rapping her trainers on their ankles. "We had to put the behavior on cue," Pryor wrote, "to stop her from choosing to be terrestrial during the show."[45]

These events, needless to say, exemplified some of Bateson's preoccupations with learning theory. Indeed, at the time they occurred, he had already restated his conception of deutero-learning in terms of Russell's Theory of Types.[46] Given the notion of repeatable context, learning was now seen in terms of an interdependent hierarchy of classes of messages. This hierarchy was the outcome of the stochastic (trial and error) process by which it occurred, and of a concomitant economy of adaptation.

> There is needed not only that first-order change which suits the immediate environmental (or psychological) demand.... But also second-order changes which will reduce the amount of trial-and-error needed to achieve the first-order change.... By super-imposing and interconnecting many feedback loops, we (and all other biological systems) not only solve particular problems but also form *habits* which we apply to the solution of *classes* of problems.... We act as though a whole class of problems could be solved in terms of assumptions or premises, fewer in number than the members of the class of problems. In other words, we (organisms) *learn* to *learn* or in the more technical phrase, we deutero-learn.[47]

First-order learning, which he now called Learning I, was defined as the codification of a specific sequence of messages: dolphin learns that certain behavior in response to certain stimuli shall be rewarded. This was indissociably accompanied by a more abstract and generally less conscious learning which was now called Learning II. The dolphin deutero-learns that there is an interactive sequence, a form of context, between himself and the trainer, that shall serve as a model for future training. These contexts are made distinguishable by signals—context markers—whose function was said to be classificatory (e.g., a dog may see his master's leash and "expect" a walk).

Changes in Learning II could be achieved by putting an animal in the wrong at the behavioral level. That which it has deutero-learned to occur in a sequence is made inappropriate. But this is a difficult and potentially painful switch. The second Sea Life Park dolphin that underwent the creativity training, for example, exhibited signs of severe distress throughout the interactions, and repeated the previously reinforced behavior numerous times before she caught on. The habits of Learning II, Bateson pointed out,

> are notoriously rigid and their rigidity follows as a necessary corollary of their status in the hierarchy of adaptation. The very economy of trial-and-error which is achieved by habit formation is only possible because habits are comparatively "hard programmed" in the engineers' phrase. The economy consists precisely in *not* re-examining or rediscovering the premises of habit every time the habit is used.[48]

By the late 1960s, it should be noted, Bateson was speculating about the rare occurrence of third-order learning, which was unique to humans. He never worked out the notion in detail so what he meant is difficult to fathom. Deriving from "contraries" generated at the deutero-level, it could result, perhaps, in total redefinition of self. If Learning I concerned specific interaction and Learning II the classification of those interactions, then Learning III seemed to concern classification itself—i.e., the process of codification by which Learning II occurs. For some, changes at this level could result in psychosis, but this was not the only possible outcome. For others, the totality constituted by the categories of deutero-learning could dissolve and reveal "a world in which personal identity merges into all the processes of relationship in some vast ecology or aesthetics of cosmic interaction."[49]

Immediately upon his arrival, amid the flurry of operant conditioning, Bateson undertook observing and conceptualizing dolphin ethology, as it was visible through the portholes of the *Essex,* a four-fifths scale model ship which sat in Whaler's Cove, the larger performance pool. For nearly two months, in the early mornings, well before preparations for the day's shows began, Bateson and Barrie Gilbert, then a graduate student in zoology at Duke

University, sat recording and videotaping the behavior of a group of seven captive dolphins.* After achieving the ability to identify them individually (two were *Stennella attenuata* and five were *Delphinus rosiventris,* or spinners—all had Hawaiian names), Bateson and Gilbert began to compile and sort the data in categories: individual behavior, dyadic interaction, triadic interaction, more complex formations, and the relations between smaller and larger groupings. At first they accumulated observations to the effect that certain dolphins acted in partnership much more often than others. From this evidence, there was confirmation of the minimal notion that the goings-on were *organized.*

Dyadic relations, in turn, Bateson classified in terms of categories which he had developed about the Iatmul in New Guinea. As pairs of Iatmul men had engaged in symmetrical sequences of behavior—boasting competitively while initiating novices—pairs of dolphins swam symmetrically, racing through the water, sometimes jumping simultaneously, sometimes in bodily contact, but "often in precise synchrony of locomotor movements."[50] The interaction between Iatmul men and women, Bateson had defined as complementary—differentiated yet integrated—e.g., the way in which the men's exhibitionism fitted together with the women's spectatorship. The interaction of dolphins, he now observed, consisted of pairs of animals who were engaged in a variety of complementary relationships: coitus, threat, body and flipper rubbing, beak-genital propulsion, and, among others, chasing. Scrutiny of these interactions revealed social stratification and status seeking. The largest male *Stennella,* called Kahili, was involved in every one of the occasions in which coitus was observed and recorded. Bateson worked out the distribution of threat behavior—sudden, sometimes brutal, lunges or beak

---

*Bateson was also pursuing his interest in their vocal signals. But this research met with little success. Underwater, the direction from which a sound has derived was nearly unidentifiable. Linking sounds to specific dolphins and distinguishing which whistles accompanied which behavior was impossible. Wayne Batteau, an acoustics engineer, was invited at one point to resolve this problem. He built large pinnae whose size was in proportion to the increased speed of aquatic sounds. That is, since sound speed is five times slower in air than in water, the pinnae were built five times the size of a man's. Hydrophones were installed within them and these were connected to earphones inside the *Essex.* Sonic discrimination was increased, evidently. (K. Pryor, *Lads Before the Wind,* p. 162.) Bateson was able to notice that dolphin whistles which he had attributed to individual animals were often the productions of pairs or triads, vocalizing in alternation or in duet. No code was cracked, however.

As a whole, this research at the Oceanic Institute achieved some celebrity. Some photographs and a small article appeared in *Life* magazine in 1967. (See "New light shed on dolphins," *Life,* 22 October 1965, pp. 122-23.) For it, Bateson was asked to don his earphones and sit in front of the observation porthole. He agreed, although somewhat petulantly—the machinery itself was left off—and he did not like to make sham out of science for the sake of publicity.

batterings—which indicated what he called "a rather clear system of ascendancy."[51] A dolphin, when threatened, would not threaten back, but might only threaten a "weaker" animal. Stratification also seemed evident in the phenomenon which he called "beak-genital propulsion." Gently, one animal, his beak inserted in the genital orifice of a second, would push the other short distances about the pool. This behavior, unlike threat, appeared to be reversible—a stronger one might push a weaker one. But predominantly, it was "rendered by animals of lower ascendancy to animals of higher ascendancy."[52] In chasing, however, the dolphins were less consistent. In the majority of cases, the chaser was "ascendant" to the chased, but a significant number of times the reverse occurred.[53] Chasing, Bateson supposed, might often be symmetrical—playful,* or competitive.

By nine o'clock every morning, the animals woke and dispersed. Before they did, Bateson and Gilbert were on hand, fascinated by their habits of sleep. These had a sustained order which, for the two ethologists, composed a diagram of their social organization. A constellation of one pair and one triad slept together while pursuing a wide, constant, circular course. The pair swam just above the triad, closest to the surface. The two were heterosexual *Stennellas*. The three spinners—two males and one female—slept beneath. Both groups surfaced alternatively to breathe, which each seemed to do synchronously. Of the two isolated male spinners, they observed that one typically swam in advance—but not leading—the group of five, while the other slept alone, suspended at the surface. The geometry, as Bateson called it, of their sleep formation was doubly crucial. Not only was it a wedge into the study of oceanic cetaceans, but when the formation was actually disrupted, the vigor of the school itself suffered.†

> No animal has been seen to circle while sleeping alone. We badly need information about sleeping in the wild. We may guess that slow circling is an efficient way of maintaining a watch against sharks and other dangers. In such a circling only one eye need be open to maintain a watch in all directions. But

---

*Bateson viewed the signal system between mother and child as a likely place to begin studying dolphins' extensive playfulness. Typically, a mother repeatedly encircles her offspring who is flapping alongside, in the course of swimming together. This Bateson construed to be a sort of aquatic playpen which might form the interactive basis of their behavior as playful adults. "Later information has to be pickled on top of the conception of the universe as constructed as a playpen." (GB, "Observations of a cetacean community," in *Mind in the Waters*, p. 164.)

†The ethologist Kenneth Norris, who became director of the Oceanic Institute in 1968, tentatively confirmed Bateson's observation of the social organization of sleep, in the course of three summers' observations of a group of wild spinning dolphins—occupants of Kealakekua Bay, off the island of Hawaii. (See K. Norris, *The Porpoise Watcher*, pp. 181-93.)

perhaps a group of animals is necessary to maintain the navigation in a circle: so that one animal sleeping by himself would have to remain stationary. . . . This raises the question of what happens to animals . . . who . . . withdraw to sleep stationary by themselves in nature. Can an animal survive in the wild if he regularly sleeps alone and stays alone in this way suspended when awake? How would he maintain contact with the school?[54]

The formation of the Whaler's Cove animals persisted until the female spinner in the triad caught her tail in a rope which had been left dangling from a boat. She could not surface, and with her death "all the patterns Gregory had been painstakingly coming to understand broke down, while the animals resorted themselves and built a new pecking order."[55] Disappointed and too short on substantive data for publication, Bateson was anticipating the investigation of sleep formations in wild schools of dolphins when he flew over some sleeping groups. The Oceanic Institute, meantime, solicited $350,000 for the construction of a new, larger pool to be used exclusively for research. If eponymy marks major achievement in scientific communities, then the new pool, which was called Bateson's Bay, was the eponymous marker of Gregory's unfinished study of sleeping dolphins. He continued to try to make sense of the dolphin interaction in following years, but, as he told John Lilly in 1967, "the rewards are very small and I can only keep myself happy by writing occasional theoretical pieces."[56]

In many of these, which he presented in conferences with anthropologists and ethologists,[57] Bateson rehearsed the view that meaning—both subjective and analytical—was synonymous with the cybernetic notion of redundancy in any *finite* set of messages, such as a sequence of phonemes, a painting, a frog, or a culture. Even when information is incomplete, he would assert, an organism should be able to guess the missing parts with better than random success—in other words, should be able to distinguish signal from noise. This order in the coding of messages inspired part-for-whole induction. An event could be an explicit signal for a whole (e.g., a cloud may stand for a storm, or a bared fang may stand for an attack), or it could be in more conditional relation to a whole, but the nature of message systems was that, having encoded a signal, a receiver's ability to make accurate predictions about the rest of a specified environment was increased. If redundancy was the basis of communication, then the converse followed as well. "All that is not information, not redundancy, not form and not restraints—is noise, the only possible source of *new* patterns."[58]

Receiving no newspaper, Bateson maintained one sort of daily isolation from the currents and countercurrents that were gaining strength in American society during the late 1960s. Still, Gregory attracted people. Anthropologists such as Raymond Firth and Edmund R. Leach and ethologists such as Konrad Lorenz appeared in Hawaii, and there was a stream of mental-health workers. The poet and social critic Paul Goodman and the novelist Philip Wylie were neighbors and friends. In general, however, Lois Bateson thought that her husband had relatively little contact with those of his own generation. "The more I lived with Gregory the more I realized that he really wasn't all that interested in his age group. ... We could call it a 'prima donna' syndrome of some kind, wanting to be *the* one to share one's information." Old friends visited. G. Evelyn Hutchinson, C. H. Waddington, and Anatol Holt all had brief sojourns in Hawaii. In particular, when Waddington came, the theoretical exchange dissatisfied Bateson, and disposed him, in part, to doubt the effectiveness of his scientific voice. "One of the repetitive yearnings," his wife said, "in the early mornings has been, 'Has anybody heard me?' ... And that's a terrible feeling to have when you are nearing the end of your life."[59]

XIV. The Ecology of Mind

In *Naven,* one side of Bateson's thinking was marked by a pained sensitivity for the falsely reified concept—in other words, for the difference between nature and thought. Consequently, his photography with Margaret Mead in Bali had been motivated, in part, by a desire to preserve the integrity of his data. During World War II, the reader will recall, his theoretical interests in learning and national character mostly excluded—even condemned—the applied concerns within which they had developed. Similarly, Bateson's years among psychiatrists and other mental-health workers were lined by revulsion against deliberate manipulation of men and against the crude manipulation of power by therapists. In a sense, his horror pushed him on to ethology, where, perhaps, the mode of investigation—a close attention to the free expression of nature—was more congenial. Arriving in the Virgin Islands, notably, his first response was critical of efforts to force human language upon dolphins. Not surprisingly, the year later, in Hawaii, it was operant conditioning of these animals which seemed brutal to him.

This lifelong preoccupation—protecting the autonomy of nature from reductive analysis by, or application of, science—was widened in the later 1960s. During these years, Bateson expressed utopian remonstrances against the incursion of Occidental rationality upon the balance of global ecology. Whether in scientific, or overtly ideological, settings, many of his performances then abounded with admonishment and exhortation. He was advocating a whole-systems view which offered a fresh outlook and possible resolution of a myriad of abiding problems. In April 1966, at a symposium sponsored by Sacramento State College, Bateson deplored symmetrical patterns of twentieth-century international relations in order to illustrate the special persistence of sick systems.[1] Two years afterward, he pointed to the interplay of religion and biology in the Occidental conceptions of mind and nature, in order to account for the shortsightedness which permitted such pathology at the international level.[2] To oscillate endlessly between the politics of imperialism and nationalism, or between sacred and scientific explanation, Bateson told a radical left-wing audience assembled by R. D. Laing, would do little but confirm the fallacious assumption that it was possible in the long run to exert unilateral power. Rather more significant, Bateson concluded, was to make and enact the "discovery that man is only a part of larger [social and ecological] systems" over which there could be little control.[3] But his was a curious ideology. It was an ideology of Bateson's curiosity, attempting at once to identify standards of ethical action and to define a science of mind.

Until the beginning of the nineteenth century, Bateson said in 1966, Occidental men invoked their deity—a sacred Mind—to explain the natural world. This was a view arranged in a timeless, unchanging, descending hierarchy, from the perfect Mind at the top down to the simplest infusoria. Then in 1809, exactly one-half century before Darwin, the *Philosophie Zoologique* appeared, in which Lamarck declared the mutability of species.[4] A major shift of scientific paradigm was announced in this book. Lamarck stood the direction of the received hierarchy on its head: instead of mind explaining nature, nature, or evolution, was taken as the basis of an explanation of mind. As a result, Lamarck was "probably the greatest biologist in history."[5]* The significance of his contribution, as Bateson construed it, was to emphasize the unity of mind and body. Lamarck "formulated a number of very modern ideas: that you cannot attribute to any creature psychological capacities for which it has no organs; that mental processes must always have physical representation; and that the complexity of the nervous system is related to the complexity of mind."[6] Aside from heroic heretics such as Samuel Butler, however, the notion of mind was dropped from materialist evolutionary thinking for the next 140 years, until the development of the cybernetic model during World War II. With the acceptance of the self-corrective attributes of systems, discussion of mind had become admissible again.

---

*Although Bateson's interest in Lamarck, of course, did not include a belief in the inheritance of acquired characters, it did extend to the man's disciplinary and public outcome. At the end of his life, blind from strain in microscopic work, Lamarck was scorned both by his colleagues and by a Parisian public who not only rejected his theories of transformation but rejected the idea itself. He was then received by Napoleon at the Tuileries. The scientist presented the Emperor with a copy of his latest work, the *Philosophie Zoologique*. "'What is this?' said the Emperor. 'Is it your absurd *Météorologie* with which you are disgracing your old age? Write on Natural History, and I will receive your works with pleasure. This volume I only accept out of consideration for your grey hair. Here!,' and he handed the book to an aide-de-camp. Lamarck, who had been vainly endeavoring to explain that it *was* a work on natural history, was weak enough to burst into tears." (J. B. Lamarck, *Zoological Philosophy*, p. xxi.)

Bateson agreed with Freudian conceptions of the unconscious as composed of primary process, creating dreams and metaphors, and as a cellar to which feared or painful memories were consigned. But he also thought this view was limited.

I believe that much of early Freudian theory was upside down. At that time many thinkers regarded conscious reason as normal and self-explanatory while the unconscious was regarded as mysterious, needing proof and needing explanation. Repression was the explanation, and the unconscious was filled with thoughts which could have been conscious but which repression and dream work had distorted. Today we think of consciousness as the mysterious, and of the computational methods of the unconscious, e.g., primary process, as continually active, necessary, and all-embracing.[7]

Bateson was fond of quoting Pascal, that *"le coeur a ses raisons que la raison ne connaît point,"** to suggest that there were additional unconscious processes which operated automatically without inspection. For the mind to function economically, the assumption he made was that necessary limits had to be imposed upon consciousness. (Was this an echo of Butler's judgment that thought was flawed to the extent it was conscious?) Consciousness was like a television set—able to display only a part of itself, the screen, and unable to transmit messages about the total system which produces the picture. "Such a report ... of the total process would require extra circuitry. But to report on the events in this extra circuitry would require a still further addition of more circuitry, and so on. Each additional step toward increased consciousness will take the system farther from total consciousness."[8] Perception, being imperceptible and involuntary, was akin to the television. An organism, Bateson asserted, need only know what it perceives, not how this happens. The quandary of a skilled artist seemed similar. He must practice the craft of his ability, but in so doing, he becomes less aware of the totality of his accomplishment. Artistic creations were multireferential, containing messages not merely about intent but about unwitting skill. An artist therefore may give only a partial, and likely distorted, account of his work. Isadora Duncan was not quite accurate when she supposed that if she could articulate the meaning of a dance, there would no longer be reason to dance it.[9] "I believe that what ... any artist is trying to communicate is ... like: 'This is a particular sort of partly unconscious message, let us engage in this particular sort of partly unconscious communication."[10]

---

* "The heart has reasons of which the reason knows nothing."

If the dancer's wordlessness suggested the limits of consciousness, then contemporary medical science illustrated some malignant ramifications of these. By probing specific diseases one by one, without relating developing knowledge to a unified conception of an interdependent organism, medicine has presented an atomized picture of the human body. The problem was not with the profession but with the nature of consciousness, said to be composed of invidious and shortsighted purposes, posing ad hoc questions within no overall frame. Wisdom, which Bateson defined as "the knowledge of the total interactive system," was everywhere lacking.[11] Bateson would joke that the Biblical Fall was the beginning of purposive, lineal thinking. In eating the apple, Adam and Eve had capitulated to the first intention, and had "cast out from the Garden the concept of their own total systemic nature and of its total systemic nature."[12] Planning began to contaminate their lives. Plants became weeds, animals became pests, work became toil, and personal relations then appeared intrusive. "Eve began to resent sex and reproduction and when it came to parturition she found this process very painful."[13] Consciousness, in short, did not possess a wider sense of cybernetic repercussion. Life "depends upon interlocking circuits of contingency, while consciousness must always involve man in the sort of stupidity of which evolution was guilty when she urged upon the dinosaurs the common sense values of an armaments race."[14] This situation, made lethal by powerful technology, had rendered conscious purposes capable "of upset[ting] the balance of the body, of society and of the biological world around us. A pathology—a loss of balance—is threatened."[15]

By contrast, appreciating art might be redressive because it focused the mind on the *integration,* of conscious intent, of habituated skill, and of the atemporal metaphors of primary process. Bateson had been enlisted by Raymond Firth, the English social anthropologist, to give a paper during the summer of 1967, on a subject related to primitive art, in a conference sponsored by the Wenner-Gren Foundation.* He prepared an analysis of a Balinese painting, "Style, Grace and Information in Primitive Art."[16] Ques-

---

*The Wenner-Gren Foundation played a large part supporting Bateson's work during the 1960s. Founded in 1941, as the Viking Fund, it was the first such institution exclusively to support anthropology. The foundation was the result of the enterprise of Paul Fejos, a Hungarian polymath, and the endowment of Axel Wenner-Gren, a somewhat mysterious Swedish industrialist with worldwide holdings. Fejos, in 1957, acquired a European conference center, for international as well as interdisciplinary meetings of behavioral scientists—Burg Wartenstein—a twelfth-century Austrian castle which had been a prince's hunting lodge. This was the site, grandiose and-isolated, of the Wenner-Gren Conferences. (See J. W. Dodds, *The Several Lives of Paul Fejos,* pp. 68-107.)

tioning the sorts of systemic wisdom which might be gleaned from the work, the Taoist in him emerged.

> The picture can be seen as an affirmation that to choose either turbulence or serenity as a human purpose would be a vulgar error. The conceiving and creating of this picture must have provided an experience which exposed this error. The unity and integration of the picture assert that neither of these contrasting poles can be chosen to the exclusion of the other, because the poles are mutually dependent. This profound and general truth is simultaneously asserted for the fields of sex, social organization, and death.[17]

Bateson's presentation, and central role in Firth's meeting provoked Lita Osmundsen, the research director of the Wenner-Gren Foundation.

> I heard him talking [she said] . . . about grace, and he used dolphins in terms of discussing grace. He then sailed into a throwaway line. . . . "What a conference it would be, to discuss human consciousness!" That evening, after dinner, we were sitting around the fire. He was alone with me and my assistant. I turned to him and said, "What about this? . . . Would you organize a conference for us, on this topic?" And he got terribly excited. I remember . . . he almost started to shake, it seemed to me, about this prospect, that he could do a conference of that kind, and have come whomever he wanted.[18]

Leaving the Austrian conference center, Bateson and family visited England for three weeks, to attend R. D. Laing's conference. For Gregory this was the first time in twenty-seven years that he set foot on native soil. Quartering themselves at Wendover with his father's former student, Nora Barlow, they visited old haunts and old friends. Bateson took John, his sixteen-year old, to Grantchester to visit the old Queen Anne house in which he had spent part of his childhood. A neighbor watched the two of them wandering about the house, the father evidently more interested in telling the old stories than the son was in hearing them.[19] In the forefront of these weeks, however, was the work Bateson was doing, elaborating themes for the following summer's conference which he thought to call The Effect of Conscious Purpose on Human Adaptation. The possibility of organizing a group to examine a recurrent tension in his life—the relations between science and nature—struck a chord in him of breathless enthusiasm. There was little restraint to his ambition for the meeting. "It has always been clear," he wrote Lita Osmundsen from Wendover, "that the philosophical ground of cybernetics would entirely change our social philosophy and ethics but I think our conference will be [a] first big step towards doing this."[20]

By the fall of 1967, he had enumerated a list of theses, the sum of which had ominous introduction. "A question of great scientific interest and perhaps grave importance is whether the information processed through consciousness is adequate and appropriate for the task of human adaptation."[21] Three systems—the individual, the social, and the larger ecological—were to be "coupled" by conscious thought, and to be constrained from exponential runaway by self-corrective loops. As the rotation speed of an engine with a governor is conserved by variation of the fuel supply, so this triadic system would maintain a steady state by continuous alteration of its interconnected subsystems. An external variable, of course, might impact and change the bias. In such a complex multilooped system, however, change would occur slowly, and once adapted the new equilibrium would then act to maintain itself—whatever the degree of pathology. During Prohibition, American society "generated" the bootlegger to sustain a level of alcohol supply in the population. In response, to manage this new profession, changes resulted in the police system. "When the question of repeal was raised, it was expectable that certainly the bootlegger and possibly the police would be in favor of maintaining Prohibition."[22] Just as systemic change was conservative in cybernetic terms, so experiential change—learning—was similarly oriented toward the preservation of the status quo. Learning was aversive in the sense that a rat will accept a reward to avoid changes induced internally by hunger. "We call an external event 'reward' if its occurrence corrects an 'internal' change which would be punishing."[23]

Unwittingly, the task Bateson was setting and his indictments of human consciousness echoed those of the classic nineteenth-century utopians.[24] The matter of change and adaptation for the individual and society was one of combining these self-corrective systems within the ecology. Yet this was the domain of the conscious mind, whose particular purposes diminished and obscured holistic vision. Left to his own preferences, man consistently has preferred to change his environment rather than himself, and with advanced technology, the parochialisms of consciousness were endowed with a deadly potency. "The argument of purpose tends to take the form 'D is desirable; B leads to C; C leads to D; so D can be achieved by way of B and C.' But if the total mind and the outer world do not, in general, have this lineal structure, then by forcing this structure upon them, we become blind to the cybernetic circularities of the self and external world."[25] This was Bateson showing his most syncretic self. Amid a densely phrased call—not to action but to ecological wisdom—there were references to *Alice in Wonderland* and invocations of Scripture. He pointed to the common sense and narrow piety of the Biblical Job, his faith ultimately stigmatized for lacking, among other things, knowledge of nature.

Existing political and economic organizations could offer no solutions, for they merely engaged "parts of persons,"[26] and oriented them toward the limited goals of rational self-maximization, "which perhaps threatens to isolate conscious purpose from many corrective processes which might come out of less conscious parts of the mind."[27] The previous summer in London, in front of an audience of radical left-wing activists, Bateson had condemned conventional ideological politics. Such human purposes were at the heart, he said then, of contemporary problems of adaptation.[28] On the other hand, planning an interdisciplinary conference in an Austrian castle—selecting the participants, then presiding over their deliberations—was an ideological gesture he himself would make.

Concerned about gathering a proper balance of age and expertise, he corresponded attentively, trying to arouse the particular interests of each prospective participant. Bateson was meticulous, in the impressions of the Wenner-Gren administrators, and "very clear about exactly whom he wanted. He always maintained a very calm and assuring air toward us, and was not one to get into a flap about the status quo of the conference, or to doubt that we on our side were doing our best."[29] Bateson asked his daughter, Mary Catherine Bateson, by then a linguist and anthropologist, to join him as rapporteur of the proceedings. Willing to listen to her father's current enthusiasms, she agreed to do so, noticing that "in the emerging awareness of the ecological crisis [Gregory] had decided to care again."[30] Bateson induced twelve others to meet around his memorandum: two cyberneticists, Warren S. McCulloch, M.D., and Gordon Pask; three ecologists, Barry Commoner, Horst Mittelstaedt, and Peter H. Klopfer; one theoretical mathematician, Anatol W. Holt; one anthropologist, Theodore Schwartz; one philosopher, W. T. Jones; two psychologists, Frederick Attneave, Bertram Kaplan; one psychiatrist Bernard Raxlen, M.D.; and one mathematics teacher, Gertrude Hendrix.

"I think that Gregory tried to create spokesmen for the various aspects of his own psyche," one of them said, to gather "a group of people to speak for various parts of him. It was [to be] psychodrama."[31] In advance of the conference, it seemed, he had a general view of its orchestration. That is, to have presented certain data, certain theoretical terminology, and to have represented certain tensions within a group of biologically oriented intellectuals. They would hear data on Melanesian cargo cults, on nitrate pollution, on child rearing in the Azores Islands, and on learning mathematics. They would come to terms with aspects of cybernetic theory. They would also play out the opposition between the word and the deed—between ideological passion and scholarly contemplation, and between applied and basic science. Conforming with the Wenner-Gren conference rule, Bateson insisted that for seven days in July 1968, participants be prepared to spend the entire time together, interacting. Indeed, when Arthur Koestler expressed interest in the conference* but was unable to fit the period it demanded into his summer schedule, Bateson was firm that partial involvement would not do.

> This is not the sort of conference at which participants can speak their piece and go their way. We shall be a working group and it will take us two or three days to become a working group. Our program will only be very loosely outlined by me, but if I succeed as chairman, a sort of unity will appear in the overall structure of our discussion. You know more about the creative process than I. Frankly I do not know how a work of art comes to have a unity the artist scarcely perceived when he began to paint. . . . Anyhow this is the sort of process which I hope we shall work through and I do not believe that it is possible to do this if the composition of the group changes in important ways during the process.[32]

The problem at large, which Bateson set his group, was global survival. The problem in particular, which he set himself, was that of being chairman. "I've had a job," he said at the conclusion of the conference, "of trying to weave the . . . no, of trying to *let* weave the fabric of conversation, so that it would be a small model of the larger thing we're concerned about."[33] What ensued was peculiar. Sober discourse was greeted by hostility. Apocalyptic engaged utopian visions. The meld of ideology with the scientific exchange of data and theory made for intense experience, ranging between conversion and repulsion. Perhaps only a trace of their proceedings remain, for the version of the conference Cathy Bateson has since published is somewhat polished.[34] Even so, it is clear that, as a chairman, Gregory was both demanding and indulgent. Throughout the conference, the Wenner-Gren administrator, Lita Osmundsen, accused him of exhausting his people by pursuing overlong hours. Yet during the discussions themselves, Bateson spoke little, except occasionally to suggest more precise language,[35] or to distinguish between spheres of scientific explanation.[36] "What I'm mainly interested in is a formal description of the ways in which human planning and applied science tend to generate pathology," he said at the outset, "in the society or in the ecology or in the individual."[37]

They began with Barry Commoner, tabulating "the appalling roster" of technological disaster—exhaust toxicities, insecticide poisoning—and narrating "an epic of destruction" in which lakes and soils were transformed into gutters and wastelands.[38] While denouncing ignorance of cybernetic circuitry,

---

*See A. Koestler, *The Call Girls*.

they made self-mocking confessions about their own daily disavowals of the severity of the ecological crisis. They then shifted to Theodore Schwartz's material on social change in Melanesia.* In response to prolonged contact with Western technology, cargo cults had occurred among the Manus people, in which native belief was that the material advantages of white civilization would be bestowed upon them in a single beneficent stroke. To many in the conference, these were tragic data—the willing abandonment of traditional patterns. To Schwartz, they were rather an illustration of a people trying to establish new social goals. Damning Western imperialism, he said, was easy self-righteousness. "I don't think there's a person in this room that deviates from a general humanistic concern with the survival and welfare of the human race, and a more human life. . . . We shouldn't occupy our time with showing that we're the right kind of person."[39] As well, their moralisms prevented Schwartz from elaborating the theoretical schema which he saw represented in the cargo cult phenomenon. Cathy Bateson, startled by the friction, thought it resonated something of the larger conflicts in which they were interested.

At the end of the second day, which was taken up with learning theory, child rearing in the Azores Islands, and an analysis of the dangers of overpopulation, tension arose again when it was suggested that the time had come to consider what collective action might derive from the conference. Bateson would have none of it and moved to adjourn, saying that conventional politics, composed of ad hoc measures, were themselves symptomatic of current problems. To act within them would promote the shortsightedness typical of applied science. Action must be predicated upon a new mode of thought, the creation of which was their first problem.

> The ills with which we are concerned are those of application of an epistemology which somehow doesn't lie flat against the phenomena which we are trying to represent. This gives us now a much clearer picture of our agenda than we had when we came in. . . . We may have to continue the conference for a month . . . or do it all again, but we are, I think, beginning to be in a position where we can talk with some care about epistemology.[40]

The next day, Anatol W. Holt explained an observer-inclusive systems theory which he proposed to be a method of description exposing the unity of

---

*In 1954, Schwartz had participated, as a young graduate student, in Margaret Mead's restudy of Manus—as Bateson's intellectual surrogate—collaborating with Mead as he had, photographically and conceptually. (T. Schwartz, "The Paliau Movement in the Admiralty Islands, 1946–54.")

complicated mutual processes. They worked on the problem of differentiating Holt's system from the traditional language of cybernetics until a passionate Luddite criticism interrupted the discussion. Was the machine appropriate as a model for the organization of humans and their society? Machines have explicit purposes, it was argued, given by a designer, but men, irreducibly, create their own purposes. "The problem," as Bateson posed it, "is how to go on thinking like a biologist in spite of having tools."[41]

By the end of the fifth day, his group had split badly, struggling to combine scientific interests with normative concerns. At this point, Bert Kaplan, a personality psychologist, developed the notion that history was a narrative of human events independent of nature. To illustrate this, Kaplan used Leonardo's painting "St. Anne, Mary and Child" in which the love within a little family is vivid, by contrast with the indistinct swirl of the natural world. To the ecologist Commoner, this view was unspeakable. To argue that social and ideological change need only focus on man, as Kaplan was, merely reiterated the false dichotomy which had given rise to their conference, namely that man and nature were opposed or separable. "We are concerned here," Bateson piously announced, "with an extension not to the creatures of nature, but to a total system of interrelationships involving the whole of nature."[42] As it had been defined, the central issue of the conference was to begin to resolve such false dichotomies in modern life.

By the end of their week together, many of the conferees evidently felt a sense of confederation. During the final meeting, according to Cathy Bateson, a variety of metaphors of integration occurred to some of them.

> We had struggled for hours over the relationship between man and the rest of nature, realizing more and more that man needs a deeper sense of himself as a part of natural processes than has existed since the beginning of civilization, and yet must keep sufficient distance to take responsibility, must feel a kinship of care and fostering like the child who learns to build peace between his quarreling parents.[43]

She initiated the last afternoon's discussion by describing the sort of solipsistic coupling in which she felt man must engage in order to establish unity either with other men or with nature. The self must recognize and express the complex similarity between its own organization and that organization in the external world. Others were self-congratulatory. "I think the brilliance of Gregory's move," Commoner had decided, "is that he sensed the need of a new kind of 'thinking beast' in order to cope with the crisis that the world is in."[44] To Bateson himself, the conference had been a success because it had not succumbed to facile solutions that would only exacerbate the pathologies which had brought about the convening of the group. Their achievement was rather to have allowed contact between ideas.

> I think the thing that most frightened me was the feeling that, as you go towards action, what you in fact do is lose understanding gained from the interlocking of the various things that have been said, the extra value that those things had by virtue of being said in the same conversation with each other. . . . As you précis, as you make policy and such things, you obscure the vast darkness of the subject, and you obscure the very real elegance and significance of the interlocking plexus.[45]

The integration of the group was inconsistent, however. They agreed, in all, on no manifesto, nor on any public gesture beyond publishing their proceedings. The majority, perhaps, were bespelled by Bateson's developing cybernetic utopianism but others were threatened by the intimacy and fatigue upon which this convergence rested. For Cathy Bateson, the deliberations had taken on an "intoxicating felicity."[46] On the other hand, for the cyberneticist Gordon Pask, the conclusion of the conference demanded a stern statement of his professional identity.[47]

Bateson left Burg Wartenstein euphoric. The meeting had touched him intellectually and emotionally. "It boiled down at the end to an analysis of those many pathologies of our culture," he wrote Taylor Pryor of the Oceanic Institute, "which result from the premise that mind is transcendent instead of being immanent in the body; and God transcendent instead of immanent in the planetary ecology."[48] The Wenner-Gren Foundation evidently shared the excitement, having agreed to sponsor a sequel for the following summer of 1969. For the second conference, Bateson planned to elaborate a cybernetic theory of action based in standards and perceptions of beauty. "At heart," prospective conferees were informed, "I believe that action, if it be planned at all, must always be planned upon an aesthetic base."[49] He entitled the meeting the Moral and Aesthetic Structure of Human Adaptation, and developed it from his romantic notion that residing within some artistic expression and aesthetic judgment was a holistic view of mind and self, somehow capable of correcting the diseased partiality of Occidental consciousness.

> It seems to me that, quite without an exhaustive analysis of the relevant cybernetic factors, some people are guided away from the courses of action which would generate ugliness—that there are people who have "green thumbs" in their dealing with other living systems. I am inclined to associate this phenomenon with some sort of aesthetic judgment, an awareness of criteria of

elegance and of the combinations of process that will lead to elegance rather than to ugliness.[50]

Approximately the same group gathered in Austria.* At the beginning of the conference, Bateson read a description of the futile efforts by the anthropologist, Sol Tax, on behalf of the peyote cult of the Native American movement. Tax wanted to film their central ceremony in order to advocate the authenticity of their religious practices which were under attack for using drugs.[51]† For some of the Indians, however, allowing the film to be made would be a defilement of their sacred ritual rather than a means for preserving it. At the same time, they understood that rejecting the making of the film would also threaten the integrity of their belief. Bateson's opening parable evoked a confusion that persisted throughout the meeting. It was unclear to the group, according to the notes of the systems theorist, Geoffrey Vickers,‡ to what Bateson was alluding by this story. Was it that any gesture of assistance threatens that which it wishes to preserve? Or was it that the conference itself was analogous to the well-intentioned anthropologist trying to help a people maintain their pristine faith? Yet, if the group was akin to the anthropologist, whose faith was to be protected? Certainly not that of Western society against whose monstrous hubris they had been summoned to convene.

Vickers attributed Bateson's frustration with this discussion and with the whole conference "to the [group's] common ambivalence toward any kind of action above the personal level.... But this [problem] never came to the surface sufficiently to generate ... discussion."[52] Lita Osmundsen seconded this interpretation, but focused it on Bateson in particular. "I think what he really wanted to do was to see if he could develop a theory of action ... which he could find palatable. ... That was what was interesting because ... down deep he believes that life is not to be tampered with."[53] From a more mortal perspective, she also pointed out that the gravity of the first conference had been enhanced by an immediate sense of grief—several members had lost relatives prior to it.[54] The second one seemed to have a less compelling

---

*Exchanging membership with Attneave, Hendrix, Jones, and Raxlen were a filmmaker, Guy Brenton; a philosopher, S. A. Erickson; a psychiatrist, Shepard Ginandes, M.D.; Bateson's patron, Taylor A. Pryor; an anthropologist, Roy A. Rappaport; and a sociologist and systems theorist, Sir Geoffrey Vickers.

†This incident was first recited by Tax himself at an earlier Wenner-Gren conference on a similar theme, Man's Role in Changing the Face of the Earth, held at Princeton in June 1952. (W. L. Thomas, ed., *Man's Role in Changing the Face of the Earth*, pp. vii-viii.)

‡Cf. Vickers' notion of "the ecology of ideas" in *Value Systems and Social Process*.

emotional basis, and perhaps suffered from the problems of contrived spontaneity which can beset sequels.

> At the end [Osmundsen recalled], Gregory asked me cold, in front of everybody, "What about a third conference?" I had to tell him no, in open session, which I hate to do. But he caught me short. . . . They were all kind of annoyed with me that night because there wasn't going to be a glorious third conference. But the conference didn't click. It didn't have an impact on the participants.[55]

The Wenner-Gren conferences, and the voluminous correspondence enveloping them, did not resolve Bateson's complicated reticence about the application of science (as if this was possible). Instead, they provided an encouraging yet critical forum. From them, he went on to several other ideological performances, which surprised him, as he wrote a psychiatric colleague in the spring of 1970. "I find as I grow older, I have less and less impulse to collect data and more . . . tendency to want to interfere on the social scene."[56] Testifying before the Hawaiian State Senate, Bateson supported a measure to endow an Office for Environmental Quality.[57] A decision by the California State Board of Education, which required that the teaching of evolutionary theory give Darwin and Genesis equal footing, prompted a note in *BioScience* to the effect that guidelines should rather be adopted emphasizing the "evolution of evolutionary theory," rather than competitive alternatives.[58] He also chaired another Wenner-Gren conference in New York City, which brought city officials and urban planners together with cyberneticists and ecologists.[59]

Late in 1968, still in the flush of the first conference, Bateson returned to an interest begun in early Palo Alto years. In a major paper which was published later as "Cybernetics of self: a theory of alcoholism," he sought to work out the logic of alcoholic addiction and the logic of the ethical therapy which the Alcoholics Anonymous organization employed so successfully.[60] The one, he thought, might stand for the pathologies that a variety of false dichotomies had brought upon Western man, while the other might stand for a way out.

> Alcoholics are philosophers in that universal sense that all human beings (and all mammals) are guided by highly abstract principles of which they are either quite unconscious or unaware that the principle governing their perception and action is philosophic. A common misnomer for such principles is "feelings." . . . This misnomer arises naturally from the Anglo-Saxon epistemological tendency to reify or attribute to the body all mental processes which are peripheral to consciousness.[61]

Bateson viewed addiction in terms of the habitual patterns of interaction in which the alcoholic drank. In Occidental societies, he argued that normal drinking is symmetrically competitive. Drinks are matched. The addict then applies this same competitive pattern to his attempts to stay sober. What takes place between ego and John Barleycorn is a match in which the alcoholic takes intense pride in his conscious ability to will permanent sobriety. "I," he says, "can stay sober." Friends, indeed, enforce this view. But successful sobriety liquidates the addict's challenge. In order to test the strength of his will, he will risk a drink. The competitive patterning of his pride requires a battle. Having deutero-learned to expect competition in connection with his drinking, he continues to assume it about his sobriety. The logic of addiction which Bateson construed had the alcoholic's sobriety schismogenically decreasing with his ability to sustain it. His drinking may have stopped for the moment, but his symmetrical pride about not drinking persists unabated. The longer he is on the wagon, the less he is challenged by not drinking. At the same time, to have a drink is also to confess his weakness.

Bateson supposed that this double bound sobriety was a species of the Cartesian dualism, separating and opposing mind and matter. The conscious will, in this case, opposed the rest of the alcoholic personality. Inebriation was thus a temporary escape from an insoluble situation. Drunk, the individual could conceive of himself and act as part of a group. "In ritual," Bateson noted, "partaking of wine has always stood for the social aggregation of persons united in religious 'communion' or secular Gemütlichkeit."[62] The alcoholic self, the integrity of which has been denied in sobriety, is reunited in drunkenness. If it is assumed that the addict's sober life in some degree gives rise to his alcoholism, then it is unlikely that reinforcing "his particular style" of sobriety will divest him of that which promotes his addiction.[63] "If his sobriety drives him to drink, then that style must contain error or pathology; and intoxification must provide some—at least subjective—correction of this error."[64]

A central tenet of the Alcoholics Anonymous rehabilitation program requires that the addict discover and admit his powerlessness over the bottle: once an alcoholic always an alcoholic. To do so, he must "hit bottom" in some way. "The panic of the alcoholic who has hit bottom is the panic of the man who thought he had control over a vehicle but suddenly finds that the vehicle can run away from him. Suddenly, pressure on what he knows is the brake seems to make the vehicle go faster. It is the panic of discovering that *it* (the system self *plus* vehicle) is bigger than he is."[65] Addiction must be understood to be a full-time business. Sobriety merely belies the presence of the pathology. This realization, which may be the result of great pain, repeatedly experienced, brings the alcoholic "to a threshold point at which he has bankrupted the epistemology of 'self-control.'"[66] The addict must reconceptualize his addiction as a dominant system in which his participation is based in a complementary epistemology—as if he were perpetually drunk—and hence no longer double bound by his competitive pride. He must accept the double identity of an alcoholic who does not drink. "The myth of self-power is thereby broken by the demonstration of a greater power."[67]*

The logic of alcoholic pathology was an extended metaphor—reviling the somatically defined Occidental self. To believe that the self is limited to the body "is a false reification," Bateson concluded, "of an improperly delimited part of this much larger field of interlocking processes."[68] At the same time, the Alcoholics Anonymous theology of submitting to a systemic power greater than self espoused the post conference ecological moralisms Bateson was advocating. Symmetrical competition was not in itself pathogenic, but to construe certain basic relationships (e.g., man-nature, man-society) in symmetrical terms must end in disaster. "The unit of survival—either in ethics or in evolution—is not the organism or the species but the largest system or "power" within which the creature lives. If the creature destroys its environment, it destroys itself."[69] The dilemma of Western man, fighting to control and destroy nature, appeared in the opposition "self vs. bottle." It also appeared in the evolution of theological man-nature relations. The shift in belief from totemic, to animistic, to transcendent gods reflected the rise of modern egoism toward the environment. Totemic man used the natural world as a sacred model of his own social and psychological organization. Animistic man took his own social and psychological self to model the organization of nature. In both conceptions, man and environment were identified in some way.† The contemporary Occident, however, divided man from nature and separated him from his deity.

---

*Notably, the same constraints that the "power" of the addiction exert upon the alcoholic—and Western man—applied to the "power" as well. Not capable of arbitrary reward or punishment, the "power" itself could not possess unilateral power, subject as it was to the same "systemic determinism." (GB, "The cybernetics of 'self,'" in Steps, p. 333.)

†Coming across the exceptional episode of Occidental totemism pleased Bateson. Finding one such, "The Story of Tuan MacCairill," he sent it to the French anthropologist, Claude Lévi-Strauss (10 May 1967). This was a pre-Christian Irish myth, circa A.D. 500, that James Stephens had collected, of a confrontation between missionary and pagan who convert each other in the course of their conversations. MacCairill, the pagan, recounts his successive dreams in which he is transformed from a man into a stag, a boar, a hawk, a salmon, and back, having been eaten by the King of Ulster's wife, into a man. "I awoke from the dream, and I was that which I dreamed" ("The Story of Tuan MacCairill," in A James Stephens Reader, ed.

If you put God outside and set him vis-à-vis his creation and if you have the idea that you are created in his image you will logically and naturally see yourself as outside and against the things around you. And as you arrogate all mind to yourself, you will see the world around you as mindless and therefore not entitled to moral and ethical consideration. The environment will seem to be yours to exploit. Your survival unit will be you and your folks or conspecifics against the environment of other social units, other races and the brutes and vegetables.[70]

Bateson's mind treasured general ideas whose formal characteristics recurred in the multiple spheres of his interest. Describing its manifestations is possible, although appreciating the prismatic quality is less so. The notion of immanence, for example, circulates throughout his thinking on alcoholism, genetics, and evolutionary theory. But this sort of thematic integration, entangled between scientific disciplines, was not easily given to definition. A moment of lucidity occurred to Bateson in January 1970, when, at the invitation of the Institute for General Semantics, he went to New York to give that year's Alfred Korzybski memorial lecture. As we shall see, for theoretical reasons, the occasion suited him.* "Everything he thought, everything he

---

L. Frankenberg, pp. 211-28.) Similarly, when lecturing, the ethologist Konrad Lorenz was in the habit of mimicking involuntarily the particular animal he was discussing.

The point which Bateson liked to make of such phenomena was that the West required just this intimate identification of man and nature. "What man needs," he wrote Joseph Wheelwright, "in order to correct the shortsightedness of conscious planning is a model which would be cybernetic, homeostatic, etc., in its nature. This model I suggest, is in fact provided by personified totemic animals, personified gods, etc. The image of god or the animal can be endowed with many characteristics which man . . . does not clearly see in himself and in his society." (22 December 1967)

*The founder of the Institute of General Semantics, Alfred Korzybski (1879–1950) was a naturalized Pole, who led something of an apostolic life, devoted to the cumulative progress of human thought, which he saw best exemplified in the critical and fastidious linguistic traditions of modern science. To Korzybski, men were unique for their ability to transmit ideas across time, and were uniquely enmired by language, the basis of this ability. Confusion of symbol and object, inattention to the limits of abstraction, dogmatic eagerness to dualize either-or distinctions, and rigid automatic behavior, typified the "unsane" human condition. Korzybski's preoccupations were ethical: Could a scientific conception of sanity be constructed which extended beyond mere social conformity? He devised a value orientation, in response to this question, founded upon the propagation of thought, which he called "time-binding." The main work, *Science and Sanity,* presented complex theoretical doctrine drawn from relativity theory, quantum mechanics, colloidal chemistry, neurology, and mathematical logic. Korzybski also developed practical therapeutic training—exercises in a set of linguistic conventions emphasizing precision in language. (A. Korzybski, *Science and Sanity.*)

believed, everything he knew, everything he saw, and saw beyond, he got into that lecture."[71] Only then, Bateson felt, did he realize the abiding intellectual project of his life—to pioneer a science of mind. "With the Korzybski lecture, 'Form, Substance, and Difference,' I found that my work with primitive peoples, schizophrenia, biological symmetry, and in my discontent with the conventional theories of evolution and learning, I had identified a widely scattered set of benchmarks or points of reference from which *a new scientific territory* [italics added] could be defined."[72]

The boundaries of this new territory—the sciences of communication— were immaterial. "If you kick a stone, it moves with the energy which it got from your kick. If you kick a dog, it moves with the energy which it got from its own metabolism."[73] As a result, explanation of living patterns of communication must diverge from explanation in the physical sciences. In the one, effects have discrete causes (impacts, forces, energy exchange), whereas in the other, effects occur in response to information. In a simple cybernetic circuit, a governor engages when it receives a message composed of the difference between the actual running speed of the engine and some ideal speed. It then transforms this difference into "efferent" messages so as to increase or lessen the fuel supply or to activate the brake. In systems of communication, it is this sort of difference between messages in space and time which stimulates response. Messages depend fundamentally upon abstraction—upon differences which make differences. Cause in communication may therefore derive from nothing. "Zero differs from one, and zero therefore can be a cause, which is not admissible in hard science. The letter which you did not write can precipitate an angry reply"[74] Differences can not be localizable. They are not things or events. "There is a difference between the color of this desk and the color of this pad," Bateson said, typically illustrating the point with immediately available objects. "But that difference is not in the pad, it is not in the desk, and I cannot pinch it between them. The difference is not in the space between them. In a word, *a difference is an idea.*"[75] The map is not the territory, Korzybski had pointed out; similarly messages are not phenomena. What appears on a map are tranforms of differences in the territory, boundaries, altitudes, or variation of population. Never the territory itself. "Always the process of representation will filter it out so that the mental world is only maps of maps. . . . All 'phenomena' are literally 'appearances.'"[76]*

---

*The year before, at a 1969 meeting of the American Psychological Association, Bateson criticized his research group's initial formulation of the double bind sequence. Confusing abstraction with phenomenon in 1956, they had been guilty of false reification. "We talk in that paper as though a double bind were a something and as though somethings could be counted."

The science of communication was an immaterial science of mind. Just as the universe was characterized by a physical determinism, there was a concomitant mental determinism.[77] The mental determinism was particularly evident, Bateson thought, in nature. His definition of mind was synonymous with the organization of a cybernetic circuit.

1) The system shall operate with and upon *differences*.

2) The system shall consist of closed loops or networks of pathways along which differences and transforms of differences shall be transmitted.

3) Many events within the system shall be energized by the respondent part rather than by the impact from the triggering part.

4) The system shall show self-correctiveness in the direction of homeostasis and/or the direction of runaway. Self-correctiveness implies trial and error.[78]

Given these criteria, coral reefs, redwood forests, and human societies all displayed the attributes of mind. That is, in each, interlocking aggregates of organisms exchanged messages. In each, the energy of component organisms derived from within the organism itself. And, in each, the whole system acted destructively and self-correctively. Mind inhered—was immanent—within those natural systems admitting of "the appropriate complexity whenever that complexity occurs."[79]

To identify a mind in nature required designating the correct totality. A computer, for example, could not itself think. It was the larger dynamic unit, man-plus-computer-plus-environment, which exhibited the characteristics of mind.

Consider a man felling a tree with an axe. Each stroke of the axe is modified or corrected according to the shape of the cut face of the tree left by the previous

---

In communication exchange there could be no quantities or substances, however, only transformations of patterns. "Are there double binds in the mind? The question is not trivial. As there are in the mind no coconuts but only percepts and transforms of coconuts, so also, when I perceive (consciously or unconsciously) a double bind in my boss's behavior, I acquire in my mind no double bind but only a percept or transform of a double bind. And that is *not* what the theory [was] about." (GB, "Double bind—1969," in *Steps*, p. 272.) Bateson frequently referred to two personal experiences, when discussing the importance of perceptual transformation: to the hallucinations (which he never saw) induced by drug, LSD 25, and to the experiments with optical illusions in depth perception by Adalbert Ames, Jr., in which Bateson had participated. Both underscored the sort of epistemology William Blake described so powerfully in 1822. "Nature has no outline: but Imagination has. Nature has no Tune: but Imagination has. Nature has no Supernatural, and dissolves: Imagination is Eternity." ("The Ghost of Abel," in *The Prose and Poetry of William Blake*, p. 268.)

stroke. The self-corrective (i.e., mental) process is brought about by a total system, tree-eyes-brain-muscles-axe-stroke-tree; and it is this total system that has the characteristics of immanent mind.[80]

Within the man-ax-tree interaction, the ax controlled the behavior of the man, while the tree controlled the ax. Construing it as a mere part of circular feedback processes, Bateson again diminished the effect of human will, while he widened the conceptual boundaries of mind.

> The individual mind is immanent but not only in the body. It is immanent also in pathways and messages outside the body; and there is a larger Mind of which the individual mind is only a sub-system. This larger Mind is comparable to God and is perhaps what some people mean by "God," but it is still immanent in the total interconnected social system and planetary ecology.[81]*

Charging the sacred meaning of the cybernetic ideas were more immediate implications. These, however, were only within reach of Bateson's imagination. He confessed, to conclude the Korzybski lecture, that his ego was immured in the diseased Western premises of transcendence.

> The most important task today [January 1970] is . . . to learn to think in the new way. Let me say that *I* don't know how to think that way. . . . If I am cutting down the tree, I still think "Gregory Bateson" is cutting down the tree. *I* am cutting down the tree. "Myself" is to me still an excessively concrete object, different from the rest of what I have been calling "mind."[82]

As the decade of the 1960s ended, this excessively "concrete" self was again sustained by a patchwork of institutional ties. "My motto," he wrote a

---

*These views developed, in part, in discussion and correspondence with Bateson's sometime neighbor in Hawaii, the philosopher-critic Paul Goodman. In 1969, Bateson was attacking the very impulse to dualize in a letter to his friend, then in New York. "You will probably tell me that this has all been said better by Plato, Aristotle, Kant and Confucius" (15 May 1969). Goodman agreed, mind and body, form and substance, and God and Universe were all of them falsely understood as oppositions. But to Goodman, dualisms in dialectic were the necessary and not entirely "neurotic" product of any finite creature. "Establishing any boundary probably involves projection of one's own unconscious across the boundary, so that tension builds up. The new resolution will be different since growth or change has meantime occurred on both sides. Yet I guess a finite creature has to have its boundaries" (19 May 1969). For just this reason, Bateson answered, minds ought to be defined within the appropriate context or system, rather than within the individual body. "Darwin's mind still bothers us even though his body has been disposed of. The same of course goes for spatial boundaries. You mind and mine can interact at 5,000 miles range. All we need is paper and pencil" (21 May 1969).

psychiatric colleague, "is 'divide in order that you may not be conquered.'"[83] He split time between the Oceanic Institute and the Anthropology Department of the University of Hawaii, where he held a visiting professorship until 1970. There, Bateson gave a seminar called Living Systems, in which, from a poetic and cybernetic perspective, he teased students with his ethical and ecological concerns. What could one conclude, he asked in one exam, from William Blake's *Songs of Innocence and Experience,* given the notion that God created both the "Tyger" and the "Lamb"? Or what systemic ramifications should politicians consider before distributing an invention, making a new law, or introducing a new organism into a preexisting ecological system?

Keeping himself aloof from its politics, Bateson was nevertheless privileged by the University of Hawaii department to conduct a class which deviated from conventional anthropology. The National Institute of Mental Health, on the other hand, withdrew its funding of him in 1969, amid suggestions that his science was no longer based in experimental or clinical data. At the age of sixty-five, indeed, the possibility of new fieldwork seemed vague, at best. He briefly considered returning to Bali or observing parent-child relations among native Hawaiians, until, impatient with restrictions and inductive research in general, Bateson became starkly insensible to the etiquette of grant application. Soliciting untheoretical data, he wrote the N.I.M.H. review board, had "wrecked" the behavioral sciences.[84] Through Taylor Pryor's administrations, in the summer of 1970, Bateson secured a half-time appointment in the Culture Learning Institute of the East-West Center at the University of Hawaii. "They don't want me to alter what I do very much," was his characteristic understanding of the new employment, "but they do want me to mingle in their affairs and to give my studies an east-west angle."[85]

Encouraged by the lucidity of the Korzybski lecture, that year Bateson also went ahead with plans to put together an anthology of his lifework. With the assistance of two young Americans, his secretary, Judith Van Slooten, and a student, Mark Engel, thirty-five representative essays were selected, which he had produced between 1935 and 1970. Bateson added short comments connecting the groups of them. In end-linkage terms, an odd reversal then took place. In English families, it may be recalled, the parental roles of exhibitionism, protectiveness, and dominance were linked to the child's roles of spectatorship, feebleness, and submission. But in American families, according to the formulation, rather than watching their parents, children showed off to them, while they remained feeble and submissive. Acting like an American parent, Bateson invited Engel, his young student, to write a preface to his new collection, which would be called *Steps to an Ecology of Mind.* Acting like an American parent to an English child, Engel did so, acknowledging his mentor's display and his own unequivocal spectatorship. "This book," he wrote, "is a sample of the best thinking I've found. I commend it to you, my brothers and sisters of the new culture."[86]

While the student endorsed *Steps to an Ecology of Mind* to American youth, circa 1971, Bateson addressed it to his professional colleagues. He introduced the book by ridiculing conventional behavioral science for having made not a single contribution to fundamental "eternal verities" of scientific thought,[87] such as the second law of thermodynamics, the tautologies of mathematics, or the conservative laws of energy and mass.[88] The self-validating process of inductive research, rocking from data to ad hoc cause and hypothesis, falsely reified, back to data, had bedeviled integration of knowledge in the behavioral sciences, which Bateson viewed as a disparate "mass of quasi-theoretical speculation unconnected with any core of fundamental knowledge."[89] A surveyor must match his measurements with Euclidean geometry, but behavioral scientists had no comparable knowledge within or against which to place their thinking.

Students of human behavior in the nineteenth century had looked for models from the physical sciences and had chosen energy as their guiding analogy. "Metabolism obeys an energy budget ... and energy expended in behavior must surely be included in this budget; and therefore it seemed sensible to think of energy as a determinant of behavior."[90] Bateson did not fault the impulse to bring together behavioral data with paradigms from the physical or chemical sciences. His criticism, rather, was that the wrong paradigm had been chosen and a bridge of conceptual language had therefore developed which was inappropriate to the exact expression of the problems. "After all, energy *is* Mass x Velocity^2 and no behavioral scientist really insists that 'psychic energy' is of these dimensions."[91]

The question to pose then was where and how to look for a new analogy. Convinced of the poverty of inductive research, he considered the essentials of scientific thought to be foreshadowed in sacred imaginations. Both Genesis and Iatmul origin myths were built around an opposition between *substance*— the problems of material creation—and *form*—the problems of order, differentiation, and classification. In both, that which was differentiated—substance—was less significant than the *process* of differentiation. The problems which Bateson called central to contemporary behavioral science—mental process, communication, organization, and differentiation—followed the emphases of these mythologies. They were also matters in which form took priority over substance. *Steps to an Ecology of Mind* was thus concerned with "building a bridge between facts of life and behavior and what we know today of the nature of pattern and form."[92] It was meant to stimulate research which fit empiricism within cybernetic and evolutionary paradigms.

With this book completed, and with a renewed sense of design in the diversity of his research and thinking, Bateson was offered thirty American undergraduates. Karl Jaeger, an independent educator, proposed that he and Lois take a small group of students through several Asian nations. The opportunity coincided with Bateson's budding interest in the parallels between cybernetics and Buddhism, and his experience leading small-group conferences, of course, had been particularly rewarding. As final inducement, Jaeger added a stop in Kenya to the end of the itinerary because Bateson had never seen the big African wildlife. As the group traveled by air through Japan, Hong Kong, Bali, Sri Lanka, India, and Kenya, the subject of the course would be of Bateson's choosing. He planned to spend it comparing major cultural premises of the Orient with those indicated by modern ecological theory, and to observe the expression of such premises in family life, in mythology, in drama, and in film. There was also an intention to synthesize cultural and genetic data which Daniel Freedman, a psychologist from the University of Chicago, was to collect from comparative infant behavior. As it was conceived, Bateson wrote prospective students, The Nature and Culture of Man was to be an "exploratory rather than didactic" program.[93]

As it happened, the academic year 1971–1972 did not work out as planned. Two months before the trip was to begin, Bateson—throughout his life an inveterate cigarette smoker—was hospitalized, pallid and hacking with emphysema. He recovered in time to leave, but remained so weak during the first months en route that his organizational abilities were impaired. "The only plan is that there is no plan," was the gist of his cryptic remarks to the group gathering in Hawaii.[94] The students, in any case, found experience more compelling than the theory being developed in class, and found each other less than compatible. There was, in short, little intellectual and human focus to the year. Even so, this was the situation in which I, as a member of that group, met Gregory Bateson.

It is difficult to extract the clutter of ensuing work from my first impressions of him. But obviously I grew fond of him. Bateson's enormous capacity for playful conversation delighted me. And his reactions were often mysteriously counterintuitive. I once walked with him and his daughter Nora, then three years old. We lumbered slowly up a hill behind Kyoto, Japan, pausing often so that he could catch his breath, to watch a troop of free-ranging macaques push each other around. Amid the bustle of monkey politics, Gregory began to mutter about the social consequences for the troop should a bored alpha animal give up his dominance.

Hitherto, social science had meant to me the intentional politics of modern economic and ethnic interest groups. Lauding the artistic imagination, Bateson dismissed such politics. The creation and appreciation of great art had for him social and even scientific value. Drawing recklessly, it seemed, upon all manner of phenomena, he was always suggesting unsuspected connections between them. One somehow felt that imbedded in the stories, formulations, humor, and pessimism was an integrated view of the world which, for some reason, he would only imply and not articulate. I began to wonder about the elements of self-disclosure hidden within his peculiar thought. Being then quite aroused by Erik H. Erikson's interpretive biographies,[95] I was led to question Bateson about the background of his career.

For his part, during the year Bateson held sympathetic discussions in Japan with Zen monks, in Sri Lanka with Theravada Buddhists, and in Pondicherry, India, with devotees of Sri Aurobindo. In Bali, returning for a day to Bajoeng Gede, the former field site, he was unhappy about the intrusion of tourism, which seemed to be infecting the trance dances. This was an epoch of impending ecological disaster, he would say, while admitting that he was not altogether certain of this. By the end of the academic year, he had regained strength enough to relish visiting the Kenya game reserves. During one evening in Nairobi, we dined with his former Cambridge classmate, the anthropologist, L. S. B. Leakey. Gregory had charge of Nora that evening, so it was difficult for the two "old boys" to converse. At one point, however, Leakey—a man of some exuberance—rushed out of the room to fetch more fossils to show us. Looking over those already on the table, hefting them, then cocking an eyebrow, "Bones," Bateson said; "I never liked them."[96]

XV. As Man of Knowledge

The Batesons returned to Hawaii in midsummer 1972 to find the Oceanic Institute beset by financial problems and closing down its operations. Deciding to retire, they moved to the superb coast of central California, at Gorda, just south of Big Sur. They owned a small property there, acquired in Palo Alto days, on which sat a large, somewhat isolated, one-room octagon, then in final stages of construction. Although building at this location and living there together had been a fond dream, by the end of 1972, when I visited to interview him, Gregory was bleak and alone. Lois, also feeling the strain of the unsettled situation, had taken their daughter Nora to visit relatives in North Carolina. She was eventually to return, but at that time had not set a date.

The move from Hawaii had left Bateson feeling burdened, he said, like a snail dragging his life on his back.[1] A grant application submitted to investigate the training and learning of religious enlightenment had been rejected, and though the possibility of returning to Cambridge University had arisen, it too had come to nothing. Instead, he had taken a part-time lectureship at the Santa Cruz campus of the University of California.* But the

---

*Every year between 1965 and 1972, the University of California at Santa Cruz opened a new residential college—each marked by a particular focus. A major experiment in American undergraduate education, envisioned by the former president of the university, Clark Kerr, Santa Cruz was to be a synthesis of intimate intellectual community and large-scale institution. The original intention was to establish an innovative climate based in extensive student-faculty interaction. There were to be no disciplinary departments. Rather the provost of each college was to be responsible for recruiting faculty around interdisciplinary themes. By the time the university opened, however, intercollege "boards," resembling departments, had been established. (G. Grant and D. Riesman, *The Perpetual Dream;* V. Stadtman, *The University of California.*)

difficult commute was long for a man of sixty-eight, and he was making it twice weekly. We spent a few days together, during which Bateson was forthcoming, readily guided back to a narrative of his life, as he wandered into global or theoretical topics, which were of greater interest to him. The most one could do for the world, he supposed at one juncture, was scientific work which might reconcile Occidentals to death.[2] Some weeks before, as it happened, driving home from Santa Cruz, he had dozed at the wheel and had smashed his car against the side of a Big Sur hill. Such was his mood; Bateson wanted to muse about the degree of intention the accident might have involved.

The following month, in January 1973, when Lois and Nora returned, all three took up residence at the University of California in Santa Cruz. At the end of the year, Gregory affiliated himself with Kresge College, the most radical of the Santa Cruz experiments in undergraduate education. Founded in 1970, with an ecological focus to "explore educational innovation through a human relations approach,"[3] the college program was inspired by the humanistic psychology of Abraham H. Maslow and Carl Rogers. During Kresge's first years, students and faculty participated in "encounter groups" which asked for emotional candor and for consensual decisions about life and education. Students were organized into small "kin groups," meeting once a week with a faculty "facilitator'" to air their feelings and, in the more enduring groups, to discuss their studies. In content, education tended toward crafts, meditation, utopias, gardening, and poetry writing. There was also a core curriculum which included both natural and social sciences. By January 1974, Robert Edgar, a geneticist who had come from the California Institute of Technology to be Kresge's founding provost, felt that the college lacked "major academic mission."[4] The early enthusiasm for the encounter group had withered, and the interests of students and faculty were dividing among women's studies, politics, and the California sun.

In these circumstances Edgar met Bateson for the first time. "I had not heard of him or read anything by him," he recalled. "I was captivated by Gregory's presence—large, awkward, shy in a way, yet bound to be the center of the conversation. His clothes were ill-fitting and he wore no socks—clearly a man who did not fit comfortably into this world."[5] By persuading him to join Kresge College, the provost hoped that his troubled institution might coalesce around Bateson's interests. Edgar then arranged for six of the college faculty—a marine biologist, a historian, an astronomer, a novelist, a psychologist, and an ex-Dominican poet—to work as teaching assistants in the Ecology of Mind, a large undergraduate lecture course Bateson was to teach. The subject was to be epistemological premises in perception and behavior, as they were found in human cultures, in plant morphology, and in animal behavior. Reading would include culture-and-personality anthropology, biological philosophy, mysticism, poetry, philosophy of mathematics, and autobiographies of madness.

After concluding the academic year of 1974, the Batesons moved from Kresge to a house near the village of Ben Lomond, in the redwooded hills northeast of the university. The few remaining artifacts were deposited there: a library dominated by nineteenth-century biology and art, the old upright Sheraton cabinet, mementos from New Guinea and Bali, and a long oak table in their dining room, which was bounded by the *Encyclopaedia Britannica* on one side and by a large salt-water aquarium on the other. Bateson based the rest of his four-year association with Kresge in this rented house, teaching such seminars as Aesthetic Process, and the Epistemology of Molecules there. (In the former, he had students analyze a poem by Rilke and then asked them to go find a leaf which had a pattern similar to the poem.) But although his hospitality was continuous, Bateson exerted only minimal influence upon faculty, and Edgar's hopes for his college were unfulfilled. "It was much easier for the students to grasp Gregory's ideas than for the faculty, [who were] already trained in traditional modes of thinking."[6]* Yearly, hundreds of undergraduates flocked to his lecture course. "He ... care[d] about being heard," a colleague said of his pedagogy, "and about reaching young people with ideas which he believed were useful to a future he was unlikely to enjoy."[7] Many students were in awe of Bateson, delighting in his ecological parables, and in his experience with primitives, schizophrenics, and dolphins. This sort of rapt attention was unusual to a man whose culture heroes—Lamarck, Blake, Samuel Butler, and William Bateson—were great, isolated dissenters. It disconcerted him, evidently.

> I begin to feel embarrassed when I stand up in a big auditorium where a third of the audience have a sort of primary assumption that they will agree with me. It is ... rather strange and improbable that ideas which my father was groping for should have become almost fashionable. And it feels very strange for me, accustomed to be a voice crying in the wilderness, to find myself more famous than infamous.[8]

---

*A handful of the Kresge faculty, however, appreciated him. One of them, Carter Wilson, a novelist, recalled his empathy and his humor, "Gregory and I had been talking one evening about LSD. After protracted discussion, I finally asked him if he thought there was something truly different about the *kind* of experience LSD provides. Long pause. Then Gregory said slowly that yes, he did think you could say that the experience under LSD was different in kind from other experiences. And that once you had had it then you knew—a very long pause—that it was an experience you could have again for a dollar." (C. Wilson to D. Lipset, 3 November 1978.)

Bateson judged that students in the 1974 version of his lecture courses found it difficult.[9] Most were exceptionally kind people, he later told Gerald Grant, a sociologist of education, but they were intellectually disappointing. They spoke a "horrible touchy-feely jargon," were unmotivated to learn, and seemed academically unskilled.[10]

A few students, one of whom was Ernestine McHugh, knew him closely. When, as an undergraduate at Kresge, she decided to do ethnographic research in Nepal, Bateson became her formal adviser. She must not waste time choosing a field site, he wrote her. The point was to get settled and concentrate on her first impressions. "My old teacher, Alfred Haddon, always asserted that anthropologists are precisely *not* travellers. They are sitters and should sit until they get callouses on their behinds."[11] During McHugh's first months in Nepal, an American woman, Jane Martin, with whom she stayed while selecting a village, died suddenly. Sending Bateson field notes of her initial activities, McHugh also wrote lengthily of her friend's death, ashamed that she felt compelled to do so. His response, she recalled, was bolstering.[12]

> Please get this absolutely straight: that what you say about Jane's death is worth a hundred of pages of "field notes" about minor magic. That solves half the problem: Just don't pretend to be a folklorist when what matters is your guts and the guts of your friends in Nepal. . . . The other half of the problem is more difficult, and it is, quite simply, to record what goes on in everyday life with as much of your lifeblood and theirs on the paper as if you were writing about birth and death. In Eliot's phrase, "an ultimate simplicity costing not less than everything."[13]

While McHugh was in Nepal in early 1974, Bateson made a small anthropological expedition of his own. A journal of psychological anthropology—*Ethos*—was dedicating its summer 1975 issue to Margaret Mead. To honor her as one of the founders of the subdiscipline, articles were solicited concerning the theme of "socialization as cultural communication," and Bateson was asked to contribute. For this occasion, he returned to the subject for which earlier there had been no funding—the socialization of trance.[14] Although the focus of his paper was to be a sequence of Balinese photographs, he began it with a discussion of the assumptions and cognitive methods—in the epistemology—from which such a study might be based. Positing that socialization required the interaction of two or more learning organisms, Bateson argued that identifying the contexts of these sequences (be they in play, aggression, or exploration) would involve the empathy and introspection of the investigator. However, the use of subjectivity as a research tool presented theoretical difficulties, since the universe was not created and maintained by discrete things, events, forces, systems, persons, or processes, except insofar as scientists attributed these separate concepts to it. Given this dissociation between nature and thought, Bateson asked, is the human mind suited to the study of socialization? "Precisely at this point there is a paradoxical reversal: the socialization that we try to study is a mental process and therefore only the productions of mind are relevant."[15]

For the *Ethos* paper, he proceeded from a series of photographs chosen from *Balinese Character.*[16] In one plate, a child is seen holding a beam while learning to walk, a girl is pictured stooping to pick up offerings, and a boy is shown scratching his knee. These pictures were to illustrate that, as infants, the Balinese learn a delicate balance and an economy of motion. To scratch his knee for example, a boy will raise his leg to his waist rather than bend over to it. On the other hand, a second plate showed that when the young learn to dance, they undergo brutal manipulations of their muscles. Teachers wrench their students' limbs as if they were disconnected, utterly disregarding their earlier kinaesthetic socialization. Bateson saw that this resulted in "discrepant muscular tensions" in the bodies of Balinese dancers "and the independent movement and posturing of the separate fingers" in their hands.[17] Similarly, in their mythology the body appeared to sway between falling to pieces and complete integration. Graveyards were believed to be haunted by the ghosts of separate limbs. Bateson presented a third plate depicting shadow puppets of some of these "boggles of Balinese fantasy"—personified headless bodies, jumping hands, and unattached feet.[18] Obversely, there were gods of unity— such as Sangiang Tjintjia—who was "completely integrated, sexless, enclosed within his own effulgence and totally withdrawn."[19]

In the altered consciousness of trance which the Balinese enter during the dance, the body becomes "an autonomous, ego-alien entity."[20] Bateson suggested that this experience was based in the physiology of rapidly oscillating successions of muscular contractions and relaxations—called clonus—which seem to the dancer to occur involuntarily.* "If the arm or the leg can act of its own accord—(and indeed, clonus is a complete self-corrective circuit; it is a true aliveness)—then a similar aliveness can be expected and can be found in any limb."[21] In all, he concluded, trance in Bali combined mystical native thought with aspects of bodily movement which are affected

---

*By the time of the Macy cybernetics conferences, Norbert Wiener had begun to identify the mathematics of feedback circuitry in servomechanisms with neurophysiological feedback circuitry—exemplified by experimentally induced clonus in cats. (See S. Heims, "Gregory Bateson and the mathematicians," *Journal of the History of the Behavioral Sciences,* 13[1977]:146.)

by physiological reflex and by particular assumptions about balance according to which the young grow up.

Perhaps this theme of oscillating between fragmentation and integration, which Bateson identified in Balinese body imagery, also pertained to a pattern in his own aging. It is apparent in his relations with his family, with Kresge students, and with professional and lay publics. The publication of *Steps to an Ecology of Mind,* being hailed widely,[22] brought Bateson invitations to appear before conferences, lectures, seminars, and psychologically oriented small groups throughout the United States. His performances in such situations were confusing and done without notes, but admirers now fawned over him as a sage and man of knowledge.[23]* Some of this feeling is evident in facets of two conferences which Bateson attended in 1975. The first one, on the collapse of industrial society, occurred in August. It was convened by William I. Thompson, a renegade historian-mystic who had quit his position at M.I.T., convinced that history had ended and that the modern university was a moral failure. It took place at the Lindisfarne Association, a college and spiritual community which Thompson founded in 1973, in Southampton, New York. The name of the venture came from a seventh-century Irish monastery established by Celtic Christian mystics fleeing the confusion of their times. Utopian in overtone but partially based in Rockefeller money, Thompson's community is said to be oriented toward fostering planetary culture and toward developing meditative alternatives to industrial careers.[24] To his conference, Thompson invited Bateson, Jonas Salk, M.D., the discoverer of the polio vaccine, Lewis Thomas, M.D.,[25] the essayist and president of the Memorial Sloan-Kettering Cancer Center, Pir Vilayat Khan, a Sufi master, John Todd, an oceanographer interested in aquaculture, and Saul Mendlovitz, a professor of law and president of the Institute for World Order.

Answering Salk's opening remarks that the world was verging upon an epoch of enlightened peace, Bateson said he doubted that the human species had more than thirty years before the destruction of one or more nations. The lineal nature of Western thought—having resulted in overpopulation and pollution—clashed so with the steady-state circuitry of biological systems, that no "new age" would emerge without major cognitive change. Bateson attacked contemporary man's relationship to his environment, and condemned

---

*Discussing his approach to big audiences, an acquaintance, the anthropologist Roy Rappaport, dismissed the idea that Bateson tried deliberately to be obscure. "I think that he feels that the writing it out and planning it forestalls any real touching. . . . I know Gregory best in face-to-face settings . . . and in the context of small groups, where it seems to me, he tries very hard to be understood. What makes it complicated, I suppose, is that he wants to be understood, but at a level, or in a way, which is of low specificity, at a level which does not forestall . . . your own kinds of processes" (Personal communication: 26 May 1977).

progress in the name of which addictive pollutants had been introduced. Whereas Salk saw man overcoming his quandaries, thanks to the "survival of the wisest," Bateson saw man destroying a planet he did not understand. A *New York Times* reporter concluded that the issue of malignant ignorance—over which Bateson presided as "high priest"—became central in the conference.[26]

Two months later, in October 1975, Bateson went to Paris to attend a five-day meeting entitled Ontogenetic and Phylogenetic Models of Development which was held at the Centre Royaumont pour Une Science de L'Homme. Before a group of virtuosi, he then discussed premises for a unified theory which would encompass the fields of genetics, morphogenesis, and learning. And he affirmed that an epistemology be developed which would connote the unity of mind and body. It should be capable, that is, of describing both environmental impact upon the phenotype (learning) *and* patterns of genetic message.[27]

Directly after the Paris conference, Bateson went to London for a few days, as the guest of R. D. Laing. Of the participants in the Paris meeting, Laing recalled, Bateson was most impressed by the compassion of the child psychologist, Jean Piaget.

> He thought Piaget was a bit of a saint. And I said, "What are your criteria of sainthood?" He said, "Well, he's not terribly bright but that isn't the prerogative of saints." "Well, what is?" "Well," he said, "looking at the world with regret, looking at what people do in the world with regret, but without anger."[28]

Although tired, Bateson had a full schedule in London. In deference, Laing deliberately restrained his eagerness to bend his guest's ear. At dinner one evening, Gregory evidently noticed that his host seemed to have no appetite.

> Without changing his tone he said, "Ronnie's anorexic!" He'd got me because I was slightly anorexic. There was not very much to it, but I wasn't eating very much when he was here. . . . We started talking about Freud's *Totem and Taboo*, about eating the father. I suddenly realized that he was wanting to be eaten, that he wanted everything he had, all the juices . . . incorporated in his sons, in his spiritual sons, in his scientific sons. I thought he was doing the rounds almost, to make sure that everyone had a last chance to suck the last thought. . . . He never used to do that.[29]

Whether or not Bateson was seeking attention more directly than in previous years, after the publication of *Steps* he was sought and adored. This was typified by Stewart Brand, an ecologically motivated entrepreneur who was the founder-editor of *The Whole Earth Catalog*.[30] Preoccupied "with biology, world-saving and mysticism," Brand read *Steps* when it first appeared in 1972 to find that it spoke to the "clear conceptual bonding of cybernetic whole-systems thinking with religious whole-systems thinking."[31] Writing a stalwart's review of the book for *Rolling Stone,* a popular culture magazine of American youth,[32] Brand then went to Bateson in December 1972 with the idea of presenting him to the more generalized readership of *Harper's* magazine.[33] During their ensuing conversation, Bateson reviewed the double bind concept, expressed anxiety about the balance of global ecology, and affirmed his faith in cybernetics. Relations between the two men expanded in the spring of 1974, when Brand founded the *CoEvolution Quarterly* in which he continued the interests of his defunct *Catalog*—the evaluation of ecologically minded technology and ideas. Part of his focus was now in homage of Bateson. Brand staged a conference for him, arranged a nostalgic quarrel with Margaret Mead for him, deposited him among politicians, and if all this were not enough, the *CoEvolution Quarterly* published transcripts of his conversations, as well as some of Bateson's articles, letters, and aphorisms.

In March 1976, Bateson met with Margaret Mead at his home in Ben Lomond. Aside from fond reminiscences of the Macy cybernetics conferences and the affection they shared for Konrad Lorenz, their conversation seemed to turn on a disagreement over how best to use a camera in ethnographic filmmaking. At one point, Bateson supposed that "the photographic record should be an art form,"[34] in which the cameraman follows behavior, rather than leaving the camera on a tripod. But artists, Mead said, produce unreliable data. In Bali, Gregory's ability as a cinematographer had been to stay in one place for a long shot of some sequence of behavior. The purpose of ethnographic film, she believed, was to produce footage so that others could restudy it. And this was precisely the success of their Balinese material.

Mead. There are sequences [in it] that are long enough to analyze.
Bateson. Taken from the right place!
M. Taken from one place.
B. Taken from the place that averaged better than other places.
M. Well, you put your camera there.
B. You can't do that with a tripod. You're stuck. The thing grinds for twelve hundred feet. It's a bore.
M. Well, you prefer twenty seconds to twelve hundred feet.
B. Indeed, I do.
M. Which shows you get bored very easily.
B. Yes, I do.

M. Well, there are other people who don't, you know? Take the films that Betty Thompson studied. . . . That Karba sequence, it's beautiful, she was willing to work on it for six months. You've never been willing to work on things for that length of time, but you shouldn't object to other people who can do it, and to giving them the material to do it.[35]

Did Bateson's increasing silence, so audible in this part of their conversation, invite Mead's browbeating about collecting quantities of data? Certainly, the pattern was not new between them. As he withdrew, she asserted, and the more she asserted, the more he withdrew. What was new was the attempt to resist her. "Had we had more quarrels like that one," Gregory said after her death two years later, "we might have stayed together."[36] From their dispute in 1976, Bateson and Mead went on to criticize other behavioral cinematographers and then began to acclaim *Balinese Character*—the ethnographic monument of their marriage. Perhaps to lighten things, Brand asked why the public reaction to conceptual cybernetics had been so small in the United States in comparison to Russia. Mead said she was not surprised in light of the facts that Americans always preferred piecemeal solutions to social problems and were more comfortable with lineal sequences of causation. Wondering what cybernetics meant in Russia, Bateson kept quiet.[37]

An essential part of his life had been spent battling the late nineteenth century materialism which had separated mind and biology. The disregard of autonomous intelligence in nature which he had found everywhere in his career—in the manipulation of natives, sick men, playful animals, and in the mistreatment of the environment as a whole—horrified him instinctively. Vis-à-vis nature, Bateson maintained a deeply passive attitude. On the other hand, in an active way, he had continued to wonder if any deliberate social planning could be developed which preserved the complexity and spirit of the biological world. Often he had thought that this question might be related to the creation of art and to an appreciation of aesthetics in biological form. Yet organizing discussion of this problem among a group of biologically oriented intellectuals had yielded little. Yet he seemed to resist himself and continued to get involved with the use of science in society.

The year before the encounter with Mead, Stewart Brand had proposed a meeting with Edmund G. (Jerry) Brown, Jr., the governor of California. Expectably, Bateson did not jump at the opportunity. Brand persuaded him that Brown's politics, being influenced by Jesuit training, might not be objectionable. The three men were to meet at the governor's office in Sacramento during an early evening in late June 1975, but Brown was detained by a few hours of budgetary negotiations. Brand, Bateson, and Jacques Barzaghi, the governor's special adviser for the arts, were talking about the problems of translating the premise of circular causality into effective action when Brown finally appeared, in the company of William Honig, an educator. Politics ought to be based in sympathy, Bateson was saying, and in an appreciation of redundant biological patterns, expressed in an acute honesty like that which schizophrenics demanded from their therapists. Aware that Brown had come from a meeting on the state education budget, Bateson began to complain about his Santa Cruz undergraduates: "They don't know the Lord's Prayer." Brown asked if he meant in English or in Latin. "Certainly not in Latin, but they don't even know it in English. They don't know Shakespeare or Blake. They don't even know what a segmented animal looks like. They don't know how the leaves are arranged on a plant." Despite this ignorance, there were a notable few, perhaps 10 percent, who yearned for committed education and who were worth teaching. As a child, Bateson recalled, education had a structure, which it now lacked. All the rote memorization of poetry he had suffered was also a sort of character training. "We have no orthodoxy," Brown answered. "It's just a sort of general malaise."[38]

Having established the existence of social problems, they exchanged views of political leadership in the United States. The governor thought public officials ought to develop personal styles which might decelerate consumption. This could be done, in part, by confronting the electorate with searing questions designed to unmask their illusions that money was the key to a better society. Bateson agreed. "Pouring money, which is a quantity, into a system that has a shape, will not really generate a new shape."[39] Bringing about changes of attitudes, Brown continued, demanded leadership which would model them in daily life. Society must learn to look to itself for solutions to social problems rather than to government. But how to do this? Bateson was reminded then of his end-linkage formulation. The natural history of American family patterns, he said, made government extremely complicated. If parents admired the performances of their children, as they do in the United States, then the American electorate—which similarly watches its governors perform—corresponded to a parental role, while leadership took a child's role. "That's why politicians have to take polls," Brown suggested.[40] Bateson recalled World War II, when Churchill argued that polling Englishmen would be beneath the dignity of a ruling body in time of crisis. Since spectatorship was a child's duty among the English middle classes, performers in England—be they politicians or actors—did not construe their audiences as supportive or instructive. They rather assumed them to be subordinate and fragile. In the United States, these relationships are reversed.

Bateson. The governors are always children in America.

Brown. The hell. I don't identify with that at all.

Brand. You're what, the youngest governor in the country?

Brown. I don't think that's what [Bateson] meant. You meant the general role of governor is one of seeking parental approval of the electorate?

Bateson. It puts leadership in a very difficult position in America, or so it seems to me with an English eye.

Honig. Somebody who is struggling with certain things inside of themselves comes to some understanding and then is able to communicate that to other people who are going through the same struggle. A Gandhian type of thing.

Brown. Well, that's what the leader is. Someone who sums up in his own experience the experience of his time, and articulates the unarticulated, "forges in the smithy of his soul the uncreated conscience of his race." That's what Stephen Daedalus said. That was rather pretentious.[41]

Their conversation then moved into other areas: the self-limiting character of effective leadership, women's liberation, and the benefits of monastic seclusion. At one thirty in the morning, they decided to meet again for breakfast. The next day, when they did, Bateson admired the governor's ability to keep up with the pace. To him, political life always seemed to demand action based upon "insufficient data," and to demand a precision of language before any conceptual clarity had been achieved.[42] As Brown disagreed, Bateson recounted standing up in a small boat as a young man, trying to punt it from the bow end like a gondolier. "How does one do this? One is only part of the system.... And the way you balance it is by making it rock.... If it rocks you, you fall in the water."[43] The image confused the governor, "I'm not sure," he said, "that when you try to make things so abstract, that you really convey much information.... The good thing about politics is you're dealing with something practical. You're dealing with something that's going to alter."[44]

Their points of departure did not make Brown and Bateson incompatible. Six months later, the governor invited him to deliver a sermon to California's annual Prayer Breakfast—a gathering of about one thousand politicians, businessmen, and state officials typically addressed by a member of the established clergy.* In January of the American bicentennial year,

---

* "I first heard about this Prayer Breakfast," Brown said after Bateson's talk, when "I was in the seminary about fifteen years ago and was horrified to learn that my father [former governor Edmund G. Brown, Sr.] was going to pray with Protestants. Since that time we've all come a long way ... because many of the apparent divisions that separate people and their ideas, and their philosophies and their roles are not quite as different and separate as we thought." (GB and E. G. Brown, "Prayer breakfast," *CoEvolution Quarterly,* Spring 1976, p. 84.)

backdropped by a Sufi choir from San Francisco, Bateson identified himself as an anthropologist who was concerned with the nature of sacred belief. "I am here to relate this strange place to other strange places in the world where men gather together in prayer, perhaps in celebration, perhaps simply to affirm that there is something bigger in the world than money and pocket knives and automobiles."[45] Bateson again narrated the episode between the well-intentioned anthropologist Sol Tax and the members of the Native American Church whose peyote sacrament was threatened. By rejecting Tax's offer to film their ceremony so as to advocate it, because it too would have been a violation, the Indians illustrated an element of the sacred—the rejection of pragmatic compromise. Bateson then recited a few stanzas of the "The Rime of the Ancient Mariner," in which the surviving sailor blesses the beauty of moonlit watersnakes swimming beside his ship. The spell, which has killed all his fellows, then breaks, and he is able to pray. Often, Bateson concluded, and especially in Buddhism, the sacred moment is one of perceptual change, when "the biological nature of the world in which we live" is suddenly recognized.[46] Finally, there was the false righteousness of Job. "Job, you will remember, is like little Jack Horner. He sticks his finger in the pie and gives to the poor, and says 'what a good boy am I.'" [47] To counter Job's pride, God prescribed natural history.

> Knowest thou the time when the wild goats of the rock bring forth?
> Or canst thou mark when the hinds do calve?
> Canst thou number the months that they fulfill?
> Or knowest thou the time they bring forth?[48]

Bateson felt that politicians might also learn to treat the world from a basis in biology.*

The sermon scandalized California, or at least scandalized its press, which represented it as a lecture about peyote, pocket knives, and pregnant goats. In the governor's judgment, however, Bateson merited further recognition. At the end of 1976, in December, they met at the Zen Center in San Francisco—a Mahayana Buddhist organization with affiliated centers throughout the United States. Brown then appointed him to the board of regents of the University of California which is an honorary committee, ordinarily occupied by an elite of businessmen, financiers, lawyers, politicians, and high society. The regents have authority over university fiscal matters but rarely assume policy leadership. Having some idea of this—and

---

*Afterward, Brown asked if he knew when the hinds brought forth. Bateson said he did not.

longstanding doubts about the whole project of policy leadership—Bateson wanted nothing to do with the job. "I argued with the governor for two hours about it and finally told him, 'Well, I guess you have something in mind. You see, I'm a field scientist, and for most of the things the regents do—physical sorts of problems and administrative functions—I don't know what they're talking about.'"[49] But Brown wanted him for his views about education. If politicians conventionally use scientists to legitimize their positions, then in the governor's mind, Bateson was to be a "cage rattler," among a group who he felt did little but attend teas and meet Nobel Laureates.[50] "The regents' meetings are so boring," Brown told a reporter, "I thought he might liven them up."[51]

The legality of the appointment was brought into question. Since Bateson already held a position at Kresge College, there was no immediate problem. In six months, though, when his lectureship would expire, renewing it would violate a by-law which made regents ineligible for appointment to any salaried job within the University of California. David Saxon, its president, viewed the situation as awkward. Another regent suggested that the anthropologist's year-to-year lectureship not be renewed. "Bateson could not be reached for comment," said the San Francisco Examiner.[52] He had gone with Lois to South India, to visit a guru to whom his wife had become devoted.

Confirmed by the state senate (and later the beneficiary of a rule waiver), Bateson attended his first meeting in January 1977. The local press noticed that instead of quartering himself with his colleagues at a stately San Francisco hotel, the new regent slept at the Zen Center. During the meeting itself, he heard discussion of the comparative quality of the university's professional schools, which the governor—an ex-officio member of the board—criticized for being unresponsive to social needs. Responding to these charges, the regent's chairman, William Coblentz, argued that this was the responsibility of government and the professions themselves. At this point, Bateson made his opening statement. Employing his best Cambridge drawl, he said nothing about the passion of past generations of Bateson educators, who reformed the curriculum and social structure of English higher education. Instead, he discussed his own American experiences as a teacher since World War II, referring particularly to the university turbulence of the late 1960s. Students, he said, had no sense of the value of learning and had few role models. "What we have here is the demon, Accidie, who whispers in your ear that what you are doing is really not worth doing, whatever it is."[53] On the other hand, American medical education was purposeful—students believed in healing. As a teacher he had always tried to instill such a sense of value in students and to develop goals for them, although only a small minority acquired it. The board of regents ought to be a similar bridge to students. Puzzled silence answered his lengthy discourse. No comment was made, except by the student regent, who said that it was "a tough act to follow."[54]

After nine meetings, Bateson felt that the bridge he wanted built was going nowhere.* "I keep wondering what perhaps Saint Augustine might say if he sat in on a meeting of the board."[55] Following the September 1977 vote on the question of university financial investments in South Africa, he wrote Coblentz, the chairman, that the meetings were bewildering and on the edge of academic concern. Bateson's letter was distributed among the board and then publicly circulated in the national press.

> I do not think it matters much whether ten thousand boys like Bakke get into the University. They will be the lowest 10 percent of our students anyway. Obviously Bakke himself, with his very mediocre qualifications and probable tendencies to fritter his "energies" in politics ... would make only a mediocre doctor at best, even if he passes through the mill which grinds out the medical man.[56]

Bateson dismissed debate about admissions policies and about the status of standardized tests. The crucial question rather was how to orient the university. Toward the vast majority of students who then disappear into society? And toward education exemplified by the standardized test, in which knowledge was little more than a mass of items? "Break the pattern which connects the items of learning," he asserted, "and you necessarily destroy all quality."[57] Standardized tests were undeniably biased against minorities, but this was subsidiary to the problem of a mediocre system of education filling society with people who aggravate the pathologies of Western civilization: hatred of nature and intellect. "In the end, 90% or 98% of them disappear into fields which are not vitally important where our former students *cannot*

---

*In addition to the business of running an enormous university, the issue of revising standards of admission for undergraduates dominated several of their monthly meetings. Eight years before, a program had been instituted to lower admissions standards by 2 percent in order to favor "the economically disadvantaged" (the U.C. system normally accepts the top 12 percent of high-school classes). While the intent of this policy was then in litigation in the Supreme Court—Alan Bakke, a white applicant rejected from a U.C. medical school, had challenged the constitutional grounds of "quotas" —the regents pondered expanding the special admissions program by 2 percent. There was also discussion of a related question: Were standardized tests an accurate means of appraising potential students, when they might be culturally biased in favor of the white middle-class majority?

remember what it was all about. What was it they saw under the microscope? What was it Sophocles or Shakespeare said?"[58]

Given the calamitous power of technology, the main responsibilities of a university were to nurture the "eternal verities" of civilized life such as the equations of relativity, mathematics, basic ecological propositions, and humanistic wisdoms about love and hate.

This orientation was, he believed, a realistic and necessary elitism. "Those who prefer the middle and the temporary placebos of applied science are looking for pie in the sky."[59] To evaluate a university in terms of its best students and researchers was a difficult but worthwhile subject for the regent's concern.

> How can we minimize the *distractions* which take up most of our debating time? I do not grudge the time we spend in ritual confirmation of matters which have been carefully worked on before they come before us. . . . I do grudge time spent on matters which are not our prime business as I see it. South Africa is surely a monstrous tragedy and, as a human being, when it came to a vote, I found I could only vote the idealistic ticket—voting as a human being, not as a regent. I don't think it was a matter for regents. . . . Excellence is our business.[60]

The public response to these opinions outstripped its effect upon the twenty-six member board. According to a San Francisco newspaper, Bateson thought little of contemporary students and even less of the business of his fellow regents.[61] He wanted to make the latter into a debating society, *Newsweek* wrote, which attended to more than the fiscal minutiae of management.[62] "I'm not here to make decisions and I don't care whether I vote," Bateson said later of his role as a regent. "But I would like the votes . . . in a few years, to be out of a background of some sort of human and biological wisdom and valuation for the learned world."[63]

Alongside the politics of education, another arena of applied knowledge continued to occupy Bateson's attention. During these years, various segments of the American mental-health profession—psychiatrists interested in research on schizophrenia, family therapists, humanistic psychologists, and Gestalt or personal-growth therapists—all engaged him repeatedly.[64] Something of the content of these occasions reached publication during 1975, when Bateson twice reconsidered the history and prospects of his work on schizophrenic communication.[65] He had no love for psychotherapy, indeed had left the profession in 1962, then construing double bind learning sequences not as a possible basis for therapeutic experimentation but as an example of the bankruptcy of simplistic behaviorism. "I must also confess that I was bored and disgusted by the Augean muddle of conventional psychiatric thinking, by my colleagues' obsession with power, by the dumb cruelty of the families which (as we used to say) 'contained' schizophrenia, and appalled by the richness of the available data."[66]

The pertinent issue in 1975 was: Were there "any fictions that will do for psychiatry what the Newtonian particle did for physics?"[67] A definitive answer would be premature; however, it was clear that such a paradigm could not derive from physical or hard-science analogies. As the realm of mind could not be separated from the realm of physical appearance, an idealist epistemology was required, forming around the relationship between the name and that which is named, around the theoretical organization of recursive systems, and around the nature of information. Double bind communication, for instance, was a class of behavior—not behavior itself—and therefore was not quantifiable. "You cannot count the number of double binds in a sample of behavior, just as you could not count the number of jokes in a comedian's spiel or the number of bats in an inkblot."[68]

In March 1977, professional interest in the double bind theory crystallized a major conference in New York City, which was sponsored by the South Beach Psychiatric Center, of Staten Island. Milton M. Berger, M.D., designed a two-day meeting, called Beyond the Double Bind, to review the theory and to assess its consequences.[69] In addition to Bateson, Jay Haley and John Weakland attended, as did the prominent family clinicians, Murray Bowen, M.D., and Carl A. Whitaker, M.D., and the noted researchers in schizophrenia, Albert E. Schefflin, M.D., and Lyman C. Wynn, M.D. The conference, which drew an audience of nearly one thousand people, heard Bateson regret that the initial formulation of his theory had been interpreted so literally, and stress that it had been meant only as a crude matrix of abstractions.

> The matrix, after all, is an epistemology, and specifically it is a recursive epistemology; at the same time, it is an epistemology of recursiveness, an epistemology of how things look, how we are to understand them if they are recursive, returning all the time to bite their own tails and control their own beginnings.[70]

The critical point to remember was that training in double bind communication had *both* pathogenic and creative potentials. The schizophrenic who, when presented with an inkblot, must think so concretely that he is unable to see anything more than the blot of ink is very sick. On the other hand, repeated double bind experience could be enriching, as Bateson had observed among the Sea Life Park dolphins.

The fascinations of the large group of therapists evidently lay elsewhere. Most were more interested in clinical demonstrations, especially in Haley's recommendations for strategies of short-term therapy.[71] "I'm not very happy," Bateson said after Haley's paper, "Ideas which handicap therapists,"[72] "at feeling myself the father of the unsaid statement that 'double bind is a theory of therapy.' I do not think it is or was."[73] Divorcing himself—again—from the applied consequences of his idea put Bateson in the somewhat convoluted position of having to join his theory's detractors when, in the aftermath of the conference, controversy developed about its use. In November 1977, Janice R. Stevens, M.D., responding to a report about the meeting in the *Psychiatric News*,[74] criticized double bind theory for doing a "major disservice" to schizophrenic patients and to their families. At a time when "the entire mental health profession" recognized schizophrenia to be a disease of the brain, Stevens was astonished that the theory still attracted notoriety, especially when it remained unsubstantiated by controlled experimentation. Worse, the theory had also caused suffering. Whole families felt blamed for the illness within them, which sometimes created hostility between generations and even between parents. "It is time for families of schizophrenic patients to demand . . . honesty from the psychiatric profession and to give up hypotheses that . . . have led to no useful treatment."[75]

Bateson's answer was fierce. Undoubtedly double bind theory had precipitated its share of suffering among those called schizophrenics. This suffering arose from the hurry of action-oriented clinicians to apply theoretical concepts before they had taken the time to understand them.

> Metrozol, insulin, lobotomy, EST, and the inhumanity of gross contempt have contributed to the mass of human sufferings that radiates from "schizophrenia," and the modern solution—chronic intoxification by chemotherapy—is not the last word. The matter is simple! We are all deeply ignorant and there can be no competition in ignorance.[76]

Nonetheless, Stevens had distorted the claims of the theory. It had concerned the interpenetration of formal logic and cybernetics in a general description of a variety of creative *and* pathological human behavior in a way that the phenomena of schizophrenia were "not in any way central."⁻⁻⁻ The theory had not judged the participants in double bind sequences in any normative way. It had not excluded other relevant etiologies.

> The appearances of schizophrenia may be produced by parasitic invasion and/or by experience: by genes and/or by training. I will even concede that schizophrenia is *as much* a "disease" of the "brain," as it is a "disease" of the "family," if Dr. Stevens will concede that humor and religion, art and poetry are likewise "diseases" of the brain or of the family or both.[78]

Double bind theory, he gathered, may have been helpful to some patients and to some therapists. But it remained at odds with empiricists because it was a theory.*

This was not merely another defense of the concept, however. At stake, Bateson seemingly felt, was the scope of his scientific imagination. "I do not need schizophrenic patients or unhappy families to give my thinking empirical roots. I can use art, poetry, or porpoises, or the cultures of New Guinea and Manhattan, or my own dreams, or the comparative anatomy of flowering plants. After all, I am not limited to inductive reasoning."[79] Disciplinary conformity had been a longstanding issue in Bateson's life and family history, as we have seen. In zoology and genetics, his father had always told students to emphasize exceptions. In a similar vein, Gregory despised textbooks because he believed that they represented knowledge in too finalized form. Quite simply, he could never conclude discovering. This was precisely the courage of his life—an unwillingness to stop challenging the fragmenting assumptions of science. This was also his failure—an unwillingness, as Mead said, to comply with its normal empirical demands. But being a pioneer, he was an elusive man. While appearing to be a sort of empirical anarchist from a disciplinary vantage point, he would nevertheless persist in fitting together data and theory in new ways.

Perhaps, the key to the theory of communication to which he had devoted so much attention in the last thirty-five years was that, obliquely or directly, exchanges of messages had bearing upon the social relationships

---

*This exchange concluded three months later when two St. Louis psychiatrists wrote that over the years they had failed to reconcile double bind theory with clinical reality. They also agreed that the theory had only added to the misery of the parents of schizophrenics. They still welcomed Bateson's clarification of the concept, hoping that their "dwindling faith" in it might, be renewed. "However, having read, reread, and read yet again Mr. Bateson's prolix, paralogical pontification, we are unable to extract any consistent meaning from the actual sentences. . . . Are we in a double bind?" (I. V. Jackson, J. L. Barton, letter to *Psychiatric News* 13(1978):2.)

occurring between the participant organisms. As a behavioral scientist, Bateson's sensitivity for the social level of communication had been sharp and exceptionally extensive. This was only slightly less the case as he got older. Increasingly, during the 1970s, many of those to whom Bateson appealed reflected aspects of his own restless thought: the ecological candor of students at Kresge College, the psychological anthropology of readers of *Ethos,* the utopians of the Lindisfarne Association, the ecological mysticisms of the readers of the *CoEvolution Quarterly,* the fashionable governor of California, and the thousands of mental-health professionals. Although Bateson recited his ideas in a genuine way before these sympathetic audiences, for the most part he did so captiously—and with some frustration. Many people in his widening circles misunderstood him. Spreading celebrity was new in Bateson's life, but the misunderstanding was not merely a result of this enlarged lay interest.

He explained the confusion as inevitable, given the nature of theoretical creativity. In fact, its sources were many. Perhaps at their center were the late Victorian antagonisms between spiritual and materialist thinking which had enshrouded William Bateson. For Gregory the tension, most vivid in his father's belief that art and science were mutually exclusive endeavors, was compounded by a grandiose hope to make a magnificent synthesis of the false dichotomies which were misdividing contemporary Western thought. The push and pull of his legacy made for a profound awkwardness—for a yearning to answer an ever-enlarged question—which at times cost Bateson credibility with specialist colleagues. But it also served as the basis of a legacy which brimmed with inventive insights.

Turning away from the frontier genetics of his youth to become an anthropologist, he refined functionalist constructions of society in a number of ways that presaged directions which that discipline then took. His theoretical concepts stressed the interaction of order and conflict, of feeling and thought, of culture and society. Bateson, moreover, was a candid theorist. Long before it became acceptable (if indeed it has), the subjective scientist appeared openly in his work as part of the field of study. With Margaret Mead, Bateson initiated the use of film as a major ethnographic tool, and influenced by her milieu, he began a lifelong attempt to develop an antireductionist theory of learning.

Enthralled by the theoretical implications of self-corrective machinery, Bateson devised conceptions not of perpetually motionless systems, but of systems which could undergo severe stress and which could change. He originated views of animal play and human humor, developed the major modern experiential theory of schizophrenia, and introduced a communications model to psychiatric researchers and family therapists. Finally, while attempting to advance theoretical knowledge of the message, Bateson made suggestive contributions to the study of dolphin social behavior. Withdrawing from active fieldwork, he involved himself in creating theoretical views of primitive art, alcoholism, trance, evolution, and became concerned with working out the idealist premises which distinguished the science of communication from materialist physics.

Throughout, Bateson held to the unity of what he came to call, mind, a belief which allowed him to draw analogies between pairs of disparate phenomena. In past research, for example, he had compared the structure of logical paradox with that of schizophrenic communication, and the radial symmetry of a sea anemone to Iatmul social organization. Such analogies, however intended to enrich his understanding, had repeatedly isolated Bateson from the conventional idiom of colleagues. From futile attempts to explain his concepts of schismogenesis to Malinowski's seminar, to his presentation of ideas about play in a Macy conference, to his first explanations of double bind sequences to members of his own research team, to his Wenner-Gren conferences, Bateson's analogies made communication difficult for him. At the same time, analogies constituted his curiosity and his pleasure. Identifying relationships among scientific, cultural, theoretical, pathological, and ethological realms had been a central focus of his life. Bateson also adored the play of ideas as a patient teacher and rarely tired of explaining or illustrating them. It is not yet the time to assess the long-term imprint of his voice upon the disciplines to which he contributed or upon recent students. For Bateson, suffice it to say, making analogies—and making relationships—was vital and had both problematic and rewarding consequences.

The elements to which I have been alluding—the prejudice against textbooks, Bateson's acute sense of social relationships in communication, the misunderstanding audiences, the antagonisms between spiritual and materialistic thinking around which his itinerant career turned, and his use of analogies—all had their place in *Mind and Nature: A Necessary Unity*,[80] the primer-like book he dictated while in seclusion at the Lindisfarne Association in the autumn of 1977. The task which then occupied him was an openly didactic attempt to synthesize one of the late Victorian tensions. His primer was concerned with working out an analogy between mental and evolutionary process. "What pattern connects the crab to the lobster and the orchid to the primrose and all four of them to me? And me to you? And all the six of us to the amoeba in one direction and to the back ward schizophrenic in another?"[81] Bateson recapitulated the idealist premises of his science in the book, presented naturally occurring and analytical examples of the generativity of "double or multiple comparison,"[82] and he enumerated a slightly amended definition of mind.

But it would be misleading to imply that this was mere simplification of old ideas for Bateson's latest perplexed audiences. One of the comparisons which *Mind and Nature* explored was a general analogy between evolutionary and intellectual change. Bateson observed that both occurred stochastically—according to processes in which random mutations were selected to endure within wider on-going sequences. Both were also constrained by similar pressures: to conform to the internal conditions of their maternal environments, yet to maintain flexibility while not diverging sharply from predecessor forms. Just as the immense diversity of species in nature depended upon the relentless repetition of the generations, so imagination depended upon the rigor of cultural traditions. "Rigor alone is paralytic death, but imagination alone is insanity."[83] Fluctuations were always mutually involved with self-corrective processes. Evolution—like thought—demanded *both* the randomizing and the conservative stresses. Change without recourse to stability and stability without recourse to change were equally threatening. Industrial societies, Bateson warned, were increasingly capable of administering changes upon the environment from which there could be no stabilizing self-correction.

As a whole, Bateson's book itself exemplified the combination of processes to which he was pointing in evolution and thought. It was both summary and search. Indeed, the conclusion, which took the familiar format of a father-daughter conversation, posed a suggestive question for a succeeding book—how might beauty, consciousness, and the sacred be said to relate?

In January 1978, a draft of the manuscript of *Mind and Nature* far from completed, Bateson returned to teach at Kresge College. Some weeks later, disease interrupted his course and his newfound productivity. In late February, after spitting up blood, he went into the hospital for a chest X-ray which showed a large spot on his left lung. A biopsy, performed in San Francisco, indicated that he had a malignant tumor growing there, which was too large to be removed. I went to visit him in the hospital ten days later, fearful that the cancer would leave him little time. When I arrived, there was Bateson, cramped into a hospital bed, dictating a letter. He was taking issue with a piece in the spring issue of the *CoEvolution Quarterly* which argued that many physical diseases—such as acne and even cancer—were the result of a patient's perceptual and semantic inaccuracies.[84]

Recovering from the surgery he was in good spirits. I was encouraged by a bottle of port on the windowsill, encircled by small glasses. Before we inquired—I had arrived with Eric, his stepson—Bateson announced that he was in no pain from the pathology but that the incision hurt. I asked if he had been afraid. "No, that's not the right word. Death does not create in me fear.

It simplifies a great many things . . . actually. Many things, such as teaching classes, won't need to be thought about. The technology of death bothers me, spitting up and the like."[85]

Bateson's family regrouped momentarily around his crisis. Lois was keeping an emaciating vigil, struggling in her mysticism to become reconciled to the idea of her husband's death.[86] Gregory's son, John, had come from British Columbia with Candy, his wife, and their three-year-old son, Gregory. Nora, now nine, visited the next day. Eric delivered her from Ben Lomond, bringing a number of copies of *Steps to an Ecology of Mind,* which Gregory had requested to give to well-wishers and doctors. Climbing up on her father's bed, Nora asked, "Daddy, could I understand *Steps?*"[87] He was doubtful, looking over the table of contents. "I suppose some of these metalogues might be possible."[88] I stood by, unnerved, saying little and asking less. Bateson noticed my silence soon enough and teased me that now my project might not be as premature as he had once thought.

To slow the growth of his tumor, radiotherapy was prescribed. Bateson declined it, however, thinking that the side effects would diminish his strength. The solution to moments of chronic doubt was still intellectual work, even at the age of seventy-four. Cathy, his elder daughter, would be asked to come from Iran, where she lived and worked, to assist her father in the hectic project of concluding *Mind and Nature.* There was much hospital-room talk given over to planning how to facilitate work at the Ben Lomond house: terminating his appointment at Kresge, protecting his privacy, rehiring his secretary, and building a bedside desk. A few days later, Bateson went home, assured by a gleeful Filipino spirit healer whom a friend had brought to see him, that what the doctors found "was a dying cancer."[89]

He spent part of the spring of 1978 with his daughter, revising the manuscript. The presence of death seemed to have revitalized him wonderfully. The cancer was in remission and he was healthy and content. His short-term memory seemed improved and his interest in people had returned. I joined him in July outside Bloomington, Indiana, for the wedding of Lois' son Eric, to Laurie Fais. The night before the ceremony, there was a dinner for Eric's North Carolina and Greek relatives and for Laurie's Ohio family. After everyone had served himself, Gregory looked at me playfully, wondering, "Should we impose a little ritual on this group?" I agreed, and he gestured that everyone take hands. I asked if he was going to say something. "No, this is enough."[90] We let go of each other. But as we did, at the opposite end of the lengthy table, Lois' father began to recite the Lord's Prayer. Quickly, we grabbed hands again. The circumstances prohibited conversation. However, a week or so earlier, his stoic candor unfazed, Bateson had characterizied his impending death as that of a Iatmul ecologist who was vacating his niche.

> It's very important that I shall die; you need me to. . . . If I stuck around, I'd go on writing on blackboards, and, in the end there'd be no room left for you or anyone else to put words on blackboards. As they say in New Guinea, "The shit would come up to the floor." This is the moral of their myth about the origin of death. You see, the people I studied in New Guinea live on platform houses that are built about eight feet off the ground. If you want to go in the middle of the night, especially if it's raining you move back a board, squat over the gap, go, and go back to bed. According to the myth, people were immortal until, finally, the shit came up level with the floor. At this point, they decided that death was necessary. But it's one thing to have a self-limiting individual and quite another to have a self-limiting society and species.[91]

By August 1978, *Mind and Nature* was settled. Before it appeared in the winter of the following year, Lois and Gregory left their Ben Lomond home to live at the Esalen Institute, a community of alternative and supernatural psychotherapists in Big Sur, California. Public life slowly resumed: attending conferences and meetings of the University of California regents (during the latter, he actively favored terminating university research and development of nuclear weapons). In June 1979, Bateson returned to Kresge College to give that year's commencement address. How many of the assembled graduates, he then wondered, were certain that they knew the difference between irony and sarcasm?

Gregory also began to work on the promised book, *Where Angels Fear to Tread*. Although no conventional deist, he had been somewhat involved in religious thought during the past ten years of his life. As he had said so often, a big part of the problem of human adaptation was that Western religions dangerously misconceived their deities in transcendent, rather than in immanent, terms. Comparative, and especially Oriental, beliefs about the sanctified totality of nature had for him more than prescriptive import, however. Keeping with the realization that he too belonged to the totality of which he spoke, Bateson also kept referring to the growth of his own personal identification with nature. "I do not believe that there is a god separate from the ocean out there," he told an inquisitor, as they watched the undulations of the Pacific. "On the other hand, I do have a sense that the ocean is alive. Is that . . . religious?"[92]

Bateson's last winter was much like the ones before it. Except for a few weeks in England and Germany, Lois and Nora and Gregory continued to live on the spectacular cliffs of the Esalen Institute. He lectured occasionally, led a few workshops under the auspices of his hosts, and tried to outline *Where Angels Fear to Tread*. The few times we spoke during the early months of 1980, I got the impression that his life was going on in usual style. He was unhappy about his work. The central idea in *Mind and Nature*—the analogy between evolutionary and mental processes—was not getting critical attention. Biologists, he suspected, were ignoring it because he was merely an amateur. Meanwhile, his new book was progressing slowly and only a few hundred pages of midnight notes were finished. He decided to send again for his daughter, Cathy, to come help him write.

In late May, a few weeks after his seventy-sixth birthday, I telephoned him to settle some questions about depositing a portion of William Bateson's correspondence. Lois called him from bed and he came to the phone cursing. In addition to a chest cold, he said a pain that felt like a "sea urchin" in his side was keeping him horizontal. He reckoned that traumatized nerves were regenerating at the site of his 1978 surgery. "But my friends," he said lightly and then paused sardonically, "all think it is cancer again."[93] I remembered that he had coughed up bloody sputum the summer before.

The chest cold turned into pneumonia and Gregory's breathing became even more labored than usual. On 10 June, the day after Cathy reached Big Sur to help him work, his condition—he was blue in the face—demanded a move. His family decided to drive him up to San Francisco, where they checked him into the University of California Medical Center. The esoteric healers at Esalen who had been lining up to treat him may have felt betrayed by this decision to get a medical diagnosis, but Gregory wanted to know what was going on with him and what could be done about it.

During his initial days in the hospital, he received a round of antibiotics for the pneumonia. He was correct about the cancer. No further spread was detected in x-rays. The excruciating burning was not diagnosed and remained mysterious. Gregory reworked his will before agreeing to undergo morphine injections to relieve the pain in his side. After a few days Lois requested that the injections be stopped so that Gregory could help decide what to do next.

Meanwhile his two sons and their wives and children arrived from Canada and Kuwait. Knowing how much he hated being alone in the dark, Lois, Cathy, John, and Eric arranged to sit with him through the nights. Though only fitfully conscious, weak, and retching, he continued to relate in "different ways to different people, compliant but skeptical."[94] Later Lois would remark that these nighttime sessions with him were a special privilege. He had been a teacher all his life, she felt, "and continued to teach in the manner of his death."[95]

Friends also came to the UC Medical Center to visit, and Gregory did his best to be gentle, especially with women. A former neighbor who went to see him found him studying the symmetry of his hands with great admiration. "I asked him, 'Gregory, do you want anything?' And he looked at me with those blue eyes which go right through you and said he wanted to go home."[96] Late one evening he even tried to break out of his hospital bed. Standing up, he demanded scissors to cut the IV and oxygen tubes, but was persuaded to lie down again.

During the third week of June there were a few optimistic days. The pain diminished to an ache and was finally diagnosed as a herpesvirus attacking his nervous system. Then the pneumonia returned and another round of antibiotics had to be administered. It became increasingly clear that Gregory did not want to go through another convalescence. He did not want to go on living. Lois, who understood this, had the IV removed and transferred him from the hospital to the Zen Center in San Francisco where she and the rest of the family were staying.

Accompanied there by a chorus of Zen students who had been instructed to breathe with him, Gregory's family continued to look after him around the clock. Now and then he would ask if someone he seemed to see were actually there, but in general he did not say much. His pain went on for another week. On the night of 2 July, Gregory demanded that his son John beat him to death with a stick. The next day he began to brush the oxygen tube out of his nose. By the end, just able to greet people, he appeared to be comfortable. Cathy has written of reading the final chapters of the Book of Job to him during his last hours and of showing him a flower that represented, she felt, "the order to which he had been most true." But she recorded no reaction on Gregory's part.[97]

He died at noon on the Fourth of July 1980 in the company of his wife and oldest daughter.

Cremation followed three days later in Marin County. Lois kept the ashes until 10 July, when the first of two memorial services took place on a lawn at the Esalen Institute. Affiliates of Esalen and friends living in the area sat on the grass in a wide semicircle around a little Zen altar which contained Gregory's ashes. People came forward and spoke. A graduate student read a poem Gregory had written upon completing a draft of *Mind and Nature*. A physicist discussed the epistemological advantages of Gregory's definition of mind. A psychiatrist sobbed. A young friend recited Samuel Butler's poem "The Life After Death."[98] A Catholic priest commented on the startling variety of people with whom his brother Gregory had been able to interact. Afterward everyone honored him by lighting incense. Then Lois led a line of people along the zigzag path, down the cliff to throw half the ashes into the ocean surf. I thought I felt the unruliness of the man in the onshore wind that blew his ashes back into our eyes.

Ten days later the second service took place at Green Gulch, the Zen Center's retreat and farm in Marin County. About two hundred and fifty friends, colleagues, and students—the outgrowth of Gregory's twenty or more years in California—turned up to join his family. Inside an austere meeting hall, the institution's roshi presided over a mildly ritualized recollection of the man. There were chants and stories. Passages were also read from William Blake, the Bible, Wallace Stevens, and T.S. Eliot. In the middle of the gathering a photograph of Bateson rested at the feet of a large Buddha. The bittersweet smell of incense filled the cool July air.

Will the whole of Bateson's accomplishment be said to compare with that of the luminaries of his childhood—the art of Blake or the laws of Mendel? While they lived, of course, very few knew anything about what they had accomplished. But Gregory's innovations do not seem to be of their scale. Theirs remains his scale though, and like them, he envisaged the great issues of the epoch into which he was born—the position of mind in the physical world and the complex matters of form and process. If not to create a major synthesis, part of Bateson's ingenuity was rather to adapt the theory and technology which developed during his lifetime to these larger issues. But the genuine aspiration to make the singular contribution was there all the same, pushing him along the way from St. John's to Kresge College.

In addition to the enormity of his purposes, the ideals of intellectual life—skepticism, generosity, and autonomous curiosity—guided Bateson's life and career. With a twinkle in his eye, I often heard him decry the trappings of greatness—a systematic theory, or an organized school of students, or even a thick set of collectable works—because he thought they generated dogma. Although there has been no paradigm change at the level of those initiated by his namesake, Gregor Mendel, or led by his father, William Bateson; still, the immediate consequences of his thought are not insignificant: books and articles known as classic in their field and influence upon leading members of every discipline to which he associated. By the end of his life, he may have fallen short of the highest realms of scientific achievement, and not simply as great or fanciful. But if his questions and ideals sometimes exceeded him, they did so from a tantalizing distance rather than from an impossible one. It remains to be seen what the future will make of them and of him.

Appendix

Three Poems by Martin Bateson

*Theist and Atheist**

T. When all attempts to find a great First Cause
Have failed, when there remains so much the mind
Can never grasp; when, after all, we find
Knowledge can never come—then, why not pause
And postulate a God who planned the Laws
of Nature? This is not a task declined—
Is Blindness crime?—and who denies the Blind
His dog? The drowning man must clutch at straws.

A. Well, if he does, he drowns. But in the name
Of all that's good and noble, right and true
In Man—and firstly of his Intellect—
I challenge the premise: I assert the claim
That he will, one day, know the First Cause too
—God, let not man thy greatest gift reject!

8 July 1917

Morality†

God, will thy people never understand
The Trinity of Man? Heart, Mind and Soul
Are but three aspects of a single whole
—The Intellect. Accurséd those who brand
Great men as "wanting morally." Such bland
Self-praise is not forgiven—it's the mole
Presuming on its Blindness to extol
Eyes which can not distinguish Sky from Land.

---

*The poem's title is taken from an epigram by Samuel Butler. "Theist and Atheist: The fight between them is as to whether God shall be called God or shall have some other name." (S. Butler, *Notebooks of Samuel Butler,* p. 337.)

†Written after hearing it said that Rugby School was in danger of confounding Intellectual with Moral Excellence.

Morality is doing what we ought;
Not what we think we ought. His love's a lie,
His soul but Self-deceit, who has not Thought,
Man's one unbestial quality, to try
His every conscious act. Christ did not rule
"Thou Knave" Hell-fire's insult, but "Thou Fool."

Math. V 22
9 Nov. 1917

A Leader of Men

"We miss his cheery laugh." Oh! is this all
Captain? This all, from you, who these long months
Have lived one life with him: talked, eaten, suffered,
Watched in agony? Yet the words ring true:
You do not wear his mask, could not. Well he
Desired it so—he would not father grief
In any man: "a few laments must be,
But Mourners, no." So said he, so succeeded,
Yes, God forgive you Captain—But you stood
All that eternity in waist high filth
Beside him (as he wrote) and did not catch
The fire of his soul? "You heard his laugh, took cheer
And smiled back: No more? "Yes, set him down
A man, and that is more indeed," you say?
Oh yes, what a man! He fooled you well.
Perhaps you knew not what he said on leave
Getting his Cross? "These blockheads," meaning you,
You, who admired him so, "whisper behind
My back 'a leader of men.' What irony!
I, who detest their every thought, who loathe
All that they count most high; who hate
Their gods, themselves, their war, their peace—I leader!
O what's there glorious in leading men
When men are still men, and no man's a man?"
       We miss his cheery laugh.

O James, then we shall never walk again
As on that last leave-taking; not speaking—
Friends have no need of speech, the world's device
To trick poor fools into a false accord—
No walking silently and drinking in
Each other's thoughts. The streets were dark and empty;

We were late but—At the camp gate, I turned,
—Well did I? Yes, we said "goodbye," Goodbye.
Never again. Well you cannot feel it—
That is something. Had we never met. O life
Is rot—who signed that note—but what's the good?
Why give another what I cannot bear?
But *he* has no such friend. O now I am dead
To sin. God you're one up. Or do I live?
I feel my pinch. O curse! The White Star Line
Has made five million more, than double what
      They made before the war—and James is dead.
                    28 July 1917

Notes

Preface

1. B. Latour and S. Woolgar, *Laboratory Life: The Social Construction of Scientific Facts* (Beverly Hills, Calif: Sage, 1979), pp. 27-33.

I. Between Determinisms: Samuel Butler

1. G. Himmelfarb, *Darwin and the Darwinian Revolution* (New York: Norton, 1968), p. 37.
2. S. Butler quoted in *The Earnest Atheist*, M. Muggeridge (London: Eyre and Spottiswoode, 1936), p. 58.
3. B. P. Webb, *My Apprenticeship* (London: Longmans, Green, 1926), pp. 130–31.
4. F. M. Turner, *Between Science and Religion: The Reaction to Scientific Naturalism in Late Victorian England* (New Haven: Yale University Press, 1974), p. 8.
5. F. Galton, *English Men of Science: Their Nature and Nurture* (New York: Appleton, 1875), p. 195.
6. B. Willey, *Darwin and Butler: Two Versions of Evolution* (New York: Harcourt, Brace, 1960), p. 52.
7. Ibid., pp. 51–52.
8. Ibid., p. 54.
9. Ibid., pp. 56–57.
10. J. P. Ravetz, *Scientific Knowledge and Its Social Problems* (Oxford: Clarendon Press, 1971), p. 18.
11. R. G. Collingwood, *The Idea of History* (Oxford: Oxford University Press, 1947), p. 134.
12. E. Tylor, *Primitive Culture* (London: J. Murray, 1871).
13. A. Gauld, *The Founders of Psychical Research* (New York: Schocken, 1968), p. 63.
14. K. Amis, "Afterword," to S. Butler, *Erewhon* (New York: New American Library, 1961), p. 238.
15. A. Silver, ed., *The Family Letters of Samuel Butler* (Stanford: Stanford University Press, 1962), p. 16.
16. Ibid., pp. 76–88.
17. H. F. Jones, *Samuel Butler, Author of Erewhon, A Memoir*, 2 vols. (London: Macmillan, 1919), 2: 382.
18. S. Butler, *Erewhon*, p. 173.

19. S. Butler, "The deadlock in Darwinism," *Essays on Life, Art and Science,* ed. R. A. Streatfield (London: Grant Richards, 1904), pp. 307–08.
20. S. Butler, *Life and Habit* (London: A. C. Fifield, 1919), p. 9.
21. Ibid., pp. 51–52.
22. Ibid., p. 54
23. Ibid., p. 134.
24. S. Butler, *The Notebooks of Samuel Butler,* ed. H. F. Jones (London: Jonathan Cape, 1926), pp. 357–58.
25. S. Butler, *Life and Habit,* p. 28.
26. Ibid., p. 29.
27. Ibid., p. 18.
28. Ibid., p. 30.
29. Ibid., p. 34.
30. F. Turner, *Between Science and Religion,* p. 173.
31. S. Butler, *Unconscious Memory* (New York: Dutton, 1911), p. 39.
32. E. Wilson, *The Triple Thinkers* (New York: Harcourt, Brace, 1952) pp. 215–16.
33. S. Butler, *Evolution Old and New* (London: A. C. Fifield, 1911).
34. N. Barlow, ed., *The Autobiography of Charles Darwin* (New York: Norton, 1969), pp. 187–88.
35. S. Butler, *The Notebooks of Samuel Butler,* p. 183.
36. S. Butler quoted in *Between Science and Religion,* F. Turner, p. 187.
37. *Times Literary Supplement* (London), 8 October 1908, p. 329.
38. S. Butler, *Luck or Cunning?* (London: A. C. Fifield, 1887), p. 155.
39. H. F. Jones, *Samuel Butler,* 2: 303.
40. S. Butler, *The Notebooks of Samuel Butler,* p. 33.
41. S. Butler, *The Way of All Flesh* (New York: New American Library, 1960), p. 112.
42. Ibid., p. 91.
43. H. F. Jones, *Samuel Butler,* 1: 389–90.

II. A Geneticist's Ancestry

1. William Bateson, "Notes on the Bateson family tree," unpublished, 1909.
2. E. Miller, *Portrait of a College,* (Cambridge: Cambridge University Press, 1961), p. 81.
3. J. P. C. Roach, "The University of Cambridge," in *The Victoria History of the Counties of England,* ed. R. B. Push (London: Dawsons of Pall Mall, 1967), 3:444.
4. E. Miller, *Portrait,* p. 49.
5. Personal communication: C. D. Darlington, 23 December 1975.
6. C. B. Bateson, *William Bateson, F.R.S.: Naturalist, His Essays and Addresses Together with a Short Account of His Life* (Cambridge: Cambridge University Press, 1928), p. 10, hereafter cited as WBN.
7. Personal communication: Gregory Bateson, 27 December 1972 (hereafter cited as GB).
8. "Obituary of Anna Bateson," *Common Cause,* 19 July 1918, p. 8.
9. C. B. Bateson, *WBN,* pp. 1–2.

10. W. Bateson, "Notes on the Bateson family tree."
11. GB to W. Coleman, 8 January 1968.
12. "In Memoriam: William Bateson, 1861–1926," *The Eagle*, St. John's College, 44(1926):232.
13. C. B. Bateson, *WBN*, p. 8.
14. Ibid.
15. W. Bateson, *Letters from the Steppe*, (London:Methuen, 1928), p. v.
16. C. B. Bateson, *WBN*, p. 7.
17. W. Bateson et al., "William Keith Brooks: a sketch of his life by some of his former pupils and associates," *Journal of Experimental Zoology*, 9(1910):6–7.
18. W. Bateson, "Evolutionary faith and modern doubts," in *WBN*, p. 389.
19. "In Memoriam," pp. 227–28.
20. C. B. Bateson, *WBN*, p. 12
21. Ibid., p. 23.
22. Ibid., p. 24.
23. Ibid., p. 49.
24. Ibid., pp. 48–49.
25. R. C. Punnett, "William Bateson," *Edinburgh Review*, July 1926, p. 72.
26. W. Bateson et al., "William Keith Brooks," p. 7.
27. Ibid.
28. W. Bateson, "The ancestry of the Chordata," in *Scientific Papers of William Bateson*, 2 vols., ed. R. C. Punnett (Cambridge: Cambridge University Press, 1928), I:1–32.
29. Ibid., p. 1.
30. R. C. Punnett, "William Bateson," p. 73.
31. W. Bateson, *Letters from the Steppe.*
32. Ibid., p. 142.
33. Ibid., p. 193.
34. C. B. Bateson, *WBN*, pp. 33–34.
35. W. Bateson, *Materials for the Study of Variation treated with especial Regard to DISCON-TINUITY in the Origin of Species* (London: Macmillan, 1894), p. 33.
36. Ibid.
37. W. Bateson quoted in "Bateson and chromosomes: conservative thought in science," *Centaurus* 15(1971):284.
38. C. B. Bateson, *WBN*, pp. 42–44.
39. W. Bateson, "Heredity and variation in modern lights," in *WBN*, C. B. Bateson, p. 228.
40. W. Bateson, *Problems of Genetics* (New Haven: Yale University Press, 1913), p. 80.
41. W. Bateson, "Evolution and education," in *WBN*, C. B. Bateson, p. 422.
42. GB quoted in "Bateson and chromosomes," W. Coleman, p. 300.
43. C. B. Bateson, *WBN*, p. 43.
44. Ibid., p. 114.
45. Ibid., p. 115.
46. Ibid., p. 162.
47. Ibid., p. 28.
48. W. Bateson, *Materials.*
49. W. Bateson, "Materials for the study of variation: Introduction," in *Scientific Papers* I: 218.
50. Ibid., p. 306.
51. Ibid., p. 217.

52. W. Coleman, "Bateson and chromosomes," p. 242.
53. "In Memoriam," p. 229.
54. Ibid., p. 230.

III. Early Genetics

1. "Obituary: A. E. Durham," *Guy's Hospital Reports,* ed. E. C. Perry and W. H. A. Jacobson, 52 (1895): xliii–civ.
2. Personal communication: Gregory Bateson (hereafter cited as GB), 27 December 1972.
3. B. Durham, "At a conversazione," *The English Illustrated Magazine,* September 1895, p. 551.
4. Ibid., p. 552.
5. W. Bateson to C. B. Bateson, 2 April 1896.
6. W. Bateson to C. B. Bateson, 5 June 1896.
7. C. B. Bateson, *William Bateson, F.R.S.* (Cambridge: Cambridge University Press, 1928), hereafter cited as *WBN,* p. 58.
8. Ibid.
9. Ibid.
10. Personal communication: Geoffrey Keynes, 18 December 1975.
11. C. B. Bateson, *WBN,* p. 61.
12. W. Bateson, "Presidential address to the British Association: 1904," in C. B. Bateson, *WBN,* p. 243.
13. C. B. Bateson to W. Bateson, 11 May 1902.
14. C. B. Bateson, *WBN,* p. 86.
15. R. C. Punnett, "Early days of genetics," *Heredity* 4(1950): 7.
16. Ibid., p. 6.
17. W. Bateson, "Heredity and variation in modern lights," in *WBN,* p. 215.
18. R. C. Punnett, "William Bateson," *Edinburgh Review,* July 1926, p. 71.
19. J. B. S. Haldane, "William Bateson," *The Nation,* 20 February 1926, p. 763.
20. C. B. Bateson, *WBN,* p. 124.
21. Ibid., p. 97.
22. Ibid., p. 78.
23. Ibid., pp. 81–82.
24. Ibid., p. 127
25. Ibid., p. 63.
26. W. Bateson, "Hybridization and cross-breeding as a method of scientific investigation," in *WBN,* p. 166.
27. W. Bateson, "Problems of heredity as a subject for horticultural investigation," in *WBN,* p. 172.
28. G. Mendel, "Experiments in plant hybrids," trans. E. R. Sherwood, in *The Origin of Genetics: A Mendel Source Book,* ed. C. Stern and E. R. Sherwood (San Francisco: W. H. Freeman and Co., 1966), pp. 1–48.
29. W. Bateson, *The Methods and Scope of Genetics* (Cambridge: Cambridge University Press, 1908), pp. 5-6.
30. J. B. S. Haldane, *Possible Worlds and Other Essays* (London: Chatto and Windus, 1949), p. 143.

31. W. Bateson, "Problems of heredity," in *WBN*, p. 175.
32. Ibid., p. 171.
33. C. B. Bateson, *WBN*, p. 70.
34. W. Bateson quoted in *The Case of the Midwife Toad*, A. Koestler (New York: Random House, 1973), p. 54.
35. W. Bateson, "Presidential address to the British Association: 1914," in *WBN*, p. 296.
36. W. Bateson quoted in "William Bateson," R. C. Punnett, p. 80.
37. C. D. Darlington, *Genetics and Man* (New York: Schocken, 1969), p. 98.
38. A. H. Sturtevant, *A History of Genetics* (New York: Harper and Row, 1965), pp. 31–32.
39. R. A. Fisher, "Has Mendel's work been rediscovered?," in *The Origin of Genetics*, ed. C. Stern and E. R. Sherwood, p. 142.
40. C. B. Bateson, *WBN*, p. 97.
41. Ibid., p. 98.
42. Personal communication: C. D. Darlington, 23 December 1975.
43. W. Bateson quoted in "Appendix," in *WBN*, p. 464.
44. W. F. R. Weldon, "Mendel's laws of alternative inheritance in peas," *Biometrika* 1(1902): 228–253.
45. W. Bateson, *Mendel's Principles of Heredity: A Defense* (Cambridge: Cambridge University Press, 1902).
46. G. Udney Yule, "Mendel's laws and their probable relation to intraracial heredity," *New Phytologist* 1(1902): 194, 204.
47. P. Frogatt and N. C. Nevin, "The law of ancestral heredity and the Mendelian-Ancestrian controversy in England, 1889–1906," *Journal of Medical Genetics* 8(1971): 24.
48. R. C. Punnett, "Early days of genetics," *Heredity* 4(1950): 7–8.
49. P. Froggatt and N. C. Nevin, "The law of ancestral heredity," p. 36.
50. W. Bateson, "Albinism in Sicily—a fresh look," *Biometrika* 4(1905):231.
51. P. Froggatt and N. C. Nevin, "The law of ancestral heredity," p. 36.
52. C. B. Bateson, *WBN*, p. 97.
53. Personal communication: Nora Barlow, 14 December 1975.
54. Personal communication: Geoffrey Keynes, 18 December 1975.
55. C. B. Bateson, *WBN*, p. 109.
56. Ibid., p. 121.
57. W. Bateson quoted in "Bateson and chromosomes," W. Coleman, *Centaurus* 15(1971): 265.
58. C. B. Bateson, *WBN*, p. 123.
59. Ibid., p. 122.

IV. A Didactic Family

1. N. Annan, "The intellectual aristocracy," in *Studies in Social History: A Tribute to G. M. Trevelyan*, ed. J. H. Plumb (London: Longmans, Green, 1949), p. 245.
2. Ibid., p. 249.
3. G. Raverat, *Period Piece* (London: Faber and Faber, 1952), p. 173.
4. Diary of C. B. Bateson, 12 October 1899.
5. C. B. Bateson, *William Bateson, F.R.S.* (Cambridge: Cambridge University Press, 1928), hereafter cited as *WBN*, pp. 65–66.

6. Personal communication: GB, 27 December 1972.
7. Martin Bateson to John Bateson, 26 November 1907.
8. C. B. Bateson *WBN*, pp. 68–69.
9. Ibid., p. 68.
10. Personal communication: GB, 16 January 1976.
11. Ibid.
12. Diary of C. B. Bateson, 14 January 1899.
13. Personal communication: Nora Barlow, 14 December 1975.
14. Personal communication: P. P. C. Bateson, 23 December 1975.
15. C. B. Bateson, *WBN*, pp. 110–11.
16. Personal communication: GB, 27 December 1972.
17. C. B. Bateson, *WBN*, p. 69.
18. W. Bateson to John Bateson, 13 May 1909.
19. Personal communication: GB, 17 November 1975.
20. Diary of C. B. Bateson, 9 May 1904.
21. Personal communication: Margaret Mead, 20 November 1972.
22. Martin Bateson to C. B. Bateson, 21 November 1907.
23. Personal communication: GB, 30 September 1975.
24. Ibid.
25. Martin Bateson to W. Bateson, 1906.
26. Personal communication: GB, 30 September 1975.
27. Martin Bateson to C. B. Bateson, 2 August 1910.
28. Delphi A. Taylor to C. B. Bateson, 11 August 1910.
29. Personal communication: G. Evelyn Hutchinson, 16 January 1976.
30. Martin Bateson to C. B. Bateson, 27 November 1910.
31. Martin Bateson to C. B. Bateson, 30 October 1910.
32. John Bateson to C. B. Bateson, 30 October 1910.
33. Personal communication: GB, 22 September 1975.

V. Before the War

1. G. B. Shaw, "Preface to *Major Barbara*," in *The Collected Works of Bernard Shaw,* (New York: William H. Wise, 1930), 11: 220–21.
2. W. Bateson, "Heredity and variation in modern lights," in *William Bateson, F.R.S.*, C. B. Bateson (Cambridge, Cambridge University Press, 1928), hereafter cited as *WBN*, p. 218.
3. W. Bateson quoted in *Samuel Butler,* H. F. Jones (London: Macmillan, 1919), 2:424.
4. W. Bateson, "Presidential address to the British Association, Australia: 1914," in *WBN*, p. 313.
5. Ibid, p. 309.
6. Ibid, p. 315.
7. W. Coleman, "Bateson and chromosomes," *Centaurus* 15(1971):297.
8. W. Bateson, "Biological fact and the structure of society," in *WBN*, p. 353.
9. Ibid., p. 355.
10. W. Bateson "Presidential address to the British Association," p. 305.
11. W. Blake, "Letter to Butts," 10 January 1802, in *The Complete Writings of William Blake,* ed. G. Keynes (New York: Random House, 1957), p. 811.

12. W. Coleman, "Bateson and chromosomes," p. 297.
13. W. Bateson, "Address to the Salt Schools," in *WBN*, p. 411.
14. Personal communication: GB, 27 December 1972.
15. GB to W. Coleman, 9 May 1967.
16. C. B. Bateson, *WBN*, p. 61.
17. GB to W. Coleman, 9 January 1968.
18. Personal communication: GB, 8 October 1975.
19. C. B. Bateson, *WBN*, p. 124.
20. Personal communication: G. Evelyn Hutchinson, 16 January 1975.
21. C. B. Bateson, *WBN*, p. 124.
22. J. B. S. Haldane, "William Bateson," *The Nation*, 20 February 1926, p. 713.
23. W. Bateson, "The methods and scope of genetics," *WBN*, p. 324.
24. J. B. S. Haldane, "William Bateson," p. 713.
25. Personal communication: GB, 30 September 1975.
26. Personal communication: GB, 8 October 1975.
27. Ibid.
28. Ibid.
29. Ibid.
30. Ibid.
31. Ibid.
32. Ibid.
33. Ibid.
34. Ibid.
35. Ibid.
36. Ibid.
37. Ibid.
38. Ibid.
39. Ibid.
40. Ibid.
41. Ibid.
42. Personal communication: GB, 2 December 1975.
43. Personal communication: GB, 8 October, 1975.
44. C. B. Bateson, *WBN*, p. 126.
45. Ibid., p. 127.
46. Ibid.
47. Ibid., p. 129.
48. Ibid., p. 128.
49. W. Bateson, "Address to the Salt Schools," p. 419.
50. C. B. Bateson, *WBN*, p. 134.
51. W. Bateson, "Gamete and zygote," in *WBN*, p. 203.

VI. Boarding School

1. Personal communication: GB, 30 September 1975.
2. Ibid.

3. Personal communication: GB, 28 December 1972.
4. E. C. Mack, *Public Schools and British Opinion* (New York: Columbia University Press, 1969), p. 276.
5. W. Bateson, "Address to the Salt Schools," in *William Bateson, F.R.S.*, C.B. Bateson (Cambridge, Cambridge University Press, 1928), hereafter cited as *WBN*, p. 413.
6. Personal communication: GB, 8 October 1975.
7. GB to C. B. Bateson, 4 June 1916.
8. John Bateson to C. B. Bateson 21 May 1912.
9. Ibid.
10. John Bateson to Martin Bateson, 6 July 1916.
11. J. Bateson, "Coleoptera," *The Entomologist's Record and Journal of Variation*, 26(1914):116.
12. Ibid.
13. Personal communication: GB, 8 October 1975.
14. John Bateson to C. B. Bateson, 8 February 1917.
15. S. Butler, "Life After Death," *The Meteor* (Rugby school), 3 December 1917, p. 185.
16. Diary of Martin Bateson, 16 June 1917.
17. Ibid.
18. Ibid., 27 May 1917.
19. Martin Bateson to C. B. Bateson, 14 July 1917.
20. C. B. Bateson to Martin Bateson, 17 July 1917.
21. Ibid.
22. Ibid.
23. C. B. Bateson to Martin Bateson, 3 November 1917.
24. W. Bateson to Martin Bateson, 19 July 1917.
25. Diary of Martin Bateson, 27 May 1917.
26. Martin Bateson to C. B. Bateson, 31 October 1917.
27. W. Bateson to Martin Bateson, 3 November 1917.
28. Ibid.
29. Ibid.
30. Ibid.
31. Ibid.
32. Ibid.
33. Ibid.
34. Martin Bateson to W. Bateson, 3 November 1917.
35. Ibid.
36. Diary of Martin Bateson, 26 January 1918.
37. Martin Bateson to C. B. Bateson, 14 October 1917.
38. Diary of Martin Bateson, 26 January 1918.
39. Ibid., 15 April 1918.
40. Ibid.
41. Ibid.
42. W. Bateson to Martin Bateson, 15 April 1918.
43. Martin Bateson to C. B. Bateson, 28 September 1918.
44. Martin Bateson to C. B. Bateson, 12 December 1918.
45. John Bateson to C. B. Bateson, 30 January 1918.
46. John Bateson to Martin Bateson, 29 July 1916.
47. John Bateson to C. B. Bateson, 20 May 1917.

48. John Bateson to C. B. Bateson, 5 November 1917.
49. John Bateson to Martin Bateson, 25 May 1917.
50. *The Times* (of London), 9 July 1918, p. 2.
51. John Bateson to C. B. Bateson, 17 June 1918.
52. John Bateson to C. B. Bateson, 5 September 1918.
53. John Bateson to Martin Bateson, 10 October 1918.
54. G. E. Tatham to W. Bateson, 19 December 1918.
55. C. B. Bateson, *WBN*, p. 135.
56. C. B. Bateson to Martin Bateson, 24 October 1918.
57. W. Bateson to Martin Bateson, 13 December 1918.
58. Ibid.
59. Ibid.

VII. William and Martin Bateson

1. GB to W. Coleman, 1 December 1966.
2. I. Shine and S. Wrobel, *Thomas Hunt Morgan* (Lexington: Kentucky University Press, 1976), pp. 46–81.
3. C. D. Darlington, *Genetics and Man* (New York: Schocken, 1969), p. 100.
4. GB to W. Bateson, 6 March 1923.
5. W. Bateson, "Gamete and zygote," in *William Bateson, F.R.S.*, C. B. Bateson (Cambridge: Cambridge University Press, 1928), hereafter cited as *WBN*, p. 209.
6. W. Bateson, "Evolutionary faith and modern doubts," in *WBN*, C. B. Bateson, p. 390.
7. W. Bateson, *Methods and Scope of Genetics* (Cambridge: Cambridge University Press, 1908), p. 34.
8. W. Bateson, "Genetic segregation," in *Scientific Papers of William Bateson*, ed. R. C. Punnett (Cambridge: Cambridge University Press, 1928), 2:315.
9. W. Bateson, "Evolutionary faith," in *WBN*, p. 392.
10. W. Bateson, *Methods and Scope of Genetics*, pp. 2–3.
11. W. Bateson to B. Nichols, May 1923.
12. W. Bateson, "Common sense in racial problems," in *WBN*, p. 381.
13. Ibid., p. 380.
14. W. Bateson, "Science and nationality," in *WBN*, p. 356.
15. W. Bateson, "Classical and modern education," in *WBN*, p. 445.
16. W. Bateson, "Science and nationality," in *WBN*, pp. 365–66.
17. Ibid., p. 366.
18. Ibid., p. 364.
19. Ibid., pp. 360–61.
20. W. Bateson, "Classical and modern education," in *WBN*, p. 444.
21. Personal communication: GB, 12 June 1976.
22. Personal communication: GB, 26 January 1976.
23. GB to Martin Bateson, 13 December 1918.
24. W. Bateson to Martin Bateson, 31 August 1919.
25. Martin Bateson to C. B. Bateson, 16 January 1919.
26. S. Sassoon, *The Memoir of George Sherston* (New York: Doubleday, 1937); R. Slobodin, *W. H. R. Rivers* (New York: Columbia University Press, 1978).

27. Martin Bateson to C. B. Bateson, 1 March 1919.
28. Ibid.
29. Martin Bateson, "Goodbye," unpublished (25 January 1918).
30. Martin Bateson, untitled play, 1918.
31. W. Bateson to Martin Bateson, 8 August 1919.
32. Martin Bateson to W. Bateson, 3 August 1919.
33. W. Bateson to Martin Bateson, 9 August 1919.
34. Martin Bateson to C. B. Bateson, 16 August 1919.
35. Martin Bateson to W. Bateson, 5 November 1919.
36. W. Bateson to Martin Bateson, 3 December 1919.
37. Martin Bateson to C. B. Bateson, 23 November 1919.
38. A. Silver, ed., *The Family Letters of Samuel Butler* (Stanford: Stanford University Press, 1962.)
39. W. Bateson to Martin Bateson, 16 November 1919.
40. C. B. Bateson to Martin Bateson, 2 November 1919.
41. W. Bateson to Martin Bateson, 30 August 1919.
42. Ibid.
43. W. Bateson to Martin Bateson, 11 September 1920.
44. W. Bateson to Martin Bateson, 31 January 1920.
45. W. Bateson to Martin Bateson, 11 September 1920.
46. Ibid.
47. E. E. V. de Peyer to D. Lipset, 31 August 1976.
48. W. Bateson to Martin Bateson, 11 September 1920.
49. W. Bateson to Martin Bateson, 24 February 1921.
50. Martin Bateson to W. Bateson, 4 March 1921.
51. W. Bateson to Martin Bateson, 28 February 1921.
52. Martin Bateson to W. Bateson, 26 February 1921.
53. W. Bateson to Martin Bateson, 28 February 1921.
54. Ibid.
55. Martin Bateson to W. Bateson, 4 March 1921.
56. Martin Bateson to W. Bateson, 28 February 1921.
57. Martin Bateson to W. Bateson, 1 June 1921.
58. W. Bateson to Martin Bateson, 3 June 1921.
59. Ibid.
60. W. Bateson to Martin Bateson, 29 September 1921.
61. Martin Bateson to C. B. Bateson, 1 October 1921.
62. W. Bateson, "Evolutionary faith," in *WBN*, pp. 389–98.
63. Personal communication: GB, 26 January 1976.
64. M. Graham to W. Bateson, 27 April 1922.
65. Ibid.
66. Martin Bateson to E. E. V. de Peyer, 16 February 1922.
67. Martin Bateson to E. E. V. de Peyer, 18 January 1922.
68. Ibid.
69. C. B. Bateson, *WBN*, p. 148.
70. Ibid., p. 398.
71. W. Bateson to Martin Bateson, 14 March 1922.
72. Ibid.

73. M. Graham to W. Bateson, 22 May 1922.
74. Personal communication: GB, 22 September 1975.
75. M. Graham to W. Bateson, 27 April 1922.
76. Report of the work of Martin Bateson, Royal Academy of Dramatic Art, 20 April 1922.
77. K. Barnes to W. Bateson, 24 April 1922.
78. C. B. Bateson to GB, 23 April 1922.
79. W. Bateson to GB, 22 April 1922.
80. G. Wilson to Martin Bateson, 22 April 1922.
81. Martin Bateson in the postmortem notes of W. Bateson, n.d.
82. Martin Bateson, 22 April 1922.

VIII. A Tear Is an Intellectual Thing

1. Personal communication: GB, 27 December 1972.
2. W. Bateson to GB, 22 April 1922.
3. P. Dimmer to GB, 29 April 1922.
4. C. B. Bateson to GB, 23 April 1922.
5. W. Bateson to GB, 11 May 1922.
6. Ibid.
7. Ibid.
8. *The Weekly Dispatch*, 27 April 1922, p. 1.
9. W. Bateson, letter to the editor of *The Daily Mirror*, unpublished, 27 April 1922.
10. W. Bateson to M. Graham, n.d.
11. M. Graham to W. Bateson, 25 September 1922.
12. W. Bateson to GB, 11 May 1922.
13. C. B. Bateson to GB, 12 June 1922.
14. C. B. Bateson *William Bateson, F.R.S.* (Cambridge: Cambridge University Press, 1928), p. 148.
15. W. Bateson to GB, May 1922.
16. C. B. Bateson to GB, 4 June 1922.
17. W. Bateson to GB, 23 April 1922.
18. W. Blake, "A Grey Monk," in *The Portable Blake*, ed. A. Kazin (New York: Viking, 1969), p. 155.

IX. As Youngest Son in Cambridge

1. E. B. Worthington to D. Lipset (hereafter cited as DL), 10 March 1976.
2. R. Kipling, "Kaa's Hunting," in *The Jungle Book*, vol. 7, in *The Writings in Prose and Verse of Rudyard Kipling* (New York: Charles Scribner's, 1898), pp. 33–74.
3. GB, Circular for Noel Porter's retirement gift, mimeographed, n.d.
4. R. Hill to DL, 23 February 1976.
5. Personal communication: GB, 2 December 1975.
6. Personal communication: G. Evelyn Hutchinson, 16 January 1976.
7. Personal communication: Margaret Mead, 22 January 1976.

8. Personal communication: GB, 30 September 1975.

9. Personal communication: G. Evelyn Hutchinson, 16 January 1976.

10. GB to C. B. Bateson, 22 April 1923.

11. R. Hill to DL, 23 February 1976.

12. Personal communication: GB, 30 September 1975.

13. Ibid.

14. GB to C. B. Bateson, 23 January 1923.

15. GB to C. B. Bateson, 9 October 1923.

16. GB to C. B. Bateson, 1 February 1923.

17. GB to W. Bateson, 5 November 1922.

18. GB to C. B. Bateson, 22 October 1922.

19. GB to C. B. Bateson, 5 November 1922.

20. GB to C. B. Bateson, 22 October 1922.

21. Ibid.

22. Ibid.

23. G. E. Hutchinson, Record of the Biological Tea Club, unpublished, 1922.

24. GB to C. B. Bateson, 30 November 1922.

25. GB to W. Bateson, 1 February 1923.

26. GB to C. B. Bateson, March 1923.

27. GB to W. Bateson, 6 March 1923.

28. GB to W. Coleman, 6 March 1967.

29. GB to C. B. Bateson, 7 May 1923.

30. G. Pickford to DL, 2 February 1976.

31. W. Blake, "Satan Exulting over Eve," in *Symbol and Image in William Blake*, G. W. Digby, (Oxford: Clarendon Press, 1957), p. 28, fig. 31.

32. GB to W. Coleman, 9 May 1967.

33. W. Blake quoted in *Literature and Western Man*, ed. J. B. Priestly (London: Heineman, 1962), p. 111.

34. Personal communication: GB, 8 February 1976.

35. Personal communication: Margaret Mead, 20 November 1972.

36. Personal communication: GB, 8 February 1976.

37. GB to C. B. Bateson, 6 May 1924.

38. GB to C. B. Bateson, 29 August 1923.

39. GB to C. B. Bateson, 6 March 1924.

40. I. Montagu to DL, 17 April, 1976; I. Montagu, *The Youngest Son: Autobiographical Sketches* (London: Lawrence and Wishart, 1970), pp. 181–249.

41. R. Hill to DL, 23 February 1976.

42. Personal communication: G. Evelyn Hutchinson, 16 January 1976.

43. GB to C. B. Bateson, 2 June 1924.

44. GB, "Experiments in thinking about observed ethnological material," in *Steps to an Ecology of Mind* (San Francisco: Chandler Press, 1972), p. 80.

45. Ibid., pp. 80–81.

46. GB to C. B. Bateson, 22 October 1924.

47. Personal communication: GB, 27 December 1972.

48. Personal communication: GB, 6 February 1976.

49. W. and G. Bateson, "On certain aberrations of the redlegged partridges *Alectoris rufa* and *saxatilis*," in *Scientific Papers of William Bateson*, ed. R. C. Punnett (Cambridge: Cambridge University Press, 1928) 2:383.

50. Idem, *Journal of Genetics* 16(1925):101–23.
51. C. B. Bateson to GB, 1 September 1924.
52. Ibid.
53. Personal communication: GB, 30 September 1975.
54. Ibid.
55. Ibid.
56. I. Chodat to GB, 23 September 1924.
57. Personal communication: GB, 30 September 1975.
58. GB to I. Chodat, 22 September 1924.
59. GB to C. B. Bateson, 20 November 1924.
60. G. E. Hutchinson to DL, 7 March 1977.
61. GB to C. B. Bateson, 10 December 1924.
62. W. and G. Bateson, "On certain aberrations of the redlegged partridges," 2:400.
63. Ibid., p. 402
64. Personal communication: GB, 11 September 1975.
65. GB to C. B. Bateson, 11 January 1925.
66. GB to C. B. Bateson, 18 January 1925.
67. Ibid.
68. Personal communication: GB, 11 September 1975.
69. GB to C. B. Bateson, 28 January 1925.
70. GB to C. B. Bateson, 6 February 1925.
71. GB to C. B. Bateson, 29 March 1925.
72. N. Barlow ed., *The Autobiography of Charles Darwin* (New York: Norton, 1969), p. 119. See also D. Lack, *Darwin's Finches* (Cambridge: Cambridge University Press, 1947).
73. Personal communication: GB, 11 September 1975.
74. Ibid.
75. Ibid.
76. Ibid; W. Beebe, *The Arcturus Adventure* (New York: G. P. Putnam's, 1926).
77. H. D. Osborn to W. Bateson, 23 May 1925.
78. T. H. Morgan to W. Bateson, 30 June 1925.
79. Personal communication: GB, 27 December 1972.
80. GB to W. and C. B. Bateson, 21 July 1925.
81. Personal communication: GB, 27 December 1972.
82. Ibid.
83. Personal communication: G. Evelyn Hutchinson, 16 January 1976.
84. Personal communication: GB, 27 December 1972.
85. GB to C. B. Bateson, 17 November 1925.
86. GB to W. and C. B. Bateson, 21 July 1925.
87. A. H. Quiggin, *Haddon: The Head Hunter* (Cambridge: Cambridge University Press, 1942).
88. GB to C. B. Bateson, 31 August 1925.
89. GB to W. and C. B. Bateson, 21 July 1925.
90. Personal communication: GB, 27 December 1972.
91. W. Bateson to GB, 22 July 1925.
92. Personal communication: C. D. Darlington, 23 December 1975.
93. C. B. Bateson, *William Bateson, F.R.S.* (Cambridge: Cambridge University Press, 1928), hereafter cited as *WBN*, p. 159.

94. GB to W. Coleman, 1 December 1966.
95. W. Bateson to GB, 1 February 1926.
96. W. Bateson, "Science in Russia," *Nature* 115 (1925): 715.
97. C. B. Bateson, *WBN*, p. 153.
98. Ibid., p. 158.
99. GB to C. B. Bateson, 4 February 1926.
100. Personal communication: GB, 13 November 1975.
101. Personal communication: GB, 27 November 1972.
102. "In Memoriam, William Bateson: 1861–1926," *The Eagle,* St. John's College, 44:228.
103. C. B. Bateson, *WBN,* preface.
104. GB to C. Guillebaud, 29 July 1926.
105. H. Iltis, *Life of Mendel,* trans. E. and C. Paul (New York: Hafner, 1966).
106. W. Bateson, "Mendeliana," *Nature* 115(1925):827.

X. As Anthropologist

1. Personal communication: GB, 27 December 1972.
2. J. O. Brew, *One Hundred Years of Anthropology* (Cambridge, Mass: Harvard University Press, 1962), p. 132.
3. Personal communication: GB, 27 December 1972.
4. R. Firth, ed., *Man and Culture: An Evaluation of the Work of Bronislaw Malinowski* (New York: Humanities Press, 1970), pp. 8–9.
5. H. Powdermaker, *Stranger and Friend* (New York: Norton, 1966), p. 35.
6. Personal communication: GB, 27 December 1972.
7. A. R. Radcliffe-Brown to R. Lowie, 6 May 1938, *History of Anthropology Newsletter* 3 (1976): 5–8.
8. A. R. Radcliffe-Brown, *Structure and Function in Primitive Society* (New York: Free Press, 1965), p. 189.
9. Ibid., p. 179.
10. Ibid., pp. 192–193.
11. Ibid., p. 190.
12. Ibid.
13. Ibid., p. 180 .
14. Ibid., pp. 190–191.
15. A. R. Radcliffe-Brown, *The Andaman Islanders* (Glencoe: Free Press, 1948), p. 243.
16. A. C. Haddon, "Report to the Electors to a Fellowship at St. John's College," unpublished, n.d.
17. Personal communication: GB, 29 December 1972.
18. C. B. Bateson (hereafter cited as CBB) to N. Barlow, 8 August 1926.
19. Personal communication: GB, 27 December 1972.
20. GB to A. C. Haddon, 16 July 1926.
21. Personal communication: GB, 27 December 1972.
22. GB to CBB, 10 February 1927.
23. Personal communication: GB, 27 December 1972.
24. GB to CBB, 29 February 1927.

25. GB to CBB, 13 March 1927.

26. Ibid.

27. GB to CBB, 9 April 1927.

28. GB to CBB, 25 April 1927.

29. GB to CBB, 13 April 1927.

30. GB to CBB, 7 October 1927.

31. GB to CBB, 8 June 1927.

32. B. Malinowski, *The Argonauts of the Western Pacific* (New York: Dutton, 1922), pp. 18–19.

33. C. Doughty, *Travels in Arabia Deserta* (New York: Random House, n.d.).

34. GB to CBB, 2 October 1927.

35. GB to CBB, 8 October 1928. See also W. H. R. Rivers, *The History of Melanesian Society*, Vol 2 (New York: Humanities Press, 1968), pp. 537–42.

36. Ibid.

37. GB to CBB, 9 October 1928.

38. GB to CBB, 8 December 1928.

39. GB to CBB, 27 November 1928.

40. GB to CBB, 8 December 1928.

41. GB to CBB, 15 February 1928.

42. GB to B. W. F. Armitidge, 28 January 1929.

43. GB to CBB, 29 March 1929.

44. Ibid.

45. GB to CBB, 20 June 1929.

46. GB to CBB, 10 July 1929.

47. GB to CBB, 19 January 1930.

48. Ibid.

49. Ibid.

50. GB to A. C. Haddon, 28 January 1929.

51. GB to CBB, 19 January 1930.

52. GB to CBB, 6 September 1929.

53. GB to CBB, 17 January 1929.

54. GB to CBB, 1 November 1929.

55. Personal communication: GB, 27 December 1972.

56. GB, "Social structure of the Iatmul people of the Sepik River, Parts I, II, and III," *Oceania* 2 (1932): 246–89, 401–53.

57. Ibid., p. 279.

58. Ibid., p. 245.

59. A. C. Haddon, "Report to the electors."

60. GB, "Social structure of the Iatmul people," p. 440.

61. Ibid.

62. CBB to GB, 7 October 1931.

63. CBB to GB, 11 August 1932.

64. GB, *Naven: A Survey of the Problems suggested by a Composite Picture of the Culture of a New Guinea Tribe drawn from Three Points of View*, 2d ed. rev. (Stanford: Stanford University Press, 1958), p. x.

65. Ibid., p. 257.

66. GB to CBB, 30 December 1932.

67. M. Mead, *Blackberry Winter: My Earlier Years* (New York: Morrow, 1972), p. 194.

68. Ibid., p. 164.
69. GB to CBB, 30 December 1932.
70. M. Mead, *Blackberry Winter,* p. 209.
71. Ibid., p. 219.
72. Ibid., p. 216.
73. Ibid., p. 217.
74. G. W. Stocking, "Ideas and institutions in American anthropology: toward a history of the interwar period," in *Selected Papers from the American Anthropologist: 1921–45,* ed. G. W. Stocking (Washington D.C.: American Anthropological Association, 1976), p. 22.
75. M. Mead, *Coming of Age in Samoa* (New York: Morrow, 1967): idem., *Growing Up in New Guinea* (New York: Morrow, 1968).
76. R. Benedict, *Patterns of Culture* (Cambridge, Mass.: Riverside Press, 1934), p. 46.
77. M. Mead, *Blackberry Winter,* p. 217.
78. Ibid., p. 220.
79. Personal communication: GB, 27 December 1972.
80. N. Wood, *Communism and British Intellectuals* (New York: Columbia University Press, 1959), p. 121.
81. M. Polanyi, letter to *Nature* 147 (1941): 119.
82. C. H. Waddington, *The Scientific Attitude* (Harmondsworth: Penguin Books, 1941); P. G. Werskey, *The Visible College* (London: Allen Lane, 1978).
83. Personal communication: GB, 27 December 1972.
84. Personal communication: Edmund Leach, 17 December 1975.
85. GB, *Naven,* pp. 1–2.
86. R. Firth, *We, The Tikopia* (New York: Beacon Press, 1963); and A. I. Richards, *Hunger and Work in a Savage Tribe* (London: George Routledge and Sons, 1932).
87. GB, *Naven,* pp. 280–81.
88. Ibid., p. 280.
89. Ibid., p. 118.
90. Ibid., p. 198.
91. Ibid., p. 121.
92. Ibid., pp. 230–31.
93. Ibid., p. 116.
94. Ibid., p. 267.
95. Ibid., p. 258.
96. GB, "Bali: the value system of a steady state," in *Steps to an Ecology of Mind* (San Francisco: Chandler Press, 1972), p. 125.
97. GB, *Naven,* p. 176.
98. Ibid., p. 177.
99. Ibid., p. 197.
100. Ibid., p. 246.
101. A. R. Radcliffe-Brown to GB, circa 1932.
102. GB, *Naven,* p. 192.
103. A. R. Radcliffe-Brown, "Review of *Naven,*" *American Journal of Sociology* 43 (1937):174.
104. GB, *Naven,* p. 3.
105. Ibid., p. 254.
106. A. R. Radcliffe-Brown "Review of *Naven,*" p. 174.
107. G. B., *Naven,* p. 278-79.

108. K. H. Wolff, "A critique of Bateson's *Naven,*" *Journal of the Royal Anthropological Institute* 74(1944):72.
109. GB, "Experiments in thinking about observed ethnological material," in *Steps,* p. 84.
110. G. B., *Naven* p. 263.
111. R. Redfield, R. J. Linton, M. J. Herskovits, "Memorandum for the study of acculturation," *American Anthropologist* 38(1936): 149–52.
112. GB, "Culture contact and schismogenesis," in *Steps,* p. 64.
113. A. Arbor, "Analogy in the history of science," in *Studies and Essays in the History of Science and Learning in Honor of George Sarton,* ed. M. F. Ashley Montagu (New York: Henry Schuman, 1944), pp. 221–33, B. Barnes, *Scientific Knowledge and Sociological Theory* (Boston: Routledge and Kegan Paul, 1974), pp. 53–57, 86–92; T. S. Kuhn, "The essential tension: tradition and innovation in scientific research," in T. S. Kuhn, *The Essential Tension: Selected Studies in Scientific Tradition and Change* (Chicago: University of Chicago Press, 1977); pp. 225–40.
114. GB, "Experiments in thinking,"in *Steps,* p. 74.
115. Ibid., p. 75.
116. Ibid.
117. GB, *Naven,* p. 3.
118. Ibid., p. 276.
119. M. Mead, *Blackberry Winter,* p. 222.
120. GB to CBB, 25 March 1936.
121. GB to E. J. Lindgren, 23 June 1936.
122. GB to CBB, 31 March 1936.
123. GB to Electors of St. John's College, 3 January 1937.
124. CBB to E. J. Lindgren, 14 June 1938.
125. GB to CBB, 31 March 1936. Cf. M. Mead, *Letters from the Field, 1925–1975* (New York: Harper & Row, 1977), p. 157.
126. G. Bateson, M. Mead, *Balinese Character: A Photographic Analysis* (New York: New York Academy of Sciences, 1942), p. xiii.
127. Ibid.
128. GB to E. J. Lindgren, 23 June 1936.
129. M. Mead, *Blackberry Winter,* p. 236.
130. GB to E. J. Lindgren, 20 September 1936.
131. GB, M. Mead, *Balinese Character,* p. 49.
132. Ibid.
133. M. Mead, *Blackberry Winter,* p. 224.
134. G. B., M. Mead, *Balinese Character,* p. 50.
135. Ibid., p. 49.
136. GB to E. J. Lindgren, 20 September 1936.
137. Personal communication: Margaret Mead, 20 January 1976.
138. Ibid.
139. M. Mead-Bateson to CBB, 21 March 1938.
140. GB to B. MacKenzie, 18 April 1938.
141. M. Mead, *Blackberry Winter,* p. 237–38.
142. Ibid., p. 252.
143. Ibid., p. 257.
144. GB to E. J. Lindgren, 27 April 1940.

145. M. Mead, *Blackberry Winter*, p. 260.
146. Ibid., p. 263.
147. GB, "Bali: the value system of a steady state," in *Steps*, p. 108.
148. GB, M. Mead, *Balinese Character*, p. xii.
149. Ibid.
150. GB, "Cultural determinants," p. 729.
151. GB, M. Mead, *Balinese Character*, p. 172.
152. Ibid.
153. Ibid., p. 84.
154. Ibid., p. 87.
155. Ibid., p. 86.
156. Ibid., p. 84.
157. GB, "Bali: the value system of a steady state," in *Social Structure: Studies Presented to A. R. Radcliffe-Brown*, ed. M. Fortes (Oxford: Clarendon Press, 1949)
158. GB, M. Mead, *Balinese Character*, p. 68.
159. Ibid., p. 255.
160. GB, "Bali: the value system of a steady state," in *Steps*, p. 115.

XI. Deus ex Machina: Cybernetics

1. D. Fleming and B. Bailyn, eds., *The Intellectual Migration* (Cambridge, Mass.: Harvard University Press, 1969), p. 96; D. P. Kent, *The Refugee Intellectual* (New York: Columbia University Press, 1953); H. S. Hughes, *The Sea Change* (New York: Harper and Row, 1975); W. R. Crawford, ed., *The Cultural Migration* (Philadelphia: University of Pennsylvania Press, 1953).
2. P. F. Lazarsfeld, "An episode in the history of social research: a memoir," in *The Intellectual Migration*, p. 302.
3. T. W. Adorno, "Scientific experiences of a European scholar in America," in ibid., p. 367.
4. D. J. Kevles, *The Physicists* (New York: Knopf, 1978), pp. 281–83.
5. L. Fermi, *Illustrious Immigrants* (Chicago: University of Chicago Press, 1968), pp. 368–69.
6. Personal communication: Philomena Guillebaud, 13 January 1976.
7. GB to CBB, 8 June 1940.
8. Personal communication: Margaret Mead, 20 January 1976.
9. Personal communication: Philomena Guillebaud, 13 January 1976.
10. Ibid.
11. M. C. Bateson, *Our Own Metaphor* (New York: Knopf, 1972), p. 3.
12. GB to CBB, 20 August 1940.
13. Personal communication: Anatol W. Holt, 11 January 1976.
14. M. Mead, *Blackberry Winter* (New York: Morrow, 1972), p. 261.
15. GB to CBB, 10 December 1940.
16. GB to CBB, 9 January 1941.
17. M. Mead, *Blackberry Winter*, p. 283.
18. Ibid.
19. GB to CBB, circa April 1941.
20. M. Mead, *Blackberry Winter*, p. 260.
21. Personal communication: Margaret Mead, 20 January 1976.
22. Ibid.

23. GB and M. Mead, "Principles of morale building," *Journal of Educational Sociology* 15(1941):206–20.

24. M. Mead-Bateson to CBB, 19 February 1941.

25. GB, "Social planning and the concept of deutero-learning," in *Steps to an Ecology of Mind* (San Francisco: Chandler Press, 1972), p. 162.

26. GB, "Morale and national character," in *Steps*, p. 90.

27. Ibid., p. 92.

28. Ibid., p. 91.

29. Ibid., p. 92.

30. Ibid., p. 91.

31. Ibid.

32. Ibid., p. 96.

33. GB, "Some systematic approaches to the study of culture and personality," in *Personal Character and Cultural Milieu*, ed. D. G. Haring (Syracuse: Syracuse University Press, 1948), p. 112.

34. GB, "Morale and national character," p. 102.

35. Ibid., pp. 102-3.

36. Ibid., p. 103.

37. Ibid., p. 104.

38. Ibid.

39. M. Mead, "The study of culture at a distance," in *The Study of Culture at a Distance*, eds., M. Mead and R. Metraux (Chicago: University of Chicago Press, 1953), p. 4.

40. M. Mead, "The organization of group research," in *The Study of Culture*, p. 97.

41. M. Mead, "Editor's note to 'An analysis of the Nazi film *Hitlerjunge Quex* by Gregory Bateson,'" in *The Study of Culture*, p. 302.

42. GB, "Cultural and thematic analysis of fictional films, in *Personal Character*, p. 117.

43. GB, "An analysis of the film *Hitlerjunge Quex* (1933)," in *The Study of Culture*, p. 314.

44. D. G. Haring, ed., *Personal Character.*

45. GB, "Sex and culture," in *Personal Character*, p. 140.

46. GB, "Experiments in thinking," in *Steps*, p. 84.

47. GB, "Social planning," in *Steps*, p. 163.

48. GB, "Review of *Conditioning and Learning* by E. R. Hilgard and D. G. Marquis," *American Anthropologist* 43(1941): 115–16.

49. GB, "Social planning," in *Steps*, p. 166; cf H. F. Harlow, "The formation of learning sets," *Psychological Review* 56(1949):51–65.

50. GB, "Social planning," in *Steps*, p. 171.

51. Personal communication: GB, 19 March 1978.

52. GB, "Social planning," in *Steps*, p. 173.

53. Ibid., p. 174.

54. Ibid.

55. Ibid., p. 175.

56. Ibid., p. 176.

57. GB quoted in "Introduction," in *About Bateson*, ed. J. Brockman, p. 6–7.

58. GB, "Symptoms, syndromes and systems," *The Esalen Catalog*, October–December, 1978, p. 5.

59. Personal communication: Geoffrey Gorer, 27 December 1975.

60. GB to H. and F. Durham, 20 April 1946.

61. M. Mead, *Blackberry Winter*, p. 240.

62. Personal communication: Margaret Mead, 20 November 1972.

63. Personal communication: GB, 27 December 1972.

64. Ibid.

65. Personal communication: John H. Weakland, 20 February 1976.

66. Ibid.

67. Personal communication: Margaret Mead, 20 November 1972.

68. Personal communication: GB, 27 December 1972.

69. GB quoted in "Introduction," in *About Bateson*, ed. J. Brockman, p. 6; cf. L. S. Kubie, "Some unsolved problems of the scientific career," *American Scientist* 42(1954):104–12.

70. N. Wiener, *Cybernetics or Control and Communication in the Animal and the Machine* (New York: J. Wiley and sons, 1948), p. 8.

71. Ibid., p. 13.

72. A. Rosenblueth, N. Wiener, J. Bigelow, "Behavior, purpose and teleology," *Philosophy of Science* 10(1943):18–24.

73. The Josiah Macy, Jr., Foundation, *A Review of Activities: 1930–55* (New York: Josiah Macy, Jr., Foundation, 1955), p. 20.

74. GB and M. Mead, "For God's sake, Margaret," *CoEvolution Quarterly*, summer 1976, p. 32.

75. GB quoted in "Introduction," in *About Bateson*, ed. J. Brockman, pp. 6–7.

76. N. Wiener, *Cybernetics or Control*, p. 26; H. von Foerster, ed., *Cybernetics: Circular Causal and Feedback Mechanisms in Biological and Social Systems* (New York: Josiah Macy, Jr., Foundation, 1949–53); W. R. Ashby, *An Introduction to Cybernetics* (New York: J. Wiley, 1956); J. Singh, *Great Ideas in Information Theory, Language, and Cybernetics* (London: Constable Press, 1967).

77. L. Frank, "Foreword," *Annals New York Academy of Science* 50(1948):192.

78. Personal communication: G. Evelyn Hutchinson, 16 January 1976.

79. GB and M. Mead, "For God's sake, Margaret," p. 34.

80. GB quoted in "Introduction," in *About Bateson*, ed. J. Brockman, p. 6.

81. S. Heims, "Gregory Bateson and the mathematicians; from interdisciplinary interaction to societal functions," *Journal of the History of the Behavioral Sciences* 13(1977): 145.

82. G. T. Guilbaud, *What Is Cybernetics?* (New York: Criterion, 1959).

83. C. Maxwell, "On governors," *Processes Royal Society* 16(1868):270.

84. L. Frank, "Forward," p. 191.

85. GB, *Naven*, p. 288.

86. N. Wiener, *The Human Use of Human Beings* (Cambridge: Houghton Mifflin Company, 1950), pp. 8–9.

87. GB, "Cybernetic Explanation," in *Steps*, pp. 410–411.

88. N. Wiener, *Cybernetics or Control*.

89. Ibid., pp. 33–34.

90. S. Heims, "Gregory Bateson and the mathematicians," p. 144.

91. W. Hagstrom, *The Scientific Community* (New York: Basic Books, 1965), p. 213.

92. S. Heims, "Gregory Bateson and the mathematicians," p. 147.

93. GB, "The patterns of an armament race," in *Personal Character*, ed. D. G. Haring, pp. 124–32.

94. GB, "Bali: the value system of a steady state," in *Steps*, pp. 107–26; GB to N. Wiener, 22 September 1952, quoted in "Gregory Bateson and the mathematicians," S. P. Heims, p. 148.

95. GB, *Naven*, "Preface."

XII. As Communications Theorist

1. Personal communication: William F. Fry, 27 February 1976.
2. GB to DL, 27 May 1973.
3. M. C. Bateson, *Our Own Metaphor* (New York: Knopf, 1972), p. 12.
4. GB to M. Mead, 28 August 1949.
5. J. Ruesch and GB, "Structure and process in social relations," *Psychiatry* 12(1949):1105–25.
6. Personal communication: Jurgen Ruesch, 24 February 1976.
7. Personal communication: Elizabeth Sumner-Bateson, 22 December 1978.
8. GB to J. Ruesch, 28 August 1949.
9. Ibid.
10. Ibid.
11. GB, "Epilogue," in *Communication and Social Interaction,* ed. P. F. Ostwald (New York: Grune and Stratton, 1977), p. 332.
12. Ibid.
13. K. Z. Lorenz, *King Solomon's Ring* (New York: Crowell, 1952).
14. GB, "Epilogue," in *Communication and Social Interaction,* p. 335.
15. Personal communication: Jurgen Ruesch, 24 February 1976.
16. Ibid.
17. GB, "Description of a research project on psychotherapy," unpublished, n.d.
18. GB, Personal notes, unpublished, 15 October 1948.
19. J. Ruesch and GB, *Communication: The Social Matrix of Psychiatry* (New York: Norton, 1951).
20. Ibid., p. 249.
21. N. Weiner quoted in S. P. Heims, "Gregory Bateson and the mathematicians: from interdisciplinary interaction to societal functions," in *Journal of the History of the Behavioral Sciences* 13(1977):150.
22. C. E. Shannon and W. Weaver, *The Mathematical Theory of Communication* (Urbana, Ill.: University of Illinois Press, 1962).
23. J. Ruesch and GB, *Communication,* p. 173.
24. A. N. Whitehead and B. Russell, *Principia Mathematica,* 3 vols. (Cambridge: Cambridge University Press, 1910–13).
25. GB, *Naven* (Stanford: Stanford University Press, 1958), p. 293.
26. Ibid.
27. GB, "Minimal requirements for a theory of schizophrenia," in *Steps to an Ecology of Mind* (San Francisco: Chandler Press, 1972), p. 247.
28. J. Ruesch and GB, *Communication,* p. 213.
29. GB, "A theory of play and fantasy," in *Steps,* p. 193.
30. GB, "The human side of schizophrenia," unpublished, n.d.
31. GB, "A theory of play," in *Steps,* p. 179.
32. Ibid., p. 180.
33. C. Darwin quoted in *Sociobiology,* E. O. Wilson, (Cambridge, Mass.: Belknap Press, 1975), p. 191; S. A. Altman, "A field study of the sociobiology of rhesus monkeys *Macaca mulatta,*" *Annals of the New York Academy of Science* 102(1962): 338–435; idem, "Social behavior of anthropoid primates: analysis of recent concepts," in *Roots of Behavior,* ed. E. L. Bliss (New York: Harper and Row, 1962), pp. 277–85.

34. GB, *The Nature of Play (part I): River Otters*, a film.
35. GB, "The message 'This is play,'" in *Group Processes: 1955*, ed. B. Schaffner (New York: Josiah Macy, Jr., Foundation, 1956), pp. 145–241.
36. Ibid., p. 175.
37. Ibid., p. 176.
38. Ibid.
39. Ibid., p. 194.
40. Ibid., p. 149.
41. Ibid., p. 216.
42. Ibid., p. 228.
43. Ibid., p. 196.
44. Ibid., p. 194.
45. Ibid., p. 185.
46. Ibid., p. 241.
47. W. Shakespeare, *Hamlet, Prince of Denmark*, Act I, Sc. 1, lines 129-30.
48. GB, "Transcript of a lecture given to psychiatric residents at Langley Porter Neuro-psychiatric clinic, San Francisco, California," unpublished, 12 January 1950.
49. GB, "The message 'This is play,'" p. 195.
50. Ibid., p. 194.
51. GB, "Foreword," in *Steps*, p. xii.
52. Personal communication: William F. Fry, 27 February 1976.
53. Ibid.
54. GB, "Foreword," in *Steps*, p. xix.
55. GB, "The message 'This is play,'" p. 193.
56. Personal communication: Elizabeth Sumner-Bateson, 22 December 1978.
57. Ibid.
58. Ibid.
59. Ibid.
60. Ibid.
61. Ibid.
62. GB, Personal notes, n.d.
63. Ibid.
64. Personal communication: R. D. Laing, 12 December 1975.
65. M. C. Bateson, *Our Own Metaphor*, pp. 8–9.
66. Ibid., p. 212.
67. GB, Letter to *Science*, unpublished, 25 January 1964.
68. Personal communication: John H. Weakland, 20 February 1976.
69. Personal communication: Jay Haley, 14 January 1976.
70. W. F. Fry and M. Allen, *Make 'em Laugh: Life Studies of Comedy Writers* (Palo Alto: Science and Behavior Books, 1975), p. 7.
71. D. D. Jackson, "The question of family homeostasis," in *Communication, Family and Marriage*, vol.1, ed. D. D. Jackson (Palo Alto: Science and Behavior Books, 1970), p. 2.
72. S. P. Heims, "Gregory Bateson and the mathematicians," p. 150.
73. J. Haley, *Uncommon Therapy* (New York: Norton, 1975), p. 9.
74. J. Haley, "Development of a theory: a history of a research project," in *Double Bind: The Foundation of the Communicational Approach to the Family*, ed. C. E. Sluzki and D. C. Ransom (New York: Grune and Stratton, 1976), p. 109.
75. Personal communication: John H. Weakland, 20 February 1976.

76. Ibid.
77. Ibid.
78. W. F. Fry, *Sweet Madness: A Study of Humor* (Palo Alto: Pacific Books, 1963), pp. 137–38.
79. Personal communication: John H. Weakland, 20 February 1976.
80. Personal communication: Jay Haley, 14 January 1976.
81. GB, untitled, unpublished, 24 January 1956.
82. Personal communication: Jay Haley, 14 January 1976.
83. GB, "Foreword," in *Steps*, p. xiii.
84. GB to N. Wiener, circa April 1954.
85. GB quoted in "Gregory Bateson and the mathematicians," S. P. Heims, p. 151.
86. GB to N. Wiener, circa April 1954.
87. J. Haley, "Development of a theory," in *Double Bind*, p. 67.
88. Personal communication: Jay Haley, 14 January 1976.
89. GB, "Toward a theory of schizophrenia," in *Steps*, pp. 201–27.
90. Ibid., p. 205.
91. Ibid., pp. 209–10.
92. GB, untitled, unpublished, 1956.
93. GB, "The human side of schizophrenia."
94. GB, "Minimal requirements for a theory of schizophrenia," in *Steps*, p. 259.
95. GB, "Double bind, 1969," in *Steps*, p. 273.
96. GB, "Toward a theory of schizophrenia," p. 206.
97. Ibid.
98. GB, "Epidemiology of schizophrenia," p. 196.
99. GB, "Toward a theory of schizophrenia," p. 206.
100. Ibid., p. 217.
101. Ibid., p. 213.
102. Ibid., p. 214.
103. Ibid., p. 215.
104. Ibid., p. 208.
105. Ibid., pp. 215–16.
106. P. L. Travers, *Mary Poppins* (New York: Harcourt, Brace, 1934), p. 121.
107. GB, "A social scientist views the emotions," in *Expression of Emotions in Man*, ed. P. H. Knapp (New York: International Universities Press, 1963), p. 236.
108. W. F. Fry, "The schizophrenogenic 'who,'" *Psychoanalysis and the Psychoanalytic Review* 49(1962): 71.
109. GB, D. D. Jackson, J. Haley and J. H. Weakland, "A note on the double bind—1962," in *Communication, Family, and Marriage*, p. 58.
110. F. Fromm-Reichmann quoted in "Towards a theory of schizophrenia," GB, p. 226; H. Green, *I Never Promised You a Rose Garden* (New York: Holt, Rinehart and Winston, 1967).
111. GB, *Naven*, pp. 181–82.
112. GB, "Response to E. G. Mishler and N. E. Waxler, 'Family interaction and schizophrenia: a review of current theories,'" in *Family Processes and Schizophrenia*, ed. E. G. Mishler and N. E. Waxler (New York: Science House, 1968), p. 279.
113. Personal communication: Jay Haley, 14 January 1976.
114. GB, "Annotated transcript of an interview with a patient," unpublished, 14 January 1956.
115. Anonymous, quoted in GB, "The message 'This is play,'" p. 190.

116. Ibid.
117. Ibid., p. 230.
118. Ibid.
119. Ibid., p. 166.
120. GB, "Epidemiology of schizophrenia," p. 198.
121. Ibid.
122. Ibid., p. 198–99.
123. W. F. Fry, "The schizophrenogenic 'Who.'"
124. D. W. Harding, "Single mind, double bind," *New York Review of Books*, 19 October 1972, p. 32.
125. GB, "The group dynamics of schizophrenia," in *Steps*, p. 237.
126. GB, quoted in *Group Processes: 1956*, ed. B. Schaffner (New York: Josiah Macy, Jr., Foundation, 1957),p. 9.
127. J. Haley, ed., *Changing Families: A Family Therapy Reader* (New York: Grune and Stratton, 1971), p. 3.
128. J. Haley, "Development of a theory," p. 72.
129. Personal communication: William F. Fry, 27 February 1976.
130. Personal communication: R. D. Laing, 12 December 1975.
131. J. Haley to DL, 26 December 1977.
132. GB, "Transcript of a family interview," unpublished, 1 November 1958.
133. GB, "The biosocial integration of behavior in the schizophrenic family," in *Exploring the Base for Family Therapy*, ed. N. W. Ackerman, F. L. Beatman, and S. N. Sherman (New York: Family Service Association of America, 1961), p. 121.
134. GB, "The group dynamics of schizophrenia," p. 236.
135. GB, "Minimal requirements for a theory," p. 262.
136. GB, "The human side of schizophrenia."
137. GB, "The group dynamics of schizophrenia," p. 233.
138. GB, "Minimal requirements for a theory," p. 260.
139. GB, "The group dynamics of schizophrenia," p. 234.
140. Ibid., p. 237.
141. GB, "Minimal requirements for a theory," p. 262.
142. GB, "The group dynamics of schizophrenia," p. 243.
143. GB, "The human side of schizophrenia."
144. J. von Neumann and O. Morgenstern, *Theory of Games and Economic Behavior* (Princeton: Princeton University Press, 1944).
145. GB, "The group dynamics of schizophrenia," p. 240.
146. Ibid., pp. 240–41.
147. GB, "The human side of schizophrenia."
148. GB, "The group dynamics of schizophrenia," p. 242.
149. J. Haley, "Development of a theory," p. 78.
150. Ibid., p. 106.
151. J. Haley, "The family of the schizophrenic: a model system," *American Journal of Nervous Mental Disorders* 129(1959):357–74: J. Haley, "Observation of the family of the schizophrenic," *American Journal of Orthopsychiatry* 30(1960): 460–67.
152. J. Haley, "Development of a theory," p. 90.
153. Ibid.
154. I. Glick and J. Haley, *Family Therapy and Research: a Bibliography* (New York: Grune and Stratton, 1970).

155. D. D. Jackson and J. H. Weakland, "Conjoint family therapy: some considerations on theory, technique and results," in *Therapy, Communication and Change*, vol. 2, ed., D. D. Jackson (Palo Alto: Science and Behavior Books, 1973), pp. 222–23.

156. GB, et al., "A note on the double bind—1962," in *Communication, Family, and Marriage*, vol. 1, pp. 55–62.

157. GB, ed., *Perceval's Narrative: A Patient's Account of his Psychosis 1830–1832* (New York: Morrow, 1974).

158. Ibid., pp. 32–33.

159. Ibid., p. xix.

160. Personal communication: Jay Haley, 14 January 1976.

161. Ibid.

162. Personal communication: William F. Fry, 27 February 1976.

163. W. F. Fry, *Sweet Madness*.

164. Personal communication: William F. Fry, 27 February 1976.

165. Personal communication: Jay Haley, 14 January 1976.

166. J. Haley, "Development of a theory," p. 93.

167. GB et al., quoted in ibid., p. 92.

168. J. Haley, "Family experiments: a new type of experimentation," in *Communication, Family, and Marriage* vol. 1, p. 261–69.

169. GB, "Minimal requirements for a theory," in *Steps*, pp. 244-69.

170. Ibid., p. 245.

171. Ibid.

172. Ibid., p. 251.

173. Ibid., p. 250.

174. Ibid., p. 255.

175. Ibid., pp. 257-8

176. S. Butler, *Luck or Cunning?* (London: A. C. Fifield, 1887).

177. GB, "Minimal requirements for a theory," pp. 258–59.

178. Ibid., p. 267.

179. Ibid.

180. Ibid.

181. Ibid., p. 269.

182. W. O. Hagstrom, *The Scientific Community* (New York: Basic Books, 1965). Cf. B. Latour, *Laboratory Life: The Social Construction of Scientific Facts* (Beverly Hills, Ca: Sage, 1979), pp. 203–11.

183. R. K. Merton, "Priorities in scientific discovery: a chapter in the sociology of science," in *The Sociology of Science*, ed. B. Barber and W. Hirsch (New York: Free Press, 1962), p. 463.

184. See D. Oliver, "Review of *Naven*," *Science* 128(1958):892–893.

185. GB to J. R. Oppenheimer, 4 March 1959.

186. GB to J. R. Oppenheimer, 18 March 1959.

187. GB, "The position of humor in human communication," in *Cybernetics: Circular Causal and Feedback Mechanisms in Biological and Social Systems* (transactions of the ninth conference), ed. H. von Foerster (New York: Josiah Macy, Jr., Foundation, 1953), pp. 1–48; and J. Z. Young, "Discrimination and learning in Octopus," in ibid., p. 109–20.

188. GB, "The role of somatic change in evolution," in *Steps*, p. 346–64.

189. GB, "Problems in cetacean and other mammalian communication," in *Steps*, p. 366.

190. GB, "Patterns of relationship in Octopus," unpublished, 1962, pp. 6–7.
191. Personal communication: Lois Bateson, 25 November 1977.
192. GB, "Patterns of relationship in Octopus," p. 15.
193. Ibid.
194. Ibid., p. 16.
195. GB, "Observations of a cetacean community," in *Mind in the Waters*, ed. J. McIntyre (New York: Scribner's, 1974), p. 159.
196. Personal communication: Lois Bateson, 25 November 1977.
197. GB, "Comment on a discussion by Dr. Joseph B. Wheelwright," unpublished, circa 1962.
198. GB, et al., "A note on the double bind, 1962," *Family Process* 2(1963): 154–61.
199. GB to E. G. Mishler, 22 May 1964.
200. GB, et al, "A note on the double bind,—" p. 56.
201. Ibid., p. 58.
202. Personal communication: GB, n.d.
203. Personal communication: Jay Haley, 14 January 1976.
204. Ibid.
205. Personal communication: R. D. Laing, 12 December 1975.
206. J. Haley, "Comment on 'Haley's history,'" in *Double Bind*, p. 110.

XIII. As Ethologist

1. J. C. Lilly, *Man and Dolphin* (New York: Doubleday, 1961); idem, "Vocal behavior of the Bottlenose Dolphin," *Proceedings of the American Philosophical Society* 106 (1966): 520–29; idem, "Vocal exchanges between dolphins," *Science* 134(1961): 1873–76; and idem, "Productive and creative research with man and dolphin," *Archives of General Psychiatry* 8(1963):111–16.
2. GB, "Problems in cetacean and other mammalian communication," in *Steps to an Ecology of Mind* (San Francisco: Chandler Press, 1972), p. 365.
3. Ibid., pp. 364–78.
4. GB, "Cybernetic explanation," in *Steps*, p. 413.
5. GB, "Comment on 'The study of language and communication across species' by H. B. Sarles," *Current Anthropology* 10(1969): 215.
6. GB, "Redundancy and coding," p. 417.
7. C. Darwin, *Expression of the Emotions in Man and Animals* (New York: Appleton, 1897), pp. 50–65.
8. GB, "Problems in cetacean," p. 372.
9. Ibid., p. 374.
10. Ibid., p. 375.
11. E. O. Wilson, *Sociobiology* (Cambridge, Mass: Belknap Press, 1975), p. 201.
12. Personal communication: Lois Bateson, 25 November 1977.
13. GB to J. C. Lilly, 23 July 1964.
14. GB, "Foreword," in *Steps*, p. xiii.
15. Personal communication: Lois Bateson, 25 November 1977.
16. GB to K. Pribram, 23 March 1964.

17. Ibid.
18. GB to T. W. Kennelly, 17 January 1964.
19. GB to G. H. Zuk, 30 September 1963.
20. GB to E. Veron, 29 August 1963.
21. GB, "The role of somatic change in evolution," in *Steps*, pp. 346–64.
22. GB to J. B. S. Haldane, 1 June 1964.
23. GB, "The role of somatic change," p. 353.
24. GB to D. Ingleby, 31 August 1964.
25. GB to B. Volcani, n.d. (circa 1962).
26. GB to C. H. Waddington, 6 August 1964.
27. Personal communication: GB, 18 January 1978.
28. GB to T. Kennelly, 23 March 1964.
29. GB to J. Prusmack, 23 March 1964.
30. K. Pryor, *Lads Before the Wind* (New York: Harper and Row, 1975), p. 155.
31. Personal communication: Lois Bateson, 25 November 1977.
32. Ibid.
33. K. Pryor, *Lads Before the Winds*, p. 42.
34. Personal communication: Lois Bateson, 25 November 1977.
35. K. Pryor, *Lads Before the Wind*, pp. 159–69.
36. Personal communication: Lois Bateson, 25 November 1977.
37. K. Pryor, *Lads Before the Wind*, p. 156.
38. Ibid.
39. Ibid., p. 165.
40. Ibid., p. 162.
41. Ibid., p. 236.
42. Ibid.
43. Ibid.
44. K. Pryor, R. Haag, J. O'Reilly, "Deutero-learning in a rough-tooth porpoise *(Steno bredanensis),*" U.S. Naval Ordinance Test Station, China Lake, NOTS TP4270; idem, "The creative porpoise: training for novel behavior," *Journal of the Experimental Analysis of Behavior* 12(1969):653–61.
45. K. Pryor, *Lads Before the Wind*, p. 251.
46. GB, "The logical categories of learning and communication," in *Steps*, pp. 279–308; idem, "Double bind, 1969," in ibid., pp. 271–78.
47. GB, "Double bind, 1969," p. 274.
48. Ibid.
49. GB, "The logical categories of learning and communication," p. 306.
50. GB, "Observations of a cetacean community," in *Mind in the Waters*, ed. J. McIntyre (New York: Scribner's, 1974), p. 148.
51. Ibid., p. 150.
52. Ibid., pp. 151–52.
53. Ibid., p. 153.
54. Ibid., p. 155.
55. K. Pryor, *Lads Before the Wind*, p. 159.
56. GB to J. C. Lilly, 28 February 1967.
57. GB, "Redundancy and coding," in *Steps*, p. 416–31; idem, "Cybernetic explanation," in *Steps*, pp. 405–15.
58. GB, "Redundancy and coding," p. 416.
59. Personal communication: Lois Bateson, 25 November 1977.

XIV. The Ecology of Mind

1. GB, "From Versailles to cybernetics," in *Steps to an Ecology of Mind* (San Francisco: Chandler Press, 1972), pp. 477–85.
2. GB, "Conscious purpose versus nature," in *Steps*, pp. 432–45.
3. Ibid., p. 443.
4. J. B. Lamarck, *Zoological Philosophy*, trans. H. Elliot (New York: Hefner, 1963).
5. GB, "Conscious purpose," p. 435.
6. GB, "Conscious purpose," p. 434.
7. GB, "Style, grace and information in primitive art," in *Steps*, pp. 135–36.
8. GB, "Conscious purpose," p. 438.
9. GB, "Style, grace and information," p. 137.
10. Ibid., p. 138.
11. GB, "Conscious purpose," p. 439.
12. Ibid., p. 441.
13. Ibid.
14. GB, "Style, grace and information," p. 146.
15. GB, "Conscious purpose," p. 440
16. A. Forge, ed., *Primitive Art and Society* (New York: Oxford University Press, 1973), pp. 235–56.
17. GB, "Style, grace and information," p. 152.
18. Personal communication: Lita Osmundsen, 5 January 1976.
19. Personal communication: Mrs. Miles Burkitt, 16 December 1975.
20. GB to L. Osmundsen, 27 July 1967.
21. GB, "Effects of conscious purpose on human adaptation," in *Steps*, p. 446.
22. Ibid., p. 448.
23. Ibid.
24. F. Manuel, "Toward a psychological history of utopias," in *Freedom from History* (New York: New York University Press, 1971), pp. 119–48.
25. GB, "Effects of conscious purpose," p. 451.
26. Ibid., p. 452.
27. Ibid.
28. D. Cooper, ed., *To Free a Generation: The Dialectics of Liberation* (New York: Macmillan, 1969).
29. C. Frey to A. Brokaw, 15 February 1976.
30. M. C. Bateson, *Our Own Metaphor* (New York: Knopf, 1972), p. 12.
31. Personal communication: Anatol W. Holt, 15 January 1976.
32. GB to A. Koestler, 9 May 1968.
33. *Our Own Metaphor,* p. 293.
34. Ibid.
35. Ibid., p. 84.
36. Ibid., p. 69.
37. Ibid., p. 31.
38. Ibid., pp. 36–55
39. Ibid., p. 98.
40. Ibid., p. 162.
41. Ibid., p. 230.
42. Ibid., p. 282.

43. Ibid., p. 284.
44. Ibid., p. 306.
45. Ibid., p. 303.
46. Ibid., preface.
47. Ibid., p. 307.
48. GB to T. A. Pryor, 21 August 1968.
49. GB, "Description of an upcoming conference: the moral and aesthetic structure of human adaptation," unpublished, 5 November 1968.
50. Ibid.
51. W. L. Thomas, ed., *Man's Role in Changing the Face of the Earth* (Chicago: University of Chicago Press, 1971), pp. vii-viii.
52. G. Vickers, "Notes on a conference: the moral and aesthetic structure of human adaptation," unpublished, 1969, p. 1.
53. Personal communication: Lita Osmundsen, 5 January 1976.
54. M. C. Bateson, *Our Own Metaphor*, pp. 18–19.
55. Personal communication: Lita Osmundsen, 5 January 1976.
56. GB to S. Schoen, 1 June 1970.
57. GB, "The roots of the ecological crisis," in *Steps*, pp. 496–501.
58. GB, "On empty-headedness among biologists and state boards of education," *BioScience* 20(1970): 219.
59. GB, "Restructuring the ecology of a great city," in *Steps*, pp. 502–13.
60. GB, "The cybernetics of 'self': a theory of alcoholism," in *Steps*, pp. 309–337.
61. Ibid., p. 320.
62. Ibid., p. 329.
63. Ibid., p. 310.
64. Ibid.
65. Ibid., p. 330.
66. Ibid.
67. Ibid., p. 313.
68. Ibid., p. 331.
69. Ibid., p. 332.
70. GB, "Form, substance and difference," in *Steps*, p. 468.
71. Personal communication: Lita Osmundsen, 5 January 1976.
72. GB, "Foreword," in *Steps*, p. xviii.
73. GB, "Pathologies of epistemology," pp. 489–90.
74. Ibid., p. 489.
75. Ibid.
76. GB, "Form, substance and difference," pp. 460–61.
77. GB, "Comment on part V," in *Steps*, p. 472.
78. GB, "Pathologies of epistemology," p. 490.
79. Ibid.
80. GB, "The cybernetics of self," p. 317. Cf. M. Sahlins, *Culture and Practical Reason* (Chicago: University of Chicago Press, 1976), pp. 89–91.
81. GB, "Form, substance and difference," p. 467.
82. Ibid., p. 468.
83. GB to R. Scholte, 23 June 1970.
84. Personal communication: GB, 3 April 1978.

85. GB to S. Schoen, 1 June 1970.
86. M. Engel, "Preface," in GB, *Steps,* p. ix.
87. GB, "Foreword," in *Steps,* p. xxi.
88. See W. S. McCulloch, "What is a number that a man may know it, and what is a man, that he may know a number?," in *Embodiments of Mind* (Cambridge: M.I.T. Press, 1965), pp. 1–18.
89. GB, "Foreword," p. xxii.
90. Ibid., p. xxiv.
91. Ibid.
92. Ibid., p. xxviii.
93. GB, "The nature and culture of man," unpublished, 1971.
94. Personal communication: GB, September 1971.
95. E. H. Erikson, *Young Man Luther* (New York: Norton, 1962); idem, *Gandhi's Truth* (New York: Norton, 1969).
96. Personal communication: GB, May 1972.

XV. As Man of Knowledge

1. Personal communication: Stewart Brand, 24 October 1978.
2. GB, letter to *BioScience,* 24 (1974): 8.
3. Quoted in *The Perpetual Dream: Reform and Experiment in the American College,* G. Grant and D. Riesman (Chicago: University of Chicago Press, 1978), p. 77.
4. Ibid., p. 112.
5. R. Edgar to DL, 11 October 1978.
6. Ibid.
7. C. Wilson to DL, 15 December 1978.
8. GB to DL, 27 May 1973.
9. GB, "Instructor's evaluation," unpublished, fall 1974.
10. GB quoted in *The Perpetual Dream,* G. Grant and D. Riesman, p. 121.
11. GB to E. McHugh, 22 February 1973.
12. Personal communication: Ernestine McHugh, 16 October 1978.
13. GB to E. McHugh, 22 February 1973.
14. GB, "Some components of socialization for trance," *Ethos* 3(1975): 52–63.
15. Ibid., p. 56.
16. GB and M. Mead, *Balinese Character* (New York: New York Academy of Science, 1942).
17. GB, "Some components of socialization," p. 59.
18. Ibid., p. 61.
19. Ibid., p. 62.
20. Ibid., p. 61.
21. Ibid.
22. J. Clark, "Review of *Steps to an Ecology of Mind,*" *British Journal of Psychology* 64(1974): 630; V. Gioscia, "Review of *Steps,*" *American Journal of Orthopsychiatry* 43 (1973): 168–70; D. W. Harding, "Single mind double bind," *New York Review of Books,* 19 October 1972, pp. 29–32; R. M. Keesing, "Review of *Steps,*" *American Anthropologist* 76(1974): 370–72; K. J. Pataki-Schweizer, "Review of *Steps,*" *Etc.: A Review of General Semantics* 31(1974): 101–03;

L. B. Slobodkin, "Mind, body, and ecology," *Human Ecology* 3(1974):59–60; A. G. Smith, "Parallel lives with divergent goals," *Contemporary Psychology* 19(1974):781–83; and A. Wilden, "Bateson's double bind," *Psychology Today,* November 1973, pp. 138–40.

23. F. Znaniecki, *The Social Role of the Man of Knowledge* (New York: Octagon Books, 1965).

24. W. I. Thompson, *Passages About Earth: An Exploration of the New Planetary Culture* (New York: Harper and Row, 1974), pp. 10–29, 187–91.

25. L. Thomas, *The Lives of a Cell* (New York: Viking, 1974).

26. T. Morgan, "Epoch B," *New York Times Sunday Magazine,* 29 February 1976, p. 33.

27. GB, "The message of nature and nurture," unpublished, 1975.

28. Personal communication: R. D. Laing, 12 December 1975.

29. Ibid.

30. S. Brand, ed., *The Whole Earth Catalog* (Menlo Park, Calif.: Portola Institute, 1968–71).

31. S. Brand, *II Cybernetic Frontiers* (New York: Random House, 1974), p. 9.

32. S. Brand, "Review of *Steps,*" *Rolling Stone,* 9 November 1972, p. 77.

33. S. Brand, "Both sides of the necessary paradox," *Harper's,* November 1973.

34. GB and M. Mead, "For God's sake, Margaret," *CoEvolution Quarterly,* Summer 1976, p. 37.

35. Ibid.

36. Personal communication: GB, 30 December 1978.

37. Ibid.

38. GB and E. G. Brown, Jr., "Caring and clarity," *CoEvolution Quarterly,* Fall 1975, p. 37.

39. Ibid., p. 40.

40. Ibid., p. 42.

41. Ibid., pp. 42–43.

42. Ibid., p. 46.

43. Ibid., p. 47.

44. Ibid.

45. GB and E. G. Brown, Jr., "Prayer breakfast," *CoEvolution Quarterly,* Spring 1976, p. 82.

46. Ibid., p. 84.

47. Ibid.

48. Job 39: 1–2.

49. *The Richmond Independent,* 25 January 1977.

50. *Newsweek,* 21 November 1977, p. 141.

51. *San Francisco Examiner,* 14 December 1976.

52. Ibid.

53. *The Richmond Independent,* 25 January 1977.

54. Ibid.

55. GB to W. Coblentz, 27 September 1977.

56. Ibid.

57. Ibid.

58. Ibid.

59. Ibid.

60. Ibid.

61. *San Francisco Chronicle,* 13 September 1978.

62. *Newsweek,* 21 November 1977, p. 141.

63. *San Francisco Chronicle,* 30 August 1978.

64. R. May, "Gregory Bateson and humanistic psychology," in *About Bateson* (New York: Dutton, 1977), pp. 61–79.

65. GB, "Epilogue," in *Communication and Social Interaction*, ed. P. F. Ostwald (New York: Grune and Stratton, 1977): idem, "Foreword," in *Double Bind: The Foundation of the Communicational Approach to the Family*, ed. C. E. Sluzki and D. C. Ransom (New York: Grune and Stratton, 1976).

66. GB, "Foreword," in *Beyond the Double Bind*, pp. xii–xiii.

67. GB, "Epilogue," p. 336.

68. GB, "Foreword," p. xiv.

69. M. M. Berger, ed., *Beyond the Double Bind: Communication and Family Systems, Theories, and Techniques with Schizophrenics* (New York: Brunner/Mavel, 1978).

70. GB, "The birth of a matrix or double bind and epistemology," in *Beyond the Double Bind*, p. 41.

71. J. Wykert, "Beyond the double bind," *Psychiatric News* 12(1977): 46–47.

72. J. Haley, "Ideas which handicap therapists," in *Beyond the Double Bind*, pp. 65–80.

73. GB, "Discussion," in *Beyond the Double Bind*, p. 81.

74. J. Wykert, "Beyond the double bind."

75. J. Stevens, letter to *Psychiatric News* 12(1977):2, 11.

76. GB, "The double bind—misunderstood?," *Psychiatric News* 13(1978): 40.

77. Ibid.

78. Ibid.

79. Ibid.

80. GB, *Mind and Nature: A Necessary Unity* (New York: Dutton, 1979).

81. Ibid., p. 8.

82. Ibid., p. 87.

83. Ibid., p. 219.

84. W. C. Ellerbroek, "Language, thought and disease," *CoEvolution Quarterly*, Spring 1978, pp. 30–38. GB, letter to *CoEvolution Quarterly*, Summer 1978, p. 17.

85. Personal communication: GB, 12 March 1978.

86. Personal communication: Lois Bateson, 13 March 1978.

87. Personal communication: Nora Bateson, 13 March 1978.

88. Personal communication: GB, 13 March 1978.

89. Personal communication: GB, 30 December 1978.

90. Personal communication: GB, 12 July 1978.

91. GB quoted in D. Goleman, "Breaking out of the double bind," *Psychology Today* 12 (1978):47.

92. GB quoted in *San Francisco Chronicle*, 30 August 1978.

93. Personal Communication: Gregory Bateson, May 1980.

94. M. C. Bateson, "Six Days of Dying," *CoEvolution Quarterly*, Winter 1980, p.6.

95. Ibid., p. 4.

96. Personal Communication: Susan Murphy, August 1980.

97. M. C. Bateson, "Six Days of Dying," p. 8.

98. See footnote on page 64.

Bibliography

Alpers, A. *Dolphins: The Myth and the Mammal.* Boston: Houghton Mifflin, 1961.

Altick, R.D. *Lives and Letters.* New York: Knopf, 1969.

Altman, S.A. "A field study of the sociobiology of rhesus monkeys *macaca mulatta.*" *Annals of the New York Academy of Sciences* 102(1962): 338–435.

———"Social behavior of anthropoid primates, analysis of recent concepts." In *Roots of Behavior,* edited by E. L. Bliss. New York: Harper and Row, 1962.

———*Social Communication Among Primates.* Chicago: University of Chicago Press, 1967.

Annan, N. "The intellectual aristocracy." In *Studies in Social History: A Tribute to G. M. Trevelyan,* edited by J. H. Plumb. New York: Longmans, Green, 1955.

Appleman, P., et al., ed. *1859: Entering an Age of Crisis.* Bloomington: Indiana University Press, 1959.

Arbor, A. "Analogy in the history of science." In *Studies and Essays in the History of Science and Learning in Honor of George Sarton,* edited by M. F. Ashley-Montagu. New York: Henry Schuman, 1944.

Arieti, S. *Interpretation of Schizophrenia.* New York: Basic Books, 1974.

Arnheim, R. *Entropy and Art.* Berkeley: University of California Press, 1971.

Ashby, W. R. *An Introduction to Cybernetics.* New York: J. Wiley and Sons, 1956.

Baker, R. V. and Platt, W. "The relation of the scientific hunch to research." *Journal of Chemical Education,* 8(1931): 1969–2001.

Bald, R. C. et al., eds. *Nineteenth Century Studies.* Westport, Conn.: Greenwood Press, 1968.

Barber, S. *Science and the Social Order.* Glencoe Ill.: Free Press, 1952.

Barlow, N., ed. *The Autobiography of Charles Darwin.* New York: Norton, 1958.

Barnes, B. *Scientific Knowledge and Sociological Theory.* Boston: Routledge and Kegan Paul, 1974.

Bartlett, F. C. *Remembering, A Study in Experimental and Social Psychology.* Cambridge: Cambridge University Press, 1932.

Bateson, C. B. *William Bateson F.R.S.: Naturalist, His Essays and Addresses Together with a Short Account of His Life.* Cambridge: Cambridge University Press. 1928.

Bateson, G. "Further notes on a snake dance of the Baining." *Oceania* 2(1932): 334–41.

———"Social structure of the Iatmul people of the Sepik river (Parts I, II, and III)." *Oceania* 2(1932): 245–91, 401–53.

————"Culture contact and schismogenesis" (1935). Reprinted in *Steps to an Ecology of Mind*, San Francisco: Chandler Press, 1972 (cited hereafter as *Steps**).

————"Music in New Guinea." *The Eagle, St. John's College* 47(1935): 158–70.

————*Naven: A Survey of the Problems Suggested by a Composite Picture of the Culture of a New Guinea Tribe Drawn From Three Points of View.* Cambridge: Cambridge University Press, 1936.

————"An old temple and a new myth" (1937). Reprinted in *Traditional Balinese Culture*, edited by J. Belo. New York: Columbia University Press, 1970.

————"Experiments in thinking about observed ethnological material" (1941). Reprinted in *Steps, q.v.*

————"Social planning and the concept of deutero-learning" (1941). In *Steps, q.v.*

————"The frustration-aggression hypothesis and culture." *Psychological Review* 48(1941): 350–55.

————"Morale and national character (1942)." Reprinted in *Steps, q.v.*

————"Some systematic approaches to the study of culture and personality"(1942). Reprinted in *Personal Character and Cultural Milieu*, edited by D. G. Haring. Syracuse: Syracuse University Press, 1948.

————"Analysis of the Nazi film Hitlerjunge Quex (1933)" (1943). Reprinted in *The Study of Culture at a Distance*, edited by M. Mead and R. Metraux. Chicago: University of Chicago Press, 1953.

————"Cultural and thematic analysis of fictional films" (1943). Reprinted in *Personal Character and Cultural Milieu, q.v.*

————"Cultural determinants of personality." In *Personality and the Behavior Disorders*, Vol. 2, edited by J. McVicker Hunt. New York: Ronald Press, 1944.

————"Form and function of the dance in Bali" (1944). Reprinted in *Traditional Balinese Culture, q.v.*

————"Arts of the South Seas." *Art Bulletin* 28(1946): 119–23.

————"From one social scientist to another." *American Scientist* 34(1946): 648.

————"Physical thinking and social problems." *Science* 103(1946): 717.

————"Protecting the future." *New York Times*, 8 December 1946, Section 4, p. 10.

————"Sex and culture" (1946). In *Personal Character and Cultural Milieu.*

————"The pattern of an armament race: Parts I and II" (1946). Reprinted in *Personal Character and Cultural Milieu, q.v.*

————"Metalogue: Why do things get in a muddle?" (1948). In *Steps, q.v.*

————"Bali: The value system of a steady state" (1949). Reprinted in *Steps, q.v.*

————"Metalogue: Why do Frenchmen?" (1951). Reprinted in *Steps, q.v.*

————"Applied metalinguistics and international relations." *Etc.: A Review of General Semantics* 10(1952): 71–3.

---

*See V. Carroll, "The published work of Gregory Bateson," in *Steps*, pp. 514–24, for original citation information up to 1971.

———"The position of humor in human communication." In *Cybernetics: Circular Causal and Feedback Mechanisms in Biological and Social Sciences; Transactions of the Ninth Conference,* edited by H. von Foerster. New York: Josiah Macy, Jr., Foundation, 1953.

———"Metalogue: About games and being serious" (1953). Reprinted in *Steps, q.v.*

———"Metalogue: Daddy how much do you know?" (1953). Reprinted in *Steps, q.v.*

———"Metalogue: Why do things have outlines?" (1953). Reprinted in *Steps, q.v.*

———"A theory of play and fantasy" (1954). Reprinted in *Steps, q.v.*

———"Metalogue: Why a swan?" (1954). Reprinted in *Steps, q.v.*

———"The epidemiology of schizophrenia" (1955). In *Steps, q.v.*

———"The message 'This is play.'" In *Group Processes: Transactions of the Second Conference,* edited by B. Schaffner. New York: Josiah Macy, Jr., Foundation, 1956.

———"Schizophrenic distortions of communication." In *Psychotherapy of Chronic Schizophrenics,* edited by C. A. Whitaker. Boston: Little, Brown, 1958.

———"Analysis of group therapy in an admission ward, United States Naval Hospital, Oakland, California." In *Social Psychiatry in Action: A Therapeutic Community,* edited by H. A. Wilmer. Springfield: Charles C. Thomas, 1958.

———"Cultural problems posed by a study of schizophrenic process." In *Schizophrenia: An Integrated Approach.* edited by A. Auerback. New York: Ronald Press, 1959.

———"Language and psychotherapy—Frieda Fromm-Reichman's last project." *Psychiatry* 21(1958): 96-100.

———*Naven: A Survey of the Problems Suggested by a Composite Picture of the Culture of a New Guinea Tribe Drawn from Three Points of View.* 2d rev. ed. Stanford: Stanford University Press, 1958.

———"Panel review" In *Individual and Familial Dynamics.* Vol. 2, *Science and Psychoanalysis,* edited by J. H. Wasserman. New York: Grune and Stratton, 1959.

———"Discussion of 'Families of schizophrenic and of well children' by S. J. Beck." *American Journal of Orthopsychiatry* 30:(1959) 263–66.

———"The human side of schizophrenia" (1959). Unpublished.

———"Minimal requirements for a theory of schizophrenia" (1959). Reprinted in *Steps, q.v.*

———"The biosocial integration of behavior in the schizophrenic family." In *Exploring the Base for Family Therapy.* edited by N. W. Ackerman, et al. New York: Family Service Association of America, 1961.

———*Perceval's Narrative: A Patient's Account of his Psychosis, 1830-1832.* Reprint edited by G. Bateson. Stanford: Stanford University Press, 1961.

———"A social scientist views the emotions." In *Expression of Emotions in Man,* edited by P. H. Knapp. New York: International Universities Press, 1963.

———"The role of somatic change in evolution" (1963). Reprinted in *Steps,q.v.*

———"Observations of a cetacean community" (1965). In *Mind in the Waters,* edited by J. McIntyre. New York: Scribner's, 1974.

————"From Versailles to cybernetics" (1966). In *Steps, q.v.*

————"Problems in cetacean and other mammalian communication" (1966). Reprinted in *Steps, q.v.*

————"Comment on 'Family interaction and schizophrenia: a review of current theories,' by E. G. Mishler and N. E. Waxler" (1966). Reprinted in *Family Processes and Schizophrenia*, edited by E. G. Mishler and N. E. Waxler. New York: Science House, 1968.

————"Cybernetic explanation" (1967). Reprinted in *Steps, q.v.*

————"Review of 'Person, time and conduct in Bali,' by Clifford Geertz." *American Anthropologist* 69(1967): 765-66.

————"Style, grace, and information in primitive art" (1967). Reprinted in *Steps, q.v.*

————"Conscious purpose vs. nature" (1968). Reprinted in *Steps, q.v.*

————"Effects of conscious purpose on human adaptation" (1968). In *Steps, q.v.*

————"The logical categories of learning and communication, and the acquisition of world views" (1968). In *Steps, q.v.*

————"Redundancy and coding" (1968). Reprinted in *Steps, q.v.*

————"Comment on 'The study of language and communication across species,' by H. B. Sarles." *Current Anthropology* 10(1969): 215.

————"Double bind, 1969." In *Steps, q.v.*

————"Metalogue: What is an instinct?" (1969). Reprinted in *Steps, q.v.*

————"Pathologies of epistemology" (1969). In *Steps, q.v.*

————"Ecology and flexibility in urban civilizations" (1970). In *Steps, q.v.*

————"Form, substance, and difference" (1970). Reprinted in *Steps, q.v.*

————"The message of reinforcement." In *Language Behavior: A Book of Readings in Communication*, edited by J. Akin, et al. The Hague: Mouton, 1970.

————"On empty-headedness among biologists and state boards of education" (1970). Reprinted in *Steps, q.v.*

————"The roots of ecological crisis" (1970). In *Steps, q.v.*

————"A re-examination of Bateson's rule" (1971). Reprinted in *Steps, q.v.*

————"Introduction." In *The Natural History of an Interview*. Chicago: University of Chicago Library Microfilm Collection of Manuscripts in Cultural Anthropology, 15(1971): 95–98.

————"The cybernetics of self: a theory of alcoholism" (1971). Reprinted in *Steps, q.v.*

————*Steps to an Ecology of Mind.* San Francisco: Chandler Press, 1972.

————"Gratitude for death." *BioScience* 24(1974): 8

————"Some components of socialization for trance." *Ethos* 3(1975): 52–63.

————"The message of nature and nurture." Unpublished. Prepared for the Centre Royaumont pour Une Science de L'Homme Conference on Ontogenetic and Phylogenetic Models of Development, Paris, 10–17 October 1975.

————"Foreword." In *Double Bind: The Foundation of the Communicational Approach to the Family*, edited by C. E. Sluzki and D. C. Ransom. New York: Grune and Stratton, 1976.

————"Epilogue." In *Communication and Social Interaction*, edited by P. F. Ostwald. New York: Grune and Stratton, 1977.

————"Letter to W. C. Ellerbroeck, M.D." *CoEvolution Quarterly*, Summer 1978.

————"The double bind—misunderstood?" *Psychiatric News* 13(1978): 40–41.

————"Symptoms, syndromes, and systems." *The Esalen Catalog*, October–December 1978.

————*Mind and Nature: A Necessary Unity*. New York: Dutton, 1979.

Bateson, G., and Bateson, W. "On certain aberrations of the red-legged partridges *Alectoris rufa* and *saxatilis*." *Journal of Genetics* 16(1926): 101–23.

Bateson, G., and Brown, E. G., Jr. "Caring and Clarity." *CoEvolution Quarterly*, Fall 1975.

————"Prayer breakfast." *CoEvolution Quarterly*, Spring 1976.

Bateson, G., and Jackson, D. D. "Some varieties of pathogenic organization." Reprinted in *Communication, Family and Marriage*, Vol. 1, edited by D. D. Jackson. Palo Alto: Science and Behavior Books, 1968.

Bateson, G., Jackson, D. D., Haley, J., and Weakland, J. "Toward a theory of schizophrenia" (1956). Reprinted in *Steps*, *q.v.*

————"A note on the double bind—1962." Reprinted in *Communication, Family and Marriage*. Vol. I. edited by D. D. Jackson. Palo Alto: Science and Behavior Books, 1968.

Bateson, G., and Mead, M. "Principles of morale building." *Journal of Educational Sociology* 15(1941): 206–20.

————*Balinese Character: A Photographic Analysis*. New York: New York Academy of Sciences, 1942.

————"For God's sake, Margaret." *CoEvolution Quarterly*, Summer 1976.

Bateson, M. C. *Our Own Metaphor*. New York: Knopf, 1972.

Bateson, W. *Materials for the Study of Variation Treated with Especial Regard to DISCONTINUITY in the Origin of Species*. London: Macmillan, 1894.

————*Mendel's Principles of Heredity: A Defense*. Cambridge: Cambridge University Press, 1902.

————*The Methods and Scope of Genetics*. Cambridge: Cambridge University Press, 1908.

————*Problems of Genetics*. New Haven: Yale University Press, 1913.

————*Letters from the Steppe*. London: Methuen, 1928.

————*Scientific Papers of William Bateson*. 2 Vols. Edited by R. C. Punnett. Cambridge: Cambridge University Press, 1928.

Beebe, W. *The Arcturus Adventure: An Account of the New York Zoological Society's First Oceanographic Adventure*. New York: Putnam, 1926.

Ben David, J. "Innovations and their recognition in social science." *History of Political Economy* 7(1975): 434–55.

Benedict, R. *Patterns of Culture*. Cambridge, Mass.: Riverside Press, 1934.

————*The Chrysanthemum and the Sword*. Boston: Houghton Mifflin, 1946.

Bennett, J. "The study of cultures: a survey of techniques and methodology in field work." *American Sociological Review* 13(1948) 672–89.

Berger, M. M. "Double bind dialogue." *Psychiatric News* 13(1978): 2.

————*Beyond The Double Bind: Communication and Family Systems, Theories, and Techniques with Schizophrenics*. New York: Brunner/Mavel, 1978.

Birdwhistell, R. L. *Kinesics and Context*. New York: Ballantine, 1970.

Blake, W. *The Prose and Poetry of William Blake*. New York: Doubleday, 1970.

Bleuer, M. "Conceptions of schizophrenia within the last fifty years and today." *Proceedings of the Royal Society of Medicine* 56(1963): 945–52.

Blume, S. S., and Sinclair, R. "Chemists in British universities: a study of the reward system in science." *American Sociological Review* 38(1973): 126–38.

Blythe, R. *The Age of Illusion*. London: Hamish Hamilton, 1963.

Boas, F. "The method of ethnology." *American Anthropologist* 22 (1920): 311–21.

Boon, J. A. *The Anthropological Romance of Bali: 1597–1972*. New York: Oxford University Press, 1977.

Brand, S. "Review of *Steps to an Ecology of Mind*." *Rolling Stone*, 9 November 1972.

————"Both sides of the necessary paradox." *Harper's*, November 1973.

————*II Cybernetic Frontiers*. New York: Random House, 1974.

Brand, S., ed. *Whole Earth Catalog*. Menlo Park, Calif.: Portola Institute. 1968–1971.

Brew, J. O. *One Hundred Years of Anthropology*. Cambridge, Mass.: Harvard University Press, 1962.

Brockman, J., ed. *About Bateson*. New York: Dutton, 1977.

Brooke, R. *The Collected Poems of Rupert Brooke*. New York: John Lane, 1915.

Bruner, J. S., Jolly, A., and Sylva, K., eds. *Play: Its Role in Development and Evolution*. New York: Basic Books, 1976.

Bukharin, N. I., et. al. *Science at the Crossroads*. 2d rev. ed. London: Frank Cass, 1971.

Buss, A. H., and E. H. *Theories of Schizophrenia*. New York: Atherton., 1969.

Butler, Samuel, *Erewhon*. London: Trübner, 1872.

————*Life and Habit*. London: Trübner, 1878.

————*Evolution Old and New: Theories of Buffon, Dr. Erasmus Darwin and Lamarck as Compared with That of Mr. Charles Darwin*. London: Hardwicke and Bogue, 1882.

————*Luck or Cunning?* London: A. C. Fifield, 1887.

————*The Authoress of the Odyssey*. London: Longmans, Green, 1897.

————*The Way of All Flesh*. London: Grant Richards, 1903

————*Essays in Life, Art, and Science*, edited by R. A. Streatfield. London: Grant Richards, 1904.

————*On Unconscious Memory*. New York: Dutton, 1911.

————*The Notebooks of Samuel Butler*, edited by H. F. Jones. London: A. C. Fifield, 1912.

————*Butleriana*. London: Nonesuch Press, 1932.

Carlson, E. A. *The Gene: A Cultural History*. Philadelphia: Saunders, 1966.

Clark, J. "Review of *Steps to an Ecology of Mind*." *Journal of Psychology* 64(1973): 630.

Cock, A. G. "William Bateson, Mendelism and Biometry." *Journal of the History of Biology* 6(1973): 1–36.

Coffey, D. J. *Dolphins, Whales and Porpoises*. New York: Macmillan, 1977.

Cole, J. R. and S. *Social Stratification in Science*. Chicago: Chicago University Press, 1973.

Coleman, W. "Bateson and chromosomes: conservative thought in science." *Centaurus* 15(1970): 228–314.

————Biology in the Nineteenth Century. New York: John Wiley, 1971.

Collingwood, R. G. The Principles of Art. Oxford: Clarendon Press, 1938.

————The Idea of Nature. Oxford: Clarendon Press, 1945.

————The Idea of History. Oxford: Oxford University Press, 1947.

Cooper, D., ed. To Free a Generation: The Dialectics of Liberation. New York: Macmillan, 1969.

Cornford, F. M. Microcosmographia Academica: Being a Guide for the Young Academic Politician. London: Bowes and Bowes, 1908.

Coser, R., ed. The Family, Its Structures and Functions. New York: St. Martin's Press, 1974.

Crane, D. Invisible Colleges. Chicago: University of Chicago Press, 1972.

Crawford, W. R., ed. The Cultural Migration. Philadelphia: University of Pennsylvania Press, 1953.

Crew, F. A. E. The Foundations of Genetics. Oxford: Pergamon, 1966.

Crowther, J. G. The Social Relations of Science. London: Cresset Press, 1941.

————British Scientists and the Twentieth Century. London: Routledge and Kegan Paul, 1952.

Darbyshire, A. D. An Introduction to Biology and Other Papers. New York: Funk and Wagnalls, 1917.

Darlington, C. D. Genetics and Man, 3d rev. ed. New York: Schocken Books, 1969.

Darwin, C. The Expression of the Emotions in Man and Animals. London: John Murray, 1872.

Deutsch, K. W., et al., eds. "Conditions favoring major advances in social science." Science 171(1971): 450-59.

Devine, E., and Clark, M., eds. The Dolphin Smile. New York: Macmillan, 1967.

Dodds, J. W. The Several Lives of Paul Fejos. New York: Wenner-Gren Foundation, 1973.

Doughty, C. M. Travels in Arabia Deserta. 2d ed. London: P. L. Warner, 1921.

Dronamraju, K. R. Haldane and Modern Biology. Baltimore: Johns Hopkins University Press, 1969.

Dunn, L. C. A Short History of Genetics. New York: McGraw-Hill, 1965.

Dupree, A. H. "The great instauration of 1940: The organization of scientific research for war" (1970). In Twentieth Century Sciences, edited by G. Holton. New York: Norton, 1972.

Eiduson, B. T. Scientists: Their Psychological World. New York: Basic Books, 1962.

Erikson, E. H. Young Man Luther. New York: Norton, 1958.

————Gandhi's Truth. New York: Norton, 1969.

————Toys and Reasons. New York: Norton, 1977.

Farrall, L. A. "Controversy and conflict in science: a case study—the English Biometric school and Mendel's laws." Social Studies of Science 5(1975): 269–301.

Fermi, L. Illustrious Immigrants. Chicago: University of Chicago Press, 1968.

Filner, R. E. "The roots of political activism in British science." The Bulletin of the Atomic Scientists 32(1976): 25–29.

Firth, R. *We, The Tikopia: A Sociological Study of Kinship in Primitive Polynesia.* London: Allen and Unwin, 1936.

———"An appraisal of modern social anthropology." *Annual Review of Anthropology* 4(1975): 1-25.

———Firth, R. ed. *Man and Culture: An Evaluation of the work of Bronislaw Malinowski.* London: Routledge and Kegan Paul, 1957.

Fleming, D., and Bailyn, B., eds. *The Intellectual Migration.* Cambridge, Mass.: Harvard University Press, 1969.

Forge, A., ed. *Primitive Art and Study.* New York: Oxford University Press, 1973.

Fortes, M., ed. *Social Structure: Studies Presented to A. R. Radcliffe-Brown.* Oxford: Clarendon Press, 1949.

Fortune, R. F. *Sorcerers of Dobu.* London: George Routledge and Sons, 1932.

Frank, L. K. "Foreword to 'Teleological Mechanisms.'" *Annals New York Academy of Science* 50(1948): 189–96.

Frankenberg, L., ed. *A James Stephens Reader.* New York: Macmillan, 1962.

Frogatt, P., and Nevin, N. C. "The law of ancestral heredity and the Mendelian-Ancestrian controversy in England, 1889–1906." *Journal of Medical Genetics* 8(1971):1–36.

Fromm-Reichman, F. "Notes on the development of treatment of schizophrenics by psychoanalytic psychotherapy." *Psychiatry* 11(1948): 263–75.

Fry, W. F. "The Schizophrenogenic 'Who.'" *Psychoanalysis and the Psychoanalytic Review* 49(1962): 68–73.

———*Sweet Madness: A Study of Humor.* Palo Alto: Pacific Books, 1963.

Fry, W. F., and Allen, M. *Make 'em Laugh: Life Studies of Comedy Writers.* Palo Alto: Science and Behavior Books, 1975.

Furbank, P. N. *Samuel Butler (1835-1902).* Cambridge: Cambridge University Press, 1948.

Fussell, P. *The Great War and Modern Memory.* New York: Oxford University Press, 1975.

Galton, F. *Hereditary Genius.* New York: Appleton, 1870.

———*English Men of Science: Their Nature and Nurture.* New York: Appleton, 1875.

Gardiner, R. G. "Anthropology and film," *Daedalus* 86(1957): 344–50.

Gauld, A. *The Founders of Psychical Research.* New York: Schocken Books, 1968.

Gilbert, B. *How Animals Communicate.* New York: Pantheon Books, 1966.

Gioscia, V. "Review of *Steps to an Ecology of Mind.*" *American Journal of Orthopsychiatry* 43(1973): 168–70.

Glick, I., and Haley, J. *Family Therapy and Research: A Bibliography.* New York: Grune and Stratton, 1970.

Goodell, R. *The Visible Scientists.* Boston: Little, Brown, 1977.

Gorer, G. *Exploring English Character.* New York: Criterion Books, 1955.

Gosse, E. W. *Father and Son: A Study of Two Temperaments.* London: Heinemann, 1907.

Grant, G., and Riesman, D. *The Perpetual Dream: Reform and Experiment in the American College.* Chicago: University of Chicago Press, 1978.

Granville-Baker, H. *The 1870s* New York: Macmillan, 1929.

Graves, R. *Goodbye to All That.* New York: Blue Ribbon Books, 1930.

———*The Long Weekend.* New York: Macmillan, 1941.

Green, H. *I Never Promised You a Rose Garden.* New York: Holt Rinehart and Winston, 1964.

Greenacre, P. *The Quest for the Father.* New York: International Universities Press, 1963.

Guilbaud, G. T. *What Is Cybernetics?* New York: Criterion Books, 1959.

Hagstrom, W. O. *The Scientific Community.* New York: Basic Books, 1965.

Haldane, J. B. S. "William Bateson." *The Nation,* 20 February 1926.

———*Possible Worlds and Other Essays.* London: Chatto and Windus, 1927.

Haley, J. "The family of the schizophrenic: a model system." *American Journal of Nervous Mental Disorders* 129(1959): 357–74.

———"Observation of the family of the schizophrenic." *American Journal of Orthopsychiatry* 30(1960): 460–67.

———"Family experiments: a new type of experimentation." *Family Process* 1(1962): 265–93.

Haley, J., ed. *Changing Families, A Family Therapy Reader.* New York: Grune and Stratton, 1971.

———*Uncommon Therapy: The Psychiatric Techniques of Milton H. Erickson, M.D.* New York: Norton, 1973.

Hall, A. R. "Merton revisited: science and society in the 17th century." *History of Science* 7(1963): 1–16.

Hallowell, A. I. "History of anthropology as an anthropological problem." *Journal of the History of the Behavioral Science* 1(1965): 24–38.

Harding, D. W. "Single mind, double bind." *New York Review of Books,* 19 February 1972.

Harlow, H. F. "The formation of learning sets." *Psychological Review* 56(1949):51–65.

Harris, C. J. *Otters.* London: Weidenfeld and Nicolson, 1968.

Harrison, R. J. "Adaptations in marine mammals." *Proceedings of the Royal Institution of Great Britain* 19(1962): 136–42.

Haskell, T. L. *The Emergence of Professional Social Science.* Urbana: University of Illinois Press, 1977.

Heims, S. P. "Gregory Bateson and the mathematicians: from interdisciplinary interaction to societal functions." *Journal of the History of the Behavioral Sciences* 13(1977): 141–59.

Henderson, P. *Samuel Butler: The Incarnate Bachelor.* London: Cohen and West, 1953.

Hilgard, E. R., and Marquis, D. G. *Conditioning and Learning.* New York: Appleton, 1946.

Himmelfarb, G. *Darwin and the Darwinian Revolution.* New York: Norton, 1959.

Hinchcliff, P. B. *John William Colenso.* London: Nelson, 1964.

Hinde, R. A. *Animal Behavior.* New York: McGraw-Hill, 1970.

Hughes, H. S. *The Sea Change.* New York: Harper and Row, 1975.

Hull, C. L. *Principles of Behavior: An Introduction to Behavior Theory*. New York: Appleton, 1943.

Hutchinson, G. E. "Marginalia." *American Scientist* 32(1944): 288–93.

————"Variations on a theme by Robert MacArthur." In *Ecology and Evolution of Communities*, edited by M. L. Cody and J. M. Diamond. Cambridge, Mass.: Belknap Press, 1975.

————*The Kindly Fruits of the Earth: Recollections of an Embryo Ecologist*. New Haven: Yale University Press, 1979.

Hynes, S. *The Edwardian Turn of Mind*. Princeton: Princeton University Press, 1968.

————*Edwardian Occasions*. New York: Oxford University Press, 1972.

Iablokov, A. V. *Whales and Dolphins, Part III*. Arlington, Va.: Joint Publications Research Science, 1974.

Iltis, H. *Life of Mendel*. Translated by E. and C. Paul. New York: Hafner, 1966.

Jackson, D. D. "The question of family homeostasis." *The Psychiatric Quarterly Supplement* 31(1957): 79–90.

Jackson, D. D., ed. *Communication, Family, and Marriage*. Vol. I. Palo Alto: Science and Behavior Books, 1968.

————*Therapy, Communication, and Change*. Vol. II. Palo Alto: Science and Behavior Books, 1968.

————*The Etiology of Schizophrenia*. New York: Atherton, 1969.

Jackson, D. D., and Weakland, J. H., "Conjoint family therapy: some considerations on theory, technique, and results." *Psychiatry* 24(1961): 30–45.

Jackson, I. V., and Barton, J. L., "Double bind." *Psychiatric News* 13(1978): 2.

Jones, H. F. *Samuel Butler, Author of Erewhon: A Memoir*. 2 vols. London: Macmillan and Company, 1919.

Jones, L. E. *A Victorian Boyhood*. London: Macmillan, 1955.

Josiah Macy, Jr., Foundation. *A Review of Activities 1930–1955*. New York: Josiah Macy, Jr., Foundation, 1955.

Kasanin, J. S., ed. *Language and Thought in Schizophrenia*. Berkeley: University of California Press, 1964.

Kazin, A., ed. *The Portable Blake*. New York: Viking, 1969.

Keats, J. *The Complete Poems of Keats and Shelley*. New York: Modern Library, n. d.

Kent, D. P. *The Refugee Intellectual*. New York: Columbia University Press, 1953.

Kevles, D. J. *The Physicists*. New York: Knopf, 1978.

King, M. D. "Reason, tradition and the progressiveness of science." *History and Theory* 10(1971): 3–32.

Koestler, A. *The Case of the Midwife Toad*. New York: Random House, 1971.

————*The Call Girls: A Tragi-Comedy with Prologue and Epilogue*. London: Hutchinson, 1972.

Korzybski, A. *Science and Sanity*. Clinton: Colonial Press, 1933.

Kuhn, T. S. *The Essential Tension: Selected Studies in Scientific Tradition and Change*. Chicago: Chicago University Press, 1977.

Kuper, A. *Anthropology and Anthropologists*. Middlesex: Penguin Books, 1973.

Lack, D. *Darwin's Finches.* Cambridge: Cambridge University Press, 1947.

Lamarck, J. B. *Zoological Philosophy.* Translated by H. Elliot. New York: Hefner, 1963.

Latour, B., and Woolgar, S. *Laboratory Life: The Social Construction of Scientific Facts.* Beverly Hills, Calif.: Sage, 1979.

Leakey, L. S. B. *By the Evidence.* New York: Harcourt, Brace, Jovanovich, 1974.

Lerner, D., ed. *Propaganda in War and Crisis.* New York: Arno Press, 1972.

LeVine, R. A. "Behaviorism in psychological anthropology," In *Concepts of Personality.* edited by J. M. Wepman and R. W. Heine. Chicago: University of Chicago Press, 1963.

Lilly, J. C. *Man and Dolphin,* New York: Doubleday, 1961.

————"Vocal exchanges between dolphin." *Science* 134(1961): 1873–76.

————"Vocal behavior of the bottlenose dolphins." *Proceedings American Philosophical Society* 106(1962): 520–29.

————"Productive and creative research with man and dolphin." *Archives of General Psychiatry* 8(1963): 111–16.

————*The Mind of the Dolphin.* New York: Avon, 1967.

————*Lilly on Dolphins.* New York: Anchor, 1975.

Linebarger, P. M. A. *Psychological Warfare.* Washington: Infantry Journal Press, 1948.

Lorenz, K. Z. *King Solomon's Ring.* New York: Crowell, 1952.

Lowie, R. H. *The History of Ethnological Theory.* New York: Holt, Rinehart and Winston, 1937.

Macbride, A. F., and Hebb, D. O. "Behavior of the captive bottlenose dolphin, *Tursiops truncatus." Journal of Comparative and Physiological Psychology* 41(1948): 111–23.

Mack, E. C. *Public Schools and British Opinion.* New York: Columbia University Press, 1969.

Malcolm, J. "Reporter at large: the one-way mirror." *New Yorker,* 15 May 1978.

Malinowski, B. *Argonauts of the Western Pacific.* New York: Dutton, 1922.

Mannheim, K. *Ideology and Utopia: An Introduction to the Sociology of Knowledge.* Translated by L. Wirth and E. Shils. New York: Harcourt, Brace, 1968.

Manuel, F. *Freedom From History.* New York: New York University Press, 1971.

Maurois, A. *Aspects of Biography.* Cambridge: Cambridge University Press, 1929.

Maxwell, J. C. "On governors." *Proceedings of the Royal Society* 16(1868): 270–83.

Mayr, O. *The Origins of Feedback Control.* Cambridge, Mass.: M.I.T. Press, 1970.

McCulloch, W. S. *Embodiments of Mind.* Cambridge, Mass.: M.I.T. Press, 1965.

McIntyre, J., ed. *Mind in the Waters.* New York: Scribner's, 1974.

Mead, M. *Coming of Age in Samoa: A Psychological Study of Primitive Youth for Western Civilization.* New York: Morrow, 1928.

————*Growing up in New Guinea.* New York: Morrow, 1930.

————*Sex and Temperament in Three Primitive Societies.* New York: Morrow, 1935.

————*And Keep Your Powder Dry.* New York: Morrow, 1942.

————"National character and the science of anthropology." In *Culture and Social Character,* edited by S. M. Lipset and L. Lowenthal. Glencoe, Ill.: Free Press, 1961.

————"Anthropology and the camera." In *Encyclopedia of Photography,* edited by W. D. Morganer, New York: Greystone Press, 1971.

————*Blackberry Winter.* New York: Morrow, 1972.

————*Letters from the Field 1925–1975.* New York: Harper and Row, 1977.

Mead, M., and Metraux, R., eds. *The Study of Culture at a Distance.* Chicago: University of Chicago Press, 1953.

————*Themes in French Culture.* Stanford: Stanford University Press, 1954.

Mead, M., and Byers, P. *The Small Conference.* The Hague: Mouton, 1968.

Medvedev, R. *The Rise and Fall of T. D. Lysenko.* New York: Columbia University Press, 1969.

Mencken, H. L. *American Language.* London: Jonathan Cape, 1922.

Merton, R. K. "Science, technology and society in 17th century England." *Osirus* 4(1939): 360–632.

————"Priorities in scientific discovery: a chapter in the sociology of science" (1959). In *The Sociology of Science,* edited by B. Barber, and W. Hirsch. New York: Free Press of Glencoe, 1962.

————*Social Theory and Social Structure.* New York: Free Press, 1968.

————*The Sociology of Science, Theoretical and Empirical Investigations,* edited by N. W. Storer. Chicago: University of Chicago Press, 1973.

Miller, E. *Portrait of a College.* Cambridge: Cambridge University Press, 1961.

Miller, N. E., and Dollard, J. C. *Social Learning and Imitation.* New Haven: Yale University Press, 1941.

Mishler, E. G., and Waxler, N. E. *Family Process and Schizophrenia.* New York: Science House, 1968.

Mitroff, I. I. *The Subjective Side of Science.* Amsterdam: Elsevier Scientific Publishing Company, 1974.

Montagu, I. G. S. *The Youngest Son.* London: Lawrence and Wishart, 1970.

Morgan, T. "Epoch B." *New York Times Sunday Magazine.* 29 February 1976.

Muggeridge, M. *The Earnest Atheist.* London: Eyre and Spottiswoode, 1936.

————*The Thirties.* London: Collins, 1967.

Mulkay, M. J. *The Social Process of Innovation: A Study in the Sociology of Science.* London: Macmillan, 1972.

Nadel, S. F. "The interview technique in social anthropology." In *The Study of Society,* edited by F. C. Bartlett. London: Routledge and Kegan Paul, 1939.

Needham, J. *Time: The Refreshing River.* London: Allen and Unwin, 1943.

Norris, K. S., ed. *Whales, Dolphins, and Porpoises.* Berkeley: University of California Press, 1966.

————*The Porpoise Watcher.* New York: Norton, 1974.

Norton, B. J. "The Biometric defense of Darwinism." *Journal of the History of Biology* 6(1973): 283–316.

————"Karl Pearson and statistics: the social origins of scientific innovation." *Social Studies of Science* 8(1978): 3–34.

Nowell-Smith, S., ed. *Edwardian England, 1901–1914.* New York: Oxford University Press, 1965.

Olby, R. C. *The Origins of Mendelism.* London: Constable, 1966.

Oliver, D. "Review of *Naven*." *Science* 128(1958): 892–93.

Pataki-Schweizer, K. J. "Review of *Steps to an Ecology of Mind*." *Etc.: A Review of General Semantics* 31(1973): 101–03.

Pearson, E. S. *Karl Pearson.* Cambridge: Cambridge University Press, 1938.

Pekelis, V. *Cybernetics A to Z.* Moscow: Mir Publishers, 1974.

Penniman, T. K. *A Hundred Years of Ethnology.* New York: Macmillan, 1936.

Pope, A. U. *The Language of Drawing and Painting.* Cambridge, Mass.: Harvard University Press, 1949.

Polanyi, M. "Cultural Significance of Science." *Nature* 147(1941): 119.

Poppen, G. *Evolution and Poetic Belief.* Oslo: Oslo University Press, 1956.

Powdermaker, H. *Stranger and Friend.* New York: Norton, 1966.

Priestly, J. B. *The Edwardians.* New York: Harper and Row, 1970.

Provine, W. B. *The Origins of Theoretical Population Genetics.* Chicago: University of Chicago Press, 1971.

Pryor, K. "Behavior modification: the porpoise caper." *Psychology Today* 3(1969): 46–49.

————*Lads Before the Wind.* New York: Harper and Row, 1975.

Pryor, K., et al. "Deutero-learning in a Roughtooth Porpoise *(Steno bredanensis),*" in U.S. Naval Ordinance Station, China Lake, NOTS TP 4270. Reprinted as "The creative porpoise: training for novel behavior." *Journal of the Experimental Analysis of Behavior* 12(1969): 653–61.

Punnett, R. C. *Mendelism.* London: Macmillan, 1922.

————"William Bateson: In Memoriam." *Edinburgh Review,* July 1926.

————"Early days of genetics." *Heredity* 4(1950): 1–10.

Quiggin, A. H. *Haddon, The Head Hunter.* Cambridge: Cambridge University Press, 1942.

Radcliffe-Brown, A. R. *The Andaman Islanders.* Glencoe, Ill.: Free Press, 1922.

————"Review of *Naven*." *American Journal of Sociology* 43(1937): 174.

————*Structure and Function in Primitive Society.* (1952). New York: Free Press, 1965.

————"Letter to R. Lowie, 6 May 1938." *History of Anthropology Newsletter* 3(1976): 5–8.

Rappaport, R. A. *Pigs for the Ancestors.* New Haven: Yale University Press, 1968.

Raverat, G. *Period Piece: A Cambridge Childhood.* London: Faber and Faber, 1952.

Ravetz, J. R. *Scientific Knowledge and its Social Problems.* Oxford: Clarendon Press, 1971.

Richards, A. I. *Hunger and Work in a Savage Tribe.* London: George Routledge, 1932.

Rivers, W. H. R. *The History of Melanesian Society*, Vol. II. Cambridge: Cambridge University Press, 1914.

————*Instinct and Unconscious*. Cambridge: Cambridge University Press, 1922.

Roach, J. P. C., ed. *The History of the County of Cambridge, and the Isle of Ely*, (Vol. III). In *The Victoria History of the Counties of England*, edited by R. B. Pugh. London: Dawsons of Pall Mall, 1967.

Rosen, J. *Direct Analysis*. New York: Grune and Stratton, 1953.

Rosenblueth, A., Wiener, N., and Bigelow, J. "Behavior, purpose, and teleology." *Philosophy of Science* 10(1943): 18–24.

Rothblatt, S. *Revolution of the Dons*. New York: Basic Books, 1968.

Ruesch, J. "Creation of a multidisciplinary team." *Psychosomatic Medicine* 18(1956): 105–12.

————*Knowledge in Action: Communication, Social Operations and Management*. New York: Jason Aronson, 1975.

Ruesch J., and Bateson, G., "Structure and process in social relations." *Psychiatry* 12:(1949): 1105–25.

————*Communication: The Social Matrix of Psychiatry*. New York: Norton, 1951.

Russell, B. *Education and Social Order*. London: Allen and Unwin, 1932.

Russell, E. S. *Form and Function*. London: John Murray, 1916.

Sahlins, M. D. *Culture and Practical Reason*. Chicago: University of Chicago Press, 1976.

Sassoon, S. *The Memoirs of George Sherston*. New York: Doubleday, 1937.

Satir, V. *Conjoint Family Therapy*. Palo Alto: Science and Behavior Books, 1967.

Schwartz, T. "The Paliau Movement in the Admiralty Islands, 1946-54." *Anthropological Papers of the American Museum of Natural History* 49(1962): 211–421.

Sears, P. B. *Charles Darwin, The Naturalist as a Cultural Force*. New York: Scribner's, 1950.

Sebeok, T. A., ed. *Animal Communication*. Bloomington: Indiana University Press, 1968.

Sechehaye, M. A. *Symbolic Realization*. New York: International Universities Press, 1951.

Sedgwick, A., and G. M., *Adam Sedgwick: A Memoir*. London: Macmillan, 1906.

Shannon, C., and Wiener, W. *The Mathematical Theory of Communication*. Urbana: University of Illinois Press, 1949.

Shaw, G. B. *Major Barbara. The Collected Works of Bernard Shaw*, Vol. XI. New York: William H. Wise, 1930.

Shine, I., and Wrobel, S. *Thomas Hunt Morgan*. Lexington: Kentucky University Press, 1976.

Silver, A., ed. *The Family Letters of Samuel Butler*. Stanford: Stanford University Press, 1962.

Singh, J. *Great Ideas in Information Theory, Language and Cybernetics*. London: Constable, 1967.

Skinner, B. F. *Science and Human Behavior*. New York: Free Press, 1953.

Slobodkin, L. B. "Mind, body and ecology." *Human Ecology* 2(1974): 67–74.

Sluzki, C. E., and Ransom, D. C., eds. *Double Bind, The Foundation of the Communicational Approach to the Family.* New York: Grune and Stratton, 1976.

Smith, A. G. "Parallel lives with divergent goals." *Contemporary Psychology* 19(1974): 781–83.

Spiegel-Rösing, I., and de Solla Price, D., eds. *Science, Technology and Society.* Beverly Hills, Calif.: Sage Publications, 1977.

Stadtman, V. *The University of California 1868–1968.* Berkeley: University of California Press, 1970.

Stern, C., and Sherwood, E. R., eds. *The Origin of Genetics: A Mendel Source Book.* San Francisco: W. H. Freeman, 1966.

Stevens, J. "Double bind theory." *Psychiatric News* 12(1977): 2, 11.

Stewart, P. "Slobodkin on Bateson: A comment." *Human Ecology* 3(1975): 59–60.

Stillman, C. G. *Samuel Butler: A Mid-Victorian Modern.* London: Martin Secker, 1932.

Stocking, G. W. *Race, Culture, and Evolution.* New York: Free Press, 1968.

Stocking, G. W., ed. *Selected Papers from the American Anthropologist 1921–1945.* Washington: American Anthropological Association, 1976.

Storer, J. D. *A Simple History of the Steam Engine.* London: John Baker, 1969.

Storer, N. W. *The Social System of Science.* New York: Holt, Rinehart and Winston, 1966.

Sturtevant, A. H. *A History of Genetics.* New York: Harper and Row, 1965.

Tavolga, M. C., and Essapian, F. S. "The behavior of the bottle-nosed dolphin (*Tursiops truncatus*): mating, pregnancy, parturition and mother-infant behavior." In *The Dolphin Smile. q.v.*

Thomas, L. *The Lives of a Cell.* New York: Viking, 1974.

Thomas, W. L., ed. *Man's Role in Changing the Face of the Earth.* Chicago: University of Chicago Press, 1971.

Thompson, W. I. *Passages About Earth: An Exploration of the New Planetary Culture.* New York: Harper and Row, 1974.

Tillyard, A. I. *A History of University Reform.* Cambridge: Heffer and Sons, 1913.

Travers, P. L. *Mary Poppins.* New York: Harcourt, Brace, 1934.

Turner, F. M. *Between Science and Religion: The Reaction to Scientific Naturalism in Late Victorian England.* New Haven: Yale University Press, 1974.

Tylor, E. B. *Primitive Culture.* London: John Murray, 1871.

Vetter, H. J., ed. *Language Behavior in Schizophrenia.* Springfield, Ill.: C C. Thomas, 1968.

Vickers, G. *Value Systems and Social Process.* London: Tavistock, 1968.

Voget, F. W. *A History of Ethnology.* New York: Holt, Rinehart and Winston, 1975.

Von Bertalanffy, L. *General Systems Theory.* New York: George Braziller, 1968.

Von Foerster, H., ed. *Cybernetics: Circular Causal and Feedback Mechanisms in Biological and Social Systems.* New York: Josiah Macy, Jr., Foundation, 1949–53.

Von Neumann, J., and Morgenstern, O. *Theory of Games and Economic Behavior.* Princeton: Princeton University Press, 1944.

Waddington, C. H. *The Scientific Attitude*. Harmondsworth: Penguin, 1941.
————*The Ethnical Animal*. London: Allen and Unwin, 1960.
————*The Nature of Life*. London: Allen and Unwin, 1961.
————*The Evolution of an Evolutionist*. Ithaca: Cornell University Press, 1975.
Wasserman, P., and Mclean, J., eds. *Awards, Honors, and Prizes*, Vol. 1. Detroit: Gale Research Company, 1975.
Watzlawick, P., Beavin, J. H., and Jackson, D. D. *Pragmatics of Human Communication*. New York: Norton, 1967.
Webb, B. *My Apprenticeship*. London: Longmans, Green, 1926.
Weber, M. *The Protestant Ethic and the Spirit of Capitalism* (1904–05). Translated by T. Parsons. New York: Scribner's, 1958.
Weldon, W. F. R. "Mendel's laws of alternative inheritance in peas." *Biometrika* 1(1902): 228-53.
Werskey, P. G. "Essay Review. Haldane and Huxley, the first appraisals." *Journal of the History of Biology* 4(1971): 171–83.
————"British scientists and 'Outsider' politics, 1931–45." *Science Studies* 1(1971): 67–84.
————*The Visible College*. London: Allen Lane, 1978.
White, A. D. *A History of the Warfare of Science with Theology in Christendom*. London: Appleton, 1896.
Whitehead, A. N. *Science and the Modern World*. New York: Free Press, 1925.
Whitehead, A. N., and Russell, B. *Principia Mathematica*. 3 vols. Cambridge: Cambridge University Press, 1910–13.
Wiener, N. *Cybernetics or Control and Communication in the Animal and the Machine*. New York: Wiley, 1948.
————*The Human Use of Human Beings: Cybernetics and Society*. Cambridge, Mass.: Houghton Mifflin, 1950.
————*I am a Mathematician*. Cambridge, Mass.: M.I.T. Press, 1956.
————*The Tempter*. New York: Random House, 1959.
Wilden, A. *System and Structure, Essays in Communication and Exchange*. New York: Harper and Row, 1972.
Willey, B. *Darwin and Butler: Two Versions of Evolution*. New York: Harcourt, Brace, 1960.
Wilmer, H. A. *Social Psychiatry in Action*. Springfield: Charles Thomas, 1958.
Wilson, E. *The Triple Thinkers*. New York: Harcourt, Brace, 1938.
Wilson, E. O. *Sociobiology*. Cambridge, Mass.: Belknap Press, 1975.
Winstanley, D. A. *Late Victorian Cambridge*. Cambridge: Cambridge University Press, 1947.
Wolff, K. H. "A critique of Bateson's *Naven*." *Journal of the Royal Anthropological Institute* 74(1944): 59–74.
Wood, N. *Communism and British Intellectuals*. New York: Columbia University Press, 1959.
Wykert, J. "Beyond the double bind." *Psychiatric News* 12(1977): 46–47.

Yule, G. U. "Mendel's laws and their probable relation to intraracial heredity." *New Phytologist* 1(1902): 193-207 and 222-37.

Zirkle, C. "Some oddities in the delayed discovery of Mendelism." *Journal of Heredity* 55(1964): 65–72.

Znaniecki, F. *The Social Role of the Man of Knowledge.* New York: Columbia University Press, 1940.

Zuckerman, H. *Scientific Elite: Nobel Laureates in the United States.* New York: Free Press, 1977.

Zuckerman, S. *Scientists and War.* London: Hamish Hamilton, 1966.

Index